Constitutional Law
of the Federal System

CONSTITUTIONAL LAW
OF THE FEDERAL SYSTEM

C. Herman Pritchett
University of California, Santa Barbara

Prentice-Hall, Inc., Englewood Cliffs, New Jersey 07632

Library of Congress Cataloging in Publication Data

Pritchett, C. Herman (Charles Herman)
    Constitutional law of the federal system.

    Includes the text of the U.S. Constitution.
    Includes indexes.
    1. United States—Constitutional law—Interpretation
and construction. 2. Judicial review—United States.
3. United States. Supreme Court. 4. Federal government—
United States. 5. Separation of powers—United States.
I. United States. Constitution. 1984. II. Title.
KF4550.P744 1984   342.73   83–16108
ISBN 0–13–167932–5   347.302

Editorial/production supervision and interior design: Dee Amir Josephson
Cover design: Wanda Lubelska
Manufacturing buyer: Ron Chapman

Printed in the United States of America

10 9 8 7 6 5 4 3 2 1

ISBN 0-13-167932-5

Prentice-Hall International, Inc., *London*
Prentice-Hall of Australia Pty. Limited, *Sydney*
Editora Prentice-Hall do Brasil, Ltda., *Rio de Janeiro*
Prentice-Hall Canada Inc., *Toronto*
Prentice-Hall of India Private Limited, *New Delhi*
Prentice-Hall of Japan, Inc., *Tokyo*
Prentice-Hall of Southeast Asia Pte. Ltd., *Singapore*
Whitehall Books Limited, *Wellington, New Zealand*

Contents

Preface

Charles Evans Hughes once observed that the Constitution of the United States means what the Supreme Court says it means. The Constitution created the American governmental system, and the Supreme Court is only one of the three major components of that system. It is on a level of equality, so far as constitutional theory goes, with Congress and the President. But there is a sense in which the Court is indeed superior to the other two branches. As early as 1803, Chief Justice John Marshall established the right of the Supreme Court to declare acts of Congress unconstitutional, which it has subsequently done well over one hundred times. So far as the President is concerned, the Court has had fewer occasions to interpret or challenge executive power, but administrative programs consistently present isues of constitutionality or statutory interpretation which require judicial review.

This book is an examination and analysis of the way in which the American Constitution, as judicially interpreted, has shaped the American federal system and its institutions. Though the book is not divided into parts, the seventeen chapters are concerned with five major themes. The first three chapters deal with the Constitution itself. Chapter 1 relates the historical background of the post-Revolutionary period, and the procedures and decisions of the Constitutional Convention of 1787 that produced what Gladstone once called "the most wonderful work ever struck off at a given time by the brain and purpose of man." Then Chapter 2 discusses the procedures for amending the Constitution and the experience with use of the amending power. Chapter 3 deals with the problems that courts and scholars encounter in interpreting the language of the Constitution, and it also introduces the 103 justices of the Supreme Court who have had the major responsibility for applying the Constitution as occasions and controversies have arisen in American political, economic, and social life.

The American system of federalism, discussed in the second section, was a true invention. The Framers assumed, contrary to most earlier theory, that sovereignty could be divided, and they proceeded to divide it between the nation and the states. The Constitution rescued the feeble central government of the Articles of Confederation and made it into a national government of broad delegated powers, while preserving the states and guaranteeing their control over all other public responsibilities. Chapter 4 discusses the nature of the national union and its relations with the states, as well as representation in state legislatures. Chapter 5 concentrates on relations among the states.

The third section of the book treats the American judicial system. Because our concern is with the Constitution as judicially interpreted, it is appropriate that the courts be considered prior to the other two branches, so that the institutions and practices of judicial review will be clarified. Chapters 6 and 7 deal with judicial power, organization, and jurisdiction, whereas Chapter 8 concentrates on the authority of the courts to declare and apply constitutional principles, as well as the self-imposed restraints on that awesome power.

The fourth section of five chapters covers Congress in both its organizational and procedural character and its various delegated powers. The congressional activities that have generated more litigation than any others—taxation and regulation of commerce—are given more intensive analysis in Chapters 11, 12 and 13.

Finally, the four chapters in the fifth section discuss the presidency. Here was the Convention's second great invention—a single-headed executive institution with a fixed term of office and largely independent of legislative control. The Supreme Court has had less occasion to delineate the powers of the executive than in dealing with Congress. Each President has a great deal of autonomy and can adapt the executive office to his particular style, ability, and mission. Consequently these chapters deal to a considerable degree with executive practices rather than constitutional limits on executive powers. The President's role in the conduct of foreign relations and his position as Commander in Chief call for special attention.

Unfortunately for the author, the Supreme Court's major decision in *Immigration and Naturalization Service v. Chadha* was handed down by the Court while this book was in the final stages of preparation for publication, and consequently only limited coverage could be given to it. Furthermore, its consequences are not yet clear. What is clear is that by declaring unconstitutional the legislative veto, the Court has made its most portentous statement of this century on executive-legislative relations. Without the legislative veto, which Congress has increasingly used, and sometimes misused, the balance in the separation of powers may sharply shift toward the White House. However, over time

Congress is likely to regain some of the lost ground by writing stricter legislation, by more intensive use of the investigatory and oversight functions, backed up by the contempt power, or by stricter appropriations controls.

In considering the constitutional powers and limitations of the federal system and the three branches of government, this book necessarily attempts breadth of coverage rather than detailed analysis. Only the major judicial decisions are discussed in depth. For the remainder, the holdings are summarized, and citations to additional cases are provided for scholars who wish to go further into the constitutional issues raised. The more recent decisions of the Supreme Court have been favored, but with due recognition of earlier cases in which formative principles were established.

Although the author has generally endeavored to let the cases and the rulings speak for themselves, there has been no hesitation to criticize judicial reasoning. The author's position on constitutional interpretation is close to that of Justice Oliver Wendell Holmes, who wrote in *Missouri v. Holland* (1920):

> When we are dealing with words that also are a constituent act, like the Constitution of the United States, we must realize that they have called into life a being the development of which could not have been foreseen completely by the most gifted of its begetters. . . . The case before us must be considered in the light of our whole experience and not merely in that of what was said a hundred years ago.

The author calls attention to a companion volume, *Constitutional Civil Liberties,* which presents a comparable analysis of judicial interpretation of the Bill of Rights.

C. Herman Pritchett

1
The Making of the Constitution

"By constitution," wrote Lord Bolingbroke in 1733, "we mean, whenever we speak with propriety and exactness, that assemblage of laws, institutions and customs, derived from certain fixed principles of reason, directed to certain fixed objects of public good, that compose the general system, according to which the community hath agreed to be governed." In making this definition, Bolingbroke was naturally thinking mainly of the English constitution, but in fact his statement accorded with the traditional understanding which, as McIlwain says, applied the term "constitution" to the "substantive principles to be deduced from a nation's actual institutions and their development."[1]

The latter part of the eighteenth century, however, brought a new concept of "constitution" into existence. The French and American Revolutions introduced as an essential governmental instrument the written constitution. The general system under which the community agreed to be governed was not, under the new regime, to be left to evolution and deduction. The "laws, institutions and customs" were not to be a heterogeneous assemblage. The fixed principles of reason, the fixed objects of the public good, were to be stated specifically in a formal basic document.

---

[1] Charles H. McIlwain, *Constitutionalism Ancient and Modern* (Ithaca, N.Y.: Cornell University Press, 1940), p. 3.

To one accustomed to the older view of constitutions, this was a disturbing departure. The Englishman Arthur Young, writing in 1792, spoke with contempt of the French idea of a constitution—"a new term they have adopted; and which they use as if a constitution was a pudding to be made by a recipe." To an Englishman it was obvious that a constitution could not be made; it had to grow.

Actually, of course, constitutions can combine both qualities. The American Constitution was made in the summer of 1787 and has been growing ever since.[2] While many influences went into its making, the Constitution was shaped most directly by the political experience of the Revolutionary period and the painful lessons learned in attempting to operate a government under the Articles of Confederation from 1781 to 1789.

THE POLITICAL THEORY
OF THE REVOLUTIONARY PERIOD

The Declaration of Independence has been generally regarded as the cornerstone of American ideas about government and the preeminent statement of American political theory.[3] The basic conceptions had obviously come from Locke, but the doctrines were sharpened and intensified by the experience of resistance to British rule. These principles were so much a part of American thinking that the Declaration referred to them as "self-evident." In addition to the Declaration, the state constitutions adopted between 1776 and 1780 abound in statements of the current political theory.

The first principle of the political thought of the time was that men are by nature endowed with certain inalienable rights. This conception posited the existence of a state of nature antedating the establishment of civil government. In this primeval condition all men were free, in the sense that they were subject to no one, and equal in the right to rule themselves. A body of natural rights belonged to them as men, including the right to "life, liberty, and the pursuit of happiness." These rights not only antedated the existence of government; they were superior to it in authority. As John Dickinson expressed it, "Our liberties do not come from charters; for these are only the declaration of preexisting rights. They do not depend on parchments or seals; but come from the King of Kings and Lord of all the earth."

The exercise of coercive power by governments over men born free and equal could be justified only by the consent of the governed. The process as hypothesized by the Massachusetts Bill of Rights was that "the body politic

---

[2]The principal constitutional history is Alfred H. Kelly and Winfred A. Harbison, *The American Constitution,* 5th ed. (New York: W. W. Norton & Co., Inc., 1976).

[3]See Carl L. Becker, *The Declaration of Independence: A Study in the History of Political Ideas* (New York: Knopf, 1942).

is formed by a voluntary association of individuals: it is a social compact by which the whole people covenants with each citizen, and each citizen with the whole people, that all shall be governed by certain laws for the common good.'' The exact nature of the contract on which government was based or the circumstances under which it was entered into were little discussed, but the concept was given a sense of reality by the numerous written compacts that had figured in American development, especially the Mayflower Compact of 1620 and the colonial charters. The slogan "no taxation without representation" was a particular application of the consent theory, with deep roots in English constitutional history.

Government is created by contract to serve the welfare of the people. To quote again the Massachusetts document, the end of government is "to secure the existence of the body politic, to protect it, and to furnish the individuals who compose it with the power of enjoying in safety and tranquility their natural rights, and the blessings of life.'' A government which fails to serve the ends for which it was set up has breached the contract under which it was established and forfeited the loyalty of its citizens. Thus the right of revolution, obviously fundamental to legitimizing the American action, was defended. The Declaration of Independence stated the case as follows: "Whenever any form of government becomes destructive of these ends, it is the right of the people to alter or to abolish it, and to institute new government, laying its foundation on such principles and organizing its powers in such form, as to them shall seem most likely to effect their safety and happiness.''

The consequences of these basic political ideas quickly became visible in the constitutions adopted by the new states. Because of the contract theory, there was a widespread insistence that the constitutions be adopted by conventions especially charged with that duty, instead of by the regular legislatures, and that the draft constitutions be submitted to the voters for approval. Nine of the twelve constitutions adopted by 1778 were drawn up by this method.

Governmental power was limited in several ways. The royal governors had been the symbol of tyranny, and so the executive office in the new constitutions was deliberately weakened, while the legislature, symbol of resistance to foreign rule, was strengthened. In eight states the governor was chosen by the legislature, he had only a one-year term in ten states, his appointing power was generally limited, and he had the veto power in only three states. The one-year rule was common for all officials, not only for governors; as John Adams said, "Where annual elections end, there tyranny begins.''

The separation of powers doctrine was also vigorously professed, though the imbalance between the legislature and executive was rather inconsistent with this theory. The Massachusetts formulation earned fame by its doctrinaire quality: "In the government of this commonwealth, the legislative department shall never exercise the executive and judicial powers, or either of them: the executive shall never exercise the legislative and judicial powers, or either of them: the judicial shall never exercise the legislative and executive powers, or either of them: to the end it may be a government of laws and not of men.'' Other restrictions were sought to be achieved by clear subordination of the military to the civil power, by decentralization of governmental functions, and by bills of rights that forbade governmental interference in certain fields of individual activity. Eight states had such bills of rights, their principles derived largely from the English common law as expounded by Blackstone.

The democratic theory professed in the new constitutions was not consistently practiced, however. Under the colonial government the lower classes had been rather generally excluded from political life. The Revolutionary movement for a time gave promise of bringing the back-country folk and the unfranchised workers into the stream of politics, but actually the circle of power-holders was little changed in the new state governments.[4] Property and religious qualifications for officeholding were general. Indeed, property, religious, and racial limitations were seemingly not regarded as inconsistent with the rights of man or the principles of political philosophy so eloquently stated in the Declaration of Independence, and the exclusion of women was taken for granted.

THE POST-REVOLUTIONARY EXPERIENCE

The American Revolution was conducted by the Continental Congress, composed of delegates from the various states, which met in session after session from 1774 to 1781. It performed the functions of a de facto government—raising, directing, and financing armies, sending and receiving diplomatic agents, entering into treaties with foreign countries. But the people of the states did not conceive that they had surrendered any of their rights to the Congress, and no state government felt bound by its decisions.

It was generally agreed that something more effective in the way of intercolonial organization was required. On June 7, 1776, after Richard Henry Lee had moved his resolution in favor of a declaration of independence, he offered a second one proposing a permanent confederation. A committee was appointed on June 12 with John Dickinson as chairman. The committee's major difficulties had to do with whether the states would be represented equally or in proportion to population, how contributions to the general treasury would be apportioned, and what disposition would be made of the claims several states were making to lands stretching back into the interior of the country. The Articles of Confederation were not adopted and sent to the states until

---

[4]Charles A. Beard, *An Economic Interpretation of the Constitution of the United States* (New York: Macmillan, 1913, 1935); Forrest McDonald, *We the People: The Economic Origins of the Constitution* (Chicago: University of Chicago Press, 1958).

November, 1777. Ratification by every state was required to make them binding. The twelfth state signed in February, 1779, but Maryland was adamant, and did not agree until March 1, 1781, at which time the Articles came into effect.

The framework of government set up by the Articles was quite unlike that of the states. Virtually all functions were concentrated in a single legislative chamber, called a Congress. There was no second branch of the legislature and no separation of executive from legislative powers. Congress was to appoint such committees and civil officers as might be needed to carry on executive work, and it could provide courts only for the limited purposes of dealing with disputes between states and captures and felonies on the high seas.

The authority of Congress did not rest on the people, but on the state legislatures which had created it. Each state legislature chose and paid its delegates to Congress, and each state had one vote. A two-thirds vote of the state delegations was required for the adoption of important measures, and amendments to the Articles required the unanimous consent of the states.

The Articles did specify certain rules of interstate comity to which the states were pledged. But the essential powers necessary to an effective central government were denied to the Confederation. Congress could not levy taxes; it could only make a "requisition" on each state for its share of the estimated monetary needs of the union. Congress could not regulate interstate commerce; and although it could make commercial treaties with foreign nations, the states felt free to retaliate against countries that discriminated against their trade. Finally, Congress could not act directly on the citizens; it had to depend on the state governments for the execution of its measures. The Confederation could scarcely be called a government. As the Articles truthfully stated, it was a league of friendship entered into by sovereign states.

As for organizational arrangements, certain executive officers were immediately established. In fact, a secretary for foreign affairs, responsible to the Congress, had been created before the Articles were finally ratified, and also the offices of superintendent of finance and secretary at war. Congress chose a presiding officer with the title of president. A federal prize court had been created in 1780, and it was continued and regularized after the adoption of the Articles. The provision of the Articles for adjudicating disputes between states involved a much more cumbersome arrangement. States in dispute might by joint consent, through the Congress as intermediary, choose commissioners to decide the dispute.

In spite of its limited authority over internal affairs, the Confederation did achieve some successes. The Bank of North America was chartered by Congress in 1781, though the fact that the Articles gave no authority to grant charters of incorporation led the bank to secure a new charter from Pennsylvania. Preparations for the government of the new lands to the west led to adoption of the famous Northwest Ordinance of 1787, applying to the area between the Ohio and the Mississippi. The ordinance provided for the eventual division of this land into from three to five states. In the meantime the territory was to be governed directly by officials chosen by Congress.

In other areas Congress was less successful at temporizing solutions for the problems of the Confederation. Attempts to negotiate commercial treaties with England, France, and Spain failed, in part at least because of doubt whether the states would feel bound by any such treaties. As for internal trade, the rivalries of the states led to various forms of discriminatory taxation. The situation of New Jersey, whose goods came in through New York on one side and Philadelphia on the other, led to Madison's famous comparison of the state to a cask tapped at both ends.

The public finances were very nearly hopeless. During the first two years under the Articles, Congress requisitioned $10 million from the states and received less than $1.5 million. There were no funds to pay interest on the debt, which actually rose after the war was over. Redemption of the worthless Continental currency was impossible. Speculators bought at a heavy discount the certificates of indebtedness issued during hostilities to pay for necessary supplies. Robert Morris, superintendent of finance, resigned in 1786, not wishing, he said, to be a "minister of injustice."

With Congress incapable of dealing with the economic ills of the country, pressure fell on the state legislatures. The most widespread demand was for relief from the burden of debts incurred during the Revolutionary inflation by state issuance of legal tender paper and by various forms of moratoria on payment of debts. The paper money forces got a majority for their inflationary program in seven state legislatures. When these forces were defeated in Massachusetts, farmers under the lead of Daniel Shays resorted to violence, breaking up court sessions trying debt cases and attempting to seize arms from the government arsenal at Springfield.

Shays's Rebellion was most effective in convincing the conservative and the propertied that there were serious defects in the government both of the states and the Confederation. The Revolutionary enthusiasm for the legislature as the dominant branch of the government had diminished. Now responsible citizens were looking for some way of checking legislatures which, as Madison said, were drawing all power into their "impetuous vortex." In most states the governor was still too weak for this purpose. Here and there were the beginnings of a system of judicial review of legislation. But the only effective control over state radicalism appeared to be a strengthening of the central government. In a paper written in the spring of 1787, Madison, concerned about the absence of any "guarantee to the States of their constitutions and laws against internal violence," thought that establishing central government control over "the internal vicissitudes of State policy, and the aggressions of interested majorities on the rights of minorities and of individuals" would have a "happy effect."

THE MOVEMENT FOR A NEW CONSTITUTION

There were stirrings toward improvement of the Articles before they were even officially in force. The three main weaknesses—lack of authority to raise revenue, to regulate commerce, or to exercise general coercive powers—were obvious to all. Article 13 provided that "Every State shall abide by the determinations of the United States in Congress assembled, on all questions which by this Confederation are submitted to them." Some argued that this article implied powers of enforcement against the states, and Congress studied the problem interminably through committees but characteristically never reached any decision.

If Congress was to have no coercive power over the states with respect to revenues, an alternative was to permit Congress to levy taxes directly. A month before the Articles became effective, Congress sent to the states an amendment permitting it to levy a duty of 5 percent ad valorem on all imports. Amendment of the Articles required unanimous vote, and this proposal failed when Rhode Island rejected it in 1782. A revised revenue amendment that sought to meet Rhode Island's objection got the approval of only two states in three years. When a committee of Congress reported in 1786 that the lack of general revenue was placing the very existence of the union in jeopardy, and that the states must permit the establishment of a revenue system, New York wrecked agreement by its lone veto.

As for the commerce power, vulnerable New Jersey pressed for central regulatory power from the beginning, but unsuccessfully. Foreign discrimination against American commerce led Congress to submit a commerce amendment to the states in 1784, which failed, as did later proposals to the same end.

This continuing demonstration of what a Virginia delegate to Congress called the "imbecillity" of the Confederation could lead only to the breaking up of the union or its reconstitution under a stronger government. There was considerable speculation about and support for the first alternative from 1783 on. The conflicting interests and conditions of the different sections were stressed. The advantages of a connection with the Southern states were widely questioned in the North. Dr. Benjamin Rush of Philadelphia reported that "some of our enlightened men . . . have secretly proposed an Eastern, Middle, and Southern Confederacy, to be united by an alliance offensive and defensive. These Confederacies, they say, will be united by nature, by interests, and by manners, and consequently they will be safe, agreeable, and durable."

It was the other alternative which won out, however. In 1782 Hamilton had prevailed on the New York legislature to request that Congress call a general convention, and Massachusetts took similar action in 1785. These efforts failed. What did happen in 1785 was a meeting of representatives from Virginia and Maryland at Washington's home at Mount Vernon, for the purpose of discussing joint problems of navigation on Chesapeake Bay and the Potomac. Ignoring a provision in the Articles that required congressional consent to all agreements between states, they developed a plan for uniform import duties, regulations of commerce, and currency in the two states.

When the Maryland legislature accepted these proposals in December, 1758, it suggested that Pennsylvania and Delaware be invited to join in the plan. In Virginia, Madison saw the possibility of using this initiative to get a general meeting on commercial problems, which the Virginia assembly proposed should meet at Annapolis in September, 1786. Nine states appointed delegates to go to Annapolis, but only five were present at the opening session. They waited three weeks for more delegates and then adjourned. But a report was drafted and sent to every state legislature and to Congress, suggesting that the states designate commissioners to meet in Philadelphia in May, 1787, "to take into consideration the situation of the United States, to devise such further provisions as shall appear to them necessary to render the Constitution of the Federal Government adequate to the exigencies of the Union."

All the states complied except Rhode Island, though New Hampshire delayed until June, after the Constitutional Convention had assembled. Congress at first ignored the project but in February, 1787, recommended a convention at the time and place already set, to meet for the "sole and express purpose of revising the Articles of Confederation."[5]

THE CONSTITUTIONAL CONVENTION: MEMBERSHIP AND PROCEDURE

The Constitutional Convention was scheduled to meet at the State House in Philadelphia on May 14, 1787, but on that day representatives from only two states, Virginia and Pennsylvania, were present. On succeeding days additional delegates appeared, but it was not until May 25 that a majority of the states were represented. The Convention then organized, with George Washington the unanimous choice as presiding officer. The Convention met in its first regular session on Monday, May 28, and continued its deliberations until the completed document was ready for signature on September 17.[6]

The session of May 28 was attended by twenty-nine delegates from seven states. Some seventy-four delegates were appointed, but only fifty-five of them

[5]Although this "call for a convention" has been regarded as the source of the Convention's authority, in fact eight states had already decided to appoint delegates before the resolution was adopted. The state legislative instruments appointing delegates were the true source of authority for the Convention. See Julius Goebel, Jr., *History of the Supreme Court of the United States: Antecedents and Beginnings to 1801* (New York: Macmillan, 1971), p. 202.

[6]For accounts of the Convention, see Catherine Drinker Bowen, *Miracle at Philadelphia* (Boston: Little, Brown, 1966); Clinton Rossiter, *1787: The Grand Convention* (New York: Macmillan, 1966); Carl Van Doren, *The Great Rehearsal* (New York: Viking, 1948); Charles Warren, *The Making of the Constitution* (Boston: Little, Brown, 1928).

ever attended the sessions. Every state except Rhode Island was eventually represented, New Hampshire's delegates being the last to arrive, on July 23. By any standards, in any country, these men would have been judged a notable assemblage. The French chargé wrote that "if all the delegates named for this Philadelphia Convention are present, one will never have seen, even in Europe, an assembly more respectable for talents, knowledge, disinterestedness, and patriotism than those who will compose it."

The fifty-five delegates were comparatively young men, only twelve being over fifty-four years of age, while six were under thirty-one. About half were college graduates. They were almost without exception men of substance and status in the new country—lawyers, physicians, planters, merchants. Most of them had risked their necks in prominent military or civilian posts during the Revolution. But the fact that only eight of the fifty-six signers of the Declaration of Independence were in the Constitutional Convention is evidence that making a constitution enlisted different talents than making a revolution. Of course Jefferson and Paine were in Europe, but Patrick Henry "smelled a rat" and stayed at home, and such Revolutionary figures as Richard Henry Lee, Sam Adams, and John Hancock were also missing.

Among the Convention's leaders, some few stand out and deserve brief mention here. The two figures with greatest prestige were Washington and Franklin. When Washington resigned his commission in December, 1783, he told Congress he was taking his leave "of all the employments of public life." Though the difficulties of the new nation affected him deeply and he was firmly convinced that a stronger government was required, he resisted efforts to enlist his services in the political arena. In August, 1786, he wrote to John Jay: "Having happily assisted in bringing the ship into port, and having been fairly discharged: it is not my business to embark again on a sea of troubles." But in March, 1787, the call of duty overrode all other considerations, and he accepted designation as a delegate from Virginia. He feared that if he did not attend, it would be taken as an indication that he had lost faith in a republican form of government. He participated seldom in debates, but there can be no doubt that his influence and endorsement were essential to the adoption of the Constitution.

Benjamin Franklin, by then eighty-one years old and suffering from the gout, was nearing the end of his glorious career and was unable to take an active part in debate. But he was, after Washington, the most influential American of his time, and his talents as a peacemaker helped the Convention ease past several danger points.

The men generally ranked as exercising the greatest influence in the decisions of the Convention are Gouverneur Morris and James Wilson of Pennsylvania, James Madison of Virginia, and Roger Sherman of Connecticut. Morris made 173 speeches; Wilson, 168; Madison, 161; and Sherman, 138. Virginia was also ably represented by George Mason and Edmund Randolph, as was Massachusetts with Elbridge Gerry and Rufus King, and South Carolina with John Rutledge and Charles Pinckney. Oliver Ellsworth of Connecticut, Alexander Hamilton from New York, John Dickinson of Delaware, and William Paterson of New Jersey might also be ranked among the leaders.

Under the Convention's rules as adopted on May 28 and 29, the deliberations were to be completely secret, and they were kept so for thirty years afterward. The official journal was confined to the formal motions made and the ayes and noes. But Madison throughout the proceeding sat with his back to Washington, facing the other members, and writing down what went on in his own version of shorthand. He did this with the silent approval of the Convention. The members trusted him and helped him fill out his reports from their own notes or memories. Madison's notes provide the principal information as to the proceedings of the Convention.[7]

Edmund Randolph started off the work of the body by presenting for the Virginia delegation a series of resolutions, largely drafted by Madison, providing for a new national government. The Convention turned itself into a committee of the whole and for three weeks mulled over the Virginia proposals, as well as a more limited plan placed before the committee by New Jersey. The New Jersey proposal was defeated on June 19. The members then reverted from committee status and, as a convention, began to go over again the various features of the Virginia Plan. One month of discussion produced agreement on a substantial number of points, so that on July 23 the Convention voted to set up a committee of detail that would draft a constitution embodying the principles agreed upon. The members of this committee were Gorham of Massachusetts, Ellsworth, Wilson, Randolph, and Rutledge. This group, however, did more than redraft the Convention's resolutions into documentary form. It expanded some of the resolutions and developed some entirely new provisions. The resulting document was presented to the Convention on August 6 and was the subject of further extended discussion. On September 8 a committee was appointed "to revise the stile of and arrange the articles which had been agreed to by the House"; it consisted of Johnson of Connecticut, Hamilton, Gouverneur Morris, Madison, and King. Morris actually did the bulk of the work for the committee of style, and was responsible for much of the phrasing of the final document.

On September 17, when the Constitution was ready for signing, forty-two delegates were present. Some had departed because they disagreed with the Convention's work. Yates and Lansing of New York had left in the midst of the proceedings, and for the last two months of the Convention Hamilton was thus the sole representative from New York. Although he spoke often, he declined to take the responsibility of casting New York's vote, which was consequently never recorded during the latter part of the proceedings. Others had departed, not because they disagreed with the Convention's results, but

---

[7]All the statements at the Convention quoted in this chapter come from Madison's notes, as printed in Max Farrand, ed., *The Records of the Federal Convention of 1787* (New Haven, Conn.: Yale University Press, 1937).

because of pressure of other business or because they felt all the important issues had been decided.

Of the forty-two delegates present on September 17, three declined to sign—Mason, Gerry, and Randolph, all of whom had played important parts in the drafting process. Madison records that while the last of the other thirty-nine delegates were still signing the document,

> . . . Doctr. Franklin looking towards the Presidents Chair, at the back of which a rising sun happened to be painted, observed to a few members near him, that Painters had found it difficult to distinguish in their art a rising from a setting sun. I have, said he, often and often in the course of the Session, and the vicissitudes of my hopes and fears as to its issue, looked at that behind the President without being able to tell whether it was rising or setting: But now at length I have the happiness to know that it is a rising and not a setting Sun.

THE MAJOR DECISIONS

The various provisions of the Constitution on which the sun had thus arisen will be the subject of examination and comment at appropriate points throughout this volume. Here an attempt will be made only to place the major decisions of the Convention in their setting, outlining the considerations that were effective in the adoption of these provisions and the alternatives that were discussed and discarded.

A New Constitution

The Convention almost immediately on assembling proceeded to disregard the instructions it had received from Congress to confine its efforts to revising the Articles of Confederation. Because of the suspicions of the state legislatures, which tended to represent the small farmers and debtors, toward the proposal to hold a convention, the supporters of the movement had felt it necessary to play down the real purposes of the call. They had seen the Annapolis meeting of 1786 break up in failure when all but five states were frightened off by talk of strengthening the central government. Consequently, Alexander Hamilton drafted the call for the 1787 meeting in terms merely of revising the Articles, with any changes proposed having to go back to the states for decision as to their adoption.

But once the delegates met, it was obvious that the goals they had in mind required scrapping the Articles. It was too apparent to them that the Confederation, with its powerless Congress, could not provide what they felt the country needed—security for business development, protection against competitive state taxation, the assurance of a sound currency, encouragement and protection of foreign trade, safety against foreign countries and Indians on the frontier. Thus the Virginia resolutions, which ignored the Articles, were accepted unanimously as the basis for the initial discussions. It was only after the demand of the small states for equal representation in the Senate had been defeated that some delegates began to suggest that the Convention was contravening its instructions. Lansing of New York said his state "would never have concurred in sending deputies to the convention, if she had supposed the deliberations were to turn on a consolidation of the States, and a National Government." Paterson, presenting the New Jersey Plan, limited to revision of the Articles, added: "If the confederacy was radically wrong, let us return to our States, and obtain larger powers, not assume them of ourselves." But when only three states supported the New Jersey Plan, the die was irrevocably cast for a new Constitution.[8]

A National Government

The decision to set up a national government and the decision to draft a new Constitution were two sides of the same coin. It was because the delegates believed a strong central government essential that they could not be content with a patching job on the Articles. The two most eloquent defenses of a national government in the Convention were those of Hamilton and Madison on June 18 and June 19. Hamilton objected to both the Paterson and the Randolph plans. Believing that the British government was the best in the world, he wanted to go as far in that direction as possible, with an executive and an upper chamber both serving for life. "It seemed to be admitted," he said, "that no good [Executive] could be established on Republican principles."

Madison's was a more moderate exposition of the differences between a federal and a national plan. The New Jersey Plan, he said, would correct none of the evils that had brought the delegates together. Would it prevent state violations of the laws of nations and of treaties? Would it prevent encroachments on federal authority? Would it prevent trespass of the states on each other? Would it secure the internal tranquility of the states (mentioning particularly Shays's Rebellion)? Would it secure the Union against the influence of foreign powers over its members?

Acceptance of the national principle was settled by the vote of June 19. This meant that the government would operate directly upon the people, in contrast with the Confederation, which operated only on the states. It meant that the central government would have power to collect its own taxes, to make laws and enforce them in its own courts. Over each citizen there would be two governments, national and state, both derived from the people, to both of which their citizens would owe obedience.

[8]See John D. Lewis, ed., *Anti-Federalists versus Federalists: Selected Documents* (San Francisco: Chandler, 1967); Herbert J. Storing, *The Complete Anti-Federalist* (Chicago: University of Chicago Press, 1981).

A Separation of Powers

Under the Articles the only governmental institution was Congress, but with a national government there was a necessity of adding executive and judicial instruments, and of relating them all to each other. Montesquieu's work on the separation of powers was known in America at that time and was occasionally quoted by Madison and others, but it probably was not too influential on the decisions of the delegates. The allocation of powers to three separate branches and the division of authority so that each could impose some limits on actions of the other two were established not to fit any theoretical models but to handle the very practical problems the Convention faced.

The Founding Fathers were still so close to George III that dread of a strong executive was very real. Their experience with state legislatures had led them to fear the domination of an overweening Congress. Their experience with paper money democracy as practiced in some states left them wary of putting too much power in the hands of the people. The system of checks and balances, then, was to blunt the drive of popular emotions—to provide, in Madison's words, by a "distribution and organization" of governmental powers "better guards than are found in any other popular government against interested combinations of a majority against the rights of a minority."

A Bicameral Legislature

There was little doubt in the minds of the delegates that if a national government were to be established, it must have a two-house legislature. This was the practice in England and in almost all of the states. The New Jersey Plan for revising the Articles retained a Congress of a single house, but after it was defeated there was no further consideration of a unicameral plan. The two-house legislature of course made possible the compromise between large and small states without which probably no Constitution could have been adopted.

It was generally accepted from the beginning that the House of Representatives would be elected by the people, and that membership would be proportionate to population. Much more difficult was the composition and basis of selection of the Senate. The Randolph plan contemplated that the Senate would be elected by the House from persons nominated by the state legislatures, and that the basis of representation should be the same in both houses. The first feature of this proposal, which would have made the Senate subservient to the House, never got much support. The general sentiment was for election of the Senate by the state legislatures.

The basis of representation in the Senate was the rock on which the Convention almost foundered. The big states wanted representation by population. But in the Congress under the Confederation, and in the Convention itself, each state had one vote, and the small states would not agree to a plan that did not preserve their status in some way. On June 9 Paterson said of the proportional proposal that New Jersey "will never confederate on the plan before the Committee. She would be swallowed up. He had rather submit to a monarch, to a despot, than to such a fate." Wilson was quickly on his feet to reply that if the small states would not confederate on the proportional plan, Pennsylvania would not confederate on any other. On June 11, just after adopting proportional representation for the House by a vote of nine to two, the committee of the whole accepted the same rule for the Senate by a vote of six to five. It was this defeat for the small states that triggered the presentation of the New Jersey Plan.

The committee's decision was reconsidered by the Convention, and on June 29 proportional representation in the House was reaffirmed, but only by a vote of six to four, with Maryland divided. Ellsworth then proposed that each state have one vote in the Senate, saying that such a variation in the representation of the two houses would be an appropriate recognition of the fact that we were "partly national; partly federal." On July 2 the Convention split five to five on this issue, with Georgia divided. A committee was set up to work over the July 4 holiday for a solution to this impasse. At Franklin's suggestion they proposed equal state representation in the Senate, but the House was to have the sole right to originate all money bills, which the Senate could accept or reject, but not modify.

This compromise was bitterly attacked by some members from the large states, including Madison, Wilson, and Gouverneur Morris. The success of the Convention seemed again in grave danger, and it was at this point that Yates and Lansing of New York went home. However, the crisis passed and the Convention held together. The big states made alternative suggestions— that the Senate representation be on the basis of state wealth, or that the states be divided into three classes on the basis of population, giving the classes one, two, and three senators respectively. But these were futile. On July 16 equal representation in the Senate was adopted by a five to four vote, with Massachusetts divided and New York not voting. Madison records that the next morning the large states held an indignation meeting to discuss what could be done, but that "the time was wasted in vague conversation." And so the issue was settled.

Powers of Congress

The original Virginia Plan proposed to grant Congress its powers under four heads: (1) the same legislative rights vested in Congress by the Confederation; (2) the right "to legislate in all cases to which the separate States are incompetent, or in which the harmony of the United States may be interrupted by the exercise of individual Legislation;" (3) "to negative all laws passed by the several States, contravening in the opinion of the National Legislature the articles of Union;" and (4) "to call forth the force of the Union agst. any member of the Union failing to fulfill its duty under the articles thereof."

This last heading was dropped on May 31 at Madison's suggestion; he was afraid that "the use of force agst. a State, would look more like a declaration of war, than an infliction of punishment, and would probably be considered by the party attacked as a dissolution of all previous compacts by which it might be bound."

The power to negative state laws was eliminated by the Convention on July 17, in spite of the strong protests of Madison, who thought "the propensity of the States to pursue their particular interests in opposition to the general interest . . . will continue to disturb the system, unless effectually controuled." But Gouverneur Morris believed that such a power would "disgust all the States." Besides, "a law that ought to be negatived will be set aside in the Judiciary Department." Following the defeat of this plan for a legislative veto of state laws, Luther Martin proposed what ultimately became the supremacy clause of Article VI, which the delegates adopted unanimously as a preferable method of asserting national control over state action.

The second heading of Randolph's proposal was subjected to considerable revision on July 17. Several delegates had earlier objected to the vagueness of the term "incompetent," and wished a more "exact enumeration" of powers, but this was not attempted by the committee of the whole. On July 17 Sherman tried to sharpen up the language by provisions which would give Congress power "to make laws binding on the people of the United States in all cases which may concern the common interests of the Union; but not to interfere with the Government of the individual States in any matters of internal police which respect the Govt. of such States only, and wherein the General welfare of the U. States is not concerned."

Gouverneur Morris thought this left too much power with the states; "the internal police . . . ought to be infringed in many cases, as in the case of paper money & other tricks by which Citizens of other States may be affected." Finally the following language was adopted by a vote of eight to two: "to legislate in all cases for the general interests of the Union, and also in those to which the States are separately incompetent, or in which the harmony of the U. States may be interrupted by the exercise of individual Legislation."

The committee of detail eliminated this provision entirely, in favor of a long list of specific powers which it felt Congress might want to exercise. The list started out with the power to tax and to regulate commerce, included fifteen other grants, and wound up with the sweeping authority "to make all laws that shall be necessary and proper for carrying into execution the foregoing powers, and all other powers vested, by this Constitution, in the government of the United States." The Convention accepted the enumeration approach and went to work on this list, adding or revising some powers, and dropping others. The result was to spell out in detail, rather than to grant by broad generalizations, those powers the absence of which in the Confederation had made the movement for a new Constitution necessary.

Limitations on the Powers of Congress

The general emphasis of the Convention was on assuring that Congress had enough powers to remedy the defects of the Confederation. But conflicting sectional interests led the delegates to insist on inserting certain prohibitions on national power. The slave interest was the one that most feared discriminatory action by the new government. A majority of the Convention was opposed to "this infernal traffic," as Mason called it, but North Carolina, South Carolina, and Georgia would have refused to join the Union if the slave trade had been prohibited. The committee of detail reported a provision that no tax or duty should be laid "on the migration or importation of such persons as the several States shall think proper to admit; nor shall such migration or importation be prohibited." Opposition to this formula was intense. Apart from the moral issue, the fact that other imports would be taxed whereas slaves would not amounted, as Wilson charged, to a bounty on slaves. Ultimately, on August 25 agreement was reached on a provision that the importation of slaves would not be prohibited before 1808, and permitting a limited power of taxation on imports of slaves.

The prohibition on the power of Congress to levy direct taxes except on an apportionment basis also represented the efforts of the slavery supporters to assure that internal taxes based specifically on slaves could not be adopted. The prohibition of taxes on exports derived not from the slave interest as such, but from the different character of the economy of the eight Northern and five Southern states. The latter, being engaged primarily in the production of agricultural commodities for which the principal market was foreign, feared that a Northern-dominated Congress would adopt export taxes falling most heavily on their trade.

Limitations on the Powers of the States

The supremacy clause was relied on to prevent state legislation contrary to the national Constitution, laws, or treaties, but there were certain specific subjects on which the delegates felt so strongly that they banned state legislation in forthright language. The sharpest feeling was against state paper money and debtor relief laws. Mercer was the only delegate who ever confessed that he was "a friend to paper money," and he warned it was impolitic "to excite the opposition of all those who were friends to paper money." Gorham likewise wondered how wise it was to line up all the paper money addicts against the Constitution. But Ellsworth replied that this was a "favorable moment to shut and bar the door against paper money."

So the Convention voted to forbid the states to coin money, to print money, or to require anything but gold and silver coin to be accepted in the payment of debts. Then, taking account of the state laws that had been passed to relieve debtors of their business obligations, language forbidding the states to pass any law impairing the obligation of contracts was added with little discussion. Gerry's effort to extend the same prohibition to Congress failed.

The Presidential Office

The Virginia Plan contemplated a national executive to be named by electors chosen by Congress. In the debate which began on June 1, Randolph proposed an executive council of three men, contending that "unity in the Executive magistracy" would be "the foetus of monarchy." Wilson replied that unity in the executive would be "the best safeguard against tyranny." Gerry thought that in military matters a plural executive would be "a general with three heads." The inconvenience and impracticability of Randolph's proposal was plain, and a single executive was approved on June 4 by a vote of seven to three.

Although this issue was decided early, the method of election and term of the executive were not. These two problems were closely related. If the executive was to be chosen by Congress, then a fairly long term with no re-eligibility was favored, in order to reduce the possibility of intrigue with Congress for a second term. If the president was to be chosen in some other fashion, then reeligibility was not objectionable and a shorter term became possible. The Convention considered many proposals, changed its mind repeatedly, and did not finally resolve the issue until almost the end of its sessions. Wilson said that the question of how to elect the President was "the most difficult of all on which we have had to decide."

The discussions are too complex to follow closely. The committee of the whole left Randolph's plan for election by Congress unchanged. Wilson's alternate proposal that the people elect electors who in turn would elect the president was defeated eight to two on June 2. The Convention was not too comfortable with its decision for congressional election, however, and on July 17 Gouverneur Morris again proposed popular election of presidential electors. The people would not fail to elect a man of "continental reputation," he thought, whereas legislative choice would be "the work of intrigue, of cabal, and of faction." But Pinckney thought the people would be led "by a few active & designing men," and Mason added that "it would be as unnatural to refer the choice of a proper character for chief Magistrate to the people, as it would, to refer a trial of colours to a blind man."

The elector plan failed, and the Convention then reaffirmed legislative election unanimously. Yet two days later Morris was again preaching the need "that the Executive Magistrate should be the guardian of the people, even of the lower classes, agst. Legislative tyranny, against the Great & the wealthy who in the course of things will necessarily compose—the Legislative body." This time Madison joined in urging that the executive should be independent of the legislature, and supported the elector plan. The Convention then switched to electors, but contrary to Wilson's proposal, provided for their choice by the state legislatures, and shortened the term to six years.

This decision led to some dispute over the number of electors to be allotted to the respective states. Then on July 24 Houston from Georgia complained that capable men would be unwilling to come in from the more distant states just to ballot for President, and so the Convention flopped back to the original scheme of legislative election. This change, it was argued, made it necessary to reinstate the ban on reeligibility, which had been dropped in the meantime, or to lengthen the term to protect the President against congressional domination. The Convention was heckled by suggestions for increasing the tenure to eight, eleven, or fifteen years. King, with tongue in cheek, suggested twenty years—"the medium life of princes." Gerry ejaculated, "We seem to be entirely at a loss on this head," and then added to the confusion by suggesting that the governors of the states select the President, or that the state legislatures do the electing. Dickinson capped this by proposing that the people of each state elect "its best citizen," and that Congress then choose among the thirteen candidates.

Afraid of election by Congress, but unable to agree on a plan of election by the people, the Convention sent to the committee of detail its decision for congressional election for a seven-year term, with no reeligibility. But how would Congress vote for President? If the two houses voted separately, they might never agree on a candidate. If they voted jointly, the big states could name the President. Joint election was adopted on August 24 by a seven to four vote, and an effort to provide that the votes would be cast by states, each state having one vote, failed by six to five. At this point Morris again urged popular election of electors, and lost by only one vote, six to five. The matter was so completely in dispute that it was turned over to a committee of eleven members, one of whom was Morris.

At long last Morris succeeded. The report of the committee proposed that the states appoint electors equaling in number the senators and representatives from the state. These electors were to meet in the respective states and ballot for two persons, one of whom could not be an inhabitant of the same state with themselves. The ballots would be sent to the capital and counted in the Senate. If one candidate received the votes of a majority of the electors, he was elected President. The runner-up was vice-president, an office that this committee invented. If no candidate received a majority, or if two candidates were tied, then the Senate would choose the president from among the five highest candidates. The term was reduced to four years.

This complicated electoral plan, it was generally believed, would enable the large states in effect to "nominate" the leading candidates, none of whom would normally have a majority. Then the small states with their equal votes in the Senate would have a considerable voice in the final selection. This feature was a calculated bid to win the votes of the small states, though Morris sought to rationalize Senate election by arguing that "fewer could then say to the President, you owe your appointment to us." But Wilson pointed out in rebuttal that the Senate had to approve presidential appointments, and that a president named by the Senate would feel obligated to that body, to the point that the Senate would actually take over the appointing power. The plan would have "a dangerous tendency to aristocracy." And so in a final flurry of voting on September 6 the Convention adopted Sherman's suggestion of choice by the House, but with the members from each state having one vote, thus preserving the principle of state equality that election by the Senate would have provided. Only Delaware voted no.

The Vice-Presidency

As just noted, the committee of eleven invented the vice-presidency at a late stage in the Convention. The report of the committee of detail on August 6 had provided for the president of the Senate to exercise the powers and duties of the President in case of removal, death, resignation, or disability. The committee of eleven proposed that the vice-president be available for this purpose, and also made him ex officio president of the Senate. This latter arrangement caused a debate on September 7. Gerry and Mason thought this was an improper mixture of legislative and executive. But Sherman pointed out that "if the vice-president were not to be President of the Senate, he would be without employment."

The Judiciary

There was universal agreement on the need for a national judiciary, the absence of which was one of the weaknesses of the Confederation. Even the New Jersey Plan of revising the Articles called for the creation of a federal supreme tribunal. The Virginia Plan, however, provided for inferior tribunals as well as for a supreme court. On June 5 the proposal for inferior courts was attacked by Rutledge, who contended that the state courts should hear all cases in the first instance; the right of appeal to the Supreme Court would be sufficient to protect national rights and provide uniformity of judgments. But Madison argued that there should be "an effective Judiciary establishment commensurate to the legislative authority. . . . A Government without a proper Executive & Judiciary would be the mere trunk of a body without arms or legs to act or move." A compromise was then voted under which the national legislature was empowered to institute inferior tribunals, and this was adopted by a vote of eight to two.

The Randolph proposal that judges, like the President, be elected by Congress was soon eliminated. On June 5 Wilson argued for appointment by the President. "A principal reason for unity in the Executive was that officers might be appointed by a single, responsible person." Madison inclined toward appointment by the Senate, as the more stable and independent branch of the legislature. Franklin entertained the gathering with a Scotch plan "in which the nomination proceeded from the Lawyers, who always selected the ablest of the profession in order to get rid of him, and share his practice among themselves."

On July 18 Gorham's proposal for executive appointment, by and with the advice and consent of the Senate, was rejected by a tie vote. Senate appointment was reaffirmed on July 21, and the matter went to the committee of detail in this posture. In its report, the general appointing power was given to the President, but the appointment of justices and ambassadors remained with the Senate. It was the committee of eleven, reporting on September 4, which gave the appointment of Supreme Court justices to the President, with Senate advice and consent. This formula was accepted by the Convention on September 7, though Wilson objected that blending a branch of the legislature with the executive in appointments would destroy executive responsibility. Gouverneur Morris replied "that as the President was to nominate, there would be responsibility, and as the Senate was to concur, there would be security." There was never any disagreement that judicial tenure should be during good behavior.

The Failure to Include a Bill of Rights

The Convention adopted several provisions aimed to protect individuals against unjust punishment or government reprisal. The committee of detail worked out the treason provision, and it was subjected to intensive discussion on August 20. The Convention also adopted a prohibition on bills of attainder and ex post facto laws, guaranteed a jury trial on criminal charges, and provided that the privilege of the writ of habeas corpus could not be suspended except in cases of rebellion or invasion.

These provisions were not thought sufficient by some delegates. On September 12 Mason expressed his disappointment that the constitutional plan had not "been prefaced with a Bill of Rights," but the attempt that he and Gerry made to get a committee appointed to prepare such a document was defeated ten to zero. Sherman's reason was that "the State Declarations of Rights are not repealed by this Constitution; and being in force are sufficient." Perhaps a more pressing reason was that the delegates had been at the job for three and a half months and wanted to get home.

RATIFICATION OF THE CONSTITUTION

The Virginia Plan called for ratification of the New Constitution by special conventions popularly elected for that purpose. The Convention agreed on July 23 by a vote of nine to one, and on August 31 added the provision bringing the Constitution into operation by the favorable vote of nine state conventions. Madison thought from the beginning that ratification by conventions rather than by state legislatures was essential. The theoretical reasons were that the new government must derive its authority directly from the people. There were also some practical considerations which were frankly stated. Thus on July 23 Randolph warned of "the local demagogues who will be degraded by [the Constitution] from the importance they now hold," and who would spare no effort to defeat the proposal. "It is of great importance therefore that the consideration of this subject should be transferred from the Legislatures where this class of men have their full influence to a field in which their efforts can be less mischievous." Others were more diplomatic in referring to the conventions as "more likely to be composed of the ablest men in the States."

Abandonment of the rule of unanimity in adoption of the Constitution was obviously necessitated by Rhode Island's refusal even to attend the Convention. The delegates also contemplated that resistance might be expected from other states. Gorham said that "the present advantage which N. York seems to be so much attached to, of taxing her neighbours [by the regulation of her trade], makes it very probable, that she will be of the number." On August 30 Carroll argued that unanimity was "necessary to dissolve the existing confederacy which had been unanimously established," but Butler "revolted at the idea, that one or two States should restrain the rest from consulting their safety." Nine was finally fixed as the number of states necessary for ratification because, as Mason said, this "had been required in all great cases under the Confederaton" and was therefore "familiar to the people."

The forces favorable to adoption of the Constitution sought to get the conventions elected as promptly as possible, before the opposition had a chance to organize. Unquestionably many farmers and backwoodsmen, who would have tended to oppose the Constitution, were neutralized in this way. About three-fourths of the male white citizens over twenty-one failed to vote in the elections for convention delegates, Charles A. Beard contends, either on account of their indifference or their disfranchisement by property qualifications. He thinks it is probable that a majority of the voters in at least six states opposed ratification. His thesis that the Constitution was adopted primarily by the manufacturing, trade, shipping, and creditor interests in the country, and that the small farming and debtor interests were largely opposed to the Constitution, has been vigorously challenged by more recent studies. It now appears quite probable that class distinctions at the time were much less significant, that property qualifications for voting excluded few from the polls, and that the Constitution was adopted by people who were primarily middle-class property owners, including farmers.

Whatever the bases of the alignments, the political campaign over ratification was intense and bitter. One of its legacies was the most famous commentary on American government, *The Federalist*. These essays were newspaper articles written to influence the vote in the doubtful state of New York by Madison, Hamilton, and John Jay. Although their discussions of the proposed Constitution may not have had great influence at the time, they have been widely accepted as authoritative guides to constitutional interpretation.

The first state convention to ratify the Constitution was that of Delaware on December 7, 1787, which was less than three months after the document was signed. Pennsylvania ratified five days later. New Jersey (December 19), Georgia (January 2), Connecticut (January 9), Massachusetts (February 6), Maryland (April 23), and South Carolina (May 23) followed. New Hampshire was the ninth state, and its ratification on June 21, 1788, brought the Constitution into effect. However, without New York and Virginia the union could not have succeeded. Virginia came in by a narrow margin on June 25, and New York followed on July 26, though an attempt to attach conditions to its ratification almost succeeded. North Carolina finally ratified on November 21, 1789, and Rhode Island held out until May 29, 1790.[9]

The absence of a bill of rights provoked the most widespread criticism in the ratifying conventions; and in Massachusetts, New York, and Virginia the promise that a bill of rights would be added was instrumental in securing the votes needed for ratification. Several of the state conventions submitted lists of proposed amendments to the Constitution at the time they ratified, and there was a general agreement that addition of a bill of rights to the Constitution through the amending process would be a first order of business.

The motive force for putting the new government in operation was supplied by the Confederation Congress. On September 13, 1788, it adopted a resolution designating "the present seat of Congress," which was New York, as the site of the new government. The resolution also fixed the first Wednesday of January, 1789, as the day for choosing presidential electors, the first Wednesday of February for the meeting of electors, and the first Wednesday of March, which fell on March 4, for the opening session of the new Congress. Various delays kept Congress from convening on that day, however, and it was not until April 30, 1789, that George Washington was inaugurated as the first President of the United States.

The framing of the American Constitution has been the subject of never-ending controversy. Some have seen the Founders as little short of demigods: for others they were a "reform caucus" of practical politicians. Was the Constitution a democratic or an aristocratic instrument? Were its drafters conservatives or liberals? Was the document more concerned with establishing the powers of the new government or the limitations on those powers?

There is room for such disagreement, because the basic truth about the Constitution is that it was the product of compromise. The men who met in Philadelphia in the summer of 1787 were generally of the opinion that government

---

[9]Jonathan Elliot, ed., *The Debates in the Several State Conventions in the Adoption of the Federal Constitution,* 5 vols. (Washington, D.C.: Taylor & Maury, 1854).

is a "necessary evil"; they were jealous of individual rights and had strong loyalties to their states. But experience with the Articles had demonstrated that a weak government could not provide the security and prosperity they wanted, and the amazing thing is how unanimous the Convention was in seeing the need for a central "government of powers." As Martin Diamond has said: "This was the great and novel idea which came from the Convention: a large, powerful republic with a competent national government regulated under a wise Constitution."[10]

[10]"What the Framers Meant by Federalism," in Robert A. Goldwin, ed., *A Nation of States* (Chicago: Rand McNally, 1963), p. 37.

2
Amendment
of the Constitution

The United States thus launched its experiment in building a federal government on the basis of a written document that has conditioned the entire development of American governmental experience since 1789. Public policy has been continuously subject to the test of constitutionality. Much of the rhetoric of public debate has been in terms of invoking the support of the document for proposals favored, and throwing doubt on the constitutional legitimacy of actions opposed.

A perennial problem of American politics has been the meaning of the American Constitution. As years and decades have passed, changes have occurred in the physical world. Technical discoveries or inventions have affected the life of the country. Population has multiplied. The political party has undergone a transformation from a despised source of faction to an indispensable instrument of representative government. Public agencies have taken over responsibilities undreamed of in the eighteenth century. Standards of public morality have changed. How is a government of continental proportions and worldwide responsibilities, with a budget of $800 to $900 billion, to be accommodated within the confines of a document drafted almost two centuries earlier for a handful of people in thirteen isolated states along the Atlantic seaboard?

One answer is that the framers of the Constitution were wise enough to avoid the evil of too great specificity in drafting key provisions of the document. Their general intent was to stick to fundamentals and leave implementation to subsequent legislative decision. Thus no departmental organization of the executive branch was written into the Constitution. The question of a system of lower courts was left to Congress, as was the matter of presidential succession beyond the vice-president, and the time, place, and manner of electing representatives and senators. The powers given to the President and to Congress were typically stated in fairly broad language. Although there was a spelling out in Article I, section 8, of congressional authority in a number of areas, the section wound up with what was called "the sweeping clause," conferring on Congress the power "to make all laws which shall be necessary and proper for carrying into execution the foregoing powers, and all other powers vested by this Constitution in the government of the United States, or in any department or officer thereof."

Nevertheless, no amount of drafting skill could be expected to eliminate the necessity of revision and development to adapt the Constitution to the unforeseen and the unforeseeable. This adaptation has taken two forms: constitutional amendment and constitutional interpretation.

THE DEVELOPMENT OF ARTICLE V

Formal provision for revision of the Constitution through amendment was made by Article V. The original Virginia Plan had provided for amendments and added that "the assent of the National Legislature ought not to be required thereto." On June 11 Mason urged the necessity of an amending clause, saying: "The plan now to be formed will certainly be defective, as the Confederation has been found on trial to be. Amendments therefore will be necessary, and it will be better to provide for them, in an easy, regular and Constitutional way than to trust to chance and violence." The reason for excluding Congress from the process as he saw it was that "they may abuse their power, and refuse their consent on that very account."

The committee of detail later produced a revised plan for amendments that also eliminated Congress. On the application of the legislatures of two-thirds of the states, Congress would be required to call a convention for amendment of the Constitution. This plan was adopted on August 30, but by September 10 the Convention was quite unhappy with it. Madison said the language was too vague. Hamilton said there must be an easier way of securing amendments. The states would never "apply for alterations but with a view to increase their own powers." Congress would be "most sensible to the necessity of amendments," Hamilton thought, and should be able to initiate the process.

The Convention then began to rewrite the amending provision on the floor, with Madison putting the various suggestions into the form finally adopted.

Legislatures of two-thirds of the states could still request Congress to call a convention, but Congress itself by a two-thirds vote in each house could propose amendments to the states. Amendments initiated in either fashion would have to be ratified either by the legislatures or special conventions in three-fourths of the states, according to the mode of ratification specified by Congress.

Rutledge then objected that "he never could agree to give a power by which the articles relating to slaves might be altered by the States not interested in that property and prejudiced against it." Consequently a proviso was added protecting the clauses pertaining to slavery from amendment until the year 1808. Then on September 15 Sherman had a last-minute fear "that three fourths of the States might be brought to do things fatal to particular States, as abolishing them altogether or depriving them of their equality in the Senate." He wanted another proviso that no state should by amendment "be affected in its internal police, or deprived of its equality in the Senate." Madison warned that if the Convention once began with these "special provisos," every state would insist on some for its boundaries or exports. However, "the circulating murmurs of the small States" led Gouverneur Morris to propose adding the proviso protecting equality in the Senate, and it was agreed to unanimously. Thus Article V was completed.

USE OF THE AMENDING POWER

The presence of the amending clause was one of the factors that led Jefferson, originally inclined to oppose the Constitution, to decide in its favor. Since 1789 the procedures of Article V have been utilized to add twenty-six amendments to the Constitution. The first ten of these amendments were drafted to meet the widespread protests against the absence of a bill of rights in the original Constitution. To fill this gap, twelve amendments were proposed by the First Congress on September 25, 1789. The first two failed ratification, but acceptance of the remaining ten was completed on December 15, 1791. The substance of these and subsequent amendments will be discussed at appropriate points throughout this volume. Here we are interested only in the chronology and general circumstances of adoption.

The Eleventh Amendment was adopted in 1795, its purpose being to override the Supreme Court's holding in *Chisholm v. Georgia* (1793), which allowed federal courts to accept jurisdiction of a suit against a state by a citizen of another state. The Twelfth Amendment, ratified in 1804, was intended to prevent a repetition of the confusion attendant on the presidential election of 1800, when Jefferson and Burr received an equal number of electoral votes. As the candidates for President and vice-president of the same party, they were supported by all the party's electors, but under the original language of Article II, there was no separate designation of votes for these two offices. Thus the election had to be decided by the House, where the Federalists were tempted to vote for Burr to spite Jefferson. The Twelfth Amendment requires electors to vote for the two offices separately.

The Thirteenth, Fourteenth, and Fifteenth Amendments were adopted as a result of the Civil War. The Thirteenth Amendment, which abolished slavery, was ratified in 1865. The Fourteenth, the longest of the lot and too complex to summarize at this point, aimed to protect the rights of the newly freed Negroes.[1] It also dealt with certain political problems which were an aftermath of the war. When it appeared that the Fourteenth Amendment would not secure the right to vote for Negroes, the Fifteenth Amendment, ratified in 1870, was adopted specifically guaranteeing the right to vote against denial or abridgement on the basis of race or color.

The next two amendments reflected the progressive political philosophy of the first part of the twentieth century. The Sixteenth, ratified in 1913, reversed another Supreme Court decision, *Pollock v. Farmers' Loan & Trust Co.* (1895), and authorized the federal government to levy taxes on incomes. The Seventeenth Amendment, ratified two months later, provided for direct popular election of senators.

The Eighteenth Amendment, which became effective in 1919, was the controversial prohibition amendment. Suffrage for women was guaranteed in 1920 by the Nineteenth Amendment. The Twentieth Amendment, ratified in 1933, fixed the date for convening the regular annual session of Congress on January 3 and the beginning of presidential terms on January 20. In addition, it sought to clarify certain points with respect to presidential succession. The Twenty-first Amendment, also adopted in 1933, repealed the Eighteenth, but did give the states full powers to prohibit the transportation, importation, or use of intoxicating liquor.

The Twenty-second Amendment, ratified in 1951, limits a President to two terms in office. The Twenty-third (1961) permits residents of the District of Columbia to vote for President and gives the District three electoral votes. The Twenty-fourth (1964) forbids the states to use the poll tax as a voting requirement in federal elections. The Twenty-fifth (1967) provides for the appointing of a new vice-president when the office of the vice-president becomes vacant for any reason, and also authorizes the vice-president to act as President if the President is incapacitated. The Twenty-sixth (1971) gives the vote to eighteen-year-olds in both state and federal elections.

In 1972 Congress proposed the Equal Rights Amendment, guaranteeing equal legal rights for women. There was an initial rush of state legislative ratifications, and by 1975 thirty-four of the required thirty-eight states had ratified. But then organized opposition by conservative political and religious groups stalled the bandwagon, and by 1978 only one additional state had ratified. With the seven-year deadline for ratification specified by Congress fast

---

[1]For the sake of historical consistency, the term Negroes is being retained here.

approaching, ERA supporters induced Congress to extend the date for ratification to June 30, 1982. But this maneuver proved futile, and the proposed amendment fell three states short of ratification.

In 1978 Congress proposed an amendment to give the District of Columbia the same congressional representation it would have if it were a state. Prospects for ratification within the seven-year time period were poor, only ten states having ratified by 1982, while an equal number had rejected it. Pending in Congress in 1983 were proposed amendments to require a balanced federal budget, allow voluntary prayer in the public schools, make abortions unlawful, provide for direct popular election of the president, and other purposes.

THE "POLITICAL" CHARACTER OF THE AMENDING PROCESS

The Supreme Court has generally regarded the amending process as almost entirely a concern of Congress, subject to very little in the way of judicial supervision or control. For example, after the Civil War the states that had seceded but had not been readmitted were required by Congress to ratify the Fourteenth and Fifteenth Amendments as a condition to their readmission. The Supreme Court refused to question this requirement.[2]

Until 1939, however, the Court was willing to pass on procedural problems pertaining to the adoption of amendments. In the *National Prohibition Cases* (1920), it ruled that the two-thirds vote in each house required to propose an amendment means two-thirds of the members present—assuming the presence of a quorum—and not a vote of two-thirds of the entire membership. In *Leser v. Garnett* (1922), the validity of the Nineteenth Amendment was attacked on the ground that the ratifying resolutions in two states were adopted in violation of those states' rules of legislative procedure. But the Court regarded official notice of ratification from the states to the United States Secretary of State as conclusive upon him, and held that his certification was conclusive on the courts.

The Eighteenth Amendment was the first to specify a period of years—in this case, seven—within which ratification had to be effected. In *Dillon v. Gloss* (1921) the Court ruled that there was no doubt about the power of Congress to fix a definite period for ratification, "within reasonable limits," and it agreed seven years was reasonable. The implication of this ruling seemed to

---

[2]*White v. Hart* (1872). Likewise, in 1959 the Supreme Court declined to consider an argument by a group of Texans that the Fourteenth Amendment was put into the Constitution by fraud and so was invalid; *Buford v. Texas*. In 1957 the Georgia senate adopted a resolution declaring the Fourteenth and Fifteenth Amendments null and void because the Thirty-ninth and Fortieth Congresses, which proposed these amendments, excluded representatives from Georgia and ten other southern states and so were illegally constituted (*New York Times,* February 9, 1957).

be that an amendment could not be ratified when it had been before the country for more than a "reasonable" time. Consequently, when the child labor amendment, which Congress had proposed in 1924, with no time limit specified, was ratified by Kansas and Kentucky in 1937, efforts were made to get a judicial ruling that because of the lapse of time the amendment was no longer open for ratification.

In *Coleman v. Miller* (1939), however, the Court refused to take responsibility for deciding what was a "reasonable" period for ratification. That was an essentially political question, which Congress would have to determine. Four members of the Court went further to hold that the Court's assertion in *Dillon v. Gloss* that amendments must be ratified within a reasonable period was entirely unauthorized, and nothing more than an "admonition to the Congress in the nature of an advisory opinion." Their view was that the entire process of amendment was political and "not subject to judicial guidance, control or interference at any point."

The issue of congressional control over the amending process was raised again by the 1978 legislation extending the period for ratification of the Equal Rights Amendment, which was declared unconstitutional by a federal district judge in *Idaho v. Freeman* (1981). The "political question" doctrine had been somewhat narrowed since *Coleman* by the Supreme Court's decisions in *Baker v. Carr* (1962) and *Powell v. McCormack* (1969). Judge Callister in the *Idaho* case rejected the contention that Congress had plenary power over the amending process, and interpreted Article V to contemplate a reasonably contemporaneous process of ratifying actions by the states. Although Congress could set a time limit on state ratification, once established it could not be changed. Moreover, the extension was also unconstitutional because it was not adopted by a two-thirds vote of both houses. This ruling was a major blow to pro-ERA forces, and an immediate appeal was taken to the Supreme Court in *National Organization for Women v. Idaho* (1982). The Court granted a stay of the Callister ruling but declined to expedite its consideration. Consequently the deadline of June 30 passed without ratification or Supreme Court decision. Three months later the Court declared the case moot and vacated Judge Callister's decision, leaving it without precedential standing.

THE PROPOSING OF AMENDMENTS: CONGRESS OR CONVENTION?

Of the two methods that Article V provides for proposing amendments—by a two-thirds majority of each house of Congress, or by a convention summoned by Congress at the request of the legislatures of two-thirds of the states—only the former has been employed. On numerous occasions state legislatures have petitioned Congress to call a convention, but always unsuccessfully. In the early part of this century some thirty-one states, meeting the two-thirds requirement at that time, submitted petitions for an amendment to provide for direct election of senators. Congress failed to call a convention, but eventually proposed the amendment itself.

In 1962 the Council of State Governments asked state legislatures to petition for a convention to adopt a package of three "states' rights" amendments, but the number responding fell far short of the required two-thirds.[3] After the Supreme Court ruling in *Reynolds v. Sims* (1964), that members of both houses in the state legislatures must be elected from equal population districts, Senator Everett M. Dirksen spearheaded an effort to persuade two-thirds of the state legislatures to petition for a convention that would propose an amendment overriding that decision. He almost succeeded, securing petitions from thirty-three of the required thirty-four legislatures.

In the 1970s some thirty-three state legislatures requested Congress to call a convention to propose a budget-balancing amendment, again a number only one short of the required thirty-four. Campaigns were also organized to require conventions to propose amendments forbidding abortions, authorizing prayers in public schools, and for other "social" issues.

These efforts concentrated attention on the many uncertainties surrounding the convention device. If two-thirds of the legislatures submit petitions, must they be in identical language, and must they be received within a limited time period? May Congress refuse to act on the petitions? If Congress does refuse, can the courts force Congress to act? If a convention is called, how are the delegates chosen, and what are the voting rules in the convention? Can a convention be prevented from going beyond the subject for which it was convened, as the Constitutional Convention did in 1787?[4]

This last question, raising the so-called Pandora's box issue, is the most serious. Senator Sam Ervin sought to quiet concern about a "runaway" convention, as well as to deal with the organizational problems of a convention, by drafting the Federal Constitutional Convention Procedures Act, which passed the Senate in 1971.[5] The bill provided that convention calls to consider one or more amendments would be valid for seven years; that each state would have as many delegates as it had senators and representatives in Congress; that amendments would be proposed by majority vote; and that Congress could refuse to submit to the states any proposed amendment on a subject not included in the concurrent resolution setting up the convention.[6]

---

[3]See "Symposium: Constitutional Amendments Proposed by the Council of State Governments," 39 NOTRE DAME LAWYER 625 (1964).

[4]There is a considerable literature on the convention issue. See Gerald Gunther, "The Convention Method of Amending the United States Constitution," 14 GEORGIA LAW REVIEW 1 (1979); American Bar Association, *Amendment of the Constitution by the Convention Method under Article V.* (Chicago: American Bar Association, 1974); Walter E. Dellinger, "The Recurring Question of the 'Limited' Constitutional Convention," 88 YALE LAW JOURNAL 1623 (1979): C. Herman Pritchett, "Congress and Article V Conventions," 35 *Western Political Quarterly* 222 (1982).

[5]S. 215, 92nd Cong.

[6]Identical legislation was proposed in 1977 by Senator Jesse Helms as part of the effort to make an anti-abortion amendment by convention more acceptable. A special committee of the

Amendment by constitutional convention presents two major problems. First, it transfers the initiation of the amendment process from Congress, where national attention focuses on the issue and insures responsible consideration, to thirty-four scattered state legislatures over a period of years, which pressure groups can pick off one by one. Congress is the national forum where constitutional amendment is most appropriately considered. Second, there is no assurance, in spite of the language of the Ervin bill, that a convention can be prevented from proposing amendments on subjects other than the one it was convened to consider. The possibility of opening up the Constitution to wholesale rewriting is an unacceptable risk.

It is settled that the President plays no official role in the proposing of amendments, in spite of the provision in Article I, section 7, that "every order, resolution, or vote to which the concurrence of the Senate and House of Representatives may be necessary—shall be presented to the President." Presumably the reason is that proposing an amendment is not an exercise of ordinary legislative power.[7] Another factor is that, since proposed amendments must be passed by a two-thirds vote of each house and since that is the margin necessary to override a presidential veto, no purpose would normally be served by presidential participation in proposing amendments. The fact that the President does not pass on proposals for amendment of course constitutes no reason why he should not interest himself in proposed amendments, as President Reagan did in calling for balanced budget and school prayer amendments in 1982.

THE RATIFICATION OF AMENDMENTS

The ratification of all amendments to the Constitution except one has been by vote of three-fourths of the state legislatures. Only in the case of the Twenty-first Amendment, which repealed the Eighteenth, did Congress require the use of state conventions. The reason for this exception was the fear in Congress that the overrepresentation in the state legislatures of rural areas, which tended to be "dry," might imperil adoption of the amendment, whereas conventions would more equitably represent the views of the urban areas. The 1962 Council of State Governments' proposal would have deprived Congress of its authority to select the state convention mode of ratification.[8]

American Bar Association made similar proposals in its 1974 report, op. cit. See also "Proposed Legislation on the Convention Method of Amending the United States Constitution," 85 HARVARD LAW REVIEW 1612 (1972); Charles L. Black, Jr., "Amending the Constitution: A Letter to a Congressman," 82 YALE LAW JOURNAL 189 (1972).

[7] See *Hollingsworth v. Virginia* (1798); *Hawke v. Smith* (1920).

[8] States cannot make ratification depend upon a popular referendum vote; *Hawke v. Smith* (1920). But in 1975 the Illinois legislature required a 60 percent vote in each house for ratification of proposed amendments, a device adopted to insure defeat of the Equal Rights Amendment and upheld by a federal court in *Dyer v. Blair* (1975).

A state that has refused to ratify a proposed amendment may later change its mind and vote favorably. In *Coleman v. Miller* the Supreme Court said such action should be regarded as a political matter with the ultimate authority of decision in Congress. However, it has been thought that an affirmative vote on ratification cannot be subsequently withdrawn, even though the amendment has not been proclaimed in effect. Ohio and New Jersey attempted to withdraw their approval of the Fourteenth Amendment before its ratification had been announced. After some uncertainty, the secretary of state disregarded the withdrawal votes and proclaimed the amendment in effect. Congress supported this decision by adopting a concurrent resolution to the same effect.[9]

The rescission issue was raised again by state legislative action on ERA. By 1981, three of the thirty-five state legislatures that had ratified—Tennessee, Nebraska, and Idaho—had rescinded their approval. Also, in Kentucky a legislative rescission had been vetoed by the lieutenant governor in the governor's absence, while the South Dakota legislature had declared that its earlier ratification would become void if ERA was not ratified within the original seven-year period. The validity of the Idaho rescission was at issue in *Idaho v. Freeman,* and Judge Callister ruled that rescission of a prior ratification was valid if it occurred prior to unrescinded ratification by three-fourths of the states; Congress had no power to determine the validity or invalidity of a properly certified ratification or rescission. The Supreme Court's action vacating this decision leaves the issue still unsettled.[10]

APPRAISAL OF THE AMENDING PROCESS

Perhaps the most striking fact about the amending process is the infrequency with which it has been used. Excluding the initial ten amendments, which must be considered practically part of the original Constitution, amendments have been adopted at a rate of less than one per decade. Following the Civil War amendments, there was a period of over forty years during which the Constitution appeared unamendable. This was an era of agrarian discontent, industrial unrest, and growing interest in political and economic reforms. The conservatism of the Supreme Court, symbolized by its invalidation of the income tax in 1895, made constitutional amendment seem a necessary step toward achieving liberal legislative goals.

Under these circumstances there was much talk about the necessity of

[9]U.S. Stats., vol. 15, pp. 708–711 (July 21, 1868). In *Idaho v. Freeman* (1981) Judge Callister reviewed the controversy surrounding ratification of the Fourteenth Amendment and concluded that a sufficient number of states had ratified the amendment without the votes of Ohio and New Jersey.

[10]An affirmative view is expressed in Samuel S. Freedman and Pamela J. Naughton, *ERA: May a State Change Its Vote?* (Detroit: Wayne State University Press, 1978).

easing the amending process. In 1913, however, the long liberal campaign for the income tax and direct election of senators succeeded, and the women's suffrage amendment followed shortly thereafter. Also, adoption of the Eighteenth Amendment revealed the possibility of a small but dedicated pressure group exploiting the amending machinery successfully. With six amendments added to the Constitution between 1913 and 1933, the amending process no longer seemed so formidable. Moreover, the liberalization of the Supreme Court's views by President Franklin Roosevelt's appointments substantially eliminated liberal interest in further amendments.[11]

After the 1930s, pressure for amendments came principally from conservative political quarters. The increase in executive power and congressional expenditures, the acceptance of new welfare functions domestically and new responsibilities internationally by the federal government, the reduced role of the states, and liberal tendencies in the Supreme Court were all factors stimulating conservative recourse to the amending process. During the 1950s, the Bricker Amendment to limit the federal government's power to enter into international agreements as well as a proposal to place a ceiling on federal income taxation were conservative measures that failed of adoption. In the 1960s, efforts to override the Supreme Court's decisions on one-person, one-vote were defeated. By 1983 the only amendment secured by conservative forces was the Twenty-second, limiting the president to two terms.

However, in the different climate of the 1980s powerful forces pushed for "social" amendments to the Constitution. In a sense, the Constitution has been the victim of its own success. Veneration of the document has resulted in an "amendment mania." Constitutional amendments are attractive to reformers and propagandists of all persuasions who hope to give their causes status and glamour and place them beyond the reach of legislative challenge or later change of national mind. Loading the Constitution with policy preferences cheapens the document and freezes policies where alternatives should remain available.

[11]See Clement E. Vose, *Constitutional Change: Amendment Politics and Supreme Court Litigation since 1900* (Lexington, Mass.: Heath, 1972).

3

Interpretation
of the Constitution

More gradual but more continuous than the amending process in adapting the Constitution to changing conditions is the device of constitutional interpretation. In fact, it has been the possibility of modification of constitutional meanings over the years to meet new times and new necessities which has permitted resort to formal amendment to be relatively infrequent.

The process of constitutional adaptation goes on at many levels and in many contexts. Some adaptations develop on an entirely unplanned basis in the form of usages or customs or methods of procedure or institutions. Perhaps the most striking example in American history is the prompt development after 1789 of a party system, for which the framers had not planned and which in fact they had taken some pains to try to prevent. The development of committees in Congress, the tradition against a third term, the use of executive agreements instead of treaties, the rule that representatives must be residents of the districts they represent in Congress—these and many other customs and usages represented evolutionary adjustments of the constitutional system to practical problems with which it was confronted.

A much more intentional and sophisticated type of constitutional interpretation goes on in the decision making of the executive and legislative branches. President Truman's decision to seize the steel mills in 1952, or President Roosevelt's destroyers-for-bases deal with Britain in 1940, were consciously based on theories of executive power under the Constitution. Likewise when Congress is considering legislation of a novel character, it is sure to hear many speeches defending or attacking the constitutionality of the proposal.

The most highly rationalized type of constitutional interpretation is that engaged in by judges, and particularly by the Supreme Court of the United States, which is the focus of this volume.[1] Wherever the process of constitutional interpretation goes on, it is guided by some more or less articulate theory of the meaning of the Constitution. But in the 190 years during which the American nation has sought to relate the words of the written document to the diversity of its economic interests, political strivings, and moral goals, every conceivable rationalization has been developed for demonstrating that the policy preferences of the interpreter are in accord with the "true meaning" of the Constitution. The major theories of constitutional interpretation deserve brief consideration.

APPROACHES TO CONSTITUTIONAL MEANING

The Intention of the Framers

One widely supported proposition is that the meaning of the Constitution should be determined by reference to the intention of the men who made it. It seems natural and logical that in the famous case of *Marbury v. Madison* (1803), where the issue was whether the judiciary had authority to invalidate acts of Congress, Chief Justice Marshall should have asked about "the intention of those who gave this power." But it is significant that, 180 years later, scholars are still disputing as to whether Marshall's conclusions about the intent of the framers on this important issue were supported by the evidence.

There are more difficulties than one might imagine in determining the intent of the framers. Fifty-five delegates were present at one or more sessions of the Constitutional Convention, but some took little or no part in the proceedings. Some propositions on which they voted were carried by narrow majorities. What was said, and the reasons given for votes cast, is known almost entirely through James Madison's incomplete notes. On no issues did all members speak; on few did a majority speak. Many decisions must have been compromises that fully pleased no one.

If the intention of the fifty-five men at Philadelphia cannot be discovered

---

[1]For general discussions of the Supreme Court's role in constitutional interpretation, see Alexander M. Bickel, *The Least Dangerous Branch* (Indianapolis: Bobbs-Merrill, 1962); Paul L. Murphy, *The Constitution in Crisis Times, 1918-1969* (New York: Harper & Row, Pub. Inc., 1972); William F. Swindler, *Court and Constitution in the Twentieh Century: The New Legality, 1932-1968* (Indianapolis: Bobbs-Merrill, 1970); Congressional Quarterly, *Guide to the U.S. Supreme Court* (Washington, D.C.: Congressional Quarterly, Inc., 1979); Laurence H. Tribe, *American Constitutional Law* (Mineola, N.Y.: Foundation Press, 1978).

with assurance, what chance is there of determining the intention of the delegates to the state ratifying conventions whose votes put the Constitution into operation? The ultimate in uncertainty is reached if we seek to discover the intention of the people who elected the delegates to the state conventions.

The same problems are presented by amendments to the Constitution. What did the members of Congress who drafted the First Amendment in 1789 or the Fourteenth Amendment in 1866 intend by such broad phrases as "freedom of speech" or "equal protection of the laws"? Historical data can throw some light on the purposes behind such language, but all too often "intention of the framers" has been a rhetorical device employed by partisans to read their own policy preferences into the Constitution.

Justice Brennan had something useful to say about intentions of the framers in *School District of Abington Township v. Schempp* (1963), where the Court had to decide whether the saying of prayers and reading of the Bible in public schools constituted an establishment of religion contrary to the First Amendment. Justice Brennan thought "a too literal quest for the advice of the Founding Fathers" on this issue would be "futile and misdirected." The history was "ambiguous," the structure of American education has greatly changed since 1791, and we are a vastly more diverse people religiously than were our forefathers. Consequently, Brennan believed that, instead of looking for the intent of the framers, it would be more fruitful to inquire whether the practices challenged in the *Schempp* case threatened those consequences of interdependence between religion and the state "which the Framers deeply feared."

Where the Supreme Court has used history to support its conclusions, it has often been very bad history. Historian Alfred H. Kelly has noted two techniques used by the Court. One is the "creation of history a priori by . . . 'judicial fiat' or 'authoritative revelation.'" He suggests that several of Marshall's most notable opinions involve the creation of history by judicial fiat, with little if any inquiry into "actual history."

A second method is what Kelly calls "law-office history," that is, extended essays in constitutional history usually written for the purpose of justifying the reversal of precedent by proving that the precedent itself was contrary to the original intention of the Constitution. Nineteenth-century illustrations of law-office history are Chief Justice Taney's essay in the *Dred Scott* case on the Negro's role in early America, designed to prove that the Constitution was a "white man's document," and Chief Justice Fuller's essays in the *Income Tax Cases,* designed to break down the established precedents that income taxes were not direct taxes. The activist Court of the 1950s and 1960s also used the historical essay to justify departures from established doctrines in several fields.[2]

[2]Alfred H. Kelly, "Clio and the Court: An Illicit Love Affair," in Philip B. Kurland, ed., *The Supreme Court Review: 1965* (Chicago: University of Chicago Press, 1965), pp. 119–58. See also Charles A. Miller, *The Supreme Court and the Uses of History* (Cambridge, Mass.: Harvard University Press, 1969).

The Meaning of the Words

There is a second theory of constitutional interpretation that also employs the historical approach but for a different purpose. This is the method of interpretation on the basis of the meaning of the words at the time they were used. W. W. Crosskey's reinterpretation of the Constitution is based on this method.[3] On the flyleaf of his first volume he offers as his touchstone this quotation from Justice Holmes: "We ask, not what this man meant, but what those words would mean in the mouth of a normal speaker of English, using them in the circumstances in which they were used." As employed by Crosskey, this method of research in word usage during the era of constitutional formulation yielded a "specialized dictionary," on the basis of which he radically revised the meaning of many of the key provisions in the Constitution.

The search for original word meanings, like that for intent of the framers, assumes the binding nature of the obligations imposed by the decisions of 1787 on subsequent generations. Both approaches have the value, necessary to all law, of seeking to preserve some sense of stability and continuity in the agreements and understandings on which legitimate governmental power is based. In searching for the original meaning of the words, however, the second approach employs somewhat narrower lexicographic skills as opposed to the social history on which the first method relies. It is more closely confined by the document itself and is more directly related to the processes by which the written instruments of private law are construed.

The objections to these two methods of constitutional interpretation are likewise somewhat similar. Original meaning may be as difficult to establish as original intent. Crosskey's work is sufficient confirmation of this point. The original word meanings that his laborious research in the written materials of the time purports to establish can perhaps legitimately be challenged only on the basis of equally laborious research that reaches other conclusions. But certainly observers who have not done this research are entitled to express reservations about the validity of conclusions attributing original meaning to words, which differ so markedly from the meanings accepted for those words only a few years after adoption of the Constitution by responsible jurists and statesmen, many of whom had themselves been active in the drafting and adoption of the Constitution.

Perhaps the most serious objection to both methods, however, is the extent to which they propose to make a nation the prisoner of its past, and reject any method of constitutional development save constitutional amendment. Both reject the legitimacy of change by consensus or usage. Both deny the possibility that evolution in moral standards or political ideology can be given effect in the Constitution without changing its language.[4]

---

[3]W. W. Crosskey, *Politics and the Constitution in the History of the United States* (Chicago: University of Chicago Press, 1953).

[4]As alternative to the textual method of constitutional interpretation, Charles L. Black, Jr., proposes that constitutional law should use "the method of reasoning from structure and

Logical Reasoning

Logical analysis is an alternative to the historical methods of determining constitutional meaning, and is particularly worthy of note because of the extensive use made of it by Chief Justice Marshall in his great decisions. The method is most aptly demonstrated by reference again to *Marbury v. Madison*. There Marshall cites no judicial decisions to support his arguments. While referring to "original intention," he makes no effort to quote contemporaneous evidence or opinion. His argument is primarily an exercise in logic. "It seems only necessary to recognize certain principles," he says, "supposed to have been long and well established, to decide it." The major principle is that the Constitution is the supreme law of the land. The Supreme Court has taken an oath to uphold the Constitution. The conclusion logically follows that when an act of Congress conflicts with the superior law, the Supreme Court cannot enforce it but must declare it null and void.

This position has been so long accepted that the logic supporting it may seem unassailable. Yet is it not equally logical to argue that, since the Constitution is the supreme law of the land, and since the President has taken an oath to support the Constitution, he cannot enforce a decision of the Supreme Court that conflicts with the Constitution, but must declare it null and void?

The problem is simply not one to which logic can guarantee a correct answer. The fallacy of the logical form may be made clearer by stating a part of Marshall's argument as a syllogism.

MAJOR PREMISE: A law repugnant to the Constitution is void.
MINOR PREMISE: This law is repugnant to the Constitution.
CONCLUSION: This law is void.

Assuming the validity of the major premise, the soundness of the conclusion depends upon whether the minor premise is *factually* true. But logic cannot tell us whether a particular law is repugnant to the Constitution. That is a matter of informed opinion and judgment. This explains why Justice Holmes said, in one of the most famous passages in his lectures on common law: "This life of the law has not been logic: it has been experience. The felt necessities of the time, the prevalent moral and political theories, intuitions of public policy, avowed or unconscious, even the prejudices which judges share with their fellow-men, have had a good deal more to do than the syllogism in determining the rules by which men should be governed."[5]

---

relation"; *Structure and Relationship in Constitutional Law* (Baton Rouge: Louisiana State University Press, 1969). A useful analysis is Craig R. Ducat, *Modes of Constitutional Interpretation* (St. Paul, Minn.: West Publishing Co., 1978).

[5]Mark DeWolfe Howe, ed., *The Common Law* (Cambridge, Mass.: Harvard University Press, 1963), p. 5. But see Justice Rehnquist's critique of the idea of a "living Constitution"; William H. Rehnquist, "The Notion of a Living Constitution," 54 *Texas Law Review* 693 (1976).

Another device often employed in Supreme Court decisions is to test a constitutional argument "by pushing it to its logical conclusion." Obviously there is some utility in examining the soundness of a proposed decision by considering its logically possible implications, so long as these implications are not treated as inevitable consequents of the ruling. But all too often the purpose of this technique is to demonstrate that if the Court accepts the constitutionality of a particular legislative or executive action, which may seem comparatively mild and reasonable, there will be no logical stopping place at which the Court could forbid extensions of the same principle until a clearly unconstitutional result had been reached. Consequently it is claimed that the Court must forbid even the initial steps down the road toward an unconstitutional terminus. Thomas Reed Powell called this method "the parade of the imaginary horribles."

The Experiential Approach

Historical evidence as to the intent of the framers, textual analysis of the language of the Constitution, and application of the rules of logical thinking all have a useful place, but neither alone nor in combination can they supply the key to constitutional interpretation. There is a further factor, which Holmes designated as "experience." The experiential approach treats the Constitution more as a political than a legal document. It considers current understandings as relevant as the debates of the Constitutional Convention. It frankly recognizes that interpretation of the Constitution will and must be influenced by present-day values and by the sum total of American experience.

The intention of the framers is surely part of that experience, but so were the Vietnam War and Watergate. The meaning of the words as originally used is a relevant datum, but so also is the language of each presidential message to Congress. One may invoke logic and technical rules of construction, but one may also invoke such intangibles as "the spirit of the Constitution." The goal of constitutional interpretation, it may be suggested, is the achieving of consensus as to the *current meaning* of the document framed in 1787, a meaning that makes it possible to deal rationally with current necessities and acknowledge the lessons of experience while still recognizing guidelines derived from the written document and the philosophy of limited governmental power that it sought to express.

This approach recognizes the right of each generation to adapt the Constitution to its own needs, to the extent that such adaptations are reconcilable with the language of the Constitution. Naturally, the provision that the President shall have a four-year term cannot be reinterpreted to justify a five-year term. But the meaning of the clause giving Congress the authority to regulate commerce among the states or forbidding cruel and unusual punishment may legitimately change over a period of time. Marshall was defending this notion of a flexible Constitution when he said in *McCulloch v. Maryland*: "We must never forget, that it is a constitution we are expounding,'' one which is ''intended to endure for ages to come, and consequently, to be adapted to the various crises of human affairs.'' Holmes put the conception of the ''living'' Constitution into eloquent language when he wrote, in the case of *Missouri v. Holland* (1920):

> When we are dealing with words that also are a constituent act, like the Constitution of the United States, we must realize that they have called into life a being the development of which could not have been foreseen completely by the most gifted of its begetters. It was enough for them to realize or to hope that they had created an organism; it has taken a century and has cost their successors much sweat and blood to prove that they created a nation. The case before us must be considered in the light of our whole experience and not merely in that of what was said a hundred years ago.

The Supreme Court's experiential ventures into constitutional policy-making have engendered sharp criticism from the so-called ''interpretivist'' school, which includes Raoul Berger, Herbert Wechsler, and Justice Rehnquist. Interpretivism asserts that judicial policy-making is legitimate only when based on value judgments embodied either in a particular provision of the constitutional text or in the overall structure of government ordained by the Constitution. Perhaps the most influential of the interpretivists is John Hart Ely, who in *Democracy and Distrust* contended that leaving judges wholly free to select any set of political and moral values for special protection against majoritarian processes is irreconcilable with the requirements of representative democracy. But even Ely concedes two activist functions to the judiciary: keeping open the avenues of political change so that democratic processes may operate, and protecting what Stone called ''discrete and insular'' minorities from discrimination when the political process fails to do so.

THE PERSONAL FACTOR IN JUDICIAL INTERPRETATION

When we say that the Supreme Court has made a decision, we actually mean that the nine justices who compose the Court at a particular point in history have made the decision. Often, in fact, it is a decision made by only five members of the Court, with which the remaining four disagree. These justices, who have been fortuitously elevated to the highest judicial body by the process of presidential selection and the tests of political acceptability, are individuals of varying abilities, backgrounds, and policy preferences. How they will interpret the Constitution depends in part upon what kind of persons they are and how the world looks to them.[6]

This has not always been understood. During considerable periods of American history there has been a popular impression that when individuals

---

[6]See Leon Friedman and Fred L. Israel eds., *The Justices of the United States Supreme Court, 1789-1969: Their Lives and Major Opinions,* 5 vols. (New York: Chelsea House and R. R. Bowker, 1969-1978).

were appointed to the Supreme Court, they somehow became depersonalized and disembodied of all ordinary prejudices and passions. In the rarefied atmosphere of their chambers they were presumed to be at work discovering the law by the exercise of pure reason. This myth has typically been strongest during periods when the Court was under conservative domination, and it served the purpose of convincing the public that judicial protection of property or the thwarting of regulatory legislation was not an expression of the personal preferences of the justices but a voicing of the authentic commands of the Constitution. This myth, however, was finally and irretrievably destroyed in the years from 1935 to 1937, when it became all too apparent that the doctrine that the Supreme Court majority was expounding was their personal laissez-faire economic beliefs. As Max Lerner said, the public learned then "that judicial decisions are not babies brought by constitutional storks."[7]

It is an equally grave error, however, to jump to the conclusion that Supreme Court justices typically determine the meaning of the Constitution merely by consulting their personal preferences. There is an institutional ethos about the Court which cannot fail to have a restraining and educating effect upon the most opinionated justice. Perhaps the most important of these institutional factors is *stare decisis,* the rule of precedent. Individual judges may think that a particular precedent is wrong or outmoded. If so, they may exercise their personal judgments and state reasons for voting to override the earlier holding. They are free to do that. But they are not free to ignore the precedents, to act as though they did not exist. Judges have free choice, but only among limited alternatives and only after they are satisfied that they have met the obligations of consistency and respect for settled principles that judicial responsibility imposes upon them. Private views of the individual help to form and may be incorporated into the public views of a justice, but they are not the same thing.

From 1789 to 1983 the Supreme Court had fifteen Chief Justices and ninety-one associate justices.[8] Biographies of the more important justices provide excellent insights into the characteristic processes of judicial review as well as their own particular problems and contributions. Here it is possible to note only the principal judicial personalities and the major historical influences associated with the Court's power to interpret the American Constitution.[9]

The Pre-Marshall Court

The first decade of the Court's history was singularly unimpressive. President Washington's appointees were uniformly Federalists, and the entire ju-

---

[7] *Ideas for the Ice Age* (New York: Viking, 1941), p. 259.

[8] Three associate justices were promoted to the post of Chief Justice.

[9] See Charles Warren, *The Supreme Court in United States History,* rev. ed. (Boston: Little, Brown, 1947); Robert G. McCloskey, *The American Supreme Court* (Chicago: University of Chicago Press, 1960).

diciary quickly developed a definite partisan tone. John Jay, the first Chief Justice, spent one year in England on a diplomatic mission and ran twice for governor of New York while on the bench. After he succeeded the second time, he resigned the chief justiceship in 1795. John Rutledge, another original appointee, failed to attend a single session of the Court during its first two years. Appointed Chief Justice to succeed Jay, he served for four months before the Senate refused him confirmation, and then went insane.

Oliver Ellsworth, the next Chief Justice, resigned in 1800. James Wilson, also a member of the original Court, was an able lawyer but also a land speculator who narrowly avoided imprisonment for debt. Samuel Chase, appointed in 1795, dominated the Court in the latter part of this period. He was blatant in giving effect to his Federalist views from the bench, and in 1800 a term of the Court could not be held because he was absent electioneering for Adams. When the Jeffersonians came into power, he was impeached, but escaped conviction.

Though the Court had comparatively little business during these years, it did make some significant decisions. For one thing, it declined to advise President Washington on some legal questions in the field of foreign relations that he submitted to the Court, and thereby established a precedent against giving "advisory opinions." Also the Court strongly supported federal authority against the states in two important decisions. *Ware v. Hylton* (1796) held the treaty of peace with Britain to override a Virginia law on the sensitive issue of debts owed by Americans to British subjects. The decision in *Chisholm v. Georgia* (1793) asserted that states could be sued in federal courts by citizens of other states, a holding so bitterly resented by the states that the Eleventh Amendment was quickly adopted to void it.[10]

The Marshall Court

One month before Thomas Jefferson's inauguration in 1801, John Marshall was appointed Chief Justice by the outgoing Federalist administration. For the next thirty-five years he dominated the Court and did more than any other man in Supreme Court history to determine the character of the federal constitutional system. It was Marshall who in *Marbury v. Madison* (1803) successfully asserted the Court's power to declare acts of Congress unconstitutional. It was Marshall who in *McCulloch v. Maryland* (1819) established the broad authority of Congress to achieve national purposes under the "necessary and proper" clause and other broad grants of constitutional power. It was Marshall who in *Gibbons v. Ogden* (1824) first construed the commerce clause and struck down state regulation of commerce. It was Marshall who in *Dartmouth College v. Woodward* (1819) expanded the coverage of the contract clause and encouraged the judicial protection of vested rights that was

[10]See Julius Goebel, Jr., *History of the Supreme Court of the United States: Antecedents and Beginnings to 1801* (New York: Macmillan, 1971).

to be a theme of great significance throughout much of the Court's history. It was Marshall who by his courage, his convictions, and his intellectual vigor raised the Supreme Court from a third-rate status to a position of constitutional equality with President and Congress.[11]

The Federalist dominance in membership was soon lost on the Marshall Court as new appointments were made by Republican Presidents, but with few exceptions these colleagues were no match for Marshall. One exception was the able and much underrated William Johnson, whose disagreements with Marshall made him the first great dissenter. Another was the scholarly Joseph Story, nominally a Republican but actually closely attuned to Marshall's views.[12] Thus Marshall was able to direct the Court for more than three decades toward his twin goals—strengthening the powers of the federal government and protecting the rights of private property.

The Taney Court

Roger B. Taney, Democrat from Maryland, was appointed Chief Justice by President Jackson in 1836. Taney's Jacksonian democracy was in marked contrast with Marshall's federalism. States' rights and state police powers were emphasized more by the Court and central authority less. Property rights retained their influence with the Court, but it was agrarian property—land and slaves—rather than the commercial-creditor classes that now won judicial favor.

During his first twenty years on the Court, Taney's attachment to the economic interests of the South and West made him look like an economic liberal. But this same attachment led to the fatal *Dred Scott* decision in 1857, which permanently blackened Taney's reputation. No less intent than Marshall in his determination to preserve the prerogatives of judicial review and control, Taney's great talents were spent in his latter years in a lost and unworthy cause. He died in 1864, an embittered man who had lived too long.[13]

The Post-Civil War Court

The next three Chief Justices—Salmon P. Chase, Morrison R. Waite, and Melville W. Fuller[14]—fell far short of the stature of Marshall and Taney,

[11]See Albert J. Beveridge, *The Life of John Marshall,* 4 vols. (Boston: Houghton Mifflin Company, 1916); Leonard Baker, *John Marshall: A Life in the Law* (New York: Macmillan, 1974); Robert K. Faulkner, *The Jurisprudence of John Marshall* (Princeton, N.J.: Princeton University Press, 1968).

[12]Gerald T. Dunne, *Justice Joseph Story and the Rise of the Supreme Court* (New York: Simon & Schuster, 1970).

[13]Carl B. Swisher, *History of the Supreme Court of the United States: The Taney Period, 1836-64* (New York: Macmillan, 1974), and *Roger B. Taney* (New York: Macmillan, 1936).

[14]Willard L. King, *Melville Weston Fuller: Chief Justice of the United States, 1888-1910* (Chicago: University of Chicago Press, 1967).

and failed to mold the Court in their own image. The *Dred Scott* decision had plunged the Court to its lowest depths. Congress revealed its contempt for the Court by changing its size three times in seven years for obvious political purposes. When the Court showed signs of declaring some of the Reconstruction legislation unconstitutional in 1868, Congress brusquely withdrew the Court's jurisdiction to decide the case.[15]

With no strong leadership, the intellectual quality of the Court for the first time was to be found in its associate justices—men like Samuel Miller of Iowa (1862–1890),[16] Stephen J. Field of California (1863–1897),[17] Joseph P. Bradley of New Jersey (1870–1892), and John M. Harlan of Kentucky (1877–1911). Gradually the Court regained its prestige by reestablishing contact with the dominant trends of the times. The postwar period was one of raw and rapid industrial expansion. A continent was being harnessd with railroads, resources were being exploited, great fortunes built. At first the Court was reluctant to legitimize the economic freedom that the burgeoning corporations demanded. In the *Slaughterhouse Cases* (1873) and in *Munn v. Illinois* (1877) it declined to use the newly adopted Fourteenth Amendment to strike down state regulatory legislation.

But eventually the pressures were too strong to resist. The due process clause, interpreted by the Court as valueless to protect the civil rights of blacks, was readily adapted to protect the property rights of corporations. The high point in the Court's dedication to the new capitalism came in 1895, with no less than three significant decisions. One declared the income tax unconstitutional. Another held that the sugar trust did not violate the Sherman Act. The third upheld the jailing of the Socialist leader, Eugene V. Debs, for violating a federal court injunction against a strike by the railway workers' union.

The Holmes Decades

Fuller was Chief Justice until his death in 1910, and was succeeded by Edward D. White of Louisiana. In 1921 former President William Howard Taft took the post and held it until 1930.[18] The most influential and distinguished member of the Court during these years, however, was Associate Justice Oliver Wendell Holmes.[19] Appointed by President Theodore Roosevelt in

[15]See Charles Fairman, *History of the Supreme Court of the United States: Reconstruction and Reunion, 1864–88* (New York: Macmillan, 1971).

[16]Charles Fairman, *Mr. Justice Miller and the Supreme Court, 1862–1890* (Cambridge, Mass.: Harvard University Press, 1939).

[17]Carl B. Swisher, *Stephen J. Field: Craftsman of the Law* (Washington, D.C.: Brookings Institution, 1930).

[18]Alpheus T. Mason, *William Howard Taft: Chief Justice* (New York: Simon & Schuster, 1965).

[19]Mark DeWolfe Howe, *Justice Oliver Wendell Holmes*, 2 vols. (Cambridge, Mass.: Harvard University Press, 1957–1963); Max Lerner, *The Mind and Faith of Justice Holmes* (Boston:

1902 from the highest court of Massachusetts, he steadily grew in stature and reputation until his resignation in 1932 at the age of ninety-one.

His character and intellectual alignments defy any brief summary. The public knew him as the great dissenter, and thought of him as a liberal because his dissents were often protests against the denial of civil liberties or the judicial invalidation of liberal legislation. But these protests were less an expression of political liberalism than of a philosophy of limited judicial review which insisted that judges should not substitute their views for those of legislators so long as the legislative policy remained within the bounds of reason.

Holmes's colleagues were generally reluctant to accept such limitations on judicial power. In *Lochner v. New York* (1905) the Court struck down a ten-hour law for bakers against Holmes's warning that "the Fourteenth Amendment does not enact Mr. Herbert Spencer's Social Statics." But his position was gradually strengthened in the country and on the Court, as by the appointment of Charles Evans Hughes in 1910, fresh from his work as a reform governor of New York.[20] Hughes left the Court in 1916 to run for President, but that same year President Wilson named to the Court an ardent progressive, Louis D. Brandeis, and got him confirmed in spite of the opposition of the organized bar and big business.[21]

The phrase, "Holmes and Brandeis dissenting," quickly became a part of American folklore as these two men, though proceeding from differing premises, joined in case after case to protest the Court's policies. In 1925 the duo became a trio as President Coolidge named his liberal attorney general, Harlan F. Stone to the Court.[22] In their dissenting opinions they mapped out an alternative to the doctrinaire conservatism of the Court majority that, if adopted in time, would have averted the crisis into which the Court was heading.

The Hughes Court and the New Deal

Hughes returned to the Court in 1931 as Chief Justice. A much more flexible man than Taft, he had the responsibility of guiding the Court in its review of the constitutional aspects of the new and experimental legislation enacted by the New Deal to combat the Great Depression. On the Court he headed, Brandeis and Stone had been joined by Benjamin N. Cardozo, appointed in 1932 to fill the Holmes vacancy. These three justices could generally

---

Little, Brown, 1946); Felix Frankfurter, *Mr. Justice Holmes and the Supreme Court* (Cambridge, Mass.: Harvard University Press, 1939).

[20]Merlo J. Pusey, *Charles Evans Hughes* (New York: Macmillan, 1951).

[21]Alpheus T. Mason, *Brandeis: A Free Man's Life* (New York: Viking, 1946); Alexander M. Bickel, *The Unpublished Opinions of Mr. Justice Brandeis* (Cambridge, Mass.: Belknap Press, 1957); Samuel J. Konefsky, *The Legacy of Holmes and Brandeis* (New York: Macmillan, 1956).

[22]Alpheus T. Mason, *Harlan Fiske Stone: Pillar of the Law* (New York: Viking, 1956); Samuel J. Konefsky, *Chief Justice Stone and the Supreme Court* (New York: Macmillan, 1945).

be counted on to uphold the New Deal, but they were offset by four conservative justices—Willis Van Devanter, appointed by Taft in 1910; James C. McReynolds, named by Wilson in 1914; and two Harding appointees of 1922, George Sutherland and Pierce Butler. The balance of power on the Court thus rested with the Chief Justice himself and with the ninth member, Owen J. Roberts, appointed by Hoover in 1930.

The initial tests of 1934 seemed to suggest that the Court would accept the new legislative trends by a vote of five to four, but this forecast soon proved mistaken. In 1935 and 1936 the Court invalidated a series of important federal and state regulatory laws, usually by a vote of five to four or six to three, depending upon whether Roberts alone, or Roberts and Hughes, voted with the conservative bloc. After his electoral triumph in 1936 President Roosevelt, who had had no Court vacancies to fill during his first term, undertook to eliminate this judicial barrier to reform by a proposal to increase the Court's size to fifteen justices.

Juggling the size of the Court was no longer so acceptable as it had been in the 1860s, however, and the Court-packing plan was defeated in Congress. However, in several key cases in the spring of 1937 Roberts swung over to the liberal side, giving the administration some five to four victories. At the end of the term Van Devanter retired, and President Roosevelt had his opportunity to begin remaking the Court.

The Roosevelt Court

Between 1937 and 1943 President Roosevelt appointed eight members to the Court (one position being filled twice) and elevated Harlan Stone to the chief justiceship. All these appointees were economic liberals, and there ceased to be any danger of judicial invalidation of regulatory legislation affecting property. The characteristic problem of the Roosevelt Court dealt rather with civil liberty; and the justices, in spite of their basic libertarian leanings, quickly found themselves more divided than ever, but now over the nature of their judicial responsibility for the protection of libertarian goals.[23] Justices Hugo Black,[24] William O. Douglas,[25] Frank Murphy,[26] and Wiley Rutledge were a cohesive group as firmly committed to the use of judicial power to protect civil liberties from legislative infringement as the anti-New Deal conservatives

---

[23]C. Herman Pritchett, *The Roosevelt Court: A Study in Judicial Politics and Values, 1937–1947* (New York: Quadrangle, 1969; Macmillan, 1948).

[24]Gerald T. Dunne, *Hugo Black and the Judicial Revolution* (New York: Simon & Schuster, 1977); John P. Frank, *Mr. Justice Black: The Man and His Opinions* (New York: Knopf, 1949); Stephen Strickland, ed., *Hugo Black and the Supreme Court* (Indianapolis: Bobbs-Merrill, 1967).

[25]Vern Countryman, *The Judicial Record of Justice William O. Douglas* (Cambridge, Mass.: Harvard University Press, 1974); *William O. Douglas, The Court Years, 1939–1975* (New York: Random House, 1980).

[26]J. Woodford Howard, *Mr. Justice Murphy: A Political Biography* (Princeton: Princeton University Press, 1968).

had been in the protection of economic freedom a decade earlier. Justice Felix Frankfurter, on the other hand, argued that the Holmes tradition called for judicial restraint in both areas.[27]

The libertarian temper of the Roosevelt Court was substantially diluted by President Truman's four appointments. Chief Justice Fred Vinson replaced Stone on the latter's death in 1946. Both Rutlege and Murphy died in the summer of 1949, thus leaving only Black and Douglas in the Court's activist bloc. The most difficult problems of the Vinson Court were those generated by the cold war against communism. In its most celebrated decision, it upheld the Smith Act convictions of the leaders of the American Communist Party in *Dennis v. United States* (1951), with Black and Douglas dissenting; and it was careful to refrain from interfering with the "Red" hunts of congressional investigating committees.[28]

The Warren Court

On Vinson's death in 1953, President Eisenhower named Earl Warren of California to be Chief Justice. In the first term under his leadership the Court unanimously declared unconstitutional racial segregation in the public schools, boldly overturning the doctrine of "separate but equal" that had been used to justify segregation for almost sixty years.

President Eisenhower had the opportunity to make four additional appointments—John M. Harlan, grandson of the earlier Harlan, replacing Jackson; William J. Brennan, Jr., replacing Minton; Charles E. Whittaker, replacing Reed; and Potter Stewart, replacing Burton. With the appointment of Brennan, a liberal Catholic Democrat, a new four-judge activist bloc developed on the Court, as Brennan voted rather consistently with Warren, Black, and Douglas. The other new members of the Court, however, tended to look to Justice Frankfurter for intellectual leadership; and particularly after 1957 there was a series of five to four defeats for the activist bloc.[29]

President Kennedy made two appointments to the Court in 1962. Whittaker's place was taken by Byron R. White, forty-four-year-old ex-Rhodes scholar and famous football player who had been deputy attorney general in the Kennedy administration. When Justice Frankfurter retired because of illness, his seat was filled by Arthur J. Goldberg, secretary of labor and former

---

[27]Helen Shirley Thomas, *Felix Frankfurter: Scholar on the Bench* (Baltimore: Johns Hopkins Press, 1960); H. N. Hirsch, *The Enigma of Felix Frankfurter* (New York: Basic Books, 1981); Michael E. Parrish, *Felix Frankfurter and His Times: The Reform Years* (New York: Free Press, 1982); Joseph P. Lash, *From the Diaries of Felix Frankfurter* (New York: W. W. Norton & Co., Inc., 1975); Bruce Allen Murphy, *The Brandeis/Frankfurter Connection* (New York: Oxford University Press, 1982).

[28]C. Herman Pritchett, *Civil Liberties and the Vinson Court* (Chicago: University of Chicago Press, 1954).

[29]Wallace Mendelson, *Justices Black and Frankfurter: Conflict in the Court* (Chicago: University of Chicago Press, 1961).

general counsel for the AFL-CIO. The Court's balance was swung sharply toward the liberal side by these appointments, as was immediately evidenced by dramatic decisions dealing with such controversial matters as legislative reapportionment, prayer and Bible reading in public schools, and increased procedural protections in criminal prosecutions.

In 1965 President Johnson asked Justice Goldberg to become United States ambassador to the United Nations. To fill the vacancy the President named one of his close advisers, Abe Fortas, member of a prominent Washington law firm who in 1963 had argued the famous case of *Gideon v. Wainwright* before the Court. Justice Clark retired in 1967 to avoid any conflict of interest after his son, Ramsey, was named attorney general. To his place President Johnson appointed solicitor general and former court of appeals judge Thurgood Marshall, the Court's first black and the man who as chief counsel for the NAACP had argued the school desegregation case, *Brown v. Board of Education* (1954), before the Court.

The Warren Court was one of the most controversial in Supreme Court history.[30] Its decisions defending minority rights and civil liberties made the impeachment of Earl Warren a favorite demand of the radical right. The attacks on the Warren Court came from three principal quarters: from Southern opponents of the desegregation decision; from those who contended that the Court had handicapped the fight against Communist subversion by its limitations on congressional investigatory power and insistence on the procedural rights of "political offenders"; and from those who maintained that the Court had infringed state authority over a wide range of activities, including economic regulation, procedure in criminal cases, religious observances in the public schools, and legislative apportionment.

In Congress the assault on the Court reached a climax in the closing days of the 1958 session, when a series of measures intended to curb or reverse the Court was narrowly defeated.[31] The Court soon thereafter withdrew from some of the positions that had led to congressional anger, particularly with respect to judicial control over congressional investigating committees.

Then in 1962 the Court again stirred up a storm by declaring unconstitutional religious observances in the public schools (*Engel v. Vitale*) and opening up state legislative-apportionment practices to judicial review and control (*Baker v. Carr*). However, efforts to reverse the Court's rulings by constitu-

---

[30]John D. Weaver, *Warren: The Man, the Court, the Era* (Boston: Little, Brown, 1967); Leonard W. Levy, ed., *The Supreme Court under Earl Warren* (New York: Quadrangle, 1972); Philip B. Kurland, *Politics, the Constitution, and the Warren Court* (Chicago: University of Chicago Press, 1970); Robert G. McCloskey, *The Modern Supreme Court* (Cambridge, Mass.: Harvard University Press, 1972); C. Herman Pritchett, *The Political Offender and the Warren Court* (Boston: Boston University Press, 1958); G. Edward White, *Earl Warren: A Public Life* (New York: Oxford University Press, 1982).

[31]See C. Herman Pritchett, *Congress versus the Supreme Court, 1957–1960* (Minneapolis: University of Minnesota Press, 1961); Walter F. Murphy, *Congress and the Court* (Chicago: University of Chicago Press, 1962).

tional amendments failed, and in the legislative-apportionment field the Court proceeded to carry through a political revolution by requiring the long under-represented urban and suburban areas to be given their proper weight in state legislatures.

Warren notified President Johnson of his intention to resign in 1968, effective upon confirmation of his successor; but Justice Fortas, nominated to the post by Johnson, was unable to secure confirmation by the Senate. Warren then continued to serve for another term until replaced by Nixon appointee Warren Earl Burger. Nixon's announced goal was to return the Court to the control of conservative "strict constructionists," and he made three more appointments of men meeting this test: Harry A. Blackmun, replacing Fortas who resigned in 1969, and Lewis F. Powell, Jr. and William H. Rehnquist, on the retirement of Hugo Black and John M. Harlan.[32]

The Burger Court

On the early Burger Court, the four Nixon appointees tended to form a conservative bloc that could generally count on the support of White or Stewart or both, leaving the liberal trio of Douglas, Black, and Marshall in a minority role. However, there was no wholesale reversal of Warren Court holdings. Rather, the Burger Court acted in a mixed or ambiguous fashion, leaving many Warren era rulings intact. While retreating moderately in the area of criminal procedures, it maintained a generally strong commitment to First Amendment rights and took activist positions on such issues as abortion, sex discrimination, capital punishment, and the rights of prisoners and inmates of mental institutions.[33] The retirement of Justice Douglas in late 1975, and his replacement by John Paul Stevens, a moderate member of the Court of Appeals for the Seventh Circuit, appeared to confirm the Court's trend toward a less active policy role, and an accelerated tendency toward limitation or reversal of Warren Court precedents, which became evident from the mid-1970s on.[34]

No vacancies occurred on the Court during President Carter's single term in office. When Justice Stewart retired in 1981, President Reagan seized the opportunity to name not only a conservative but also the first woman justice in the history of the Court, Sandra Day O'Connor, a state legislator and judge from Arizona. She promptly took a judicial restraint and states' rights position close to that of Burger and Rehnquist. Justices Powell and White tended

---

[32]See the discussion of the Fortas resignation and the Nixon appointments in Chapter 6.

[33]See James F. Simon, *In His Own Image: The Supreme Court in Richard Nixon's America* (New York: D. McKay, 1973); Leonard W. Levy, *Against the Law: The Nixon Court and Criminal Justice* (New York: Harper & Row, Pub., 1974).

[34]See Bob Woodward and Scott Alexander, *The Brethren: Inside the Supreme Court* (New York: Simon & Schuster, 1979); Richard Y. Funston, *Constitutional Counterrevolution? The Warren Court and the Burger Court* (New York: John Wiley, 1977); Stephen L. Wasby, *Continuity and Change: From the Warren Court to the Burger Court* (Santa Monica, Calif.: Goodyear, 1976).

toward a pragmatically moderate stance in the middle of the Court, while Stevens and Blackmun showed considerable affinity for the Court's two liberals, Brennan and Marshall.

In summary, the American constitutional system is one in which important policy questions are frequently cast in the form of a lawsuit and brought to the Supreme Court for decision. The Court is basically a public law court, and its highest public law function is to determine the current meaning of the Constitution when that is necessary to settle a judicial controversy that comes before it. In the search for current meanings the justices inevitably consult their own policy preferences, but the institutional setting forces responsibility upon them and requires them to meet high standards of consistency and logic. Theirs is the difficult task of moving with the times, yet without departing from constitutional fundamentals or impairing that popular expectation of judicial stability that is so necessary an asset to the moral authority of the Court.

Members of the United States Supreme Court 1789-1983

CHIEF JUSTICES	STATE	TERM	APPOINTED BY	LIFE-SPAN
John Jay	N.Y.	1789–1795	Washington	1745–1829
John Rutledge	S.C.	1795*	"	1739–1800
Oliver Ellsworth	Conn.	1796–1800	"	1745–1807
John Marshall	Va.	1801–1835	J. Adams	1755–1835
Roger B. Taney	Md.	1836–1864	Jackson	1777–1864
Salmon P. Chase	Ohio	1864–1873	Lincoln	1808–1873
Morrison R. Waite	Ohio	1874–1888	Grant	1816–1888
Melville W. Fuller	Ill.	1888–1910	Cleveland	1833–1910
Edward D. White	La.	1910–1921	Taft	1845–1921
William H. Taft	Conn.	1921–1930	Harding	1857–1930
Charles E. Hughes	N.Y.	1930–1941	Hoover	1862–1948
Harlan F. Stone	N.Y.	1941–1946	F. D. Roosevelt	1872–1946
Fred M. Vinson	Ky.	1946–1953	Truman	1890–1953
Earl Warren	Calif.	1953–1969	Eisenhower	1891–1974
Warren Earl Burger	Minn.	1969–	Nixon	1907–
ASSOCIATE JUSTICES				
John Rutledge	S.C.	1789–1791	Washington	1739–1800
William Cushing	Mass.	1789–1810	"	1732–1810
James Wilson	Pa.	1789–1798	"	1742–1798
John Blair	Va.	1789–1796	"	1732–1800
James Iredell	N.C.	1790–1799	"	1751–1799
Thomas Johnson	Md.	1791–1793	"	1732–1819
William Paterson	N.J.	1793–1806	"	1745–1806
Samuel Chase	Md.	1796–1811	"	1741–1811
Bushrod Washington	Va.	1798–1829	J. Adams	1762–1829
Alfred Moore	N.C.	1799–1804	"	1755–1810

Members of the United States Supreme Court 1789–1983 (Cont.)

ASSOCIATE JUSTICES	STATE	TERM	APPOINTED BY	LIFE-SPAN
William Johnson	S.C.	1804–1834	Jefferson	1771–1834
Henry B. Livingston	N.Y.	1806–1823	"	1757–1823
Thomas Todd	Ky.	1807–1826	"	1765–1826
Joseph Story	Mass.	1811–1845	Madison	1779–1845
Gabriel Duval	Md.	1811–1835	"	1752–1844
Smith Thompson	N.Y.	1823–1843	Monroe	1768–1843
Robert Trimble	Ky.	1826–1828	J. Q. Adams	1777–1828
John McLean	Ohio	1829–1861	Jackson	1785–1861
Henry Baldwin	Pa.	1830–1844	"	1780–1844
James M. Wayne	Ga.	1835–1867	"	1790–1867
Philip P. Barbour	Va.	1836–1841	"	1783–1841
John Catron	Tenn.	1837–1865	"	1786–1865
John McKinley	Ala.	1837–1852	Van Buren	1780–1852
Peter V. Daniel	Va.	1841–1860	"	1784–1860
Samuel Nelson	N.Y.	1845–1872	Tyler	1792–1873
Levi Woodbury	N.H.	1846–1851	Polk	1789–1851
Robert C. Grier	Pa.	1846–1870	Polk	1794–1870
Benjamin R. Curtis	Mass.	1851–1857	Fillmore	1809–1874
John A. Campbell	Ala.	1853–1861	Pierce	1811–1889
Nathan Clifford	Maine	1858–1881	Buchanan	1803–1881
Noah H. Swayne	Ohio	1862–1881	Lincoln	1804–1884
Samuel F. Miller	Iowa	1862–1890	"	1816–1890
David Davis	Ill.	1862–1877	"	1815–1886
Stephen J. Field	Calif.	1863–1897	"	1816–1899
William Strong	Pa.	1870–1880	Grant	1808–1895
Joseph P. Bradley	N.J.	1870–1892	"	1813–1892
Ward Hunt	N.Y.	1872–1882	"	1810–1886
John M. Harlan	Ky.	1877–1911	Hayes	1833–1911
William B. Woods	Ga.	1880–1887	"	1824–1887
Stanley Matthews	Ohio	1881–1889	Garfield	1824–1889
Horace Gray	Mass.	1881–1902	Arthur	1828–1902
Samuel Blatchford	N.Y.	1882–1893	"	1820–1893
Lucius Q. C. Lamar	Miss.	1888–1893	Cleveland	1825–1893
David J. Brewer	Kans.	1889–1910	B. Harrison	1837–1910
Henry B. Brown	Mich.	1890–1906	"	1836–1913
George Shiras, Jr.	Pa.	1892–1903	"	1832–1924
Howell E. Jackson	Tenn.	1893–1895	"	1832–1895
Edward D. White	La.	1894–1910	Cleveland	1845–1921
Rufus W. Peckham	N.Y.	1895–1909	"	1838–1909
Joseph McKenna	Calif.	1898–1925	McKinley	1843–1926
Oliver W. Holmes	Mass.	1902–1932	T. Roosevelt	1841–1935
William R. Day	Ohio	1903–1922	"	1849–1923
William H. Moody	Mass.	1906–1910	"	1853–1917
Horace H. Lurton	Tenn.	1909–1914	Taft	1844–1914
Charles E. Hughes	N.Y.	1910–1916	"	1862–1948
Willis Van Devanter	Wyo.	1910–1937	"	1859–1941
Joseph H. Lamar	Ga.	1910–1916	"	1857–1916
Mahlon Pitney	N.J.	1912–1922	"	1858–1924

Members of the United States Supreme Court 1789–1983 (Cont.)

ASSOCIATE JUSTICES	STATE	TERM	APPOINTED BY	LIFE-SPAN
James C. McReynolds	Tenn.	1914–1941	Wilson	1862–1946
Louis D. Brandeis	Mass.	1916–1939	"	1856–1941
John H. Clarke	Ohio	1916–1922	"	1857–1945
George Sutherland	Utah	1922–1938	Harding	1862–1942
Pierce Butler	Minn.	1922–1939	"	1866–1939
Edward T. Sanford	Tenn.	1923–1930	"	1865–1930
Harlan F. Stone	N.Y.	1925–1941	Coolidge	1872–1946
Owen J. Roberts	Pa.	1930–1945	Hoover	1875–1955
Benjamin N. Cardozo	N.Y.	1932–1938	"	1870–1938
Hugo L. Black	Ala.	1937–1971	F. D. Roosevelt	1886–1971
Stanley F. Reed	Ky.	1938–1957	"	1884–1980
Felix Frankfurter	Mass.	1939–1962	"	1882–1965
William O. Douglas	Conn.	1939–1975	"	1898–1980
Frank Murphy	Mich.	1940–1949	"	1890–1949
James F. Byrnes	S.C.	1941–1942	"	1879–1974
Robert H. Jackson	N.Y.	1941–1954	"	1892–1954
Wiley B. Rutledge	Iowa	1943–1949	"	1894–1949
Harold H. Burton	Ohio	1945–1958	Truman	1888–1964
Tom C. Clark	Tex.	1949–1967	"	1899–1977
Sherman Minton	Ind.	1949–1956	"	1890–1965
John M. Harlan	N.Y.	1955–1971	Eisenhower	1899–1971
William J. Brennan, Jr.	N.J.	1956–	"	1906–
Charles E. Whittaker	Mo.	1957–1962	"	1901–1973
Potter Stewart	Ohio	1958–1981	"	1915–
Byron R. White	Colo.	1962–	Kennedy	1917–
Arthur J. Goldberg	Ill.	1962–1965	"	1908–
Abe Fortas	Tenn.	1965–1969	Johnson	1910–1982
Thurgood Marshall	Md.	1967–	"	1908–
Harry A. Blackmun	Minn.	1970–	Nixon	1908–
Lewis F. Powell, Jr.	Va.	1971–	"	1907–
William H. Rehnquist	Ariz.	1971–	"	1924–
John Paul Stevens	Ill.	1975–	Ford	1920–
Sandra Day O'Connor	Ariz.	1981–	Reagan	1930–

*Unconfirmed recess appointment.

4

Nation and State

One of the serious reservations that the framers had in setting up a new Constitution was whether a large country would be a threat to the freedom of its citizens. The delegates who opposed the Virginia Plan for a strong central government had a picture in their minds, drawn in part at least from the experience of the Greek city-states, of the "small republic" as the ideal form of government. Roger Sherman put it this way: "The people are more happy in small than large States."

The problem was that small republics were too weak, standing alone, to protect their independence and their economies, and so they had to associate in some common organization for mutual protection. But Sherman and other supporters of the New Jersey Plan believed that a confederation limited to the functions of keeping the peace among the states and defending them against foreign enemies was all that was needed.

It was James Madison's role to answer the small republic argument. He contended that, from antiquity to the current American states, small republics had been beset by conflicts between classes, which were fatal to liberty. A large republic would be preferable, for there, he argued, liberty would be protected by "the great variety of interests, parties, and sects which it embraces." An "extended republic of the United States" would be divided into many groups, no single one amounting to a majority. Only as smaller groups voluntarily associated could majorities be formed, a process that would force each group to moderate its position and protect the liberties of all.

The Constitutional Convention was persuaded by Madison's argument and even more by realization that their goals of security, peace, and economic development could be achieved only through a strong central government. But the Founders' insistence on also preserving the states as strong organs of local government forced them to invent a federal system.

We now think of the threefold distinction among the confederal, federal, and unitary forms of government as self-evident. But in 1787 only two forms, the confederal and the national (unitary), were recognized. The opening words of the resolution proposing the Virginia Plan stated these two alternatives: a "merely federal" union or "a National Government." "Merely federal" meant a confederation such as was then in existence. It was because this "merely federal" plan had failed that the Virginia delegation proposed a truly "national" government. But what actually emerged from the Convention was the blueprint for a large republic intended to achieve both liberty and security by a division of responsibilities and functions that has come to be considered the true form of federalism.

The Constitution, it should be noted, does not use the term "federalism." Because of the vague theoretical origins of American federalism, disagreement over the nature of the Union was almost inevitable. The existence of sharply divisive sectional interests led to the exploitation of these disagreements for intensely practical purposes. Regional differences were compounded by localistic patriotism and hope of economic gain. Where such animus is present in constitutional issues, judicial decisions are not likely to be accepted as final. During the first half of the nineteenth century these controversies were fostered by all the resources of the political process, and ultimately had to be resolved by a bitter civil war. Only after the nature of the Union had been determined by the arbitrament of arms was it possible for the courts to continue with adjudication of the lesser but continuing problems of adjustment in the federal system.

THE NATURE OF THE UNION

A Compact of States or of People?

The prevailing political philosophy of the eighteenth century, as we have seen, stressed contract as the basis of governmental authority. The Constitution was such a contract, but who were the parties to it—the states or the people of the United States? The language of the Constitution could be cited to support both views. Article VII provides that approval by conventions in nine states "shall be sufficient for the establishment of this Constitution *be-*

tween the states so ratifying the same.''[1] On the other hand, the Preamble to the Constitution declares that it is ''the people of the United States'' who ''do ordain and establish this Constitution,'' and conventions rather than state legislatures were chosen as the instruments of ratification precisely to emphasize the popular base of the contract. Again, it could be pointed out that, although the Articles of Confederation had specifically provided that the states were sovereign, the Constitution was discreetly silent on the location of sovereignty.

Interposition

After the establishment of the new government, the first significant theoretical attack on the authority of the national government came in the form of the famous Kentucky and Virginia Resolutions against the Alien and Sedition Acts. The first paragraph of the Kentucky Resolutions, which Jefferson drafted, reads:

> *Resolved,* That the several states composing the United States of America are not united on the principle of unlimited submission to their general government; but that, by compact, under the style and title of a Constitution for the United States, and of amendments thereto, they constituted a general government for special purposes, delegated to that government certain definite powers, reserving, each state to itself, the residuary mass of right to their own self-government; and that whensoever the general government assumed undelegated powers, its acts are unauthoritative, void, and of no force; that to this compact each state acceded as a state, and is an integral party; that this government, created by this compact, was not made the exclusive or final judge of the extent of the powers delegated to itself, since that would have made its discretion, and not the Constitution, the measure of its powers; but that, as in all other cases of compact among parties having no common Judge, *each party has an equal right to judge for itself, as well of infractions as of the mode and measure of redress.*

In a second set of resolutions passed in 1799, the Kentucky legislature proclaimed: ''That a Nullification, by those sovereignties, of all unauthorized acts done under color of that instrument, is the rightful remedy.'' Madison, who drafted the Virginia Resolutions, contributed the concept of ''interposition'' to American constitutional history in the third paragraph of those resolutions, when he concluded ''that, in case of a deliberate, palpable, and dangerous exercise of other powers, not granted by the said compact, the states, who are parties thereto, have the right, and are in duty bound, to interpose, for arresting the progress of the evil, and for maintaining within their respective limits, the authorities, rights, and liberties, appertaining to them.''

Did Madison and Jefferson mean to claim that the Union was a system of fully sovereign states, a confederation from which each state could retire at any time? Did they mean that refusal to be bound by any objectionable act of Congress was within the rights of the states, and that an attempt to enforce

[1]Italics supplied.

the act on a state would justify its secession? It seems highly unlikely. While they referred to the states as sovereign, they also conceded that the national government was sovereign. Acceptance of the divisibility of sovereignty was common at that time.

The Kentucky and Virginia Resolutions were circulated among the other states; and they elicited responses from at least seven, mostly in the Federalist Northeast, upholding the concept of federal supremacy and denying the right of a state to nullify federal law. Jefferson's victory over the Federalists in the election of 1800, due in no small part to popular resentment over the Alien and Sedition Acts, terminated this episode. But within a decade the New England states were themselves to enunciate extreme states' rights doctrine, under the pressure of the severe economic hardships they experienced as a result of President Jefferson's embargo policy. This sectional disaffection was increased by the strains of the War of 1812, during which the New England states sometimes refused to cooperate with American military operations and continued considerable trade with Britain. The Hartford Convention of 1814–1815, in which this movement culminated, recommended to the legislatures of the states represented that they pass measures to protect their citizens from the operation of unconstitutional national acts. But before the resolutions even got to Washington, the war was over, the complaints were forgotten, and the only result of the Convention was to annihilate the Federalist party.

Nullification

The theory of nullification originated with Jefferson's statement in the Kentucky Resolutions that "where powers are assumed which have not been delegated, a nullification of the act is the rightful remedy." This idea was later developed as a rationalization for Southern opposition to the increase in tariff rates between 1816 and 1828. John C. Calhoun, alarmed at the open talk of secession in the South, offered the doctrine of nullification as a substitute, contending that it was a logical extension of the Virginia and Kentucky Resolutions.

In 1832 a South Carolina convention passed an "Ordinance of Nullification" declaring the federal tariff acts null and void and forbidding federal agents to collect them in the state. President Jackson immediately challenged this action, saying that the power of nullification was "incompatible with the existence of the Union" and sent gunboats into Charleston harbor to enforce the tariff. The nullification statute was eventually repealed by the state after Congress had worked out a compromise measure on the tariff rates.

Secession

In the years preceding the Civil War, with the controversies over slavery and the tariff going on around them, Southern statesmen shifted their ground from the right of nullification to secession as the means to preserve their economic life and social institutions. Jefferson Davis pointed to the reservations that Virginia, New York, and Rhode Island had made in ratifying the Constitution, wherein they asserted that the powers granted to the federal government might be reassumed by the people in case of oppression, and concluded: "The right of the people of the several States to resume the powers delegated by them to the common agency, was not left without positive and ample assertion, even at a period when it had never been denied."[2]

For Calhoun, secession was justified as a final remedy to preserve a state's rights. According to his theory, after a state had interposed its authority to prevent federal action, the federal government could appeal to the amending process. If three-fourths of the states upheld the federal claim, the matter was settled as far as those states were concerned. But the dissenting state was not obliged to acquiesce in all instances.

Lincoln's decision to use force to keep the Southern states in the Union and the victory of the North in the Civil War closed the debate over the legality of secession. The final decision was rendered at Appomattox Courthouse. After the war, the Supreme Court tidied up a bit in *Texas v. White* (1869). The case hinged on the question whether or not Texas had ever left the Union, and the Court held:

> When, therefore, Texas became one of the United States, she entered into an indissoluble relation. . . . The act which consummated her admission into the Union was something more than a compact; it was the incorporation of a new member into the political body. And it was final. The union between Texas and the other States was as complete, as perpetual, and as indissoluble as the union between the original States.

Chief Justice Chase summed up the principle involved: "The Constitution, in all its provisions, looks to an indestructible Union, composed of indestructible States."

NATIONAL SUPREMACY

Division of Powers

In essence, American federalism is a form of political organization in which the exercise of power is divided between two levels of government, each having the use of those powers as a matter of right, and each acting on the same citizen body. The appropriate division of powers between these two levels was one of the major concerns of the Constitutional Convention, and the

[2]Jefferson Davis, *The Rise and Fall of the Confederate Government* (New York: Appleton, 1881), I:173.

pattern of allocation that emerged was fairly complex, as the following summary indicates:

1. Exclusively national powers   Since a nation obviously must speak with one voice in foreign relations, the power to declare war and make treaties was allocated to the national government. For different but equally obvious reasons, a uniform monetary system was essential, which necessitated central control of the power to coin money.

2. Exclusively state powers   Since the federal government was one of delegated powers, obviously any powers not delegated to it remained with the states. Rather than leave this matter to inference, however, the Tenth Amendment spelled it out: "The powers not delegated to the United States by the Constitution, nor prohibited by it to the States, are reserved to the States respectively, or to the people." There has been much misunderstanding about this amendment, and it has often been viewed as the principal guarantor of the rights of the states. Actually it adds nothing new to the Constitution, being simply declaratory of the relation between the national government and the states.[3]

3. Concurrent powers   The Constitution expressly gives to the national government such important powers as levying taxes and regulating commerce, but it makes no effort to prohibit the states from also exercising such authority within their own borders.

4. Powers prohibited to the national government   According to the principle that the national government is one of delegated powers, which was accepted by the framers though not spelled out until the Tenth Amendment was added, the national government has no authority to exercise powers not authorized by the Constitution. It was this argument, we have seen, that was used at the Convention to deny the necessity for a protective bill of rights. However, the framers did include in the original Constitution a few express prohibitions on federal power, such as those against the levying of direct taxes or suspending the writ of habeas corpus. When the Bill of Rights was added, the extensive prohibitions of the first eight amendments were incorporated in this group.

5. Powers prohibited to the states   In Article I, section 10, a group of activities is forbidden to the States. The purpose of these prohibitions is primarily to enforce the exclusive nature of national control over foreign relations, the monetary system, and foreign commerce. A further prohibition,

---

[3]Walter Berns, "The Meaning of the Tenth Amendment," in Robert A. Goldwin, ed., *A Nation of States* (Chicago: Rand McNally, 1963), pp. 126–48.

which does not fall into any of these three categories, is on any law impairing the obligation of contracts.

6. *Powers prohibited to both the nation and the states*   Certain prohibitions on the states in Article I, section 10, are also imposed on the national government by the preceding section. These include the ban on passing bills of attainder and ex post facto laws, and granting titles of nobility.

Legislative Supremacy

With this rather elaborate division of functions and powers between the two levels of government, disputes are bound to occur. The Constitution supplies a principle for settling them in the supremacy clause of Article VI: "This Constitution, and the laws of the United States which shall be made in pursuance thereof; and all treaties made, or which shall be made, under the authority of the United States, shall be the supreme law of the land; and the judges in every state shall be bound thereby, any thing in the Constitution or laws of any state to the contrary notwithstanding."

The effectiveness of this section was early demonstrated in the case of *McCulloch v. Maryland* (1819). In 1818 the Maryland Legislature levied a tax on the politically unpopular Bank of the United States, which had been chartered by the federal government. The cashier of the Baltimore branch of the bank refused to pay the tax and was convicted of violating the law by the state courts. The Supreme Court unanimously upheld the bank's position, Chief Justice Marshall basing his opinion squarely on the supremacy clause. "If any one proposition could command the universal assent of mankind," he wrote, "we might expect it would be this: that the government of the Union, though limited in its powers, is supreme within its sphere of action." Consequently, no state had any power "to retard, impede, burden, or in any manner control, the operations of the constitutional laws enacted by congress."

When Congress enters a field in which it is authorized to act, then, its legislation supersedes all incompatible state regulations. In practical terms, however, the question whether Congress has preempted a given area is a difficult one, since federal statutes seldom state whether all local rules on the matter are suspended. It falls ultimately to the Supreme Court to determine the relation of federal and state statutes. In *Pennsylvania v. Nelson* (1956), Chief Justice Warren attempted to codify the tests which the Court has used to guide such decisions. First, is the scheme of federal regulations so pervasive as to make it a reasonable inference that Congress has left no room for the states? Second, do the federal statutes touch a field in which the interest of the national government is so dominant that it must be assumed to preclude state action on the same subject? Third, does enforcement of the state act present a serious danger of conflict with the administration of the federal program?

In the *Nelson* case, a conviction for violation of the Pennsylvania sedition act has been reversed by the state supreme court on the ground that a federal sedition act (the Smith Act of 1940) had occupied the field and superseded the state law. The United States Supreme Court agreed. Using the three criteria just suggested, Warren concluded that Congress had taken over the entire task of protecting the country from seditious conduct when it passed the Smith Act, even though no express intention to exclude the states was stated in that statute.[4]

Dual Federalism

Congressional supremacy, thus established under Marshall, had to face a different kind of challenge from the Taney Court, grounded on the Tenth Amendment. Under the influence of Taney's states' rights constitutional theories, the Supreme Court on many occasions took its legal bearings more from this amendment than from the national supremacy clause. Espousing a doctrine called "dual federalism," the Court assumed that the two levels of government were coequal sovereignties, each supreme within its own sphere. Thus the fact that certain powers had been reserved to the states constituted a limit on the authority specifically delegated to the national government.

From 1890 to 1937 the Court with its laissez-faire philosophy found it convenient to use the Taney doctrine. On the one hand the federal government was restricted from enacting economic regulation by "invisible radiations" from the Tenth Amendment, and on the other hand the states were barred from interference with the workings of the economic system by the due process clause of the Fourteenth Amendment.

The theory of dual federalism received its clearest statement in *Hammer v. Dagenhart* (1918). By a five to four vote, the Court here invalidated a congressional statute restricting the transportation in interstate commerce of goods produced by child labor. For the majority, Justice Day wrote: "The grant of authority over a purely federal matter was not intended to destroy the local power always existing and carefully reserved to the States in the Tenth Amendment." He went on to say that in interpreting the Constitution it should never be forgotten that "the powers not expressly delegated to the National Government are reserved" to the states and the people by the Tenth Amendment.

To arrive at this conclusion Justice Day had to misquote the amendment; the term "expressly" does not appear in its text. He had to ignore judicial precedent; Marshall in *McCulloch v. Maryland* had held that the omission of the word "expressly" had left the question whether a particular power had been delegated to the national government to be answered by a "fair construction of the whole instrument." Justice Day had also to assume a position that

---

[4]Earlier significant preemption decisions were *Hines v. Davidowitz* (1941) and *Rice v. Santa Fe Elevator Corp.* (1947).

was historically inaccurate: when the Tenth Amendment was under consideration in the First Congress the anti-Federalists had tried to insert the word "expressly," but had been voted down. In any case, the commerce power had
been expressly delegated to Congress. These errors did not go unchallenged.
Speaking for the four dissenters Justice Holmes declared: "I should have
thought that the most conspicuous decisions of this Court had made it clear
that the power to regulate commerce and other constitutional powers could
not be cut down or qualified by the fact that it might interfere with the carrying out of the domestic policy of any State."

Much of the struggle in the middle 1930s between the conservative members of the Supreme Court and President Roosevelt may be seen as a clash
between Taney's dual federalism and the older national supremacy of Marshall. In the end it was the interpretation of Marshall and Roosevelt that prevailed. In a series of cases culminating in *United States v. Darby Lumber Co.*
(1941), the reconstituted and rejuvenated Supreme Court upheld a number of
federal laws that directly affected local policies. In the *Darby* opinion Justice
Stone wrote that the Tenth Amendment "states but a truism that all is retained
which has not been surrendered. There is nothing in the history of its adoption
to suggest that it was more than declaratory of the relationship between the
national and state governments as it had been established by the Constitution
before the amendment." The *Darby* decision specifically overruled *Hammer
v. Dagenhart.*[5]

ADMINISTRATIVE FEDERALISM

No specific constitutional provision other than the authorization to Congress
to lay and collect taxes to provide for the "general welfare" supports the complex network of fiscal relationships that has developed linking Washington
and the state and local governments. The federal government began very early
to provide financial aid to the states. In 1837 Congress disposed of an embarrassing treasury surplus in this way. Since that time countless state and
local activities have been financed by federal grants in good times and bad:
education, highways, health, welfare, housing, airports, hospitals, law enforcement, forestry, libraries. By 1978 federal aid accounted for 27 percent of
all state and local expenditures.

Court challenges to the grant system have been few and ineffective. The
spending power of Congress will be considered in Chapter 11. Here it is sufficient to note the principal Supreme Court decision, *United States v. Butler*
(1936), where the majority did invalidate a federal tax, the proceeds of which
were to be used to pay farmers for reducing their acreage in production. Jus-

---

[5]The limited and perhaps temporary revival of dual federalism in *National League of Cities
v. Usery* (1976) will be discussed in Chapter 12.

tice Roberts thought that the payments had the effect of invading the jurisdiction of the states. But Justice Stone asserted for the minority that congressional payment of money to the states "for a national public purpose" was "a permissible means to a legitimate end," and the cloud over the spending power was dispelled the following year in *Steward Machine Co. v. Davis* and *Helvering v. Davis.*

Federal grants to the states and localities continued to increase until challenged by the New Federalism of President Reagan. In his inaugural address in 1981 Reagan asserted: "The federal government did not create the states; the states created the federal government." In fact the federal government was created by "We, the People" in collectivity, not by the individual states. The concept of the Union as a compact of states was rejected by the Civil War. As Abraham Lincoln summed up, "The Union is older than any of the states and, in fact, it created them as States. . . . The Union and not the states separately produced their independence and their liberty."[6] Reagan's conception of the federal-state relationship, however, was at least in the short run effective in substantially reducing federal support for the states and substituting financing by "block grants" which left the states more discretion in deciding how to use decreased federal financial assistance.

Judicial Supremacy

Implementing the principle of national supremacy requires that the Supreme Court have authority to review the decisions of state courts. The Judiciary Act of 1789, in section 25, provided for such review of final judgments or decrees "in the highest court of law or equity of a State in which a decision in the suit could be had," in three classes of cases: (1) where the validity of a federal law or treaty was "drawn in question," and the decision was against its validity; (2) where a state statute was questioned as "repugnant to the constitution, treaties or laws of the United States," and the decision was in favor of its validity; and (3) where the construction of the federal Constitution, treaty, or statute was drawn in question, and the decision was against the title, right, privilege, or exemption claimed. These categories were all based on the principle that if the Constitution and laws of the United States were to be observed, the Supreme Court would have to have an opportunity to review decisions of state courts that ruled adversely on asserted federal rights.

The Supreme Court's power of review over state supreme court decisions was not established without incident. In *Fairfax's Devisee v. Hunter's Lessee* (1813) the Supreme Court (John Marshall not sitting because his brother was involved in the litigation) reversed a decision of the Virginia high court regarding the land rights of British subjects who were protected under the Jay Treaty. Virginia refused to acquiesce in the decision; the state court argued

---

[6]Samuel H. Beer, "The Idea of the Nation," 187 *The New Republic* 23 (July 19 & 26, 1982).

that although a state was bound to respect the Constitution, laws, and treaties of the United States as supreme, it was obliged to follow only its own interpretations, not those of a federal court. Because the courts of the United States represented one sovereignty, they could not review decisions of state courts, which belonged to another sovereignty.

Consequently the Supreme Court's order was returned unobeyed. The Court in *Martin v. Hunter's Lessee* (1816) strongly reaffirmed its right to review state decisions. Justice Story answered Virginia's argument with the statement that the Constitution was not ordained by the states, but by the "people of the United States," and these "people" could invest the national government with whatever powers they thought proper. "The courts of the United States can, without question, revise the proceedings of the executive and legislative authorities of the States. . . . Surely, the exercise of the same right over judicial tribunals is not a higher or more dangerous act of sovereign power."

The second Supreme Court order bypassed the Virginia supreme court and was directed to the court in which the case had originated. There the mandate was obeyed. Charles Warren, the historian of the Court, has termed Story's opinion in this case as having been ever since "the keystone of the whole arch of Federal judicial power."[7] However, the states' rights forces were not easily daunted, and they returned to the attack in *Cohens v. Virginia* (1821). Congress had passed an act authorizing the District of Columbia to conduct lotteries to finance civic improvements. The state of Virginia, which had a law forbidding lotteries, arrested and convicted two persons for selling the Washington tickets within its domain. After conviction, the defendants appealed to the Supreme Court. The Virginia Legislature was highly incensed at this reiteration of federal appellate jurisdiction over state courts, and denied the existence of any such authority. The argument for the state was that the Supreme Court could not exercise appellate powers over a state court decision to which a state was a party, since the Constitution placed all cases in which a state was a party within the Supreme Court's *original* jurisdiction. Counsel argued that the power of the federal judiciary was either exclusive or concurrent, but not paramount. Where it was concurrent, "whichsoever judiciary gets possession of the case [first], should proceed to final judgment, from which there should be no appeal."

Again the Supreme Court rejected the anarchic principles of this contention. Marshall held that where a state had obtained a judgment against an individual and in so doing had overruled a defense set up under the Constitution or laws of the United States, it was the undeniable right of the Supreme Court to review the decision. Then the Court examined the merits of the case and decided against the defendants on the ground that Congress had not in-

---

[7]Charles Warren, *The Supreme Court in United States History,* rev. ed. (Boston: Little, Brown, 1947), I:449.

tended the lottery tickets to be sold outside the District of Columbia. Many Virginia officials and newspapers were enraged at the assertion of federal jurisdiction, but because of the decision on the merits they were left with no order to disobey or resist.

Nullification and the Courts

The right to review and reverse judgments of state courts and to review state legislative or executive action through Supreme Court reexamination of state or lower federal court orders has been challenged from time to time by the theory of nullification. Rather surprisingly, the principal episodes of this kind occurred in the Northern states. The first controversy, *United States v. Peters* (1809), concerned the decision of a lower federal court in Pennsylvania on a claim growing out of a prize case from the Revolutionary War. The state legislature defied the court's judgment and declared it to be in violation of the Eleventh Amendment. In the Supreme Court's decision Marshall made short shrift of the state's claim to interfere with the actions of a federal court, saying: "If the legislatures of the several States may, at will, annul the judgments of the courts of the United States, and destroy the rights acquired under those judgments, the constitution itself becomes a solemn mockery; and the nation is deprived of the means of enforcing its laws by the instrumentality of its own tribunals."

Shortly before the Civil War, nullification reappeared in the North. In Wisconsin, Sherman M. Booth, a Milwaukee newspaper editor, helped rescue an escaped slave from a deputy federal marshal. Booth was arrested by federal authorities, and since there were no federal prisons in the area, he was placed in a local jail to await trial. A judge of the Wisconsin supreme court issued a writ of habeas corpus and declared the federal Fugitive Slave Law unconstitutional. The federal marshal appealed to the entire state supreme court against the obvious irregularity of a state judge issuing orders to federal officials. But the Wisconsin supreme court upheld the judge both on the issuance of the writ and the unconstitutionality of the law. The marshal then appealed to the United States Supreme Court. But before that Court could hear the case, Booth was convicted in federal district court and sentenced to a fine of $1,000 and a month in prison. Once again Booth applied to the Wisconsin supreme court for habeas corpus and once again that court issued the writ, freeing Booth.

In *Ableman v. Booth* (1859) Chief Justice Taney voiced the unanimous opinion of the Supreme Court that Wisconsin "has reversed and annulled the provisions of the Constitution itself, and the [Judiciary] act of Congress of 1789, and made the superior and appellant tribunal the inferior and subordinate." If Wisconsin could so control the actions of federal agencies within that state, so could every other state. The language of Article VI was "too plain to admit of doubt or to need comment." The decisions of federal courts were "as far beyond the reach of the judicial process issued by a State judge or a State Court, as if the line of division was traced by landmarks and monuments visible to the eye." In closing his opinion, Taney, himself a firm believer in states' rights, affirmed that "no power is more clearly conferred by the Constitution and laws of the United States, than the power of this court to decide, ultimately and finally, all cases arising under such Constitution and laws."

In 1956 the dust was blown off the doctrines of interposition and nullification, as they were invoked by several Southern states in protest against the Supreme Court's decision invalidating racial segregation in the schools. In its act of nullification the state of Alabama laid down the basic premise of its action.

> WHEREAS the states, being the parties to the constitutional compact, it follows of necessity that there can be no tribunal above their authority to decide, in the last resort, whether the compact made by them be violated; and, consequently, they must decide themselves, in the last resort, such questions as may be of sufficient magnitude to require their interposition.

On these grounds the legislature of Alabama declared, "The decisions and orders of the Supreme Court of the United States relating to the separation of races in the public schools are, as a matter of right, null, void, and of no effect; and . . . as a matter of right, this State is not bound to abide thereby."[8]

All such actions and arguments are condemned by their opposition to the mainstream of American history and constitutional development. In the 1958 Little Rock case, *Cooper v. Aaron,* the Supreme Court disposed sharply and decisively of the contention that the governor and legislature of Arkansas were not bound by the Court's 1954 decision declaring segregated schools unconstitutional. Later, in *Bush v. Orleans School Board* (1960) the Court quoted with approval the terse comment of a federal district court: "The conclusion is clear that interposition is not a *constitutional* doctrine. If taken seriously, it is illegal defiance of constitutional authority."

ADMISSION OF NEW STATES

With the migration to the territory between the Appalachians and the Mississippi, it was apparent even before the Constitutional Convention that new states might well be formed in the area. The claims of certain states to western territory had been ceded to the general government when the Articles of Confederation were adopted, with the understanding that Congress would eventually organize the territory into states and admit them to the Union. By the

---

[8]Act no. 42, Special Session 1956, Alabama, reprinted in 1 RACE RELATIONS LAW REPORTER 437 (1956).

Northwest Ordinance of 1787, the Confederation Congress provided that the Northwest Territory was to be divided into not less than three nor more than five states, and that 60,000 inhabitants would be requisite for admission of a state.

Article IV, section 3, provides for the admission of new states into the Union by Congress. The only stated limitations on congressional discretion are that "no new state shall be formed or erected within the jurisdiction of any other state; nor any state be formed by the junction of two or more states, or parts of states, without the consent of the legislatures of the states concerned as well as of the Congress."

Thirty-five new states were admitted to the Union between 1791 and 1912. Five were carved out of the territory of older states—Vermont, Kentucky, Tennessee, Maine, and West Virginia. In the first four cases the legislature of the older state gave its consent. But West Virginia was formed from the western counties of Virginia during the Civil War when Virginia was in military opposition to the Union. In this situation consent was given by a rump legislature from the area convened especially for this purpose. After the war, Virginia formally consented to the dismemberment.

Of the remaining thirty states, all but two went through a probationary status as organized territories before they were admitted as states. The exceptions were Texas, which upon its admission in 1845 was an independent republic, and California, which was formed out of a region ceded by Mexico in 1848.[9]

The normal procedure by which a territory becomes a state calls for Congress to pass an enabling act allowing the territorial government to convene a popular convention to propose a state constitution. If the voters ratify this constitution, it is submitted to Congress for approval. Congress then may pass a resolution admitting the new state. A statehood resolution, like other legislation, is subject to presidential veto, but unlike other statutes, once adopted it is irrepealable.

Congress may grant or withhold statehood for any reasons it chooses. Before the Civil War the primary motive in admission was to maintain a balance between slave and free states. Nevada was admitted, in spite of its sparse population, to provide a necessary ratifying vote for the Thirteenth Amendment. Hawaii and Alaska were strong candidates for admission from at least 1944, when the platforms of both political parties recommended statehood, but various political considerations delayed favorable action by Congress. Alaska finally won admission in 1958, and Hawaii in 1959.

Under the Northwest Ordinance of 1787 new states were to be admitted

[9]The joint resolution admitting Texas to the Union provided that four additional states could be formed from its territory and be entitled to admission. Some Texans have expressed interest in this possibility as a way of getting eight additional Senate seats for Texas. But in spite of the 1845 law, Congress would have to give consent for admission of the new states, which seems unlikely.

"on an equal footing with the original states, in all respects whatever." Consequently it is surprising that the Constitutional Convention of the same year voted, nine states to two, against placing a similar equal status provision in Article IV. However, this omission has had no practical effect, for the principle of equality is a fundamental part of American constitutional law. Thus the joint resolution admitting Texas in 1845 specified that Texas "shall be admitted unto the Union . . . on an equal footing with the existing States."

The Supreme Court has on many occasions recognized equality of status as an inherent attribute of the federal Union. *Coyle v. Smith* (1911) supplies the best illustration of its position. Under the enabling act admitting Oklahoma as a state. Congress had specified that the capital should be located at Guthrie for at least seven years. After four years, the Oklahoma Legislature ordered the capital moved to Oklahoma City. The Supreme Court held that the state was not bound by the congressional limitation, reasoning as follows:

> The power is to admit "new States into *this* Union." "This Union" was and is a union of States, equal in power, dignity and authority, each competent to exert that residuum of sovereignty not delegated to the United States by the Constitution itself. To maintain otherwise would be to say that the Union, through the power of Congress to admit new States, might come to be a union of States unequal in power, as including States whose powers were restricted only by the Constitution, with others whose powers had been further restricted by an act of Congress accepted as a condition of admission.

Another illustration of the ineffectiveness of preadmission restrictions after admission was supplied by the experience of Arizona, which proposed a state constitution providing for the recall of elected officials, including judges. President Taft objected to this feature, and vetoed the resolution of admission. Arizona then amended her constitution to eliminate this provision, and was then admitted. Shortly thereafter Arizona, secure in her statehood, put recall of judges back into her constitution.

An exception to the "equal footing" doctrine arose under the Submerged Lands Act of 1953, which ceded to the coastal states ownership of land and resources under adjoining seas to a distance of three miles from shore or to the state's "historic boundaries."[10] The Supreme Court interpreted this statute to grant Florida and Texas jurisdiction ten miles into the Gulf of Mexico, since their "historic boundaries" were three marine leagues, whereas all other states have only three miles.[11] That the Atlantic seaboard states have jurisdiction only to the three-mile limit was confirmed in *United States v. Maine* (1975).

---

[10]This statute reversed the Supreme Court decision in *United States v. California* (1947), which had denied states ownership rights in coastal waters.

[11]*United States v. States of Louisiana, Texas, Mississippi, Alabama, and Florida* (1960).

OBLIGATIONS OF THE NATIONAL
GOVERNMENT TO THE STATES

The Constitution imposes several obligations upon the national government with respect to the states. Under Article V no state may be denied equal representation in the Senate without its consent. Again, the government must respect the territorial integrity of the existing states in the formation of new states, as noted in the preceding section. In addition there are three other obligations, all appearing in Article IV, section 4, that deserve more extended treatment.

Guarantee against Invasion
and Domestic Violence

The protection against foreign invasion is simply a corollary of national self-defense. Article IV, section 4, goes on to provide that, on application of a state legislature, or of the governor if the legislature cannot be convened, the United States shall guarantee a state against "domestic violence." A statute adopted by Congress in 1795 spelling out this obligation uses the term "insurrection" rather than domestic violence. On at least sixteen occasions states have sought federal assistance in suppressing domestic violence. The procedure, as specified by Attorney General Clark in 1967, is as follows. First, the governor must make a finding that "serious domestic violence" exists, which cannot be brought under control by law enforcement resources available to him. The legislature or governor must then request the president to employ the armed forces to bring the violence under control.

A request from the state legislature or governor is not necessary, however, where domestic violence threatens the enforcement of national laws. Article I, section 8, authorizes Congress to provide for calling forth the militia to execute the laws of the Union, suppress insurrections, and repel invasions. In 1792 Congress adopted legislation which, as revised in 1795, provided:

> That whenever the laws of the United States shall be opposed, or the execution thereof obstructed, in any state, by combinations too powerful to be suppressed by the ordinary course of judicial proceedings, or by the powers vested in the marshals by this act, it shall be lawful for the President of the United States, to call forth the militia of such state, or of any other state or states, as may be necessary to suppress such combinations, and to cause the laws to be duly executed.[12]

An important presidential use of troops to enforce national laws occurred in Chicago in 1894. A strike by the railwaymen's union against the Pullman Company had spread to trains using Pullman equipment, causing an

[12]1 Stat. 424 (1795).

almost complete stoppage on the railroads operating out of Chicago. The federal district attorney in Chicago obtained an injunction against Eugene Debs, the leader of the union, and other labor officials, forbidding them to hinder the mails or interstate commerce in any way. When the injunction went unheeded and violence increased, the federal marshal informed the United States attorney general that an emergency existed with which he was unable to cope. President Cleveland then ordered federal troops into the city to restore order and assist in getting the trains running. This action was not taken in pursuance of a request by the state executive. In fact, Governor Altgeld strongly protested Cleveland's order.

Debs and the other leaders were arrested for contempt of court in disobeying the injunction and received sentences of from three to six months. The Supreme Court refused to issue a writ of habeas corpus, upholding the presidential action in a unanimous opinion with these words:

> The entire strength of the nation may be used to enforce in any part of the land the full and free exercise of all national powers and the security of all rights entrusted by the Constitution to its care. The strong arm of the national Government may be put forth to brush away all obstructions to the freedom of interstate commerce or the transportation of the mails. If the emergency arises, the army of the Nation, and all its militia, are at the service of the Nation to compel obedience to its laws.[13]

In 1957 President Eisenhower found it necessary to use federal troops to control violence in Little Rock, Arkansas, and enforce court orders seeking to accomplish gradual desegregation of the local high school. Again in 1962 federal troops had to be used to quell violence arising out of a school integration controversy at the University of Mississippi, which had been ordered by the federal courts to admit James H. Meredith as its first black student.[14]

In March, 1965, Alabama state troops on the order of Governor George Wallace halted a voting rights march that Martin Luther King was attempting to lead from Selma to Montgomery. Federal district judge Frank M. Johnson, Jr., enjoined state officials from interfering with the march. Governor Wallace then sent a telegram to President Johnson requesting that he provide "sufficient federal civil authorities or officers" to guarantee the safety of the marchers and citizens along the route, alleging that his state could not afford the cost of mobilizing the National Guard. President Johnson complied, but expressed regret that "the Governor and the legislature of a sovereign state [should] decline to exercise their responsibility and . . . request that duty be assumed by the Federal Government."[15]

---

[13]*In re Debs* (1895).

[14]On the general subject of civil disorder, see "Riot Control and the Use of Federal Troops," 81 HARVARD LAW REVIEW 638–52 (1968).

[15]*The New York Times,* March 26, 1965.

Guarantee of a Republican Form of Government

Article IV, section 4, provides that "The United States shall guarantee to every State in this Union a republican form of government." This is the only limitation in the Constitution on the internal governmental organization of a state. No definition is provided of a republican form of government, but the language may be interpreted as requiring a form somewhere between a monarchy or oligarchy on the one hand, and a pure or direct democracy on the other.[16]

In designating the "United States" as responsible for this guarantee, the Constitution does not specify which branch has the responsibility for its enforcement. The Supreme Court, however, has ruled on several occasions against judicial enforcement of the clause. The first occasion was in the case of *Luther v. Borden* (1849). In 1841 Rhode Island was still operating largely under the system of government established by a charter from Charles II, which made no provision for amendment. Dissident groups, protesting mainly against the limits on suffrage, combined to form a popular convention which drafted a new constitution. Elections were held the following year, and Thomas Dorr was elected governor. All the while the old charter government continued to operate and was attempting to put down what it regarded as a rebellion. When one of its agents tried to arrest a Dorr supporter, he was sued for trespass, and one of the issues at the trial was whether the charter government was "republican" under the terms of the Constitution.

Chief Justice Taney for the Supreme Court denied that a court possessed the machinery either to hold a plebiscite or to interrogate enough witnesses to determine which government had the support of a majority of the people. This was a purely political decision that had to be made by Congress. Taney wrote:

> Under this article of the constitution it rests with Congress to decide what government is the established one in a State. For as the United States guarantee to each State a republican government, Congress must necessarily decide what government is established in the State before it can determine whether it is republican or not. And when the senators and representatives of a State are admitted into the councils of the Union, the authority of the government under which they are appointed, as well as its republican character, is recognized by the proper constitutional authority. And its decision is binding on every other department of the government, and could not be questioned in a judicial tribunal.

In this case no representatives had been elected from Rhode Island while the dispute was in progress, so there had been no congressional contest over seating. But the constitutional guarantee against domestic violence had been invoked. The president had recognized one of the contending governors as the legitimate executive authority of the state, and had taken steps to call out the

---

[16]See William M. Wiecek, *The Guarantee Clause of the U.S. Constitution* (Ithaca, N.Y.: Cornell University Press, 1972); "A Niche for the Guarantee Clause," 94 HARVARD LAW REVIEW 681 (1981).

militia to support his authority, should that be necessary. The announcement of this presidential determination had in fact been responsible for terminating Dorr's rebellion against the charter government. After the president had made such a decision, Taney continued,

> . . . is a circuit court of the United States authorized to inquire whether his decision was right? Could the court, while the parties were actually contending in arms for the possession of the government, call witnesses before it, and inquire which party represented a majority of the people? . . . If the judicial power extends so far, the guarantee contained in the constitution of the United States is a guarantee of anarchy, and not of order.

The Supreme Court had occasion to reiterate that the republican form of government guarantee is judicially nonenforceable in a 1912 case where it was alleged that the insertion in the Oregon constitution of a provision for direct legislation by way of the initiative and referendum deprived the state of a republican form of government. The Court's reply was that, in the absence of any determination on this point by the political departments of the federal government, it would refuse to consider such charges. Moreover, Chief Justice White asserted that if the judiciary had the power to overthrow a state government, it must have the power to build another in its place—a power that would itself destroy the existence of a government republican in form.[17]

More recently, the Court has dealt with the republican form of government provision in connection with the problem of apportionment and representation in state legislatures, to which we now turn.

REPRESENTATION IN STATE LEGISLATURES

Until 1962 the states were free from any federal constitutional controls over apportionment and districting in their legislatures, and they followed a great variety of representation practices. David and Eisenberg divided the states into four general classes on the basis of their representation arrangements:

1. Sixteen states had an equivalent of the "federal" plan, in which one house (like the United States Senate) had a fixed apportionment of representation among fixed districts with no regard for population, while the other house was apportioned more or less on the basis of population. In seven of these states, counties were treated exactly like states in the federal union, each county having at least one representative in the lower house and equal representation with other counties in the upper house. Towns were represented in the lower houses of Vermont and Connecticut.
2. In nine states, the constitution provided for a straight population basis of representation in one house and some kind of qualified population standard in the

---

[17]*Pacific States Telephone & Telegraph Co. v. Oregon* (1912). Other early cases rejecting guarantee clause claims were *Minor v. Happersett* (1875) and *In re Duncan* (1891).

other house. Some of these states were close to the federal pattern. In California, the requirement that no county have more than one state senator limited Los Angeles County, with a population of over six million, to a single member in the state Senate.

3. In sixteen states, population was the principal criterion for both houses, but was qualified in one way or another for both.
4. In the final group of nine states, population was the constitutional criterion for representation in the entire legislature.[18]

In the nineteenth century these provisions for representation of each county or town and the various departures from population representation did not result in great inequalities of election districts. But as large urban centers developed in the present century, they were increasingly underrepresented. Moreover, in rurally controlled legislatures the power-holders took steps to protect their position, either by writing new restrictions on population representation into the constitution or by failing to redistrict when such action would have given additional representatives to urban areas.

It was a situation of this latter sort with which the Supreme Court was confronted in the famous 1962 case of *Baker v. Carr*.[19] The constitution of Tennessee provided for ninety-nine members of the House and thirty-three members of the Senate, and directed the legislature to allocate, at least every ten years, the senators and representatives among the several counties or districts "according to the number of qualified voters in each." Despite these mandatory requirements, no reapportionment had been made since 1901. During the period between 1901 and 1950, the population grew from 2,021,000 to 3,292,000, but the growth was very uneven among counties. Thus 37 percent of the voting population could control twenty of the thirty-three members of the Senate, while 40 percent of the voters could control sixty-three of the ninety-nine members of the House.

In 1959 suit was brought in federal district court by certain citizens of Tennessee against state election officials under the Civil Rights Act of 1871, alleging deprivation of federal constitutional rights. The principal obstacle to success in their suit was that in *Colegrove v. Green* (1946) the Supreme Court had declined to rule on a similar claim made against congressional districts in Illinois, where likewise a failure since 1901 to obey the constitutional mandate to redistrict every ten years had resulted in population inequalities as great as

---

[18]Paul T. David and Ralph Eisenberg, *State Legislative Redistricting* (Chicago: Public Administration Service, 1962), pp. 8–10.

[19]There is an extensive literature on the consequences of *Baker v. Carr*. See particularly Robert G. Dixon, Jr., *Democratic Representation: Reapportionment in Law and Politics* (New York: Oxford University Press, 1968); Gordon E. Baker, *The Reapportionment Revolution* (New York: Random House, 1966); Nelson W. Polsby, ed., *Reapportionment in the 1970s* (Berkeley: University of California Press, 1971); Ward E. Y. Elliott, *The Rise of Guardian Democracy* (Cambridge, Mass.: Harvard University Press, 1974); Bernard Grofman, ed., *Representation and Redistricting Issues* (Lexington, Mass.: Lexington Books, 1982).

nine to one. The Court, speaking through Justice Frankfurter, had held in a four to three decision that these election controversies constituted a political thicket that judges must avoid.

In *Baker v. Carr,* however, the Court reversed the *Colegrove* rule and held the Tennessee complaint to be justiciable. Justice Brennan asserted two main grounds for refusing to follow *Colegrove.* First, Frankfurter's position on justiciability had been supported by only three of the seven participating justices. Justice Rutledge, who supplied the fourth vote, actually agreed with the three dissenters that the issue was justiciable, and only voted as he did because he felt that it would be unwise to upset the Illinois arrangements so soon before the congressional elections of 1946.

Second, Brennan traced the "political question" doctrine, on which Frankfurter had relied, all the way back to *Luther v. Borden* to demonstrate that it did not cover the Tennessee type of election controversy. A true political question, from his view, was presented only where there was a separation of powers issue at stake. A political question was one that the courts should avoid out of deference to the President or Congress, as in *Luther v. Borden.* Since there was no such conflict here, the question was justiciable.

Justice Frankfurter, dissenting along with Harlan, argued on the contrary that the significant factors in past judicial refusals to get involved in political questions were these:

> . . . the caution not to undertake decision where standards meet for judicial judgment are lacking, the reluctance to interfere with matters of state government in the absence of an unquestionable and effectively enforceable mandate, the unwillingness to make courts arbiters of the broad issues of political organization historically committed to other institutions and for whose adjustment the judicial process is ill-adapted.

The Tennessee case, Frankfurter felt, fell squarely in this tradition of controversies that do not lend themselves to judicial standards or judicial remedies.

Justice Frankfurter made specific use of the republican guarantee clause in his argument, saying: "The present case involves all of the elements that have made the Guarantee Clause cases nonjusticiable. It is, in effect, a Guarantee Clause claim masquerading under a different label."

Legislative apportionment, Frankfurter continued, was a political problem bound to prove vastly embarrassing to courts if they got involved in it. There are no standards for decision except political preferences and competing political philosophies, while "in every strand of this complicated, intricate web of values meet the contending forces of partisan politics." This was the political thicket that the Court majority would require the federal district courts to enter, he warned, with no standards or constitutional principles to guide them, no indication of what kind of remedies they could formulate to correct legislative apportionments.

Justice Brennan, however, assumed that the Court would be equal to developing remedies when the need arose. None were required here, since the Court merely held that the complaint against Tennessee's legislative districts should not have been dismissed. This ruling opened the gates to a flood of suits.

The first one to reach the Court was *Gray v. Sanders* (1963), involving not a state legislature but rather the Georgia county-unit system of primary elections to statewide offices, a system deliberately designed to give control of the electoral process to rural minorities. The Supreme Court, with only Justice Harlan dissenting, invalidated the county-unit plan on the ground that no preferred class of voters is permissible under the Constitution and by American traditions. Every voter is equal to every other voter in the state: "The conception of political equality from the Declaration of Independence, to Lincoln's Gettysburg address, to the Fifteenth, Seventeenth, and Nineteenth Amendments can mean only one thing—one person, one vote." Applying this conception to the present case, Douglas concluded:

> Once the geographical unit for which a representative is to be chosen is designated, all who participate in the election are to have an equal vote—whatever their race, whatever their sex, whatever their occupation, whatever their income, and wherever their home may be in that geographical unit. This is required by the Equal Protection Clause of the Fourteenth Amendment.

While *Gray v. Sanders* was a voting case, not an apportionment case, the standard of "one person, one vote" had obvious relevance for legislative districting. However, there were many who expected that the court would apply this rule to only one house of bicameral state legislatures, leaving room for other principles in the makeup of the second house. But in *Reynolds v. Sims* (1964) and fourteen companion cases the Supreme Court confounded these expectations and made "one person, one vote" the constitutional rule for both houses. The legislatures of all fifteen states under review were declared unconstitutional by the Court, with varying majorities of from six to eight justices, because of substantial violations of the one-person, one-vote standard.

Chief Justice Warren wrote the opinion of the Court in all of these cases. He started with "the basic standard of equality among voters," as established in *Gray v. Sanders* and supported by general principles of representative government, majority rule, and equal protection of the laws. Representative government, the Chief Justice said, "is in essence self-government through the medium of elected representatives of the people, and each and every citizen has an inalienable right to full and effective participation in the political processes of his State's legislative bodies." He rejected any sophisticated notions about representation. "Legislators represent people, not trees or acres. Legislators are elected by voters, not farms or cities or economic interests."

The principle of representative government is majority rule, Warren went on. It is logical and reasonable "that a majority of the people of a State could elect a majority of that State's legislature. To conclude differently, and to sanction minority control of state legislative bodies, would appear to deny majority rights in a way that far surpasses any possible denial of minority rights that might otherwise be thought to result." The Chief Justice was of course not insensitive to minority rights, but he thought that "our constitutional system amply provides for the protection of minorities by means other than giving them majority control of state legislatures."

The principle of equality Warren believed to be essential to both representative government and majority rule. No one would argue that some voters could vote two, five, or ten times for state legislators, or that votes of certain citizens should be given a weight of two, five, or ten times that of voters in other areas. But this is what happens when legislative districting schemes "give the same number of representatives to unequal numbers of constituents. . . . To the extent that a citizen's right to vote is debased, he is that much less a citizen."

The Supreme Court firmly rejected the idea that the rule of equality might be applied to only one house of a bicameral legislature. The right to equal representation in one house, Warren said, "would amount to little if States could effectively submerge the equal-population principle in the apportionment of seats in the other house." The two houses might compromise on some issues, but "in all too many cases the more probable result would be frustration of the majority will through minority veto in the house not apportioned on a population basis."

The Court denied any analogy between state legislatures and the Congress, where the Senate represents states and the House population. The system of representation in the federal Congress, the Chief Justice noted, was the fruit of a compromise between the larger and smaller states that averted a deadlock in the Constitutional Convention. It arose from "unique historical circumstances . . . based on the consideration that in establishing our type of federalism a group of formerly independent states bound themselves together under one national government." At the heart of the federal system remains the concept of "separate and distinct entities which have delegated some, but not all, of their formerly held powers to the single national government." In contrast, "political subdivisions of states—counties, cities, or whatever—never were and never have been considered as sovereign entities," but only as "subordinate governmental instrumentalities created by the State to assist in the carrying out of state governmental functions."

The Court made it clear that it did not mean to impose impractically strict requirements. What was required of each state was that it make "an honest and good faith effort to construct districts, in both houses of its legislature, as nearly of equal population as is practicable." Mathematical exactness was not intended. Further, the states might use political subdivision lines in drawing districts, "so long as the resulting apportionment was one based substantially on population and the equal-population principle was not diluted in any significant way.'' In fact, ''a State can rationally consider according political subdivisions some independent representation in at least one body of the state legislature, as long as the basic standard of equality of population among districts is maintained.'' In general, ''so long as the divergences from a strict population standard are based on legitimate considerations incident to the effectuation of a rational state policy, some deviations from the equal-population principle are constitutionally permissible.'' But ''neither history alone, nor economic or other sorts of group interests,'' nor considerations of area alone, ''are permissible factors in attempting to justify disparities from population-based representation.''

Justices Stewart and Clark, who had been part of the majorities in *Baker* and *Gray,* dissented, as did Harlan, who continued the vehement opposition he had expressed in those two cases. The bulk of his opinion was devoted to two points. The first was the inapplicability of the equal protection clause to representation matters. He contended that section 2 of the Fourteenth Amendment, authorizing Congress to reduce the representation in the House of states that deny or abridge the right to vote, was the sole remedy intended for representation errors, and that there was no thought when the amendment was adopted of controlling the elective franchise by section 1.[20] Second, he contended that giving courts ''blanket authority and the constitutional duty to supervise apportionment'' was an ''intolerable and inappropriate interference . . . with the independent legislatures of the States.''

The decisions in *Baker v. Carr* and subsequent cases were surprisingly popular, considering the drastic remedies they imposed. Within a few years after *Reynolds,* the great majority of state legislatures had been reapportioned on something close to a one-person, one-vote basis, sometimes by uncoerced legislative action, sometimes by legislatures acting under court orders, and sometimes by direct court action.

Attempts to organize opposition in Congress to the Court's mandate were unsuccessful. The principal effort was the Dirksen Amendment, offered in 1965 and 1966. It would have required one house of a bicameral state legislature to be apportioned on the basis of population but would have permitted the other house to be apportioned ''among the people on the bases of population, geography, and political subdivisions in order to insure effective representation in the State's legislature of the various groups and interests making up the electorate.'' The Dirksen Amendment was defeated in the Senate in 1965, when it failed by seven votes to get the two-thirds majority needed, and it lost again in 1966 by the same margin.

[20]Justice Harlan's position on this issue is rebutted by William W. Van Alstyne, ''The Fourteenth Amendment, the 'Right' to Vote, and the Understanding of the Thirty-ninth Congress,'' in Philip B. Kurland, ed., *The Supreme Court Review: 1965* (Chicago: University of Chicago Press, 1965), pp. 33–86.

Subsequent developments in the interpretation and enforcement of the *Reynolds* ruling can be considered under six headings. First, how rigid would the Court be in applying its equal population rule? The gross variations in *Swann v. Adams* (1967) were clearly unacceptable, with ranges of 30 percent among Florida senate district populations and 40 percent among house districts. But in *Kirkpatrick v. Preisler* (1969) and *Wells v. Rockefeller* (1969), where the variations were minimal, the apportionment plans were still invalidated because of failure to show that "a good-faith effort to achieve precise mathematical equality" had been made. Even many friends of the one-man, one-vote rule felt that this was an unrealistic standard, and the Court subsequently modified its stand.

In *Abate v. Mundt* (1971), a districting plan for a New York county board of supervisors with a total deviation from equality of 11.9 percent was approved, the Court noting that the plan did not contain any built-in bias favoring particular political interests or geographic areas. Then *Mahan v. Howell* (1973) held that reapportionment of the Virginia legislature resulting in a variation of 16.4 percent from the ideal district was acceptable because it helped to maintain the integrity of traditional county or city boundaries. Similarly, *Gaffney v. Cummings* (1973) upheld a Connecticut reapportionment plan where the maximum deviation between districts totaled 7.83 percent.[21] The Court added that an otherwise acceptable plan was not made constitutionally vulnerable because its purpose was to provide districts that would achieve "political fairness" between major political parties.

A second issue was raised by the occasional use of multimember districts. Such districts are suspect because they may have the effect, and may in fact be adopted for the purpose, of denying representation to minorities within the expanded district. In *Fortson v. Dorsey* (1965) and *Burns v. Richardson* (1966), the Court held that multimember districts were not illegal per se and that any invidious effect must be demonstrated in the record. While there was substantial evidence of dilution of the votes of blacks and poor people by a multimember district in Indiana, it was not sufficient to convince the Court in *Whitcomb v. Chavis* (1971) that this was invidious underrepresentation. However, *Connor v. Johnson* (1971) held that, where a federal court was called upon to fashion an apportionment plan, it should not make any use of multimember districts because "single-member districts are preferable . . . as a general matter."[22]

In the Court's strongest action against multimember districts, *White v.*

<hr/>

[21]But *Chapman v. Meier* (1975) invalidated a Court-ordered plan with a 20 percent deviation, saying that a Court-ordered plan "must be held to higher standards than a State's own plan."

[22]This position was repeated for a state legislature in *Chapman v. Meier* (1975) and for a school board in *East Carroll Parish School Board v. Marshall* (1976). On multimember districts, see Laurence H. Tribe, *American Constitutional Law* (Mineola, N.Y.: Foundation Press, 1978), pp. 750–55.

Regester (1973) held that two such legislative districts in Texas must be disestablished because of the history of discrimination against blacks and Mexican-Americans living there. But in the *City of Mobile v. Bolden* (1980), the Court was unable to find racial discrimination in Mobile's at-large elections for the city commission. A federal district court had concluded that at-large elections diluted black residents' voting strength, and had ordered replacement of the three-person commission by a mayor and a nine-person city council. Reversing this order, the Surpeme Court reiterated that vote dilution was unconstitutional only if done with discriminatory intent. A political group, said Justice Stewart, has no "constitutional right to elect candidates in proportion to its members."

Only two years later, however, the Court in *Rogers v. Herman Lodge* (1982) found the at-large electoral system in Burke County, Georgia, was being maintained for the invidious purpose of diluting the voting strength of the black population, and ordered the utilization of single-member districts as the proper remedy. Subsequently Mobile agreed to submit a district election plan to the federal court. Also, Congress in extending the Voting Rights Act in 1982 included a provision intended to neutralize the "intent" requirement of the *Mobile* decision, by allowing election law violations to be proved on a showing that an election procedure "resulted" in denial or abridgement of the right to vote, whether intentionally or not.

A third issue concerns the relation of the one-person, one-vote rule to gerrymandering of election districts.[23] In fact, to the degree that the achievement of population equality requires the disregarding of local government boundaries, it makes gerrymandering easier.[24] While recognizing this fact, the Supreme Court has been reluctant to undertake the task of controlling gerrymanders unless there is an obvious racial motive involved.[25] Even in *Wright v. Rockefeller* (1964), where there was a strong prima facie case that congressional district lines had been drawn with racial considerations in mind, the Court held that the evidence was not compelling. And in *Gaffney v. Cummings* (1973) the Court upheld a Connecticut apportionment plan drawn with careful attention to party voting habits.

A fourth issue arose from extension of the one-person, one-vote rule to local government. *Sailors v. Board of Education of Kent County* (1967) ruled that the functions of a county board of education were essentially ad-

[23]See Gordon E. Baker, "Gerrymandering: Privileged Sanctuary or Next Judicial Target," in Nelson W. Polsby, ed., *Reapportionment in the 1970s* (Berkeley, Cal.: University of California Press, 1971), pp. 121–50; Laurence H. Tribe, *American Constitutional Law* (Mineola, N.Y.: Foundation Press, 1978), pp. 756–61.

[24]The Court's rulings in *Kirkpatrick v. Preisler* (1969) and *Wells v. Rockefeller* (1969), which imposed very strict limits on equal population in voting districts that could be met only by disregarding political boundaries, appeared to give a green light to gerrymandering without regard to the former constraints of existing county lines.

[25]An example is the case of *Gomillion v. Lightfoot* (1960), which is discussed in Chapter 9.

ministrative rather than legislative and that consequently there was no constitutional objection to a system whereby each local school board, regardless of population in its area, had one vote on the county board. But in *Avery v. Midland County* (1968), the Court did apply the rule to local government, holding that where county, city, or town governments elect their representatives from single-member districts, the districts must be substantially equal in population. The same requirement was applied to public college trustees in *Hadley v. Junior College District* (1970).[26]

Fifth, there has been a spillover of the one-person, one-vote rule from legislative elections to other voting situations. *Kramer v. Union Free School District* (1969) struck down a New York State law limiting the right to vote in school district elections to owners of real property in the district or parents of children enrolled in the local public schools. Similarly, *Cipriano v. City of Houma* (1969) held unconstitutional as a denial of equal protection a Louisiana law giving only property taxpayers the right to vote in elections called to approve issuance of revenue bonds by municipal utilities. *City of Phoenix v. Kolodziejski* (1971) extended this principle to elections for the approval of general obligation bonds.[27]

By contrast, *Salyer Land Co. v. Tulare Water Storage District* (1973) approved a plan for electing a water district's board of directors that limited the right to vote to landowners in the district and weighted their votes according to the assessed valuation of their land. However, there were only 77 persons in the area covered by the district. But in *Ball v. James* (1981), the Supreme Court by a five to four vote approved a similar plan for a large Arizona water and power district within which half of the state's residents lived. Balloting for district directors was confined to property owners, with voting power in proportion to the amount of land owned. Though the district had power to condemn land and sell tax-exempt bonds, the Court ruled that it was a business enterprise, exercising no "normal functions of government."[28]

Finally, the Court in *Fortson v. Morris* (1966) declined to interpret the one-person, one-vote rule as invalidating the provision of the Georgia constitution allowing the state legislature to select the governor from between the

[26]But it is constitutional for city council members or county commissioners to be elected at large, with the requirement that each member come from a separate election district the population of which varies widely; *Dusch v. Davis* (1967), *Dallas County, Alabama v. Reese* (1975).

[27]*Hill v. Stone* (1975) struck down an ordinance that divided voters in city bond elections into two categories: (1) those owning taxable property and (2) all other registered voters; bond issues had to be approved by majority vote of both groups.

[28]*Gordon v. Lance* (1971) upheld a state constitutional requirement that 60 percent of the voters in referendum elections must approve bonded indebtedness or tax increases. *Holt Civic Club v. City of Tuscaloosa* (1978) upheld an Alabama law that subjected residents in unincorporated areas on the outskirts of cities to the city police and sanitary regulations, criminal jurisdiction of the municipal court, and the city's licensing powers, in spite of the fact that they had no opportunity to vote in city elections.

two top candidates in an election where no candidate secured a majority. The one-person, one-vote rule applied only to "voting cases," said Justice Black; it had no relation to how a state should elect its governors.

CONTROL OVER TERRITORIES

Jefferson's doubts about the authority of the federal government to acquire new territory are well known. In making the Louisiana Purchase he felt he had been justified in seizing the opportunity to protect American rights to the Mississippi waterway, but for future defense of the Constitution he requested Congress to propose a formal amendment. No such action has ever been taken, however, and few have thought this course necessary. John Marshall supplied the constitutional justification for the acquisition of new domain when he held in 1828: "The Constitution confers absolutely upon the government of the Union, the powers of making war, and of making treaties; consequently, that government possesses the power of acquiring territory, either by conquest or by treaty.[29]

Marshall might reasonably have construed at least two other provisions of the Constitution as conferring the right to increase the territory of the United States: the power of Congress to admit new states and to govern territory. There is also the fact that the United States as a sovereign nation has the same rights under international law to obtain new land as any other nation.[30] The Supreme Court has long treated the matter as completely closed.

In contrast, the power of Congress to "dispose" of territory is explicitly written into Article IV, section 3, of the Constitution. The principal controversy over the use of this power occurred in connection with the "disposal" of the Panama Canal Zone to Panama in 1978. Ever since President Theodore Roosevelt "took" Panama in 1904, the American presence on the Isthmus had been an irritant in relations with Latin America. Continuing diplomatic efforts culminated in a treaty, negotiated by the Carter administration, turning over most of the Canal Zone to Panama. The United States was to continue to operate the Canal itself through a Panama Canal Commission, composed of five U.S. representatives and four from Panama. Panama would receive full ownership of the Canal in the year 2000.

There was bitter opposition to "giving away" the Panama Canal, and the two treaties effecting the disposal were ratified by votes of sixty-eight to thirty-two, only one vote over the required two-thirds majority. The opponents then contended that the treaties "disposed" of American property and consequently the action would require approval of the House of Represen-

[29]*American Insurance Co. v. Canter* (1828).
[30]See *Jones v. United States* (1890).

tatives as well as the Senate. But the Senate rejected this theory, and so did the federal courts.[31]

Article IV, section 3, gives Congress power to "make all needful rules and regulations" respecting territories of the United States. This is a plenary grant of authority, and in its exercise Congress may act with full national and local sovereignty. Congressional power is not wholly unlimited, however. In *The Insular Cases* (1901)[33] a badly divided Supreme Court made a distinction between territories that were "incorporated" and those that were "unincorporated." In the former, which are supposedly destined for statehood, Congress must accord all the rights and privileges of the Constitution except those clearly applicable only to state citizens, such as participation in a national election. In the "unincorporated" areas, however, it is mandatory only that "fundamental" rights be guaranteed. Since the admission of Alaska and Hawaii as states, there are no longer any "incorporated" territories.

The District of Columbia has a distinctive and unique status. By Article I, section 8, Congress has power of "exclusive legislation" in the District. Though the District was allowed home rule prior to 1874, it was thereafter completely deprived of any right to control its own affairs. To all intents and purposes it was governed by the House and Senate committees on the District of Columbia, with three presidentially appointed commissioners administering the local government.

A long succession of efforts to restore to the District's residents, the great majority of whom are black, the right to elect their own governmental officials failed in Congress. The Twenty-third Amendment, adopted in 1961, did grant District voters the right to vote in presidential elections, and the District has an elected nonvoting delegate in the House of Representatives. In 1973 Congress finally passed compromise legislation giving partial home rule to the District. The act provides for an elected mayor and thirteen-member city council. The District government has the power to tax, but its budget must be submitted to Congress, which continues to make annual appropriations for the District. Congress reserves the right to legislate for the District at any time, and acts passed by the District council must lie before Congress for thirty days and can be vetoed by concurrent resolution.[34]

Puerto Rico is in a category by itself. In 1950 Congress proposed through Public Law 600 a "compact" between Puerto Rico and the United States whereby Puerto Rico would adopt a constitution acceptable to Congress, and would then assume a "commonwealth" status. Only two advance restrictions

[31]*Edwards v. Carter* (1978). See 92 HARVARD LAW REVIEW 524 (1978).

[32]*First National Bank v. Yankton County* (1880); *Simms v. Simms* (1899).

[33]*DeLima v. Bidwell* (1901); *Downes v. Bidwell* (1901).

[34]As noted in Chapter 2, in 1978 Congress proposed an amendment treating the District for the purpose of federal elections as though it were a state, but ratification appears unlikely. In 1982 residents of the District held a "constitutional convention" to draw up a constitution for the District as a full-fledged state, an effort obviously doomed to defeat.

were placed on this constitution: that it provide for a republican form of government and that it contain a bill of rights. This compact arrangement was approved by referendum vote, and a constitution was subsequently drafted. With only minor changes Congress gave its consent to this document as the fundamental law of Puerto Rico.

The constitution is much like that of the United States, providing for popular elections, separation of powers, a bicameral legislature, judicial review, and an enumeration of certain guaranteed rights, including a maximum working day of no more than eight hours unless overtime pay is given.

Most federal laws do not apply in Puerto Rico, but Congress can pass legislation specifically applicable there. Puerto Ricans do not pay federal income tax, and Congress has given the island certain tax advantages. Puerto Ricans are of course American citizens and can move freely between Puerto Rico and the United States.

Under this commonwealth status, control over Puerto Rico's foreign policy remains with the United States. In addition to conforming to the Puerto Rican constitution, local legislation must also conform to the terms of Public Law 600, the law approving the Puerto Rican constitution, and the applicable provisions of the United States Constitution. Appellate jurisdiction over the decisions of the Puerto Rican supreme court is exercised by the Court of Appeals for the First Circuit in cases involving the writ of habeas corpus or questions of federal law.[35] It is very probable that island court determinations of local law will be treated as final.

Theoretically, Congress could at any time revoke the compact entered into with Puerto Rico and resume direct rule over the island, but such action is most unlikely. There is some sentiment for statehood, which is supported by the governor elected in 1980, and both Presidents Ford and Reagan have declared for statehood. But the Puerto Ricans would probably demand as conditions that bilingualism be recognized and that federal taxes be phased in over a twenty-year period, conditions Congress would almost certainly reject. Consequently Puerto Rico is likely to continue as a commonwealth.

There are certain other territories in the possession of the United States. The Virgin Islands and Guam have a large measure of self-government, though their governors are appointed from Washington. Their residents have full rights of American citizenship. The residents of Samoa, however, are classed as American "nationals," a condition less than full citizenship but involving allegiance to the United States and the obligation of protection by the American government. Certain former Japanese islands in the Pacific—the Marianas, Marshalls, and Carolines—are held by the United States as trust territories under the supervision of the United Nations. In 1976 Congress approved commonwealth status, involving United States citizenship and sovereignty, for the Northern Mariana Islands, which became effective in 1978.

---

[35] *Torres v. Puerto Rico* (1979) held that the requirements of the Fourth Amendment apply in Puerto Rico.

5

Interstate Relations

One of the major motivations of the Founding Fathers, we have seen, was to impose some order and limits on the states in their relations with each other. The constitutional tactics for dealing with commercial rivalries will be discussed in Chapter 13, but the Constitution foresaw five other kinds of interstate problems and adopted provisions for handling them.

INTERSTATE PRIVILEGES AND IMMUNITIES

Article IV, section 2, provides: "The citizens of each state shall be entitled to all privileges and immunities of citizens in the several states." There is no definition of the privileges and immunities to which citizens in the several states are entitled. Neither is it made clear whether citizens are entitled to these privileges in their own state, or when they are temporarily in other states, or both. Nor is any test of state citizenship suggested. Moreover, the clause "is not one the contours of which have been precisely shaped by the process and wear of constant litigation and judicial interpretation over the years since 1789."[1]

The earliest effort at interpretation of this language was that of Justice

---

[1] Justice Blackmun in *Baldwin v. Fish and Game Commission of Montana* (1978).

Bushrod Washington, sitting in federal circuit court in the case of *Corfield v. Coryell* (1823). A New Jersey statute prohibited any person who was not an actual inhabitant or resident of New Jersey from gathering oysters in the state. Was this statute in conflict with Article IV, section 2? Washington decided that it was not. The privileges and immunities that the Constitution protects, said Washington, are those "which are, in their nature, fundamental; which belong, of right, to the citizens of all free governments." The justice thought it would "be more tedious than difficult" to enumerate these rights, but then risked tedium by suggesting quite a list, including the right of a citizen of one state to pass through, or reside in, other states for purposes of trade or profession; the right to institute and maintain court actions; exemption from higher taxes than are paid by other citizens of the state; and the elective franchise, as regulated by the laws of the state in which it is exercised.

This interpretation, if it had been followed by the Supreme Court, might have made Article IV, section 2, a constitutional source of fundamental or "natural rights" guaranteed to state citizens against violation by their own states. But any such development was rendered pointless when much the same result was achieved by adoption of the Fourteenth Amendment. Shortly thereafter, in *Paul v. Virginia* (1869) the Court flatly rejected the natural rights interpretation; and the *Slaughterhouse Cases* (1873) held that Article IV, section 2, created no rights "for the citizens of the State in which they were claimed." Rather, the purpose of the clause was solely to relieve "state citizens of the disabilities of alienage in other States."

Accepting this limitation on the clause, the *Corfield* test of "fundamental" rights still had possible relevance. In *McReady v. Virginia* (1876) the Supreme Court followed *Corfield* in striking down a state law prohibiting citizens of other states from oyster farming in Virginia waters, because oyster farming was not a fundamental right attached to state citizenship. By related logic, *Geer v. Connecticut* (1896) held that states had the fundamental right of ownership of all fish and game (*naturae ferae*) within their borders, and so could monopolize them for their own citizens. As recently as 1978 in *Baldwin v. Fish and Game Commission of Montana* the Court relied on the fundamental right theory to uphold a state law charging out-of-state elk hunters a license fee twenty-five times higher than that for state citizens, saying: "Whatever rights or activities may be 'fundamental' under the Privileges and Immunities Clause . . . elk hunting by nonresidents of Montana is not one of them."

Application of the privileges and immunities clause need not involve, however, the elusive quest for fundamental rights. Greater importance now seems to attach to the impact of the challenged discrimination on successful operation of the federal system. As the Court said in *Austin v. New Hampshire* (1975), "The Clause thus establishes a norm of comity without specifying the particular subjects as to which citizens of one State coming within the jurisdiction of another are guaranteed equality of treatment." According to

Toomer v. Witsell (1948), the clause bars "discrimination against citizens of other States where there is no substantial reason for the discrimination beyond the mere fact that they are citizens of other States." Justice Brennan added: "A State's unequal treatment of nonresidents [must] be reasoned and suitably tailored. . . ."[2]

A Georgia law that forbade women from out of state to secure abortions in Georgia did not meet this test, the Court held in *Doe v. Bolton* (1973). A state could not limit to its own residents general medical care available there. Grossly discriminatory license fees for out-of-state commerical fisherman were invalidated in *Toomer v. Witsell* and *Mullaney v. Anderson* (1952). *Austin v. New Hampshire* struck down that state's effort to tax New Hampshire-derived income of nonresidents, citing "the structural balance essential to the concept of federalism."

However, under the "substantial reason" rule the Court has carved out exceptions for discriminations that could not reasonably be regarded as hostile to the rights of citizens of other states. Somewhat higher fees for hunting or fishing by outsiders can be justified on the ground that local citizens pay additional taxes that are used in part for the upkeep of the public domain, or the state may show that there is an added cost in enforcing its police regulations against people who live outside the state.

The substantial reason rule can also justify lower tuition for state citizens in state universities than for outsiders. But in *Vlandis v. Kline* (1973) the Court held that a Connecticut statute that required students admitted to state universities as nonresidents to pay nonresident tuition for their entire four years was unconstitutional as a denial of due process. A Washington law requiring one year of residence in the state to qualify as a resident for tuition purposes was upheld in *Sturgis v. Washington* (1973).[3]

Again, technical requirements for access to the courts may be somewhat different for out-of-state than for local citizens.[4] The right to engage in normal businesses is protected, but the practice of certain professions connected with the public interest, such as medicine and law, is licensed by the states; and restrictions may be imposed on licensed professionals from other states.

The earlier view that a state's "ownership" of its wildlife or natural resources entitled it to keep out citizens of other states or to burden them with discriminatory fees has been largely abandoned. In *Toomer v. Witsell* the ownership doctrine was labeled a mere fiction "expressive in legal shorthand of the importance to its people that a State have power to preserve and regulate the exploitation of an important resource." The *naturae ferae* holding in *Geer v. Connecticut* was overruled in *Hughes v. Oklahoma* (1979). *Hicklin v. Or-*

---

[2]*Baldwin v. Fish and Game Commission of Montana* (1978).

[3]*Spatt v. New York* (1973) upheld a state law requiring state scholarship award winners to go to colleges within the state.

[4]*Ward v. Maryland* (1871); *Miles v. Illinois Central Railroad* (1942).

beck (1978) held unconstitutional an "Alaska hire" law that required all oil and gas operations in the state to give hiring preference to qualified Alaska residents.

The present-day significance of the privileges and immunities clause is not great. While it still figures in an occasional controversy, to a great degree its purpose in furthering a "norm of comity" can be served as well or better by the equal protection and commerce clauses.[5] Thus in *Hughes v. Oklahoma* a limitation on transporting minnows out of the state was held to violate the commerce clause. Though the appellants in *Hicklin* did not raise the commerce issue, the Court voluntarily noted the "mutually reenforcing relationship" between the two provisions and "their shared vision of federalism."

INTERSTATE TRAVEL

Originally, protection of the right to travel from state to state was derived from general principles of federalism. *Crandall v. Nevada* (1868) held that a tax of one dollar per passenger on commercial vehicles leaving the state interfered with the government's right to call citizens to cross state lines in order to fill offices and wage wars and with citizens' rights to carry on business among the states and to seek redress of grievances from the government. In *Ward v. Maryland* (1871) the privileges and immunities clause was used to strike down a state license tax on out-of-state drummers; and in *Edwards v. California* (1941) a statute making it a misdemeanor to bring indigents into the state was invalidated on the basis of the commerce clause.

More recently, the right to travel has been related to individual freedoms. Close surveillance and control of travel has always been a central technique of the totalitarian state. The right to travel abroad, which does not involve considerations of federalism, was upheld in *Kent v. Dulles* (1958) as an element of the liberty protected by the due process clause of the Fifth Amendment. Likewise, *Aptheker v. Secretary of State* (1964) ruled that congressional denial of passports to members of the Communist party "too broadly and indiscriminately restricts the right to travel and thereby abridges the liberty guaranteed by the Fifth Amendment."[6] In *United States v. Guest* (1966) the

---

[5]But in *Austin v. New Hampshire* the Court regarded the privileges and immunities rationale preferable to equal protection. In *Zobel v. Williams* (1982) O'Connor concurred with Burger in striking down an Alaskan law distributing $415 million in oil revenues to Alaska citizens in varying shares based on length of residence in the state, but she invoked the privileges and immunities clause rather than Burger's equal protection argument.

[6]But *Califano v. Aznavorian* (1978) held that a statute denying payments under a special Social Security program for the aged, blind, and disabled for any month the recipient spends outside the United States had a rational basis and did not impose an impermissible burden on the freedom of foreign travel. And *Califano v. Torres* (1978) held that reducing the benefits under the same program for recipients who moved from the United States to Puerto Rico was not a violation of the right to travel.

right to travel was characterized as "fundamental" without reference to any particular provision of the Constitution, and interference with that right was the basis for a civil rights action charging criminal conspiracy.

The equal protection clause was invoked in *Shapiro v. Thompson* (1969) to strike down state and District of Columbia laws that denied welfare assistance to persons who had not been resident in the state or District for one year. The right of interstate travel was deemed so fundamental that there was no need "to ascribe the sources of this right . . . to a particular constitutional provision." The one-year residency requirement was a limitation on that right that was unjustified by any compelling state interest and so was an invidious classification denying equal protection. In like fashion, *Dunn v. Blumstein* (1972) held residency requirements for voting an unconstitutional limitation on the "fundamental personal right . . . to travel." And *Memorial Hospital v. Maricopa County* (1974) ruled that an Arizona durational residency requirement for free medical care "penalizes indigents for exercising their right to migrate to and settle in that State."[7]

In contrast, *Sosna v. Iowa* (1975) upheld an Iowa law requiring one year's residence in the state before a person could bring a divorce action, only the minority justices raising the right to travel issue. Though interstate travel was not involved, in *McCarthy v. Philadelphia Civil Service Commission* (1976) the Court upheld ordinances requiring municipal employees to live within a city's boundaries. The rulings in *Vlandis v. Kline* and *Sturgis v. Washington* upholding residence requirements for college tuition have already been noted. Obviously the equal protection rationale for interstate travel is subject to qualifications if they impress the Court as furthering legitimate state interests.

FULL FAITH AND CREDIT

Article IV, section 1, commands that each state accord full faith and credit to three types of official acts of sister states: public records, statutes, and court decisions.[8] Congress is given power to issue uniform regulations for authentication of the legal papers that deserve such recognition, and to determine the precise effect to be given such documents. Even without this explicit requirement some obligation of the sort would have existed under the doctrine of comity in international law. As a demonstration of friendship, nations customarily recognize as valid the public proceedings of other countries, provided there is no contrary local policy. The Constitution, however, removes the mat-

---

[7]In *Abrams v. Salla* (1980) the Court let stand a New York court's invalidation of a state law giving preference on public works to residents of the state for twelve consecutive months or more, citing the right to travel among other constitutional grounds.

[8]See Robert H. Jackson, *Full Faith and Credit: The Lawyer's Clause of the Constitution* (New York: Columbia University Press, 1945).

ter of faith and credit from considerations of mutual courtesy and amity and makes it a legal duty enforceable in federal courts.

Judicial Proceedings

Under authority of the full faith and credit clause Congress passed legislation in 1790 and 1804, providing a simple method of authentication for judicial proceedings and public records, and commanding that they be given the same effect in every court that they had in the court which issued them. Because of these explicit provisions the matter of according full faith and credit to judicial acts is relatively uncomplicated, except in divorce cases, which are considered below. In 1813 a young attorney named Francis Scott Key argued before the Supreme Court that the obligation imposed by Article IV had been met when a state merely received a sister-state judgment as evidence and weighed it with the other evidence in the case. The Court, however, rejected this contention and held that a judgment conclusive in one state must be recognized as final in all others.[9]

Such conclusiveness is not automatic. A person who has secured a court order in one state and wishes to have it enforced against a person who has since gone to another state must bring a new legal action in the latter state. In this action the court will accept the original decree, examine it, and if it finds the order to be properly authenticated, will issue an enforcement order of its own. This must be done even if the public policy of the second state would not have permitted such a decision had the case originated there. The defendant may appear in court and contest the order. He may not, however, reargue the merits of the case. The only valid line of attack open to him is the claim that the court where the original decree was handed down did not have proper jurisdiction over either the parties or the subject matter involved in the dispute.

A second situation in which the full faith and credit clause applies to judicial proceedings occurs where a judgment of a court in one state is offered *in defense* against a new proceeding in another state growing out of the same facts that were involved in the original suit. An illustration would be supplied where a decree of divorce granted in one state was offered as a bar to a divorce suit by the other party to the marriage in a second state. In the 1940s and 1950s, when only a few states had lenient divorce laws, major problems arose as to whether other states were required to give full faith and credit to "quickie" divorces.[10] The recent relaxation of divorce laws in most states has reduced the problem, since fewer persons feel obliged to resort to out-of-state divorces. As already noted, *Sosna v. Iowa* (1975) held that a one-year residency requirement for divorce was justified.

[9]*Mills v. Duryee* (1813).

[10]See *Williams v. North Carolina* (1942, 1945); also *Estin v. Estin* (1948), *Rice v. Rice* (1949), *Vanderbilt v. Vanderbilt* (1957), *Simons v. Miami Beach First National Bank* (1965).

State Legislation

The matter of the extrastate effect of state statutes has been less satis-factorily resolved than that of judgments or records. In general, no state is obliged to enforce the criminal laws of another state.[11] For other types of statutes, the general principle is that the full faith and credit clause does not abolish the dominance of local policy over the rules of comity. Thus the effect of the *Dred Scott* decision was that Scott, though he had become a free man during his residence in Illinois, where slavery did not exist, on his return to Missouri became subject to its local policy as stated in its laws and judicial decisions, and so reverted to slave status.[12]

Problems as to the extrastate effect of a state statute customarily arise when a statute of one state is set up as a defense to a suit brought under the statute of another state, or where a foreign statute is set up as a defense to a suit or proceeding under a local statute. The Supreme Court's practice in han-dling such conflicts was well summed up by Justice Stone in *Alaska Packers Association v. Industrial Accident Commission* (1935): "The conflict is to be resolved, not by giving automatic effect to the full faith and credit clause, compelling the courts of each state to subordinate its own statutes to those of the other, but by appraising the governmental interests of each jurisdiction, and turning the scale of decision according to their weight."[13] Cases involving the full faith and credit to be accorded statutes have arisen in three principal fields: commercial law, insurance, and workmen's compensation.[14]

RENDITION

The obvious gap in federalism caused by the fact that full faith and credit is never given by one state to another state's criminal laws is to a great extent closed by the obligation imposed by the command of Article IV, section 2, that: "A person charged in any state with treason, felony, or other crime, who shall flee from justice, and be found in another state, shall on demand of the executive authority of the state from which he fled, be delivered up, to be removed to the state having jurisdiction of the crime." Edmund Randolph, the first attorney general of the United States, offered the opinion that this part of the Constitution was not self-executing. Accordingly, Congress in 1793

[11]*Huntington v. Attrill* (1892).

[12]*Dred Scott v. Sandford* (1857).

[13]For example, in *Nevada v. Hall* (1979) an automobile owned by the state of Nevada figured in an accident in California. In a personal injury action Nevada was held subject to suit in California courts. But Nevada contended that California must give full faith and credit to a Nevada law limiting the state's tort liability to $25,000. The California courts refused and an award of $1,150,000 was granted. The Supreme Court approved, holding that the full faith and credit clause does not require a state to apply another state's law in violation of its own legitimate public policy.

[14]See *Thomas v. Washington Gas Light Co.* (1980).

passed a statute affirming the obligation of a governor to surrender a fugitive from another state.

Under international law there is no right on the part of one nation to demand the return of a fugitive unless there is a treaty between the two countries providing for extradition. It is usual in such treaties for the crimes for which extradition can be requested to be specifically listed. Political offenses (that is, those against a particular government or governing group rather than against the state itself) are almost universally nonextraditable; nor will a nation usually extradite its own citizens. Moreover, a person extradited under a treaty arrangement can be tried only for the crime which was alleged in the request for surrender. If other charges are to be pressed against the prisoner, he must first be allowed to return to the country to which he had fled.

The Constitution states no such restrictions. It simply specifies that "fugitives" from justice shall be turned over to the demanding executive authority. The question whether certain crimes were excluded from rendition was raised on the very eve of the Civil War in *Kentucky v. Dennison* (1861). William Lago, a free Negro, had been indicted in Kentucky for assisting a slave to escape. To avoid trial Lago fled across the border to Ohio, and the governor of Kentucky presented a request for Lago's return. Dennison, the governor of Ohio, refused to comply on the ground that the crime in question was one that the Constitution had not meant to include.

Kentucky brought suit in the Supreme Court for a writ of mandamus to compel Dennison to perform his duty. The Court was aware of the political situation in March, 1861, and realized that a direct order to the governor of Ohio would probably be disobeyed. The tactics adopted by Chief Justice Taney were, first, to reject absolutely the contention that certain crimes were outside the purview of Article IV. Neither could Taney see any doubt that it was the duty of the governor of Ohio to return the fugitive.

Then, having firmly established what was the law in the case, Taney began to extricate the Court from the position of having to issue an order which would be ignored. Whether the Court, Taney hedged, could command Governor Dennison to perform this function was an entirely different question. The statute of 1793 had not provided any means to compel the execution of the duty of rendition; nor could the federal government constitutionally coerce a state official. "Indeed, such a power would place every State under the control and dominion of the General Government." Although this is dubious doctrine so far as general nation-state relations are concerned, the rule of the *Dennison* case has been respected subsequently in rendition matters.

It should be emphasized that although governors occasionally refuse to return a fugitive, orderly rendition is the normal course of events. To eliminate serious breaches of justice, Congress in 1934 exercised its power under the commerce clause to make it a federal offense for anyone to cross a state line fleeing from justice or for anyone to help another to do so. Since this act provides that the fugitive must be tried in the federal district court in the state from which he fled, the prisoner is readily available to local officials if the federal government does not complete its prosecution. Moreover, since 1936, most states have adopted a uniform criminal extradition act.

A governor's grant of extradition is prima facie evidence that all constitutional and statutory requirements have been met, and subsequent judicial challenges in the asylum state have generally failed. In *Sweeney v. Woodall* (1952) the Supreme Court refused to block the extradition of a fugitive who contended that he had been subjected to cruel and unusual punishment in prison, while in *Michigan v. Doran* (1978) the Court refused to permit courts of the asylum state to question the constitutionality of the arrest procedures in the demanding state.

INTERSTATE COMPACTS

In recent years there have been numerous protests against the centralizing tendencies of the federal government. One means to avoid concentration of power in Washington and to permit state handling of problems that extend beyond the borders of a single state has been the interstate compact. Initially this method was used to solve relatively minor issues, such as marking disputed land or water boundaries. In the twentieth century, however, the device has been more fully exploited. Compacts between states have regulated such diverse matters as conservation of natural resources in gas, oil, water, and timber; civil defense coordination for possible emergencies; mutual sharing of water power of large rivers; water and air pollution control; development of interstate metropolitan areas and interstate facilities such as bridges and harbors; regulation of ocean fisheries; and interstate programs of graduate and professional education.

Perhaps the most famous interstate compact has been that between New York and New Jersey, which established the Port of New York Authority to develop and operate harbor and transportation facilities in the bistate area. In 1953 the same states signed another important compact regulating labor practices in the New York port area. Because of the evidence of crime and racketeering along the waterfront, the states agreed on a comprehensive set of regulations for licensing and employment on the docks. To enforce the terms of the agreement, the compact set up a two-person waterfront commission, with one member from each state. No individual can work as a stevedore or longshoreman in the port area without securing a license from the commission.

Truly sovereign states would be at liberty to make treaties at will, but the Constitution imposes definite limitations on the states in this respect. Article 1, section 10, clause 1, provides: "No state shall enter into any treaty, alliance, or confederation . . . ," while the third clause of the same section stipulates that: "No state shall, without the consent of Congress . . . enter into any agreement or compact with another state, or with a foreign power." Obviously the justification for the interstate compact must be found in the uncertain distinction between "treaty" and "agreement or compact." Presumably this distinction is a political question for Congress to determine in giving its consent.

Although congressional consent to interstate compacts is required, there is no set formula as to when and how that approval should be registered. The assent may be given before or after the agreement; it may be explicit, implicit, or tacit.[15] Nor is there any form in which Congress must cast its approval. It may be done by specific statute, by a joint resolution, by ratification of a state constitution that contains such a compact, or by means of a compact between Congress and the states involved.[16] Congress may even extend blanket approval to future agreements in certain specific areas.

No case has arisen in which a compact has been held unconstitutional by the Supreme Court. Still, there can be no doubt that interstate agreements must conform to the Constitution; otherwise the combined action of two states and a congressional majority could amend the Constitution. The presidential veto is an added safety device to that supplied by the courts.

The Multistate Tax Commission, organized in 1967 by seven states to facilitate determination of the tax liabilities of multistate taxpayers, was attacked in *U.S. Steel Corp. v. Multistate Tax Commission* (1978) because it had not been approved by Congress. But the leading case of *Virginia v. Tennessee* (1893) had held that the compact clause applied and congressional consent was required only in the case of agreements tending to increase the political power of the states at the expense of the "just supremacy" of the United States. The Court held that this commission did not enhance state power to the detriment of federal supremacy, and the justices were reluctant "to circumscribe modes of interstate cooperation."

Once a state has formally ratified a compact and the approval of Congress has been obtained, the agreement is binding on the state and all its officers—executive, legislative, and judicial. A state cannot unilaterally declare that a compact is in violation of its constitution and use this as a basis for withdrawal.[17]

DISPUTES BETWEEN STATES

There are, in general, three methods open to a nation in settling disputes with its neighbors: war, diplomacy, or submission of the controversy to some form of judicial determination. Under the Constitution only the last two methods

---

[15]*Virginia v. Tennessee* (1893).
[16]*Burton's Lessee v. Williams* (1818).
[17]*West Virginia ex rel. Dyer v. Sims* (1951).

are open to American states. Interstate diplomacy might terminate in an informal agreement between governors or in a full-fledged compact requiring the consent of Congress. Litigation between states is handled exclusively by the Supreme Court under its original jurisdiction, according to Article III, section 2, of the Constitution.

The Articles of Confederation made Congress the tribunal of last resort for interstate disputes and laid down elaborate provisions for the selection of a panel of impartial arbiters to hear the controversies. The Constitutional Convention discussed a similar proposal that would have given jurisdiction over territorial and jurisdictional disputes to the Senate, but finally decided that the scope of the federal judicial power would render this grant unnecessary.

The first question that the Supreme Court must answer in hearing a dispute between states is whether or not the matter is properly a controversy between states. This matter is not always so simple as it might appear at first glance. After the Civil War, Louisiana defaulted on certain state bonds and under the Eleventh Amendment the state could not be sued without its consent by citizens of other states. A group of bondholders from New Hampshire tried to evade this provision by nominally transferring their holdings to New Hampshire and having that state bring suit against Louisiana for payment. The Court viewed this as a mere subterfuge and refused to decide the case.[18] However, some twenty years later South Dakota bondholders gave their state government full title to some North Carolina securities on which that state had defaulted. In this case the Supreme Court by a five to four vote held that there was an actual controversy between states and that its jurisdiction had been properly invoked. Judgment was given in favor of South Dakota.[19]

On the whole, in controversies between states the Supreme Court has strictly applied its usual standards of what constitutes sufficient injury to bring about a real "case or controversy."[20] It has refused to entertain suits where a state has sought to enjoin other states from forbidding the importation of prison-made goods or levying inheritance taxes on intangibles held by its citizens in another state.[21] On several occasions, the Court has gone out of its judicial way to discourage litigation and to suggest that the disputing states settle their controversies by negotiation or compact.[22] On the other hand, the Court has accepted cases where serious and irreparable injury was allegedly threatened by such hazards as sewage pollution of large rivers or by the diversion of vitally necessary water from interstate streams. The Court has ex-

[18]*New Hampshire v. Louisiana* (1883).

[19]*South Dakota v. North Carolina* (1904).

[20]See discussion of the "case or controversy" requirement in Chapter 6.

[21]*Alabama v. Arizona* (1934); *Massachusetts v. Missouri* (1939).

[22]*Washington v. Oregon* (1909); *Minnesota v. Wisconsin* (1920); *New York v. New Jersey* (1921).

tended its jurisdiction to disputes such as those involving state boundaries, where it might have claimed that the issue was "political" rather than legal.[23]

Once a case between two states has been accepted by the Court, the next problems that arise are what law should be applied and what procedure the Court should follow. Generally the law of the case is decided on principles of international law modified by the exigencies of a federal system. In *Kansas v. Colorado* (1907) Justice Brewer noted that federal law, state law, and international law would be employed as the situation might demand. He also suggested that in judging interstate conflicts the Court had been in effect "building up what may not improperly be called interstate common law."

Where the factual issues involved in these disputes are complicated, the Court frequently appoints a "special master," usually a member of the Supreme Court bar, to act as a fact finder. He may have the right to summon witnesses and take depositions. After the findings of the master are filed, the Court will allow the parties to the case to submit exceptions and will hear argument on the objections. It is not unusual, however, for the master's report as filed to be adopted by the court in its final decree.

There always exists, potentially at least, the problem of what the Supreme Court might do if one of the states chose to ignore or disobey a judgment. The nearest this question came to a practical answer was in the historic Virginia-West Virginia dispute. As part of the terms of its becoming a separate state during the Civil War, West Virginia had agreed to assume its just share of the Virginia state debt and the compact had been duly ratified by Congress. In 1907, after four decades of negotiation had yielded no monetary results, Virginia brought suit for collection. The litigation continued to 1915, when the Supreme Court affirmed the report of its special master and fixed the amount of West Virginia's liability. However, West Virginia still made no motion to pay.

The matter came to a head in 1918. Chief Justice White spoke for a unanimous Court and warned West Virginia:

> That judicial power essentially involves the right to enforce the results of its exertion is elementary. . . . And that this applies to the exertion of such power in controversies between States as the result of the exercise of original jurisdiction conferred upon this court by the Constitution is therefore certain.[24]

The chief justice asserted that it was patent from the wording of the legislative and judicial articles in the Constitution and from the limitations placed thereby on the states, that the federal government had the power to enforce a court decision against a recalcitrant state. There were two general remedies available. First, Congress could legislate. Second, further court action was possi-

---

[23]See discussion of the "political question" doctrine in Chapter 8.
[24]*Virginia v. West Virginia* (1918).

ble. Precisely what course or compulsion could or would be pursued was not indicated. The case was postponed for reargument on the judicial remedies that should be invoked and to allow time for congressional action or further opportunity for peaceful settlement. Before the case was reopened, the West Virginia Legislature appropriated the money to meet the obligation.

6

Judicial Power and Jurisdiction

The federal judiciary, asserted Alexander Hamilton in No. 78 of *The Federalist,* is "beyond comparison the weakest of the three departments of power." He went on:

> The judiciary, from the nature of its functions, will always be the least dangerous to the political rights of the Constitution, because it will be least in a capacity to annoy or injure them. The Executive not only dispenses the honours, but holds the sword of the community. The legislature not only commands the purse, but prescribes the rules by which the duties and rights of every citizen are to be regulated. The judiciary, on the contrary, has no influence over either the sword or the purse; no direction either of the strength or of the wealth of the society; and can take no active resolution whatever. It may truly be said to have neither force nor will, but merely judgment.

This appraisal of the comparative power positions of the three branches seems accurate enough almost 200 years later. Nevertheless, for present purposes it is "judgment" rather than "force" or "will" that is most important. Since this is a study of the meaning of the American Constitution as judicially determined, it is appropriate that a survey of the three departments of government begin, not with Article I, which creates and empowers the Congress, nor with Article II, which establishes the executive, but with Article III, which pertains to the judiciary. An understanding of judicial power and organization and the conditions under which constitutional controversies are decided by the federal courts, which these chapters supply, is required both for itself and for the background it provides to the discussions in the subsequent sections of this volume.

FEDERAL JUDICIAL POWER

Article III begins with this sentence: "The judicial power of the United States shall be vested in one supreme court, and in such inferior courts as the Congress may, from time to time, ordain and establish." This language tells who is to exercise the federal judicial power, but it does not define that power. In practice, the judicial power exercised by the federal courts is an amalgam of constitutional authority, legislative authorization and interpretation, traditional forms, and prudential practice. The federal courts behave as they do partly under the directives of the Constitution and Congress, and partly because they stand in the time-honored tradition of the English common-law and equity courts. In addition, their development has been shaped by the overriding necessity of accommodation to a federal system with a dual structure of courts, which continually creates problems of adjustment and division of responsibilities.[1]

Power to Decide Cases and Controversies

The basic power of the federal courts, as indicated in Article III, section 2, is to decide "cases" and "controversies." This authorization has been interpreted to foreclose the handling of any case by the federal courts unless it meets four tests: (1) it must involve *adverse parties* (2) who have a *substantial legal interest* (3) in a controversy growing out of a *real set of facts* (4) which admits of an *enforceable determination* of the legal rights of the parties. As Chief Justice Hughes said in *Aetna Life Insurance Co. v. Haworth* (1937): "A justiciable controversy is . . . distinguished from a difference or dispute of a hypothetical or abstract character. . . . The controversy must be definite and concrete, touching the legal relations of parties having adverse legal interests. . . . It must be a real and substantial controversy admitting of specific relief through a decree of conclusive character."[2] As we shall see in Chapter 8, these conditions impose limitations of real importance on judicial review.[3]

[1]See Lea Brilmayer, "The Jurisprudence of Article III," 93 HARVARD LAW REVIEW 297 (1979); Mark V. Tushnet, "The Sociology of Article III," 93 HARVARD LAW REVIEW 1698 (1980).

[2]Moreover, the controversy must not be moot—i.e., it must not have developed to the point where judicial action is no longer possible or cannot provide the relief requested. For example, see *DeFunis v. Odegaard* (1974) and *Edgar v. Mite Corp.* (1982).

[3]See James E. Radcliffe, *The Case-or-Controversy Provision* (State College: Pennsylvania State University Press, 1978).

The power of the federal courts to enforce their decisions is likewise normally taken for granted, but in fact the courts have no enforcement machinery at their direct disposal except for a few marshals. The judiciary must look to the executive and Congress for help in case of any real resistance to its orders. Whether apocryphal or not, Andrew Jackson's comment, "John Marshall has made his decision, now let him enforce it," reveals the hollowness of the Supreme Court's authority unless it is sustained by the support of its governmental colleagues and the backing of public opinion.

The matter of the enforceability of judicial decisions was most strikingly raised by the Supreme Court's 1954 ruling on the constitutionality of racial segregation in the public schools.[4] Recognizing the bitterness of the resistance that this ruling would evoke, the Court authorized a pattern of compliance that could be varied in character and speed to meet local conditions. When in 1957, in spite of these ameliorative efforts, mob violence and official state obstruction frustrated enforcement of the court order in Little Rock, Arkansas, President Eisenhower promptly made it clear that the entire compulsive power of the government was available to enforce the judicial decree, stating: "Failure to act in such a case would be tantamount to acquiescence in anarchy and the dissolution of the Union."

The Contempt Power

In order to carry out their primary function of making binding decisions in cases or controversies, the federal courts possess certain auxiliary sanctions. First is the power to punish for contempt of their authority. The origin of the contempt power was in England, where disobedience of court orders was regarded as contempt of the king himself. Presumably the courts of the United States would have enjoyed similar power without specific legislation, but in fact the Judiciary Act of 1789 did confer power "to punish by fine or imprisonment, at the discretion of said courts, all contempts of authority in any cause or hearing before the same."

Contempts may be either civil or criminal. A civil contempt consists in the refusal of a person to obey a court order, and the purpose of the sanction is to preserve and enforce the rights of the parties in the proceeding. Civil contempt may be purged by obedience to the court order. In a criminal contempt, however, the purpose of the punishment is to vindicate the authority of the court. The act of contempt has been completed, and guilty persons cannot purge themselves of contempt by subsequent action. The same conduct may amount to both civil and criminal contempt, and the court may impose both coercive and punitive measures in the same proceeding.[5]

The judicial power to punish for contempt has often been a source of

[4]*Brown v. Board of Education* (1954).
[5]*United States v. United Mine Workers* (1947).

serious concern. It was historically a summary power—i.e., exercised by the judge without jury or other procedural protections. Moreover, as developed in England it applied to contempts committed out of court as well as those in the presence of the court. American experience has resulted in limiting the contempt power in both respects.[6] A congressional act of 1831 confined its exercise to misbehavior in the presence of the court "or so near thereto as to obstruct the administration of justice," and to disobedience to lawful writs or orders of the court.

As for summary punishment for contempt, it is now authorized by Section 42(a) of the federal rules of criminal procedure only when the judges certify that they saw or heard the conduct constituting the contempt. Most summary contempt convictions are based on some type of disruptive, indecorous, or contumacious behavior.[7] However, in *United States v. Wilson* (1975) the Court held that mere refusal to testify in a criminal trial on Fifth Amendment grounds, despite a grant of immunity, amounted to intentional obstruction of court proceedings and could be punished summarily under Rule 42(a).[8]

The discretion that a judge exercises in summarily punishing contempts occurring in court is not often successfully challenged on appeal, but it did happen in *In re McConnell* (1962), where counsel for one of the parties had been held in contempt for insisting on asking questions that the judge had barred. The Supreme Court, observing that "a vigorous, independent bar" was as necessary in our system of justice as an independent judiciary, reversed the conviction.[9]

A novel problem was presented by *Sacher v. United States* (1952), which involved the contempt of court sentences passed on the lawyers for the defendants in the 1949 Smith Act prosecution of eleven Communist party leaders.[10] The nine months' trial of the case was among the most turbulent and hectic in American court annals. The five principal defense lawyers carried on a running battle with Judge Harold Medina that appeared "wilfully obstructive" of the conduct of the trial. The trial judge was convinced that the lawyers had deliberately badgered and insulted him throughout the long months of the

[6]On the problem of out-of-court contempt by newspapers in commenting on judicial proceedings, see *Bridges v. California* (1941) and *Craig v. Harney* (1947).

[7]See, for example, *Eaton v. City of Tulsa* (1974), *In re Little* (1972), *Fisher v. Pace* (1949), and *Mayberry v. Pennsylvania* (1971). In *Illinois v. Allen* (1970), where an obstreperous defendant had been chained to his chair and gagged in court, the Supreme Court reluctantly approved the action but expressed preference for the contempt remedy.

[8]See Richard B. Kuhns, "The Summary Contempt Power: A Critique and a New Perspective," 88 YALE LAW JOURNAL 39 (1978).

[9]*Holt v. Virginia* (1965) held that a lawyer who moved for a change of venue on the ground that the judge was biased was not in contempt. Similarly *Maness v. Meyers* (1975) ruled that a lawyer may not be cited for contempt for advising a client to refuse on Fifth Amendment grounds to produce subpoenaed material.

[10]*Dennis v. United States* (1951). See C. Herman Pritchett, *Constitutional Civil Liberties* (Englewood Cliffs, N.J.: Prentice-Hall, 1984), Chapter 6.

trial. On many occasions he warned counsel that their conduct was contemptuous, but in order not to delay the trial or deprive defendants of counsel, he did not cite them for contempt until after the jury had brought in its verdict and been discharged. Immediately thereafter he asked the lawyers to stand up, read them a small portion of a lengthy "contempt certificate" he had prepared, found them all guilty of contempt, and sentenced them to prison.

The Supreme Court majority upheld Medina's procedure, on the ground that he himself had heard and seen the contempt. But Justice Frankfurter, dissenting along with Black and Douglas, contended that this rule "merely permits summary punishment" of contempts committed in the presence of the court; it does not command it. He argued that even though the contempt had occurred in the presence of the court,

> no judge should sit in a case in which he is personally involved and that no criminal punishment should be meted out except upon notice and due hearing, unless overriding necessity precludes such indispensable safeguards for assuring fairness and affording the feeling that fairness has been done.

While *Sacher* has not been overruled, the similar procedure followed by a trial judge who had been scandalously reviled by a defendant was invalidated in *Mayberry v. Pennsylvania* (1971). The Court held there that no judge who had been "cruelly slandered" in his own court could maintain "that calm detachment necessary for fair adjudication" and that therefore the fact of contempt should have been tried before another judge. Judge Julius Hoffman likewise followed the Medina procedure in the tumultuous 1969 trial of the Chicago Seven. His contempt judgments, delayed until the end of the trial, were reversed by the court of appeals, which directed a new trial before a different judge. In that trial, only one of the two lawyers and three of the seven defendants were convicted of contempt.[11]

All contempts occurring outside the court, according to Rule 42(b), must be prosecuted only after notice; there must be representation by counsel, trial by jury if provided for by act of Congress, and—where the contempt involved disrespect to or criticism of the judge—trial before a different judge.

Though criminal contempt proceedings are so similar to ordinary criminal trials, they have not been covered by the constitutional requirements of grand jury indictment and trial by jury. The objection to jury trial has been that judicial authority would be seriously compromised if judges had to depend upon a jury verdict for defense of their position against contemptuous assaults. However, Congress can, if it wishes, require trial by jury in the federal courts for contempts, and it has done so in several statutes.[12]

One reason why the unfettered judicial contempt power was accepted

---

[11] *In re Dellinger* (1972); *United States v. Seale* (1972). See also *Taylor v. Hayes* (1974).

[12] The Civil Rights Acts of 1957 and 1964 require jury trial for contempt if the penalty imposed on conviction is a fine in excess of $300 or imprisonment for more than forty-five days. The Clayton Act of 1914 requires a jury trial in contempt proceedings arising out of disobedience

was because criminal contempt sentences were generally for a relatively short period. But in *Green v. United States* (1958), contempt sentences of three years were imposed on two of the eleven Communist party leaders who had been convicted of violating the Smith Act in 1951 but had failed to appear in court for sentencing. Contempt sentences of such severity were unprecedented, and three members of the Court—Black, Warren, and Douglas—protested that severe punishment under summary conditions, where the same "functionary" lays down the law, prosecutes, sits in judgment on his own charges, and punishes as he sees fit, amounted to "autocratic omnipotence." Justice Black thought that "there is no justification in history, in necessity, or most important in the Constitution for trying those charged with violating a court's decree in a manner wholly different from those accused of disobeying any other mandate of the state."

There was an indication in *United States v. Barnett* (1964) that a majority of the Court was willing to accept absence of jury trial in criminal contempts only when the punishment was "minor" or "trivial." This hint was confirmed in *Cheff v. Schnackenberg* (1966). Though the Court still denied that a criminal contempt proceeding was a criminal prosecution within the meaning of the Bill of Rights guarantee of trial by jury, it held, in an exercise of its supervisory power over the federal courts, that sentences exceeding six months for criminal contempt could not be imposed without jury trial.

Two years later, in *Bloom v. Illinois* (1968), the Court held the six-month rule applicable to the states as well, and in its opinion accepted the position that "convictions for criminal contempt are indistinguishable from ordinary criminal convictions."[13]

In the aftermath of the Chicago Seven trial, Judge Hoffman sought to avoid the six-month limit by assessing contempt sentences of six months or less for a number of individual acts by defendants and their counsel and cumulating them for total sentences of up to four years. This stratagem was predictably voided on appeal. In the *Mayberry* case, the trial judge had by a similar method calculated sentences of eleven to twenty-two years, which were vacated by the Supreme Court ruling.[14]

---

to federal court orders provided the conduct complained of also constitutes a criminal offense under federal or state laws. A provision of the 1932 Norris-LaGuardia Act, which provided jury trial in cases of contempt arising under that act, was replaced in 1948 by a statute (U.S. Code Title 18, sec. 3692) providing a broader guarantee of jury trial "in all cases of contempt arising under the laws of the United States governing the issuance of injunctions...in any case involving or growing out of a labor dispute." Nevertheless, in *Muniz v. Hoffman* (1975), the Supreme Court held this provision inapplicable and denied jury trial in an action for criminal contempt for violation of the Labor Management Relations Act.

[13]In *Duncan v. Louisiana* (1968), the Court had ruled that jury trial must be provided in state courts for all serious crimes—i.e., those for which the statutory penalty is more than six months.

[14]Se also *Codispoti v. Pennsylvania* (1974).

Refusal to testify before a grand jury may be punished as civil or criminal contempt after a judicial order requiring the testimony has been secured. However, *Harris v. United States* (1965) held that such a proceeding is governed by Rule 42(b), requiring notice and hearing. *Shillitani v. United States* (1966) and *Pappadio v. United States* (1966) likewise involved refusal to testify before a grand jury. A federal court imposed two-year sentences of contempt but gave the witnesses the unqualified right to be released if and when they obeyed the order to testify. The Court held that the conditional nature of the sentences rendered each of the actions a civil contempt proceeding for which indictment and jury trial were not constitutionally required. However, since the term of the grand jury which had demanded the testimony had expired, imprisonment would no longer serve any useful coercive purpose, and so the Court vacated the contempt judgments.[15]

Power to Issue Writs

The Judiciary Act of 1789, in section 14, gave all courts of the United States power "to issue writs of *scire facias, habeas corpus,* and all other writs not specially provided for by statute, which may be necessary for the exercise of their respective jurisdictions, and agreeable to the principles and usages of law." In addition, the Supreme Court was authorized to issue writs of mandamus "in cases warranted by the principles and usages of law, to any courts appointed, or persons holding office, under the authority of the United States." It was this provision that was to be held unconstitutional in *Marbury v. Madison* (1803).[16]

The writ of habeas corpus, though mentioned in Article I, section 9, is issued only in accordance with statutory authorization. The historic purpose of the writ has been to challenge detention by executive authorities without judicial trial, and up to 1867 it was not available against any sentence imposed by a court of competent jurisdiction. But in that year Congress gave federal courts a broad authorization to issue writs of habeas corpus to prisoners in custody "in violation of the constitution or of any treaty or law of the United States."

[15]Gerardo Catena was imprisoned in New Jersey for civil contempt in 1970 for refusing to answer questions about organized crime posed by a state investigating commission. He remained in prison for five years, refusing to talk, and was finally released when the New Jersey supreme court concluded that the confinement had lost its "coercive power" (*The New York Times,* August 20, 1975). In *Popkin v. United States* (1973) the Supreme Court let stand the contempt citation of a Harvard professor who had refused to answer grand jury questions relating to the Pentagon Papers, on the ground that a scholar had the right to keep confidential the sources of his information.

[16]On the general issue of the use of the writ of mandamus, see *Allied Chemical Corp. v. Daiflon, Inc.* (1980), where the Court said: "Only exceptional circumstances, amounting to a judicial usurpation of power, will justify the invocation of this extraordinary remedy." But the Court did use the writ of mandamus in *Connor v. Coleman* (1979), ordering a federal district judge in Mississippi to adopt a plan for the reapportionment of the state legislature within thirty days.

Similarly the equity power to issue writs of injunction is dependent upon congressional authorization and subject to congressional limitation. In the original act of 1789, Congress provided that no equity suit should be maintained where there was an adequate remedy at law. In 1793 it passed the first of a long series of statutes limiting the power of federal courts to issue injunctions against state courts or state officers. In 1867 the federal courts were forbidden to enjoin the collection of federal taxes.[17] The Norris-LaGuardia Act of 1932 restrained the use of injunctions in labor disputes.[18] Under the Emergency Price Control Act of 1942, the Emergency Court of Appeals was the only court permitted to enjoin price control orders or regulations, and it was limited to permanent injunctions. It could not issue temporary restraining orders or interlocutory decrees. Chief Justice Stone, in upholding this limitation, said that there "is nothing in the Constitution which requires Congress to confer equity jurisdiction on any particular inferior federal court."[19]

Other Judicial Powers

Federal courts possess the power of making rules governing their process and practice, but this too is derived from statutes.[20] The process acts of 1789 and 1792 were upheld by Chief Justice Marshall in *Wayman v. Southard* (1825). Although he regarded the rule-making power as essentially legislative in nature, he thought that Congress could delegate to courts the power to "fill up the details."

The federal courts have full authority to appoint special aides required for the performance of their duties, such as masters in chancery, referees, or auditors. Insolvent enterprises that come under judicial control are normally administered by court-appointed officers. In particularly complex cases a court may appoint aides to take testimony and to make findings and recommendations.

Attorneys are officers of the courts, which have inherent power over their admission to practice and disbarment, subject to any general statutory qualifications that may be imposed. These powers, however, cannot be used, in Chief Justice Taney's words, in an "arbitrary and despotic" manner.[21] The Test Oath Act of 1862 sought to exclude former Confederates from the prac-

---

[17]See *Bob Jones University v. Simon* (1974); *California v. Grace Brethren Church* (1982).

[18]The act was held constitutional in *Lauf* v. *E. G. Shinner & Co.* (1938). See also *Boys Markets v. Retail Clerks Union* (1970) and *Jacksonville Bulk Terminals v. I.L.A.* (1982).

[19]*Lockerty v. Phillips* (1943). On injunctions generally, see "Developments in the Law: Injunctions," 78 HARVARD LAW REVIEW 994 (1965); Owen M. Fiss, *Injunctions* (Mineola, N.Y.: Foundation Press, 1972), and *The Civil Rights Injunction* (Bloomington: Indiana University Press, 1978).

[20]Rules proposed by the Supreme Court are submitted to Congress and go into effect automatically if Congress does not act on them within ninety days.

[21]*Ex parte Secombe* (1857).

tice of law in the federal courts, but the Supreme Court in *Ex parte Garland* (1867) held it unconstitutional as a bill of attainder.

LEGISLATIVE STRUCTURING
OF THE COURT SYSTEM

It took congressional action to turn the bare outlines of Article III into a functioning judicial establishment.[22] The First Congress set up the organization and defined the jurisdiction of the federal judicial system by the famous Judiciary Act of 1789. This act was the result of protracted debate during the summer of 1789 between Federalists seeking a strong and complete system of federal courts, and anti-Federalists intent on keeping the judicial establishment within the narrowest possible bounds. The Federalists won a limited victory, the statute providing for two judicial levels—district courts in every state and three circuit courts—below the Supreme Court. The circuit courts had no separate judiciary, however. They were to be staffed by the six Supreme Court justices, who would ride circuit between sessions, plus the district judge in whose district the circuit court was sitting.

The act gave to the district and circuit courts jurisdiction in admiralty and in suits between citizens of different states. It conferred little of the potentially broad jurisdiction allowed by the Constitution over cases arising under the Constitution, laws, or treaties, awarding jurisdiction over only a small number of federal crimes, plus penalties and forfeitures made under the laws of the United States. The state courts were allowed to retain jurisdiction concurrent with that of the federal courts in suits between citizens of different states and in numerous types of cases involving the enforcement of federal laws. It was not until 1875 that Congress gave the federal courts the full range of jurisdiction they were capable of exercising under the Constitution.

The act of 1789 also provided for the appointment in each district of a marshal to execute the orders of the court, and of an attorney for the United States to prosecute criminal cases and civil actions in which the United States was a party. Finally, the act set up the office of Attorney General of the United States, whose duty it was "to prosecute and conduct all suits in the Supreme Court in which the United States shall be concerned, and to give his advice and opinion upon questions of law when required by the President of the United States, or when requested by the heads of any of the departments." The attorney general was not given any supervisory responsibility over the United States attorneys, and the Department of Justice was not created until 1870.

The Judiciary Act of 1789 has been generally hailed as an outstanding

[22]See Felix Frankfurter and James M. Landis, *The Business of the Supreme Court: A Study in the Federal Judicial System* (New York: Macmillan, 1928).

piece of legislation, but there were weaknesses in it. The role of the federal court system was limited because the Supreme Court could meet only in the capital, access to which was made difficult by poor transportation; the federal trial courts could meet only at one or at most two places in each state, and had limited jurisdiction. Thus the new system of courts was remote and expensive. From 1789 to 1801 only three cases were appealed from state courts to the Supreme Court. Riding circuit over abominable roads was a judge-killing assignment for the high court's members. Moreover, sitting in circuit courts meant that they reviewed their own decisions when cases were appealed to the Supreme Court.

After their defeat by Jefferson in 1800, the Federalists passed the Judiciary Act of 1801, which terminated circuit riding by the justices. The six-member Court was to be reduced to five when the next vacancy occurred, to avoid tie votes and to give incoming President Jefferson one less vacancy to fill. More district courts were created, and the old circuit court system was abolished in favor of six new courts with increased jurisdiction, staffed by resident circuit judges. The fact that all these new judgeships were filled by the outgoing Federalist administration led the Jeffersonians to attack the "midnight judges bill" as judicial jobbery, and it was promptly repealed.

Instead, the Jeffersonians adopted a new act in 1802 providing for six circuits, each composed of one Supreme Court justice and one district judge, but allowing the circuit courts to be held by a single judge, a practice that became increasingly common. This act again tied the size of the Supreme Court to the number of circuits, and as the country expanded and more circuits were added, the size of the Supreme Court had to be increased. A seventh member was added in 1807, and in 1837 the size went to nine. A tenth justice was added for a tenth circuit in 1864. President Andrew Johnson's difficulties with Congress led it to adopt an act in 1866 reducing the Court to seven, as vacancies occurred, and reorganizing the circuits into nine. Actually, the number of justices did not go below eight. By an act of 1869 the size of the Court was again increased to nine. This statute also drastically curtailed the circuit-riding responsibilities of the justices, but the postwar development of judicial business and the territorial expansion of the country left the pressure on the Court as heavy as ever. By 1890 it had 1,800 cases on its docket.

The problem of the circuit courts also continued unabated. A panel of circuit judges had been provided by the 1869 act, but the number was quite inadequate. By the 1880s, eight-ninths of the litigation in the circuit courts was disposed of by single judges, usually district judges. Cases that came to the circuit courts on appeal from the districts were thus customarily heard by the same judge who had decided the case in the district court.

A remedy was finally found for the Supreme Court's problem in the Circuit Courts of Appeals Act of 1891. A new level of intermediate appellate courts was established, consisting of a court of appeals for each of the nine circuits and the District of Columbia. The old district and circuit courts were retained; but except for certain categories of direct appeal to the Supreme Court, their decisions were routed to the new courts of appeals for final disposition. As a gesture to tradition, the circuit duty of Supreme Court justices was not eliminated, but little was expected of them. The Supreme Court immediately felt the benefits of the act as the flood of litigation it had been receiving was shunted to the circuit courts of appeals. The one obvious error in the 1891 statute was the retention of the circuit courts, which were finally abolished by statute in 1911, through a merger of their jurisdiction with that of the district courts. Thus the present organization of the federal court system was achieved.

Keeping the Supreme Court's business under control required further legislation. Principally the problem was that in a considerable number of situations there was a statutory right of appeal from lower federal courts and from state supreme courts to the Supreme Court. A 1916 act seeking to give the Supreme Court greater discretionary review did not go far enough. With Taft's appointment as chief justice in 1921, he took the lead in urging an extension of the discretionary principle, and the Court itself developed a bill that was adopted as the Judiciary Act of 1925.

This act was based on the proposition that the Supreme Court's time had to be conserved for handling issues of national significance. Litigation that did not meet this test was to be left to state courts of last resort and to the circuit courts of appeals. To achieve these purposes, most decisions of the circuit courts of appeals were made reviewable in the Supreme Court only by the writ of certiorari, which the Court granted or denied in its own discretion. Again, cases that previously could be appealed directly from district courts to the Supreme Court were now, with some important exceptions, directed instead to the circuit courts of appeals. Finally, the act confined to two classes the cases that could as a matter of right be taken from the state courts to the Supreme Court: (1) where the validity of a state statute was challenged on federal constitutional grounds and its validity sustained; and (2) where a federal statute or treaty was invoked and its validity denied by a state court.

The size of the Court, which had been stabilized at nine since 1869, again became an issue in 1937 with President Roosevelt's proposal that Congress authorize appointment of one new justice for each sitting justice who remained on the Court after reaching the age of seventy, to a maximum limit of fifteen justices. The plan was generally disliked even by those who disapproved of what the Court had been doing, and it was defeated in Congress.[23] The episode led to a subsequent effort by the organized bar to freeze the size of the Supreme Court at nine justices by an amendment to the Constitution. The proposal passed the Senate in 1954, but failed in the House.

[23]See Leonard Baker, *Back to Back: The Duel Between FDR and the Supreme Court* (New York: Macmillan, 1967).

THE LOWER FEDERAL COURTS

The District Courts

The district courts are the trial courts of the federal system. Cases are heard by a single judge, with participation of a jury when appropriate. There are currently ninety-four district courts, including those located in Puerto Rico, Guam, and the Virgin Islands. Each state has at least one federal district court, and some have as many as four. The number of judges per district ranges from one to a high of twenty-seven in the southern district of New York, which covers New York City. In 1982 there were 516 district judgeships.

About one-third of all the civil suits tried in the district courts involve the government as a party, as either plaintiff or defendant. As for private civil suits, there are three main heads of jurisdiction: (1) federal questions, covering all cases in law and equity arising under the Constitution, laws, and treaties of the United States: (2) diversity of citizenship; and (3) admiralty. In addition, federal courts in the District of Columbia, Guam, and the Virgin Islands have general local jurisdiction and law-enforcement responsibilities.

The diversity of citizenship cases constitute one-fourth of all civil cases in the federal courts.[24] The theory of the Constitution in opening the federal courts to suits involving citizens of different states was that the state courts might well be biased against out-of-state litigants, whereas the federal courts would provide a neutral tribunal for all parties. The anti-Federalists opposed giving such jurisdiction to the federal courts, and periodically there have been efforts to abolish it. The present-day objection to diversity jurisdiction is that it congests the federal courts with a tremendous number of cases growing out of essentially local issues, many of them personal injury suits, which federal judges must determine according to state law. While in 1789 there might have been prejudice in state courts against outsiders, it is argued that this possibility is no longer important. These arguments have not prevailed, but in 1958 Congress did limit access to the federal courts in diversity cases by various restrictions.[25]

The federal district courts also deal with a heavy load of criminal prosecutions. Criminal cases begun in 1981 totaled 30,355, including prosecutions

[24]In 1981, out of 180,576 civil cases filed in federal district courts, 45,444 were based on diverse citizenship. For a general discussion, see Henry J. Friendly, *Federal Jurisdiction* (New York: Columbia University Press, 1973). Chapter 7.

[25]The amount involved in a diversity suit must be at least $10,000, and removal to federal courts from state courts of cases arising under state workmen's compensation laws is forbidden. In 1968 the American Law Institute proposed substantial modifications in diversity jurisdiction. See *Study of the Division of Jurisdiction between State and Federal Courts* (Philadelphia: American Law Institute, 1969). The House voted to abolish diversity jurisdiction in 1978, but the Senate failed to concur. See Thomas D. Rowe, Jr., "Abolishing Diversity Jurisdiction," 92 HARVARD LAW REVIEW 963 (1979); David L. Shapiro, "Federal Diversity Jurisdiction: A Survey and a Proposal," 91 HARVARD LAW REVIEW 317 (1977).

for violation of the immigration laws, fraud, transportation of stolen automobiles, and violations of the narcotics, liquor, migratory bird, selective service, white slave, and food and drug laws.

A 1968 statute created a system of federal magistrates.[26] Magistrates are attorneys, appointed by federal district judges, who serve as officers of the court authorized to issue warrants, fix bail, hold preliminary hearings, conduct trials for petty offenses, and screen petitions from prisoners seeking review of their sentences or convictions.[27] In 1979 Congress permitted magistrates to hear civil cases with the consent of the parties, and appeal from the judgment of a magistrate could be taken directly to a court of appeals. Also, changes in the jurisdiction of magistrates in criminal cases were made, and requirements for the merit selection of magistrates were strengthened.[28] There were 201 full-time magistrates in 1980, plus a substantial number of part-time magistrates.[29]

Three-Judge District Courts

There are certain situations where a district court consisting of three district or court of appeals judges must be impaneled. A three-judge trial court was first authorized by Congress in the expediting act of 1903, which empowered the attorney general, in any proceeding brought by the United States under the Sherman Act or the Interstate Commerce Act that "in his opinion . . . is of general public importance," to file a certificate to that effect with the court where the case was docketed. Thereupon the case was to be given precedence and assigned to a panel of three judges, from whose decision appeal lay directly to the Supreme Court.

A second occasion for use of this device was provided by the Supreme Court's ruling in *Ex parte Young* (1908) that lower federal courts could enjoin state officers from enforcing state statutes on the ground of their unconstitutionality. Congress was alarmed over the prospect of a single federal

[26]See "Masters and Magistrates in the Federal Courts," 88 Harvard Law Review 779 (1975).

[27]But *Wingo v. Wedding* (1974) held that magistrates could not conduct evidentiary hearings in habeas corpus cases. In response to this decision, Congress amended the 1968 act to grant wider discretion to district judges in treating recommendations of the magistrates. In *United States v. Raddatz* (1980) the Supreme Court ruled that this delegation did not violate Article III so long as the ultimate decision was made by the court.

[28]There has been some opposition to granting increased functions to magistrates, who of course do not have good behavior tenure and are not confirmed by the Senate. See "Article III Constraints and the Expanding Civil Jurisdiction of Federal Magistrates: A Dissenting View," 88 Yale Law Journal 1023 (1979). *Mathews v. Weber* (1976) had permitted district judges to refer some Social Security and Medicare cases to magistrates for initial review.

[29]The 1978 Bankruptcy Act gave federal referees in bankruptcy the status of judges, with fourteen-year terms and subject to removal by a judicial council. In *Northern Pipeline Construction Co. v. Marathon Pipeline Co.* (1982) the Supreme Court held the act unconstitutional because it granted judicial powers to appointees who did not meet Article III requirements ("good behavior" tenure and guaranteed salary).

judge enjoining a state legislative program, and in the Mann-Elkins Act of 1910 and the Judicial Code of 1911, provided that a three-judge court would have to be convened to pass on the constitutionality of state legislation before injunctions could be issued.[30]

The Mann-Elkins Act also created the five-judge Commerce Court, which was to hear all appeals of Interstate Commerce Commission cases. In 1913 this court was abolished and injunctions against ICC orders were required to be heard by a three-judge district court. Later statutes set up the same arrangements for certain other federal administrative agencies. In 1937 Congress provided that no interlocutory or permanent injunction against enforcement of an act of Congress on the ground of its alleged unconstitutionality could be issued except by a three-judge court.

Because appeal from decisions of a three-judge district court is directly to the Supreme Court and is a matter of right, the Court has tended to interpret strictly the various statutes providing for three-judge courts.[31] In 1950 Congress abolished the three-judge provision for all federal agencies except the ICC. On the other hand, the civil rights era brought many challenges to the constitutionality of state action which had to be tried before three-judge courts. For example, in 1974 three-judge courts numbered 249, of which 171 dealt with civil rights suits, 51 with review of ICC orders, and 8 with reapportionment issues. Chief Justice Burger advocated the abolition of all three-judge courts because of their "waste" of judicial resources and their erosion of the Supreme Court's discretionary control over its docket. Congress responded in 1976 by eliminating the requirement that three-judge courts hear challenges to the constitutionality of state and federal legislation, but continued their use in cases where the constitutionality of federal or state legislative reapportionment was an issue or where such a court was required by specific acts of Congress, as in the Voting Rights Act of 1965 and the Civil Rights Act of 1964. Because of the 1976 statute, the number of three-judge courts had declined to 35 in 1981.

The Federal Courts of Appeals

The courts of appeals, created by Congress in 1891, and known until 1949 as circuit courts of appeals, constitute the second level of the federal judiciary. Their purpose is primarily to relieve the Supreme Court by hearing appeals from the decisions of the district courts, and in practice they are the

---

[30]As the Supreme Court explained in *MTM, Inc. v. Baxley* (1975), "the congressional policy behind the three-judge court and direct review apparatus [was] the saving of state and federal statutes from improvident doom at the hands of a single judge. . . ."

[31]*Phillips v. United States* (1941); *Swift & Co. v. Wickham* (1965); *Gonzalez v. Automatic Employees Credit Union* (1974). See David P. Currie, "The Three-Judge District Court in Constitutional Litigation," 32 UNIVERSITY OF CHICAGO LAW REVIEW 1 (1964); also "The Three-Judge District Court," 77 HARVARD LAW REVIEW 299 (1963).

courts of last resort for the great majority of all federal cases.[32] For judicial purposes the country is divided into eleven numbered districts; a twelfth court of appeals sits in the District of Columbia. Prior to 1981 there were eleven circuits, but in that year a long effort to divide the fifth circuit was successful. The states of Louisiana, Mississippi, and Texas remained in the fifth circuit, while Alabama, Florida, and Georgia went into the new eleventh circuit.[33]

Members of the Supreme Court are assigned as supervising justices for each of the circuits. There are from 4 to 27 judges in each circuit, and a total of 132 in 1982 for the twelve courts. A panel of three normally sits in a case, but on occasions "en banc" review will be given by the entire circuit bench.[34]

All final decisions and some intermediate orders of the district courts are subject to review by the courts of appeals. In 1981, 26,362 appeals were taken to the circuit courts, and 21,391 of these were from the district courts. The balance were appeals from federal administrative boards and commissions, such as the Tax Court, the National Labor Relations Board, the Federal Communications Commission, and so on. Trials in the courts of appeals are conducted on the basis of the record made in the original proceeding before the district court or administrative agency. New evidence may not be presented.

THE SUPREME COURT

The Supreme Court is composed of the Chief Justice of the United States and eight associate justices. The Court meets annually in October for its regular term and remains in session, though with periodic recesses, until the following June or early July. The Chief Justice may call the Court into session for special terms during the summer, as was done in 1958 to dispose of the Little Rock segregation controversy and in 1942 to review the death sentences imposed on eight Germans who had come to the United States by submarine on a sabotage mission.[35] The Court formerly sat in the old Senate chamber in the basement of the Capitol, but it now occupies a palace of dazzling white marble so elegant that, when it was completed in 1935, one justice suggested that the members of the Court should ride in on elephants.

---

[32]A study by J. Woodford Howard, Jr., of all cases decided by three appeals courts from 1965 to 1967 found that the courts of appeals were the courts of last resort in 98.1 percent of the cases and made decisions that formally prevailed in 98.6 percent; *Courts of Appeals in the Federal Judicial System* (Princeton, N.J.: Princeton University Press, 1981), p. 58.

[33]For an account of the role of the fifth-circuit judges in enforcement of the *Brown* decision, see Jack Bass, *Unlikely Heroes* (New York: Simon & Schuster, 1981).

[34]See "En Banc Review in Federal Circuit Courts," 72 MICHIGAN LAW REVIEW 1637 (1974).

[35]*Cooper v. Aaron* (1958); *Ex parte Quirin* (1942). In 1974 the term was extended to permit hearing the Watergate tapes case, *United States v. Nixon*.

The Court's Operation

The Court sits for four hours daily, Monday through Wednesday, in an impressive high-ceilinged courtroom, with enormous pillars and red velvet hangings. The justices meet in the robing room behind the drapes shortly before ten o'clock. By tradition, each justice shakes hands with every colleague. Promptly at ten the court crier smashes his gavel, spectators rise, the velvet curtains part, and the justices take their places behind the long bench.[36]

During its public sessions the Court hears oral arguments in scheduled cases and announces its decisions. For every case on the docket, the record of the proceedings in the lower courts and briefs stating the arguments for each side are filed with the Court. The justices study these materials before the case comes up for hearing. The time for oral argument is strictly limited; except in the most important cases, counsel for each side will have one half hour to address the Court. Legend has it that Chief Justice Hughes once called time on a lawyer in the middle of the word "if."

Counsel seldom have an opportunity to make their arguments without interruption. The justices frequently break in with questions, comments, or requests for clarification. From the questions asked, it is often possible to predict how the individual justices are likely to vote in deciding the case. Probably their minds are not often changed by the oral argument, but it does give counsel a chance to emphasize what they feel are the main points for their side.

Thursdays are available for the justices to work on pending cases. On Friday of each week when the Court has been sitting, the justices meet in conference to decide the cases heard that week. The proceedings are absolutely secret. No one other than the justices is present. The Chief Justice presents each case that is ready for decision, making such comments and offering such views as he chooses. Discussion then goes around the table, each associate justice speaking in order of seniority. When all have given their views, voting begins. In the past it was generally understood that the reverse order was followed, the most junior justice voting first and the Chief Justice last, a procedure that maximized the role of the Chief. However, it appears that the practice of Chief Justice Burger is to vote first.[37]

Following the vote the Chief Justice assigns the writing of the opinion

---

[36]For a general discussion of the Supreme Court's operation, see Henry J. Abraham, *The Judicial Process* (New York: Oxford University Press, 1980), Chapter 5; also Stephen L. Wasby, *The Supreme Court in the Federal Judicial System* (New York: Holt, Rinehart Winston, 1978); J. Harvey Wilkinson, *Serving Justice: A Supreme Court Clerk's View* (Charterhouse, 1974); Bob Woodward and Scott Armstrong, *The Brethren: Inside the Supreme Court* (New York: Simon & Schuster, 1980).

[37]See generally David J. Danelski, "The Influence of the Chief Justice in the Decisional Process," in Walter F. Murphy and C. Herman Pritchett, *Courts, Judges, and Politics* (New York: Random House, 1979), pp. 695–703.

of the Court.[38] However, if there is a divided vote and the Chief Justice is in the minority, then the senior associate justice who voted in the majority controls the assignment. Drafts of opinions are circulated among the justices, and the author may revise the final draft on the basis of comments by his colleagues.[39]

In the early years of the Court, it was customary for all justices to give their opinions seriatim in a case, and there was no single opinion of the Court. However, when Marshall became Chief Justice, he saw that the Court would be more influential if it spoke with a single voice, and so he himself wrote the opinion of the Court in almost all important cases.

Justices were still free to write concurring or dissenting opinions, but there was a tendency for them to go along with the opinion of the Court unless their disagreement was sharp. The fame of Justices Holmes and Brandeis as dissenters was based on the quality rather than the quantity of their dissents. However, the Supreme Court's struggle with the New Deal caused dissents to become more frequent, and since the 1943 term nonunanimous opinions have outnumbered the unanimous opinions. Concurring opinions are written by justices who agree with the result reached by the Court but not entirely with the reasons given in the opinion of the Court. The number of concurring opinions written by Supreme Court justices has also increased markedly in the past four decades.[40]

The Court's decisions were formerly announced only on Mondays; since 1965, however, they may be given at the beginning of any session. While it was once customary for opinions to be read in full from the bench, now the author of the opinion of the Court usually summarizes the main points of the ruling in a few minutes. Dissenters may also outline their disagreement if they wish. No advance notice is ever given as to when a decision in a particular case will be ready, and the opinions are distributed to newsmen only after the decision has been announced from the bench. In the printing operation, each opinion is divided among several printers so they will not know what case they are working on.

The role of the Chief Justice is extremely important, for he can develop a substantial position of leadership on the Court. His formal authority stems primarily from his role as presiding officer at Court sessions and in the conference, and from his power to assign the writing of opinions. But he is also the symbolic head of the Court and the highest officer of the government after the President and vice-president; and if he has the necessary skill, he can use

[38]Numerous studies have been made of the strategy of opinion assignment; see David W. Rohde and Harold J. Spaeth, *Supreme Court Decision Making* (San Francisco: W. H. Freeman & Company, Publishers, 1976).

[39]See Walter F. Murphy, *Elements of Judicial Strategy* (Chicago: University of Chicago Press, 1964). A majority opinion, it has been said, is a "negotiated instrument."

[40]"Plurality Decisions and Judicial Decisionmaking," 94 Harvard Law Review 1127 (1981).

his position to guide the decision-making process toward consensus and keep discussion from bogging down in quibbling and personalities.

Original Jurisdiction

The Supreme Court is primarily an appellate court, but the Constitution does define two categories of cases that can be heard in the Court's original jurisdiction—i.e., without prior consideration by any other court. These are cases in which a state is a party, and those affecting ambassadors, public ministers, and consuls. This grant of original jurisdiction is self-executing and requires no legislation to make it effective. Since it flows directly from the Constitution, Congress can neither restrict it nor enlarge it. This latter point was decided in the case of *Marbury v. Madison* (1803), where the Court held a provision of the Judiciary Act of 1789 unconstitutional on the ground that it sought to add to the Supreme Court's original jurisdiction the power of issuing writs of mandamus.

Congress can, however, adopt legislation implementing the constitutional language on original jurisdiction. Thus Congress has provided that the Supreme Court shall have "original and exclusive" jurisdiction of all controversies between two or more states, whereas other cases in which a state is a party can be heard either by the Supreme Court or lower federal courts. Because of such arrangements for concurrent jurisdiction, the Supreme Court generally does not need to accept a suit invoking its original jurisdiction unless it feels there is a good reason why it should. As the Court stated in an 1895 case, its original jurisdiction "is limited and manifestly to be sparingly exercised, and should not be expanded by construction."[41]

Appellate Jurisdiction

All the remaining business of the Supreme Court comes to it in its appellate jurisdiction, which it exercises, as the Constitution says, "with such exceptions, and under such regulations as the Congress shall make." It might have been argued that the Court's appellate jurisdiction, like its original jurisdiction, flowed directly from the Constitution, and did not require legislative authorization. However, the fact is that the Judiciary Act of 1789 did legislate on the subject of appellate jurisdiction, and in 1796 the Court agreed that without a statute prescribing a rule for appellate proceedings, the Court could not assume jurisdiction.[42] In 1810 Marshall held that an affirmative statutory bestowal of appellate jurisdiction implied a denial of jurisdiction not granted.[43]

---

[41]*California v. Southern Pacific Co.* (1895). See Justice Rehnquist's complaint about use of the Court's original jurisdiction in *Maryland v. Louisiana* (1981).

[42]*Wiscart v. Dauchy* (1796).

[43]*Durousseau v. United States* (1810).

The consequences of this judicial surrender of control over appellate jurisdiction to Congress were dramatically demonstrated in the post-Civil War case of *Ex parte McCardle* (1869). Stringent Reconstruction measures establishing military rule over the South were enacted by Congress. A Mississippi editor, McCardle, held for trial before a military commission authorized by these acts, petitioned for a writ of habeas corpus under a statute passed in 1867 that gave federal judges power to grant habeas corpus to any person restrained in violation of the federal Constitution or laws, and provided for appeal to the Supreme Court in such cases. McCardle was denied the writ and appealed to the Supreme Court.

That Court had just declared Lincoln's wartime use of military commissions unconstitutional in *Ex parte Milligan* (1866), and Congress feared that it would use the *McCardle* appeal to invalidate the Reconstruction legislation. Consequently in March, 1868, the Radical Republicans rushed through Congress, and repassed over the president's veto, a statute repealing the act of 1867 so far as it granted apeals to the Supreme Court, and withdrawing "any such jurisdiction by said Supreme Court, on appeals which have been, or may hereafter be taken." The Court, which had already heard argument on the *McCardle* case when this act was passed, felt constrained to rule that its authority to render a decision had been abrogated. Congress had withdrawn the Court's jurisdiction in the clearest possible fashion. "Without jurisdiction the court cannot proceed at all in any cause. Jurisdiction is power to declare the law, and when it ceases to exist, the only function remaining to the court is that of announcing the fact and dismissing the cause."

Under the *McCardle* principle, then, it would be theoretically possible for Congress to abolish the appelate jurisdiction entirely and leave the Supreme Court with only the handful of cases that can be brought in its original jurisdiction. It is highly unlikely that this will ever happen, but threats of such "Court-stripping" are periodically used as a tactic by Court opponents. In 1957 Senator Jenner sought reprisal against the Court's decisions in certain national security cases by proposing legislation to withdraw the Court's appellate jurisdiction in five specific areas, including cases involving the investigatory power of Congress.[44]

A more serious campaign against the Court was begun in the late 1970s as bills were introduced to strip all federal courts, including the Supreme Court, of jurisdiction in school prayer, abortion, and racial integration cases. Constitutional authorities and the organized bar almost unanimously opposed these bills.[45] While the Reagan administration favored the purpose of such legisla-

[44]See C. Herman Pritchett, *Congress versus the Supreme Court: 1957–1960* (Minneapolis: University of Minnesota Press, 1961), Chapter 3; Walter F. Murphy, *Congress and the Court* (Chicago: University of Chicago Press, 1962).

[45]See Raoul Berger, *Congress v. The Supreme Court* (Cambridge, Mass.: Harvard University Press, 1969), Chapter 9; Leonard G. Ratner, "Congressional Power over the Appellate Jurisdiction of the Supreme Court," 109 UNIVERSITY OF PENNSYLVANIA LAW REVIEW 157 (1960); Law-

tion, Attorney General William French Smith warned against congressional restrictions on the Supreme Court's jurisdiction, saying that while Congress clearly had some limited authority over the Court's jurisdiction, "Congress may not, . . . consistent with the Constitution, make 'exceptions' to Supreme Court jurisdiction which would intrude upon the core functions of the Supreme Court as an independent and equal branch in our system of separation of powers."[46]

Methods of Review

Except for the Court's original jurisdiction and in the limited classes of cases where there is an appeal to the Supreme Court as of right, review is sought by filing with the Court a petition for writ of certiorari to a state supreme court or federal court of appeals.[47] This writ, if granted, directs the lower court to send up the record in the case for review.

During the 1980 term, the Court disposed of 4,280 cases, with 864 remaining on its docket. They included 7 original jurisdiction cases, 2,256 on the appellate docket (referred to as "paid cases"—i.e., with prepayment of costs), and 2,017 *in forma pauperis* cases (the miscellaneous docket). The latter cases originated mostly with convicts in state or federal prisons. The Court granted review of 10.6 percent of the cases on the appellate docket, and only 1.4 percent of those on the miscellaneous docket. The great majority of the *in forma pauperis* cases present no substantial grounds for review.

Certiorari petitions, including pertinent portions of the record, petitioner's brief, and opposing responses, are circulated among all members of the Court, who make substantial use of their law clerks in reviewing the petitions. There can be oral argument on granting petitions, but normally this does not happen. Petitions are granted on the affirmative vote of four justices. The rule of four was adopted when the Judiciary Act of 1925 was passed, to reassure Congress that access to the Court by the discretionary writ of certiorari would not be refused too easily.

Review of the flood of certiorari petitions imposes a heavy burden on

---

rence Gene Sager, "Constitutional Limitations on Congress' Authority to Regulate the Jurisdiction of the Federal Courts," (95 HARVARD LAW REVIEW 17 (1981); Laurence H. Tribe, "Jurisdictional Gerrymandering: Zoning Disfavored Rights Out of the Federal Courts," 16 HARVARD CIVIL RIGHTS-CIVIL LIBERTIES LAW REVIEW 129 (1981). Justice Douglas said in *Glidden* v. *Zdanok* (1962): "There is a serious question whether the *McCardle* case could command a majority today."

[46]*New York Times,* May 7, 1982.

[47]Certiorari may be sought to review a federal district court decision while the case is still pending in the court of appeals, but the Supreme Court will grant the writ in these circumstances only if the case is of such "imperative public importance" as to require immediate settlement. See *Aaron* v. *Cooper* (1958) and *Youngstown Sheet & Tube Co.* v. *Sawyer* (1952). In 1974 the Supreme Court took the case of *United States* v. *Nixon* for review directly from the district court, as provided for by Rule 20, *Revised Rules, Supreme Court of the United States* (1967).

the justices. The Court's Rule 19 states that review on certiorari "will be granted only where there are special and important reasons therefor." Among the circumstances cited in the rule as justifying the grant of certiorari are the following: where two courts of appeals have rendered conflicting decisions; where a state court or a federal court of appeals has decided an important question of federal law on which the Supreme Court has never passed, or in such a way as to conflict with applicable decisions of the Court; or where a federal court has so far departed from the accepted canons of judicial proceedings as to call for exercise of the Supreme Court's power of supervision.

Usually the Court announces no reason for denial of certiorari. Many petitions, particularly those *in forma pauperis,* are wholly without merit and ought never to have been filed. When the Court does state a reason, often it is a technical one—for example, that the federal question is not properly presented, or was not passed on below. But some denials are clearly for policy reasons. As Justice Frankfurter said in *Maryland v. Baltimore Radio Show* (1950):

> A decision may satisfy all . . . technical requirements and yet may commend itself for review to fewer than four members of the court. Pertinent considerations of judicial policy here come into play. A case may raise an important question but the record may be cloudy. It may be desirable to have different aspects of an issue further illumined by the lower courts. Wise adjudication has its own time for ripening.

The denial of a writ leaves the decision of the lower court in effect, but it has no other legal significance. It does not mean necessarily that the Supreme Court approves of the decision below, and is in no sense an affirmance of the decree. However, this point is difficult to get across to the public. Denials of certiorari are often cited as precedents, and it must be admitted that in practice they may have such effect, particularly since lower court decisions are reversed in a very high proportion of the cases in which certiorari is granted.

The constantly rising workload of the Supreme Court—cases filed increased 118 percent from 1960 to 1980—has caused concern and stimulated suggestions for reform. In 1972 a report on the Supreme Court's caseload, by a study group appointed by Chief Justice Burger and headed by Paul Freund, concluded that review of the flood of certiorari petitions was draining the energy of the justices and preventing them from giving adequate consideration to the cases they selected to decide.[48] The study group proposed creation of a

---

[48]*Report of the Study Group on the Caseload of the Supreme Court* (Washington: Federal Judicial Center, 1972). Comments on the plan include Charles L. Black, J., "The National Court of Appeals: An Unwise Proposal," 83 YALE LAW JOURNAL 883 (1974); "The National Court of Appeals: A Constitutional 'Inferior Court'?" 72 MICHIGAN LAW REVIEW 290 (1973); Alexander M. Bickel, "The Overworked Court," 168 THE NEW REPUBLIC 17 (February 17, 1973).

As an alternative to the Freund plan, a federal commission headed by Senator Roman L. Hruska proposed in 1975 a seven-member national court to take significant cases on assignment from the Supreme Court or the various circuit courts of appeals. Commission on Revision of the

new national court of appeals immediately below the Supreme Court. Staffed by senior circuit judges on a rotating basis, this court would resolve conflicting rulings among the circuits and screen appeals, passing on perhaps four hundred of the most important cases to the Supreme court. The plan was not favorably received. Critics, including former Chief Justice Warren, argued that deciding which cases to decide is an essential function of the Supreme Court, and that cutting off access to the Court and denying justices control over their docket would seriously damage the power and prestige of the high court.

There has been some disagreement as to the burdensome character of the Supreme Court's workload. A substantial statistical study in 1976 criticized the Freund report and concluded: "We are not persuaded that the Supreme Court's workload has reached the point at which radical changes in the Court's jurisdiction or in the structure of federal appellate review should be contemplated." The authors recommended more modest reforms, including

> abolition of the remaining obligatory jurisdiction of the Supreme Court and of direct appeals to the Court from federal district courts, the creation of supreme courts of patent and tax appeals, greater pooling of law clerks for screening applications for review, reduction in the number of concurring and dissenting opinions, denial or curtailment of oral argument in some cases, greater use of short, per curiam opinions to decide unanimous cases, and the promulgation of detailed guidelines regarding the criteria for the grant and denial of review.[49]

SPECIALIZED AND LEGISLATIVE COURTS

In addition to the regular federal courts, Congress has from time to time set up courts to perform specialized functions. The oldest of these courts was the Court of Claims, created in 1855 to try claims against the government. Other specialized courts were the Customs Court, sitting in New York, and the Court of Customs and Patent Appeals.

Federal Court Appellate System, *Structure and Internal Procedures: Recommendations for Change* (Washington, D.C., 1975).

[49]Gerhard Casper and Richard A. Posner, *The Workload of the Supreme Court* (Chicago: American Bar Association, 1976), p. 117.

The recommendation for elimination of the Supreme Court's obligatory jurisdiction was in part adopted when three-judge courts were limited in 1976. In 1978 a bill completely to terminate the Court's obligatory jurisdiction was proposed in the Senate (S. 3100, 95th Cong.) but failed of adoption. In 1982 Justice Stevens, speaking before the American Bar Association, complained of the flood of certiorari petitions and unwisely revived the idea of a new court to decide which cases the Supreme Court should decide. For views of other justices, see *The New York Times,* September 14, 1982; also William J. Brennan, Jr., "Some Thoughts on the Supreme Court's Workload," 66 *Judicature* 230 (1983). In 1983 Chief Justice Burger proposed creation of a new appeals court to resolve conflicting decisions among the thirteen federal appeals courts, staffed by present appellate judges on a rotating basis.

In 1982 Congress changed the name of the Customs Court to the U.S. Court of International Trade and gave it some additional duties. In 1982 the appellate division of the Court of Claims and the Court of Customs and Patent Appeals were consolidated in the new Court of Appeals for the Federal Circuit, on the same footing as the twelve existing appeals courts, but with specialized jurisdiction. By the same statute the new trial-level U.S. Claims Court was created.

The Commerce Court, which reviewed decisions of the ICC, was created in 1910, but had an unhappy history and was abolished in 1913. The Emergency Court of Appeals was set up during World War II to try certain suits under the price control statutes. It was staffed by judges from the regular federal courts and was authorized to sit anywhere in the United States. The so-called Tax Court, which reviews tax decisions by the Bureau of Internal Revenue, is legally not a court at all, but a part of the executive branch. The Court of Military Appeals was created by the Uniform Code of Military Justice in 1950 to hear appeals from courts martial on matters of law.[50]

The reason for specialized courts is primarily to permit certain difficult classes of litigation to be handled by judges who have particular competence in the field. In the case of the Emergency Court of Appeals, it was feared that the wartime program of price control would break down if every federal and state judge in the country could issue injunctions against price control orders, so this power was centralized in a single specialized court.

Congress provides a system of courts for the District of Columbia and for other territories under United States control. For this purpose Congress does not have to rely upon Article III. It is given complete authority to legislate for the District of Columbia by Article I, section 8, and has power to "make all needful rules and regulations" respecting territories of the United States under Article IV, section 3. Courts created by Congress under its authority to legislate for the District or the territories have consequently been called "legislative" courts, in contrast with the "constitutional" courts authorized by Article III.

The practical significance of this distinction is that Congress need not observe the provisions of Article III so far as appointments to and jurisdiction of the legislative courts are concerned. This point has been clear since *American Insurance Co. v. Canter* (1828). Congress had created an admiralty court for the territory of Florida, the judges of which were limited to four-year terms

---

[50]In 1979 the Foreign Intelligence Surveillance Court was created to approve or disapprove requests by U.S. intelligence agencies to spy on American citizens within the United States. Composed of seven federal judges, it meets secretly in a chamber like a bank vault in the Department of Justice. The Temporary Emergency Court of Appeals was created by the Economic Stabilization Act of 1970 to hear suits under that statute; see *Fry v. United States* (1975) and *Bray v. United States* (1975). The Rail Reorganization Court was created by statute in 1973 to determine the value of properties transferred by certain bankrupt railroads; it is staffed by three federal judges on assignment. Appeals from the specialized courts go to the Supreme Court on certiorari or certification of questions.

of office. This court could have been held unconstitutional because the judges did not enjoy tenure for good behavior. Instead Marshall ruled that the provisions of Article III did not apply to this court, since it was created under congressional power to legislate for the territories. It followed that the judges of a legislative court could not only be given term appointments, but could also be removed by the President, their salaries could be reduced while they were in office, and they could be given jurisdiction other than that specified in Article III.

The test of a legislative court laid down in the *Canter* case was clear enough; it was a geographical test, location in a territory. The same test made the courts of the District of Columbia legislative courts, and the Supreme Court in *Ex parte Bakelite Corp.* (1929) and *Williams v. United States* (1933) held that the Court of Customs and Patent Appeals and the Court of Claims were neither confined in jurisdiction nor protected in independence by Article III, but that both had been created by virtue of substantive powers possessed by Congress under Article I. Consequently Congress could give the District of Columbia courts nonjudicial functions such as revisionary powers over grants of patents and rates fixed by the local public utility commission. There was a conceptual hitch, however. Legislative courts had been regarded as exercising no part of the "judicial power of the United States," since they were not created under Article III, whereas the Supreme Court could exercise nothing but "judicial power." How was it possible, then, for the Supreme Court to hear appeals from legislative courts?

When this point was first raised, the Supreme Court concluded that it was not possible. In *Gordon v. United States* (1864), Chief Justice Taney ruled that Court of Claims decisions, which were in effect only advisory to the secretary of the treasury, could not be reviewed by the Supreme Court. Congress then amended the law to give finality to judgments of the Court of Claims, and on that basis the Court accepted appeals from it.[51] The same thing happened with the revisory power of courts of the District of Columbia over the Federal Radio Commission.[52] Thus the Court developed the rule that in proceedings before a legislative court that are judicial in nature and admit of a final judgment, the Supreme Court will accept appellate jurisdiction—an arrangement that Corwin calls a "workable anomaly."

It was made somewhat less anomalous but somewhat more confusing in 1933 when the Court suddenly decided that the courts of the District of Columbia were *both* legislative and constitutional courts.[53] As regards their organization and the tenure and compensation of their judges, they were constitutional courts controlled by Article III, but as regards their jurisdiction and powers they were both legislative and constitutional courts, and so could

[51]*DeGroot v. United States* (1867)
[52]*Federal Radio Commission v. General Electric Co.* (1930)
[53]*O'Donoghue v. United States* (1933).

be vested with nonjudicial powers while sharing the judicial power of the United States.

The difficulties of this dual status were only partially resolved by the decision in *Glidden Co. v. Zdanok* (1962). Congress had sought to clear up the status of the Court of Claims in 1953 by legislation flatly declaring it to have been established under Article III, and it did the same thing for the Court of Customs and Patent Appeals in 1958. The validity of this legislation came into question when judges of these two courts were assigned temporarily by the Chief Justice to sit in regular federal courts that were short of judges because of disability or disqualification. The contention in *Glidden* was that they were not Article III judges, and so could not sit in Article III courts.

By a five to two vote the Supreme Court upheld the Article III status of these judges, but the majority was split as to the reasons. Three justices held that the two courts were now Article III courts because Congress had said so, and they overruled *Bakelite* and *Williams,* which had said they were not. The other two justices in the majority held that the two courts had become Article III courts because Congress had withdrawn questionable jurisdiction from those courts since the *Bakelite* and *Williams* decisions, which they would not overrule. The two dissenters, Douglas and Black, thought that these two specialized courts were still performing legislative and executive functions, that *Bakelite* and *Williams* were still the law, and that it was as improper for their judges to be assigned to sit in a regular federal court as it would be for a member of the Interstate Commerce Commission to sit there.[54]

There appears to be something about the legislative court concept that breeds confusion. It might be better if Marshall had never invented it.

STAFFING THE FEDERAL JUDICIARY

The appointment of federal judges is frankly and entirely a political process.[55] During the present century over 90 percent of all judicial appointments have gone to members of the President's party. For example, of the 258 judges named to the federal bench by President Carter, 240 were Democrats.[56] Ap-

---

[54]*Northern Pipeline Construction Co. v. Marathon Pipe Line Co.* (1982) held that federal bankruptcy courts, which under the Bankruptcy Act of 1978 had the status of "adjuncts" to federal district courts, could not be regarded as "legislative courts" and consequently were unconstitutional because bankruptcy judges did not enjoy good behavior tenure or protection from reduction in salaries. Disagreement between House and Senate on new legislation left the situation unresolved in 1983.

[55]See Harold W. Chase, *Federal Judges: The Appointing Process* (Minneapolis: University of Minnesota Press, 1972); Henry J. Abraham, *Justices and Presidents: A Political History of Appointments to the Supreme Court* (New York: Oxford University Press, 1974); John R. Schmidhauser, *The Supreme Court: Its Politics, Personalities, and Procedures* (New York: Holt, Rinehart & Winston, 1960), part I; Robert Scigliano, *The Supreme Court and the Presidency* (New York: Free Press, 1971), Chapters 4–5.

[56]Sheldon Goldman, "Carter's Judicial Appointments," 64 JUDICATURE 344 (1981).

pointees have typically been active in state or national party affairs, perhaps unsuccessful candidates for office. The posts are also prestigious rewards for administrative officials or members of Congress.

In the nomination of judges for the lower federal courts, senators of the president's party play an important role, although not always a dominant one. The Department of Justice, acting through the deputy attorney general, also conducts an active search for promising talent. If there is a conflict of views between the senator and the Justice Department, the senator can threaten to block a nomination at the confirmation stage, and so a compromise is usually arranged. Since the courts of appeals cover more than one state, vacancies must be allocated to the various states on some basis satisfactory to the party organizations. When the list of candidates has been narrowed, the FBI runs a full loyalty-security check, and the Justice Department seeks the approval of the American Bar Association Committee on the Federal Judiciary. This committee conducts its own inquiry, securing the views of the legal profession in the candidate's area.[57] The committee then reports to the Justice Department, rating potential appointees as exceptionally well qualified, well qualified, qualified, or not qualified.[58]

The creation of 152 new judgeships by Congress in 1978, plus the normal turnover of lower court judges, gave President Carter an opportunity to make more judicial appointments than any president in history, some 40 percent of all federal judges. On taking office he created screening commissions in each circuit, before which candidates for appointment had to appear. Senatorial resistance made it unwise to create similar commissions for district judgeships, but Carter encouraged senators to set up their own merit commissions, and this was done in over half the states. Of Carter's 258 appointees, 40 were women, 37 were black, and 16 Hispanic. The commissions were abandoned by the Reagan administration.[59]

Vacancies on the Supreme Court present major policy problems for the President. He receives suggestions from many sources and particularly from his attorney general, but he makes his own decisions, and often he has his own ideas on the subject, either as to specific candidates or as to the qualifications he wants. Presidents are usually interested in the political viewpoint of a possible nominee and the line he is likely to take in deciding cases. Of course, predicting the future decisions of a man to be placed in a lifetime position on the bench is risky business. Theodore Roosevelt was unusually careful in picking men who could be expected to vote right on the big issues, and he was very angry when Justice Oliver Wendell Holmes, soon after his appointment

[57]See Joel B. Grossman, *Lawyers and Judges: The ABA and the Politics of Judicial Selection* (New York: John Wiley, 1965).

[58]Of President Carter's 258 nominees, 17 were rated exceptionally well qualified, 128 well qualified, 110 as qualified, and 3 as not qualified (one on the basis of age); Goldman, op. cit.

[59]Sheldon Goldman, "Reagan's Judicial Appointments at Mid-Term," 66 *Judicature* 335 (1983).

to the Court, disappointed his expectations in an important antitrust case. President Taft felt that the most significant thing he had done during his administration was to appoint six justices who shared his conservative views. "And I have said to them," Taft chuckled to newspapermen when his term was expiring, "Damn you, if any of you die, I'll disown you."[60] President Nixon announced on taking office that he would appoint only "strict constructionists" to the Court.

The Senate must confirm all judicial appointees and can thus impose effective restraints on executive choice. Washington saw one of his Supreme Court nominees rejected by the Senate, and in the nineteenth century over 25 percent of the nominations failed to negotiate the Senate hurdle. By contrast, during the first two-thirds of the twentieth century, only one nominee was rejected by the Senate: John J. Parker was defeated in 1930, partly because of the opposition of labor and black organizations. There had been strong conservative opposition to Louis D. Brandeis in 1916, while liberals sought to defeat Charles Evans Hughes in 1931; but both were confirmed by substantial majorities. It was therefore a stunning reversal of precedent when within the space of two years, 1968 to 1970, both President Johnson and President Nixon saw two of their nominees fail to secure confirmation.

Johnson's trouble arose out of his effort to elevate his longtime friend and legal adviser Associate Justice Abe Fortas to the post of Chief Justice. In June, 1968, Earl Warren notified Johnson of his desire to retire, effective upon confirmation of his successor. Johnson transmitted Fortas's name to the Senate, at the same time nominating another old friend, Court of Appeals Judge Homer Thornberry of Texas, to the post to be vacated by Fortas. Opposition to Fortas quickly developed for a variety of reasons: partisan politics, objections to the liberal decisions in which he had participated, revelation of Fortas's continuation as presidential adviser while on the bench, and the argument that there was no vacancy since Warren had not actually retired. When a filibuster prevented the Senate from voting on the nomination, Fortas asked the President to withdraw his name, and he remained as associate justice.[61] Thus the vacancy for which Thornberry had been nominated was rendered nonexistent, and Warren continued as Chief Justice for one more term and into the Nixon administration.

President Nixon selected Warren Burger as successor to Warren as chief justice, and Burger was confirmed almost without opposition. He had been a conservative member of the Court of Appeals for the District of Columbia. The next vacancy was a different matter. It was created by the resignation of Justice Fortas, who was revealed in 1969 to have committed an indiscretion by agreeing to accept an annual fee for advisory services to a private foun-

[60]Henry F. Pringle, *The Life and Times of William Howard Taft* (New York: Holt, Rinehart & Winston, 1939), p. 854.

[61]See Robert Shogan. *A Question of Judgment: The Fortas Case and the Struggle for the Supreme Court* (Indianapolis: Bobbs-Merrill, 1972).

dation, funded by a man who was under federal investigation at the time and who was subsequently convicted for violations of the Securities and Exchange Act.

President Nixon nominated appeals court Judge Clement Haynsworth for the Fortas vacancy. But the Senate had been so alerted to the issues of judicial ethics by the Fortas affair, and the Democrats in the Senate so embarrassed by it, that Haynsworth's record was subjected to intense scrutiny. Certain indications of ethical insensitivity related to stock holdings in companies involved in cases in which he participated, as well as opposition to his conservative political views, led to his rejection by the Senate after a classic battle by a vote of fifty-five to forty-five.

Nixon's next "strict constructionist," G. Harrold Carswell, another appeals court judge, was also rejected by the Senate, fifty-one to forty-five, because of his lack of intellectual qualifications and past opposition to civil rights.[62] Not since 1894 had two successive Supreme Court appointments been defeated in the Senate.

When Justices Black and Harlan retired in the summer of 1971, Attorney General Mitchell submitted to the ABA committee six names of possible nominees, all of whom were unknown nationally or obviously lacking in qualifications for the high court. The committee's response was to rate as unqualified the two candidates listed as Nixon's preferences, ratings that immediately became known to the public. Nixon then dropped these candidates and, without notifying the committee, named two much abler conservatives, Lewis Powell and William Rehnquist.[63]

Carter had no opportunity to make an appointment to the Supreme Court. During his campaign Reagan said that one of his first appointments to the court would be a woman, and indeed he did replace Justice Potter Stewart with Sandra Day O'Connor.

It is sometimes argued that only persons with previous judicial experience should be given federal judicial appointments. In fact, this frequently happens.[64] It would be unfortunate, however, if presidential freedom of selection were to be limited by a judicial experience requirement, particularly at the Supreme Court level. The major questions with which the Supreme Court deals require political judgment more than technical proficiency in private law. If judicial experience had been a prerequisite in the past, many of the greatest Supreme Court justices would have been ineligible for appointment, including

[62]See Richard Harris, *Decision* (New York: Dutton, 1971).

[63]See James F. Simon, *In His Own Image: The Supreme Court in Richard Nixon's America* (New York: D. McKay, 1973).

[64]One third of the district judges named between 1953 and 1971 had had prior judicial service, while 59 pecent of the appointees to the courts of appeals during this period were former judges; Sheldon Goldman, "Judicial Appointments to the United States Courts of Appeals," 1967 WISCONSIN LAW REVIEW 186; and "Johnson and Nixon Appointees to the Lower Federal Courts," 34 JOURNAL OF POLITICS 936 (1972). Of Carter's 258 appointees, 139 had had prior judicial experience.

Marshall, Story, Taney, Miller, Bradley, Hughes (at his first appointment), Brandeis, Stone, Black, Frankfurter, and Warren.[65] In spite of all criticisms, it should be recognized that the present system of selecting judges has resulted in a federal bench of high prestige, a satisfactory level of ability, and unquestioned honesty.[66]

JUDICIAL TENURE AND COMPENSATION

Appointment of federal judges for "good behavior" is one of the great pillars of judicial independence. A federal judge can be removed from office only by conviction on impeachment.[67] Only one Supreme Court justice has ever been subjected to impeachment proceedings, Samuel Chase, whose judicial conduct was marked by gross and violent Federalist partisanship. In 1804 the triumphant Jeffersonians sought his removal by impeachment, but failed to secure a conviction. They were successful, however, in impeaching and convicting a district judge, John Pickering, who was a Federalist but also apparently insane. Only seven other federal judges have been impeached, three successfully, and in no case were any partisan political motives involved. But in 1970 Gerald Ford, then House minority leader, sought to initiate impeachment proceedings against Justice William O. Douglas in a transparently partisan effort to remove the Court's most liberal member and clear the way for another Nixon appointment. A House judiciary subcommittee found no grounds for impeachment.

A long congressional effort to provide a method of judicial discipline short of impeachment was successful in 1980. The Judicial Conduct and Disability Act gives disciplinary authority over federal judges to the judicial councils of the circuits. Under the act any person can file a complaint against a federal judge or magistrate, alleging conduct prejudicial to administration of judicial business or mental or physical disability. Complaints not dismissed as frivolous are assigned to an investigating committee composed of an equal number of circuit and district judges. On the basis of the committee report, the council can censure or reprimand, temporarily suspend case assignments, request "voluntary" retirement, or take other appropriate action. Final orders

[65]Justice Frankfurter himself, after a detailed study of this problem in 1957, concluded: "One is entitled to say without qualification that the correlation between prior judicial experience and fitness for the functions of the Supreme Court is zero." "The Supreme Court in the Mirror of Justices," 105 UNIVERSITY OF PENNSYLVANIA LAW REVIEW 781 (1957).

[66]But see a critical and rather sensational analysis of the federal judiciary by Joseph C. Goulden, *The Benchwarmers: The Private World of the Powerful Federal Judges* (New York: Weybright and Talley, 1974).

[67]Raoul Berger, *Impeachment: The Constitutional Problems* (Cambridge, Mass.: Harvard University Press, 1973), and "Impeachment of Judges and 'Good Behavior' Tenure," 79 YALE LAW JOURNAL 1475 (1970); Irving Brant, *Impeachment: Trials and Errors* (New York: Knopf, 1972).

may be appealed to the Judicial Conference. Removal of an Article III judge is expressly prohibited.

Federal judges can be indicted for criminal behavior while on the bench, and conviction would require resignation. Five judges have been indicted and two convicted.

Congress is of course free to encourage the resignation of federal judges by attractive retirement arrangements. The absence or inadequacy of retirement allowances has in the past been responsible for some judges retaining their posts long after they were physically or mentally incapacitated for the work. When Justice Grier had become senile in 1870, a committee of his colleagues, headed by Justice Field, finally waited on him and suggested that he retire. Twenty-six years later Field himself became mentally incompetent. His worried colleagues deputed Justice Harlan to approach Field and ask him if he could recall the course of action he had suggested to Grier. Field finally got the point and, momentarily recovering his acuteness, burst out: "Yes! And a dirtier day's work I never did in my life!" His colleagues then abandoned their efforts, but within a few months Field submitted his resignation.[68]

The age of Supreme Court justices was one of the key issues in President Roosevelt's 1937 "Court-packing" plan. As an aftermath of this controversy, Congress passed a liberalized retirement act that permits federal justices to retire after seventy on full pay without resigning, remaining thereafter subject to recall for further judicial duty in the lower courts.

The provision that a judge's compensation may not be reduced while he is in office is a subsidiary support for judicial independence.[69] In 1920 the Supreme Court in *Evans v. Gore* ruled that a federal judge could not be assessed income tax because it would amount to an unconstitutional reduction of his salary. Justices Holmes and Brandeis dissented, Holmes saying that judges were not "a privileged class, free from bearing their share of the cost of the institutions upon which their well-being if not their life depends."

The Court persisted, and in 1925 compounded its error when in *Miles v. Graham* it ruled that a judge appointed after the effective date of the tax was also entitled to the immunity. Congress overrode this decision by express legislation, and in 1939 a more sensible Court reopened the matter and overruled *Evans v. Gore,* Justice Frankfurter saying in *O'Malley v. Woodrough:* "To suggest that [the tax] makes inroads upon the independence of judges. . .

---

[68]Carl B. Swisher, *Stephen J. Field* (Washington, D.C.: Brookings Institution, 1930), p. 444. Justice William O. Douglas remained on the Court for eleven months after suffering a stroke, but physical incapacity forced him to retire in November, 1975. He had served for 36½ years on the Supreme Court, the longest period of service in the Court's history.

[69]In 1976 130 federal judges, whose salaries had not been increased for over six years, unsuccessfully brought suit in the Court of Claims contending that Congress had violated the compensation clause by not increasing judicial salaries to compensate for inflation (*Atkins v. United States* [1978]). However, the compensation clause was successfully invoked in *United States v. Will* (1980).

is to trivialize the great historic experience on which the framers based the safeguards of Article III.''[70]

The immunity of judges from liability for damages for acts committed within their judicial jurisdiction was firmly established at common law, and the Supreme Court recognized this doctrine in *Bradley v. Fisher* (1871). This immunity applies even when the judge is accused of acting maliciously or corruptly. The doctrine is not "for the protection of a malicious or corrupt judge, but for the benefit of the public, whose interest it is that the judges should be at liberty to exercise their functions with independence, and without fear of consequences.''[71]

[70]In *Duplantier v. United States* (1981) the Supreme Court refused to hear an appeal by seven federal judges against disclosing their assets as required by the Ethics in Government Act of 1978, alleging violation of the separation of powers.

[71]But see Frank Way, "A Call for Limits to Judicial Immunity," 64 JUDICATURE 390 (1981). Way studied 163 federal and state cases (1966-1978) in which a judge who claimed judicial immunity was a defendant in an action for damages or in an equity proceeding, and found that equitable relief or monetary awards were secured in eight cases. (One case involved phyical assault by a justice of the peace against a courtroom spectator.) Way criticizes the immunity doctrine as "pre-democratic," and advocates a qualified immunity standard, under which a plaintiff would be required to prove negligence or malice on the part of the judge, while the judge would have the defenses of good faith and reasonableness.

In a very controversial case, *Stump v. Sparkman* (1978), the Court upheld the immunity of a judge who had approved the sexual sterilization of a young girl where his jurisdiction was highly questionable.

Imbler v. Pachtman (1976) held that prosecutors are also immune from civil damage suits, even if they deliberately violate the civil rights of defendants. Judicial immunity does not require dismissal of an action against private parties accused of conspiring with a judge; *Dennis v. Sparks* (1980). Police officers giving perjured testimony at a criminal trial are immune from damage claims under the Civil Rights Act of 1871; *Briscoe v. LaHue* (1983).

7
Federal Judicial Power and Jurisdiction

Article III, section I, provides that the "judicial power of the United States shall be vested in one Supreme Court, and in such inferior courts as the Congress may from time to time ordain and establish." As we know, the Constitution thus left undecided the basic question as to whether there would be a system of lower federal courts, but the First Congress proceeded to create a complete hierarchy of courts.[1]

The "judicial power" is defined in Article III, section 2, which set out the various classes of cases and controversies over which the federal courts can be given jurisdiction. "Jurisdiction" in the judicial sense means the power of a court to hear (or try) a case. A court may exercise judicial power only within its authorized jurisdiction. The terms "judicial power" and "jurisdiction" are often used synonymously. However, so far as the federal courts are concerned, it is necessary to distinguish between "the judicial power of the United States" and "the jurisdiction of the federal courts," because, in spite

[1]See generally Paul M. Bator et al., *Hart and Wechsler's The Federal Courts and the Federal System* (Mineola, N.Y.: Foundation Press, 1973); David P. Currie, *Federal Courts* (St. Paul, Minn.: West Publishing Company, 1968); Charles Alan Wright, *Handbook of the Law of Federal Courts* (St. Paul, Minn.: West Publishing Company, 1970); Martin H. Redish, *Federal Jurisdiction: Tensions in the Allocation of Judicial Power* (Charlottesville, Va.: Michie Bobbs-Merrill, 1980).

of the word "shall," the judicial power of the United States is not automatically vested in the lower federal courts by Article III.

These courts are creatures of Congress, and Congress has assumed from the beginning that it can control their jurisdiction. The Judiciary Act of 1789 conferred jurisdiction on the lower federal courts, but not all the jurisdiction they were capable of receiving under the federal judicial power. The Supreme Court has acquiesced in congressional exercise of this power in a long series of decisions.[2]

The situation, then, is that for the lower federal courts to have jurisdiction of a case of controversy, (1) the Constitution must have defined it as within the judicial power of the United States, and (2) an act of Congress must have conferred jurisdiction over such cases on the courts.

FEDERAL JUDICIAL POWER: SUBJECT MATTER

The judicial power of the United States is defined by Article III on two different bases: subject matter and nature of the parties involved. The subject-matter classifications are: (1) all cases in law and equity arising under the Constitution; (2) all cases in law and equity arising under "the laws of the United States"; (3) all cases in law and equity arising under treaties made under the authority of the United States; and (4) all cases of admiralty and maritime jurisdiction. The federal judicial power extends to any case falling in these four fields, regardless of who the parties to the controversy may be.

The Constitution as a Source of Judicial Power

Cases "arising under this Constitution" are those in which an interpretation or application of the Constitution is necessary in order to arrive at a decision. They usually arise when individuals challenge the enforcement against themselves of federal or state legislation or executive action, which they assert to be in violation of federal constitutional provisions. Suits raising a constitutional issue may be filed in the federal courts, or if filed in state courts are subject to review by the Supreme Court after they have progressed through the highest state court to which appeal is possible.[3] The most striking aspect of the American judicial system is the power of courts, both federal and state, to invalidate legislation, both federal and state, on the ground of its conflict with the Constitution. This power of judicial review is so significant that it is reserved for treatment in the following chapter.

---

[2]*Turner v. Bank of North America* (1799); *United States v. Hudson and Goodwin* (1812); *Cary v. Curtis* (1845); *Sheldon v. Sill* (1850).

[3]The case of *Thompson v. City of Louisville* (1960) went directly from the Louisville police court to the Supreme Court; it involved two fines of $10 each, and police-court fines of less than $20 on a single charge were not appealable to any other Kentucky court.

Laws and Treaties as Sources of Judicial Power

The "laws of the United States" referred to in Article III are statutes passed by Congress. At first there was some contention that the phrase also covered federal common law. It was asserted that a new political system must carry over and enforce, until revised or repealed, the customary law previously prevailing, which in this case was the English common law. The Supreme Court, however, took the general position that "courts which are created by written law, and whose jurisdiction is defined by written law, cannot transcend that jurisdiction."[4] In 1812 it specifically ruled that there was no common law of crimes enforceable by the federal courts.[5]

Under Article VI, "all treaties made, or which shall be made, under the authority of the United States" share with the Constitution and the laws of the United States the status of the "supreme law of the land." A treaty that is self-executing—i.e., which operates of itself, without the aid of any legislative enforcement—thus has the status of municipal law and is directly enforceable by the courts. This distinctive feature of the American Constitution resulted from experience under the Articles, when the fulfillment of treaties entered into by Congress was dependent on the action of state legislatures. Laws and treaties are of course subordinate to the Constitution, but as to each other are on the same level of authority. Thus in the case of a conflict between a law and a treaty, the later one in point of time will be enforced by the courts.[6]

Issues arising under the Constitution, laws, or treaties of the United States are referred to generally as "federal questions." A plaintiff seeking to bring a case in the federal courts on one of these grounds must set forth on the face of the complaint a substantial claim as to the federal question involved. The mere allegation that such a question is present will not suffice; its presence must be clearly shown. The right or immunity created by the Constitution, laws, or treaties must be such that it will be supported if they are given one construction or defeated if given another. The question alleged to exist must not be insubstantial, or have been so conclusively settled as to foreclose the issue entirely. The Supreme Court often declines to review cases because they do not raise a "substantial federal question."

Admiralty and Maritime Jurisdiction

Under the Articles, decisions of state admiralty courts could be taken to an admiralty court of appeals set up by the Congress. The Constitution, in pursuance of its goal of promoting uniform regulation of commerce, provided for admiralty and maritime jurisdiction in the federal courts. The Judiciary

[4]*Ex purte Bollman* (1807).
[5]*United States v. Hudson and Goodwin* (1812).
[6]*Head Money Cases* (1884).

Act of 1789 vested this jurisdiction exclusively in the federal district courts,[7] although parties were enabled to avail themselves of common-law remedies in the state courts.

In England admiralty jurisdiction, which dealt with local shipping, harbor, and fishing regulations, extended inland only as far as the ebb and flow of the tide. In a small country like England where practically all navigable streams are tidal, this was an adequate definition, but it did not prove so in the United States. It was gradually expanded until a congressional act of 1845 extended admiralty jurisdiction to all the navigable waters of the country. The Supreme Court upheld this law in the case of *The Genesee Chief* (1852).

Admiralty and maritime jurisdiction covers two general classes of cases. The first relates to acts committed on the high seas or other navigable waters, and includes prize and forfeiture cases as well as torts, injuries, and crimes. Locality is the determining circumstance in this class of jurisdiction. The second category relates to contracts and transactions connected with shipping, including seamen's suits for wages, litigation over marine insurance policies, and the like.

FEDERAL JUDICIAL POWER: PARTIES

Apart from the four subject-matter classifications, federal judicial power is defined in terms of parties. Article III extends federal power to controversies (1) to which the United States is a party; (2) between two or more states;[8] (3) between a state and citizens of another state; (4) between citizens of different states; (5) between citizens of the same state claiming lands under grants of different states (a category that quickly became obsolete); (6) between a state, or the citizens thereof, and foreign states, citizens, or subjects; and (7) to all cases affecting ambassadors, other public ministers, and consuls. Matters involving these classes of parties can be brought in the federal courts, no matter what the subject matter.

Suits to Which the United States is a Party

Obviously no constitutional provision would have been necessary to give the United States authority to bring suit as party plaintiff in its own courts. Nor is congressional authorization necessary to enable the United States to sue.[9] Like other parties, however, the United States must have an interest in

---

[7]The general principle of exclusiveness of federal admiralty jurisdiction does not prevent the states from retaining their general or political powers of law enforcement on navigable waters, as was established when the Supreme Court invalidated a federal court conviction for a murder committed in Boston Harbor. *United States v. Bevans* (1818).

[8]The problem of suits between states has already been discussed in Chapter 5.

[9]*Dugan v. United States* (1818).

the subject matter and a legal right to the remedy sought. Thus in 1935 the Supreme Court refused to take jurisdiction of a suit by the United States against West Virginia to determine the navigability of certain rivers in that state on the ground that there were no legal issues, merely differences of opinion between the two governments.[10]

The principal problems arise, not where the United States is a plaintiff, but where it is a defendant. The principle of sovereign immunity establishes that the government cannot be sued without its consent. Where such consent is given by Congress, the United States can be sued only in accordance with the conditions stated. The government has been suable on contracts in the Court of Claims since 1855, but could not be sued in torts until the passage of the Federal Tort Claims Act in 1946. Even under the statute, there are considerable limits on the government's liability for torts of its employees.[11]

Government corporations are in a special category so far as liability to suit is concerned. They have generally been created in order to operate business enterprises for the government with something like the freedom of private corporations, and this includes freedom to sue and be sued. Congress can of course relieve government corporations from liability to suit, but where it makes no provision one way or the other, the Supreme Court has held the practice of corporate liability to be so well established as to render the corporation subject to suit.[12]

When no consent to sue the government has been given, it may be possible to sue officials acting for the government. In practice it is often very difficult for courts to decide whether a suit that is nominally against a government official is actually a suit against the government. For example, a suit against the secretary of the treasury to review a decision about the rate of duty on sugar was held to be suit against the United States because of its effect on the revenue system of the government.[13] One general rule which courts have tended to apply is that a suit in which the judgment would affect the United States or its property is a suit against the United States.[14] On the other hand, cases in which action adverse to the interests of a plaintiff is taken by a government official who is alleged to be acting beyond his statutory authority or under an unconstitutional statute are generally held not to be suits against the government.

The leading case on establishing official liability to suit is *United States*

---

[10]*United States v. West Virginia* (1935).

[11]*United States v. Orleans* (1976).

[12]*Keifer & Keifer v. Reconstruction Finance Corporation* (1939).

[13]*Louisiana v. McAdoo* (1914). See Louis L. Jaffe, "Suits against Governments and Officers: Sovereign Immunity," 77 HARVARD LAW REVIEW 1 (1963); Edgar S. Cahn and Jean C. Cahn, "The New Sovereign Immunity," 81 HARVARD LAW REVIEW 929 (1968).; Laurence H. Tribe, "Intergovernmental Immunities in Litigation, Taxation, and Regulation," 89 HARVARD LAW REVIEW 682 (1976).

[14]See *Larson v. Domestic & Foreign Commerce Corp.* (1949).

v. Lee (1882), which involved the claim of the government to possession of the Robert E. Lee mansion in Arlington, Virginia, through a tax sale. Lee's heirs brought suit for ejectment against the federal officials in charge, and by a five to four vote the Supreme Court held this was not a suit against the United States until it had been determined whether the officers were acting within the scope of their lawful authority. Here the Court found that government possession was based on an unlawful order of the President, and concluded: "No man in this country is so high that he is above the law. No officer of the law may set that law at defiance with impunity."

Controversies Between a State and Citizens of Another State

This provision of the Constitution was generally assumed to extend federal jurisdiction only to suits by a state as plaintiff against citizens of another state as defendants. However, in *Chisholm v. Georgia* (1793), the Supreme Court imprudently interpreted it as permitting a state to be made a defendant in a suit brought by citizens of another state. Georgia then refused to permit the decree to be enforced[15] and widespread protests against the Court's action resulted in its prompt reversal by adoption of the Eleventh Amendment. Later the Court itself admitted that the *Chisholm* decision had been erroneous.[16]

Since states cannot be sued by citizens of other states in the federal courts, or in their own courts without their consent, no judicial means may be available to compel a state to honor debts owed to private citizens. As already noted, an effort by citizens of New Hampshire to use their state government as a collection agency to recover on defaulted Louisiana bonds failed.[17] When similar bonds were donated outright to South Dakota, however, that state was successful in collecting from North Carolina on them, though four justices thought that even this was a violation of the Eleventh Amendment.[18]

In general, the question as to when a suit is one against a state, and so forbidden by the Eleventh Amendment, is determined on much the same rules as govern federal immunity to suit.[19] Thus, suits against state officers involving state property or suits asking for relief that call for the exercise of official

[15]In fact, the Georgia House of Representatives made any attempt to carry out the Supreme Court's ruling a felony punishable by hanging without benefit of clergy.

[16]*Hans v. Louisiana* (1890).

[17]*New Hampshire v. Louisiana* (1883).

[18]*South Dakota v. North Carolina* (1904).

[19]See *Governor of Georgia v. Madrazo* (1828); *Kennecott Copper Co. v. State Tax Commission* (1946); Clyde E. Jacobs, *The Eleventh Amendment and Sovereign Immunity* (Westport, Conn.: Greenwood Press, 1972). *Lake County Estates v. Tahoe Regional Planning Agency* (1979) held that a bistate agency created by compact between California and Nevada was not entitled to immunity. *Nevada v. Hall* (1979) ruled that Nevada could not claim immunity in a suit brought in a California court by California residents to recover for injuries sustained on a California highway involving a vehicle owned by the state of Nevada. *Quern v. Jordan* (1979) held that the Civil Rights Act of 1871 did not abrogate the Eleventh Amendment immunity of the states.

authority are considered suits against the state and so prohibited. But suits against state officials alleged to be acting in excess of their statutory authority or under an unconstitutional statute are maintainable.[20] Likewise suits can be brought by other states or by the United States, and the Supreme Court can review state court judgments in suits where the state is a party.

Federal legislation can create rights enforceable against states or state officials in spite of the Eleventh Amendment. *Scheuer v. Rhodes* (1974) held that parents of students killed by the Ohio National Guard on the Kent State campus in 1970 could bring suit for damages under the Civil Rights Act of 1871 against the governor of Ohio and other officials for depriving their children of a federal right under color of state law. The immunity of state executive officials is not absolute, the Court said, but depends upon the scope of their discretion and responsibilities and the circumstances existing at the time. *Parden v. Terminal Railway* (1964) held that employees of a railroad owned by the state of Alabama could sue the state for injuries under the Federal Employers' Liability Act.[21]

As a plaintiff suing citizens of another state, a state may act to protect its own legal rights, or as *parens patriae* to protect the health and welfare of its citizens. The *parens patriae* concept will justify suits brought to protect the welfare of the people as a whole, but not to protect the private interests of individual citizens, though this distinction is often difficult to make. In 1945 the Court permitted Georgia as *parens patriae* to sue twenty railroads in its original jurisdiction for alleged rate-fixing conspiracy. "If the allegations of the bill are taken as true," the Court said, "the economy of Georgia and the welfare of her citizens have seriously suffered as the result of this alleged conspiracy."[22]

Under this clause states are limited to civil proceedings. They cannot seek to enforce their penal laws against citizens of other states in the federal courts.[23] Moreover, states may not seek judicial redress that would be inconsistent with the distribution of powers under the federal Constitution.[24]

Controversies Between Citizens of Different States

Interesting jurisdictional questions are created by the "diversity of citizenship" clause. For natural persons the tests of state citizenship are domicile

---

[20]See *Osborn v. Bank of the United States* (1824).

[21]But the Fair Labor Standards Act did not authorize employees of state nonprofit institutions to sue the state; *Employees of Department of Public Health and Welfare v. Missouri* (1973). *Edelman v. Jordan* (1974) held that state participation in a federal welfare program did not in itself signify consent by the state to be sued in federal court.

[22]*Georgia v. Pennsylvania R. Co.* (1945). But in *Ohio v. Wyandotte Chemicals Corp.* (1971), the Court declined to permit Ohio to sue companies polluting Lake Erie in its original jurisdiction.

[23]*Wisconsin v. Pelican Insurance Co.* (1888).

[24]*Massachusetts v. Mellon* (1923).

in a state, which may be established by residence there, acquisition of property, payment of taxes, or acquisition of the suffrage. If there are multiple parties in a diversity suit, all the persons on one side of the case must be citizens of different states from all persons on the other side. In the case of corporations the Court has adopted the fiction that all the stockholders of a corporation are citizens of the state of incorporation.[25]

The ease of access to the federal courts thus provided for corporations led to substantial abuses. The classic example was the *Kentucky Taxicab Case* (1928). Here a taxicab company, incorporated in Kentucky and doing business in a Kentucky city, wanted to enter into an exclusive contract to provide taxicab service at a railroad station. Knowing that Kentucky courts would invalidate such a contract as contrary to state law, the corporation dissolved itself and reincorporated the identical business in Tennessee. In its new guise it entered into the contract, and then brought suit in federal court to prevent a competing company from interfering with the carrying out of the contract. Since the federal court was not bound by the Kentucky law, this stratagem succeeded.[26]

The *Kentucky Taxicab Case* would be decided differently today, because in 1938 an extremely important reversal of doctrine occurred on the Supreme Court with respect to the law to be applied in diversity cases. This is an interesting story, which goes back to the original Judiciary Act of 1789. Section 34 of that act provided that in diversity cases at common law the laws of the several states should be the rules of decision of the federal courts. In *Swift v. Tyson* (1842) Justice Story for the Supreme Court decided that "the laws of the several states" referred only to state statutes, and did not cover the unwritten or common law of the states. Thus in the absence of state statutes controlling a case, federal courts were free to adopt and apply such general principles of law as they thought fitting and applicable.

The principle of the *Tyson* case was subsequently extended from negotiable instruments to other matters, such as wills, torts, real estate titles, and contracts, until by 1888 there were twenty-eight kinds of cases in which federal courts were free to apply rules of law in diversity cases different from those of the state courts. Thus in every state the federal and state courts had their own version of commercial common law, with all attendant confusion that was bound to result, and plaintiffs were free to shop around for the court in which their case would have the best chance of success.

Profound discontent developed with the *Tyson* rule, which was attacked as a wasteful and confused way to handle a delicate problem of federal-state relations. Justice Holmes, who became the spearhead in the fight on *Swift v. Tyson*—Miller and Field had preceded him—was motivated not only by re-

---

[25]*Strawbridge v. Curtis* (1806); *Muller v. Dows* (1877).
[26]*Black & White Taxicab Co. v. Brown & Yellow Taxicab Co.* (1928).

spect for state courts, but also by his pragmatic view of law. Law, he said, "does not exist without some definite authority behind it." He had no patience with the notion of a "transcendental body" of law hanging in the air waiting to be divined by the independent judgment of federal courts. An impressive literature of protest against *Swift v. Tyson* appeared in the law reviews. Charles Warren in 1923 published an article with newly discovered evidence that seemed to shown that Story's interpretation of section 34 was incorrect. Liberals in Congress proposed legislation to terminate the *Tyson* rule.

All this had an effect. In 1934 the Court decided that in a case "balanced with doubt," the federal court's independent judgment should be subordinated to the state decisions.[27] This was the only warning given before the roof fell in. *Erie Railroad v. Tompkins* was decided in 1938. Counsel in the case had not questioned the *Tyson* precedent. The interpretation of section 34 was not before the Court. Yet Justice Brandeis not only overruled *Swift v. Tyson,* he also held that by its previous interpretation of section 34 the Court had committed an unconstitutional action. This is the first and only time in its history that the Supreme Court has accused itself of having made an unconstitutional decision. What it was saying, in effect, was that if Congress should wish to reinstate the *Tyson* rule, it could not do so without amending the Constitution.

The facts of the *Erie* case may help to show the policy considerations that went into this decision. Tompkins, a citizen of Pennsylvania, was seriously injured by a freight train while he was walking along the railroad right of way. He was a trespasser, and by the common law of Pennsylvania railroads were not liable to trespassers except for wanton or willful negligence. So his attorneys filed suit, not in the state courts of Pennsylvania, but in the federal court in New York, the state in which the railroad was incorporated. The lower federal courts awarded Tompkins a judgment of $30,000, holding that it was unnecessary to consider what Pennsylvania law provided, for the question was one of general law to be decided by the federal courts in the exercise of their independent judgment. To this situation Justice Brandeis reacted by stating a new rule of decision:

> Except in matters governed by the Federal Constitution or by Acts of Congress, the law to be applied in any case is the law of the State. And whether the law of the State shall be declared by its Legislature in a statute or by its highest court in a decision is not a matter of federal concern. There is no federal general common law.

The essential intent of the ruling, Justice Frankfurter said in 1945, was to ensure that, in all diversity cases, "the outcome of the litigation in the

[27]*Mutual Life Insurance Co. v. Johnson* (1934).

federal court should be substantially the same, so far as legal rules determine the outcome of a litigation, as it would be if tried in a State court.[28] At first the Supreme Court's tendency was to push its mandate rather far. For example, the Court held that the *Erie* rule required the enforcement of state procedural as well as substantive law. Again, in situations where the highest state court had not passed on a matter of state law, the Supreme Court held that the federal district court must descend the state judicial hierarchy until it did find a court that had ruled on the matter, and then be guided by that ruling.[29]

However, increasing experience with the *Erie* rule led the Supreme Court to recognize "countervailing factors" that reflect a federal interest in diversity litigation, and where these are deemed to be of overriding importance, to apply federal policy rather than state law.[30] In 1965 Justice Harlan confessed that "up to now Erie and the cases following it have not succeeded in articulating a workable doctrine governing choice of law in diversity actions." His approach toward determining whether to apply a state or federal rule was to inquire whether "the choice of rule would substantially affect those primary decisions respecting human conduct which our constitutional system leaves to state regulation. If so, Erie and the Constitution requrie that the state rule prevail.[31] But Laurence Tribe has warned against interpreting *Erie* to require "a mechanical application of state precedent. . . . [F]ederal diversity courts were and are common law courts, with all the flexibility which that designation implies."[32]

Cases Involving Foreign States and Citizens

The language giving federal jurisdiction over controversies "between a state, or the citizens thereof, and foreign states, citizens or subjects" is not quite as broad as it sounds. Under principles of international law foreign states cannot be sued in American courts without their consent, not even by American states, and conversely foreign powers cannot sue American states in the federal courts.[33] But an American state can sue foreign citizens, foreign states can sue American citizens, American citizens can sue foreigners, and vice versa.

---

[28]*Guaranty Trust Co. v. York* (1945).

[29]*West v. American Telephone & Telegraph Co.* (1940); *Fidelity Union Trust Co. v. Field* (1940); but see *King v. Order of United Commercial Travelers* (1948).

[30]See *Textile Workers Union v. Lincoln Mills* (1957); Alexander M. Bickel and Harry H. Wellington, "Legislative Purpose and the Judicial Process: The Lincoln Mills Case," 71 Harvard Law Review 1 (1957); *Prima Paint Corp. v. Flood & Conklin Mfg. Co.* (1967).

[31]*Hanna v. Plumer* (1965). See John Hart Ely, "The Irrepressible Myth of Erie," 87 Harvard Law Review 693 (1974); Abram Chayes, "The Bead Game," 87 Harvard Law Review 741 (1974).

[32]*American Constitutional Law* (Mineola, N.Y.: Foundation Press, 1978), p. 119.

[33]*The Exchange v. McFaddon* (1812); *Monaco v. Mississippi* (1934).

Giving foreign states access to American courts is in accord with the general principle of comity in international law. To be able to sue in American courts, a foreign government must be recognized by the United States, and of course it must submit to the procedures and rules of decisions of American courts.

Cases Affecting Ambassadors, Ministers, and Consuls

When Article III gives the federal courts jurisdiction over cases affecting ambassadors, other public ministers, and consuls, naturally it is referring to diplomatic personnel accredited by foreign states to the United States, not to American ambassadors to other countries.[34] Since ambassadors and ministers representing foreign governments in the United States are exempt from jurisdiction of American courts under international law, the effect of this provision is principally to permit foreign diplomats to bring suit in American federal courts against private individuals.

Consuls are not entitled to the same immunity, and federal courts can take jurisdiction of cases concerning them. They may also be dealt with in state courts where appropriate.[35]

CONGRESSIONAL CONTROL OF FEDERAL COURT JURISDICTION

We have seen that the lower federal courts receive their jurisdiction by congressional authorization. Since 1875, when Congress granted full "federal question" jurisdiction, the federal courts have exercised substantially the full panoply of "judicial power" defined by the Constitution. To be sure, Congress has imposed occasional limits on the jurisdiction granted. As noted in Chapter 6, there are statutory limits on judicial issuance of injunctions, including the well-known Norris-LaGuardia Act. Congress has limited diversity jurisdiction to controversies exceeding $10,000, and the same requirement applied to "federal question" cases until abolished by Congress in 1980. As another example, the Emergency Price Control Act of 1942 provided that price regulations could be attacked only in a newly-created Emergency Court of Appeals, withdrawing jurisdiction from all other lower federal courts.

Such jurisdictional restrictions can be justified as intended to avoid overloading the federal courts or to promote efficiency. But there have also been many efforts in Congress, so far generally unsuccessful, to curtail or abolish jurisdiction because of substantive disagreement with judicial decisions—a

[34]*Ex parte Gruber* (1925).
[35]*Popovici v. Agler* (1930).

"kill the umpire" reaction. For example, the Tuck bill, passed by the House in 1964, intended to make the Supreme Court's decision in *Baker v. Carr* (1962) unenforceable by forbidding any district court from reviewing state reapportionment legislation. During the 1950s and 1960s over sixty bills were introduced in Congress to curtail some aspect of federal jurisdiction in areas where Warren Court rulings had aroused congressional opposition. Efforts of this kind were intensified after conservative victories in the 1980 elections, with emphasis on school desegregation, school prayer, abortion, and sex discrimination issues.

The general argument in support of such legislation is that since Congress created the lower federal courts, it can abolish them, and that the power to abolish completely must include the lesser power to withdraw certain controversies from their jurisdiction. This contention is unacceptable. In the first place, it is not true that as a general proposition the power to create necessarily includes the right to destroy. In the second place, this argument posits a "right" to destroy the lower federal court system that is both practically impossible and constitutionally unjustifiable. While in 1789 it was possible to conceive of a federal judicial structure consisting of "one Supreme Court," almost two centuries of living with a complete system of federal trial and appellate courts is a fact of national political and economic existence. The thousands of civil and criminal cases arising under "the judicial power of the United States" heard annually by lower federal courts cannot conceivably be transferred to state courts, nor can "one Supreme Court" review the constitutional rulings of fifty state supreme courts.

It is argued, however, that withdrawing specific subject-matter areas from the jurisdiction of the lower federal courts does not destroy the system. But what such measures do destroy is the conception of the federal judiciary as a coequal branch of the government and the long-established understanding that constitutional rights are enforceable in the federal courts. As Tribe says, what is at stake "is nothing less than the survival of a distinctly American institution, that of review of legislative and executive action by an independent judiciary entrusted to enforce the Constitution."[36]

It is of course possible for the power of Congress over federal court jurisdiction to be used for nonpunitive purposes. We have noted the 1976 limitation on the use of three-judge district courts. There is a strong case for abolishing the obligatory jurisdiction of the Supreme Court. The House Judiciary Committee has long pursued its goal of abolishing the diversity jurisdiction of the federal courts, contending that diversity cases have become

---

[36]Laurence H. Tribe, "Jurisdictional Gerrymandering: Zoning Disfavored Rights out of the Federal Courts," 16 HARVARD CIVIL RIGHTS-CIVIL LIBERTIES LAW REVIEW 129, 131 (1981). See also Theodore Eisenberg, "Congressional Authority to Restrict Lower Federal Court Jurisdiction," 83 YALE LAW JOURNAL 498 (1974).

too burdensome (45,000 in 1981) and that the federal courts should be reserved for federal questions.

FEDERAL-STATE COURT RELATIONS: CONCURRENCY OF JURISDICTION

Though the Judiciary Act of 1789 provided for a complete system of lower federal courts, the statute, as already noted, withheld from the federal courts much of the jurisdiction they were capable of exercising. In fact, from 1789 to the Civil War the lower federal courts were in effect subsidiary courts, principally designed as protection to citizens litigating outside their own states. But after the Civil War the new feelings of nationalism motivated Congress to invest the federal judiciary with enormously increased powers. The Removal Act of March 3, 1875, provided that any suit involving a right given by the Constitution, laws, and treaties of the United States could be begun in the federal courts, or if begun in state courts could be removed to the federal courts for disposition.

Jurisdiction over cases within the judicial power of the United States may thus be exercised by either federal or state courts, except in certain areas where Congress has entrusted jurisdiction *exclusively* to the federal courts. Important areas now exclusively within federal jurisdiction include crimes defined by the United States, federal seizures on land or water, admiralty and maritime jurisdiction, bankruptcy proceedings, actions arising under patent and copyright laws, suits for penalties and forfeitures incurred under the laws of the United States, and most of the remedies against the United States or federal agencies that have been specially defined by statute.

States have occasionally sought to place restrictions on the right of removal of civil suits from state courts, particularly in dealing with foreign (i.e., out-of-state) corporations. These efforts have usually been held unconstitutional. *Terral v. Burke Construction Co.* (1922) concerned a state law providing that when a foreign corporation removed a suit into federal court, its license to do business within the state would be revoked. The Supreme Court held this was an attempt to curtail the free exercise of a constitutional right, and consequently invalid.

When state courts exercise jurisdiction over cases falling within the judicial power of the United States, they operate under the control of the supremacy clause of the Constitution. Article VI, after making the Constitution, laws, and treaties of the United States "the supreme law of the land," continues: "And the judges in every state shall be bound thereby, any thing in the Constitution or laws of any state to the contrary notwithstanding."

Enforcement of this obligation through Supreme Court review of state court decisions, as established in the cases of *Martin v. Hunter's Lessee* (1816) and *Cohens v. Virginia* (1812), has been discussed in Chapter 4. All things considered, the Supreme Court, like Congress, has been extremely considerate of the position of state courts. This deference is exemplified in its practice of not reviewing a decision of a state court if that decision rests on a nonfederal ground adequate to support it. Section 25 of the Judiciary Act of 1789 limits the Supreme Court to reviewing "final" judgments of the highest state court in which a decision could be had. This ensures that state systems of justice will have full opportunity to settle their own questions before the Supreme Court intervenes.

An interesting aspect of concurrency is the postive obligation that the federal government has sometimes imposed on state courts to enforce federal laws. During the early decades, before the federal courts were so well established, this practice was fairly common. The Fugitive Slave Act of 1793, the Naturalization Act of 1795, and the Alien Enemies Act of 1798, all imposed positive duties on state courts to enforce federal law. In 1799 Congress authorized state trial of criminal offenses under the Post Office Act. Great reliance was placed on state courts for the enforcement of Jefferson's Embargo Acts.

This early effort to relieve the federal courts came to grief. The New England courts were hostile to the Embargo Acts, and the Northern courts generally resisted enforcement of the Fugitive Slave Law. The argument was widely heard that one sovereign cannot enforce the penal laws of another, and the Supreme Court for a time endorsed this position by its holding in *Prigg v. Pennsylvania* (1842).

More recently, the Federal Employers' Liability Act of 1908, covering injuries to railroad employees, not only gave concurrent jurisdiction in suits arising under the act to state courts, but even prohibited removal of cases begun in state courts to the federal courts. The purpose was to prevent railroads from fleeing to the federal courts if the injured workman felt he would be better off in the state court. Under this statute a state court can be compelled to enforce federal remedies that are contrary to state policy, the Supreme Court ruled in *Second Employers' Liability Cases* (1912).

The basic constitutional issue was reconsidered in *Testa v. Katt* (1947). The Emergency Price Control Act of 1942 provided that persons who had been overcharged in violation of the act could sue for treble damages in any court of competent jurisdiction. When such a suit was brought in Rhode Island, the state supreme court held this to be "a penal statute in the international sense" that state courts could not be required to enforce. The Supreme Court unanimously reversed this ruling, Justice Black reminding Rhode Island that "state courts do not bear the same relation to the United States that they do to foreign countries." Although Congress could not require Rhode Island to provide courts for the enforcement of these suits, since the state does have courts that enforce similar claims, it may require the state to apply the federal law.

Suitors who seek to defend rights under the federal Constitution, laws, or treaties by filing suits in federal court cannot be denied a federal forum merely because state courts are also available to hear such claims. And a federal judge cannot transfer a diversity suit to a state court merely because state courts are less burdened and could try the suit more promptly.[37] But *Moore v. Sims* (1979) held that federal courts should have refused to hear a child custody case while it was still pending in a state court.

In *Railroad Commission of Texas v. Pullman Co.* (1941) the Court announced a judge-made rule of "equitable abstention" which provides that when an injunction is sought in federal court against a state statute on grounds of its unconstitutionality, the federal courts might suspend action to allow state courts an opportunity to adopt an interpretation of the challenged law that would avoid the constitutional problem. Abstention is not a consistent practice; rather, it is an instrument of judicial diplomacy that the Court uses as a matter of grace and prudence. Abstention cannot be ordered simply to give the state courts the first opportunity to vindicate the federal claim. In *Zwickler v. Koota* (1967) the Supreme Court held that abstention should not have been applied in a case where a state statute was attacked as repugnant to the First Amendment on its face. And in *Monroe v. Pape* (1961) the Supreme Court approved consideration of the plaintiff's Fourteenth Amendment claim notwithstanding a second claim that the police action was also violative of state law.[38]

FEDERAL-STATE COURT RELATIONS: CONFLICTS OF JURISDICTION

A dual system of courts faces, in addition to the confusions of concurrency, the frictions of jurisdictional conflicts. Coercive writs may be sought in one jurisdiction against the operation of the other. States may try to impose barriers to removal of cases to federal courts. States may attempt to punish in state courts federal officials who commit some transgressions in the execution of their official duties within the state. State courts have on occasion even refused to comply with Supreme Court orders.

Such frictions may require adoption of appropriate federal legislation, but to a considerable extent the two systems of courts handle their own problems by application of principles of comity. Comity, says Corwin, is "a self-imposed rule of judicial morality whereby independent tribunals of concurrent or coordinate jurisdiction exercise a mutual restraint in order to prevent interference with each other and to avoid collisions of authority."[39] Exercise of

---

[37] *Thermtron Products, Inc. v. Hermansdorfer* (1976).

[38] See also *Wisconsin v. Constantineau* (1971); *Harris County Commissioners v. Moore* (1975); "Federal Question Abstention," 80 HARVARD LAW REVIEW 604 (1967).

[39] Op. cit., p. 626. In *Fair Assessment in Real Estate Assn. v. McNary* (1981) the Court held that the principle of comity barred a state taxpayers' suit brought in federal court to protest allegedly unconstitutional administration of the Missouri tax system.

the principles of comity is most often required where writs of injunction or habeas corpus are used by one system of courts against the other level of government.

Judicial Conflict Through Injunctions

In general, neither state nor federal courts may enjoin each other's proceedings or judgments. State courts have been forbidden to take such action by Supreme Court decisions.[40] The reason given has been not the paramount jurisdiction of the federal courts, but rather the complete independence of the two judicial systems in their respective spheres of action.

Federal courts were forbidden to enjoin proceedings in state courts by act of Congress in 1793. But this bar is not applicable where Congress has expressly authorized a stay of proceedings in state courts, or where an injunction is necessary to protect the lawfully acquired jurisdiction of a federal court or to prevent the relitigation of issues previously adjudicated and finally settled by federal court decree.[41]

Congress has also limited the power of federal courts to issue injunctions affecting the states by other statutes. The tax injunction act of 1937 forbids federal district courts to enjoin the collection of state and local taxes where an adequate remedy exists in state courts. Again, the Johnson Act of 1934 forbids the federal courts to enjoin or suspend the operation of public utility rates that have been fixed by state order after reasonable notice and hearing, if there is an adequate remedy in state courts.

Federal courts do, however, exercise the extremely important power of restraining state officials from enforcing unconstitutional state statutes. This power to enjoin state officials from bringing criminal or civil proceedings to enforce an invalid statute was first asserted by the Supreme Court in *Osborn v. Bank of the United States* (1824), but the rule then was that an injunction could issue only after a finding of unconstitutionality had been made in a lawsuit. In 1908 this requirement was abandoned in *Ex parte Young,* which held that the attorney general of a state could be enjoined from proceeding to enforce a state statute in the state courts *pending* a determination of its constitutionality.

The *Young* decision was sharply criticized in Congress, which in 1910 passed a law prohibiting the issuance of injunctions by a single federal judge to restrain the enforcement of state laws; a three-judge court was required to sit in all cases seeking "to interpose the Constitution against enforcement of a state policy." The Supreme Court has also since about 1940 tended to exercise a moderating influence on such invalidation of state legislation through injunctions against state officials.[42]

---

[40]*McKim v. Voorhies* (1812); *United States ex rel. Riggs v. Johnson County* (1868).

[41]"The Federal Anti-Injunction Statute and Declaratory Judgments in Constitutional Litigation," 83 HARVARD LAW REVIEW 1870 (1970).

[42]See *Railroad Commission v. Rowan & Nichols Oil Co.* (1940, 1941); *Burford v. Sun Oil Co.* (1943); *American Federation of Labor v. Watson* (1946).

The civil rights problems of the 1960s imposed new strains on relations between federal and state courts, which may be illustrated by the case of *Dombrowski v. Pfister* (1965). Officers of a civil rights organization active in Louisiana filed suit in a federal district court requesting an injunction against imminent prosecutions under two state anti-Communist laws. The complaint alleged that the statutes were unconstitutional and that the defendants, who were various state officials, had threatened prosecution solely for the pupose of discouraging the organization's civil rights activities. The Supreme Court held that the provisions of these statutes were so vague and so susceptible of unconstitutional application that their very existence tended to have a "chilling effect upon the exercise of First Amendment rights." Therefore, an injunction should issue immediately, restraining state officials from enforcing or threatening to enforce the statutes until they received an adequate "narrowing construction" in a state declaratory judgment proceeding.

The *Dombrowski* precedent was substantially limited by *Younger v. Harris* (1971), involving a California socialist who was charged with violation of the state Criminal Syndicalism Act. This statute had been upheld by the Supreme Court in *Whitney v. California* (1927), but *Whitney* had been overruled in 1969 by *Brandenburg v. Ohio*. Harris alleged that the very existence of the statute inhibited him in the exercise of his rights of free speech, and on this claim he secured a federal court injunction against prosecution under the statute. However, the Supreme Court reversed, Justice Black arguing that "a federal lawsuit to stop a prosecution in a state court is a serious matter," conflicting with the principles of what he called "Our Federalism."

The *Younger* doctrine has been elaborated and refined in a number of subsequent rulings. It was limited by *Steffel v. Thompson* (1974), which approved a federal court declaration that a state statute was unconstitutional where prosecution under the statute had been threatened but not begun. But *Huffman v. Pursue, Ltd.* (1975) extended the *Younger* ban on federal injunctions from state criminal prosecutions to civil proceedings, unless the federal court found that the state case was conducted in bad faith or that the state statute involved was flagrantly and patently unconstitutional.[43] Again, *Justice v. Vail* (1977) ruled that a debtor who had ignored state contempt proceedings could not challenge the constitutionality of the state's contempt statute in federal court.[44]

A more questionable application of *Younger* occurred in *Hicks v. Miranda* (1975). A theater owner sued in federal court to have the California obscenity law declared unconstitutional and to enjoin officials from seizing

---

[43]The *Huffman* rule was applied in *Trainor v. Hernandez* (1977), and *Younger* was applied in *Samuels v. Mackell* (1971) and *Doran v. Salem Inn, Inc.* (1975). See the general discussion of *Younger* in Tribe, op. cit., pp. 152–156.

[44]*Kugler v. Helfant* (1975) denied a federal court injunction sought by an indicted New Jersey municipal judge who contended he could not get a fair trial in the New Jersey courts. *Middlesex County Ethics Committee v. Garden State Bar Assn.* (1982) ruled that federal courts should abstain from interfering with ongoing state disciplinary proceedings.

certain films. After the federal complaint was filed but before any proceedings of substance had occurred, state criminal proceedings were begun against the federal plaintiff. This obvious tactic to frustrate the federal case succeeded, as the Supreme Court voted five to four that the *Younger* rule applied. Stewart, dissenting, thought that this distorted the principle of "Our Federalism" beyond recognition. If federal courts should not interfere with the legitimate functioning of state courts, neither should state courts interfere with federal courts.[45]

Judicial Conflict Through Habeas Corpus

The first important controversies in this area arose during the Civil War period from the attempted use of habeas corpus by state courts to release prisoners in federal custody. The most famous case was *Ableman v. Booth* (1859) in which the Supreme Court took a strong and correct line on national supremacy in dealing with the action of a Wisconsin judge who had released a prisoner held by a federal officer on charges of violating the Fugitive Slave Law. As late as 1872, in *Tarble's Case,* Wisconsin again asserted power to release persons in federal custody; and again the Supreme Court denied this power, saying that neither government "can intrude with its judicial process into the domain of the other, except so far as such intrusion may be necessary on the part of the National government to preserve its rightful supremacy in cases of conflict of authority."

The use of habeas corpus by the federal courts to test the constitutionality of state court convictions for violations of state criminal laws is based on a statute of 1867 extending the remedy of the writ to any person in custody "in violation of the Constitution, or of any treaty or law of the United States."[46] This measure was adopted by the Radical Republican Congress in anticipation of Southern resistance to the new constitutional guarantees. As Justice Brennan has commented: "A remedy almost in the nature of removal from the state to the federal courts of state prisoners' constitutional contentions seems to have been envisaged."[47]

The result of the 1867 statute has been to create "an utterly unique relationship between the state and federal sovereigns," under which the "state and federal courts jointly and severally administer federal law relevant to state

---

[45]The *Younger* doctrine was mistakenly invoked by Justice Rehnquist in *Rizzo v. Goode* (1976). In *Moore v. Sims* (1979) Justice Stevens charged that the Court had applied "the *Younger* doctrine where it simply does not belong."

[46]See the comprehensive discussion in "Developments in the Law—Federal Habeas Corpus," 83 HARVARD LAW REVIEW 1038–1280 (1970); also David L. Shapiro, "Federal Habeas Corpus: A Study in Massachusetts," 87 HARVARD LAW REVIEW 321 (1973). Justice Holmes established habeas corpus as a postconviction remedy by his eloquent opinion in *Moore v. Dempsey* (1923), after he had failed in *Frank v. Mangum* (1915).

[47]*Fay v. Noia* (1963).

criminal proceedings."[48] The major accommodation between the two systems has been the Supreme Court's requirement that the defendant exhaust state remedies before seeking review on habeas corpus in a federal district court.[49] However, where a state prisoner fails to comply with a state procedural requirement and consequently loses the opportunity to present in the state court federal questions relevant to the power of the state to hold him in custody, the Supreme Court ruled in *Fay v. Noia* (1963) that he is not barred thereby from subsequent resort to the federal courts for relief through habeas corpus.[50]

On federal habeas corpus (referred to as "collateral" review), the basic standard that state criminal convictions must meet is "fundamental fairness." The classic grounds for issuance of the writ, as Justice White noted in *Rose v. Lundy* (1982), have been "that the proceeding was dominated by mob violence [*Moore v. Dempsey* (1923)]; that the prosecutor knowingly made use of perjured testimony [*Mooney v. Holohan* (1935)]; or that the conviction was based on a confession extorted from the defendant by brutal methods [*Brown v. Mississippi* (1936)]." Errors of this kind justify relief on habeas corpus, no matter how long a judgment may have been final and even though not properly preserved at the original trial.

But applications for habeas corpus have not been confined to "classic" situations. The number of petitions from convicted state prisoners rose from 127 in 1941 to 9,419 in 1981. In 1953 Justice Jackson made reference in *Brown v. Allen* to this multiplicity of petitions, "so frivolous, so meaningless, and often so unintelligible that this worthlessness of the class discredits each individual application."[51] In *Schneckloth v. Bustamonte* (1973) Justice Powell attacked "the escalating use, over the past two decades, of federal habeas corpus to reopen and readjudicate state criminal judgment." He contended that the Court had extended habeas corpus "far beyond its historic bounds and in disregard of the writ's central purpose," resulting in unwise use of limited judicial resources, repetitive criminal litigation, and friction between federal and state systems of justice. Powell was particularly opposed to reversal of state convictions because evidence had been admitted in violation of the Fourth Amendment if the defendant had been provided a fair opportunity to raise the unlawful search and seizure issue in state courts; Powell would limit habeas corpus review to constitutional issues "bearing on innocence."

[48]Curtis R. Reitz, "Federal Habeas Corpus: Impact of an Abortive State Proceeding," 74 HARVARD LAW REVIEW 1315, 1324 (1961).

[49]*Ex parte Hawk* (1944); *Darr v. Burford* (1950); *Brown v. Allen* (1953); *Pitchess v. Davis* (1975).

[50]See also *Irvin v. Dowd* (1959). *Fay v. Noia* overruled the *Darr v. Burford* requirement that exhaustion of remedies must include application for review of the state court decision on certiorari to the United States Supreme Court.

[51]In 1966 Congress amended the habeas corpus act to require federal judges to defer to state court decisions on matters of fact unless there was a substantial reason to question the correctness of the decision. See *Sumner v. Mata* (1981, 1982). In 1980–81 prisoner petitions to district courts totalled 27,711, of which 9,419 were habeas corpus.

The Burger Court adopted this position by a six to three vote in *Stone v. Powell* (1976). The majority ruled that collateral attacks on state convictions would no longer be permitted where the only challenge to the convictions was that evidence had been secured in violation of the Fourth Amendment, provided the defendant had been given a "full and fair" opportunity to make the Fourth Amendment claim in state court. Powell's opinion stressed that state judges were still obligated by *Mapp v. Ohio* (1961) to exclude illegally seized evidence, and he was confident that state courts could be relied on to enforce federal constitutional rights.[52] Burger would have gone further; he proposed to wipe out the *Mapp* exclusionary rule, or at least limit it to instances of "egregious, bad faith" conduct by the police.[53]

The Burger Court's policy on collateral review of state criminal convictions has been increasingly restrictive. In *Francis v. Henderson* (1976) the Court held that a defendant in state court who failed to challenge the constitutionality of the grand jury that indicted him had waived his right to raise that issue on habeas corpus.[54] *Rose v. Lundy* (1982) required federal courts to dismiss a prisoner's habeas corpus petition if it contained any claims that had not been exhausted in state courts. In *Holmberg v. Parratt* (1977) the Court agreed with the Eighth Circuit that a "full and fair" adjudication does not include the right to a correct decision.[55]

The 1867 habeas corpus act may also be utilized by persons held under state authority for criminal acts done under federal authority. The constitutionality of this usage was upheld in *Tennessee v. Davis* (1880). A federal revenue officer was arrested in Tennessee on a murder charge. His defense was that he had acted in pursuance of official duties and he petitioned to have the case removed to the federal court. The Supreme Court admitted that Davis's crime was one against state rather than federal law, but upheld the removal, pointing out that the federal government must act through its officers within the states.

The complication of a dual system of courts is one that other leading federal governments, such as Australia, Canada, and India, have avoided. In those countries there is only one federal court, superimposed on a complete system of state courts. By contrast, the American system, as Justice Douglas has noted, may seem to be in many respects "cumbersome, expensive, and productive of delays in the administration of justice. . . . It has required ju-

---

[52]See Burt Neuborne, "The Myth of Parity," 90 HARVARD LAW REVIEW 1105 (1977), for a contrary view.

[53]It was widely anticipated that the Court would adopt this position in *Illinois v. Gates* (1983), but it postponed the issue.

[54]See *Estelle v. Williams* (1976); *Engle v. Isaac* (1982); *U.S. v. Frady* (1982).

[55]James Turner, "Habeas Corpus after *Stone v. Powell,*" 13 HARVARD CIVIL RIGHTS-CIVIL LIBERTIES LAW REVIEW 521 (1978); Neil D. McFeeley, "A Change of Direction: Habeas Corpus from Warren to Burger," 32 WESTERN POLITICAL QUARTERLY 174 (1979); William F. Duker, *A Constitutional History of Habeas Corpus* (Westport, Conn.: Greenwood Press, 1980).

dicial statesmanship of a high order to prevent unseemly conflicts between the two judicial systems." But, he concludes, "the days of crisis have passed; regimes and attitudes of harmony and cooperation have developed; and the tradition of deference of one court system to the other has brought dignity and a sense of responsibility to each."[56]

[56]William O. Douglas, *We the Judges* (New York: Doubleday, & Inc., 1956), p. 135.

8

Judicial Review

The phrase "judicial review" may be applied to several types of processes. It may describe the control that courts exercise over subordinate corporations or units of government, such as municipalities, or over public officials exercising delegated legislative and administrative powers. Courts will customarily review the actions of such officers or units of government to determine whether they are acting within their powers, and will punish or grant redress for acts found to be *ultra vires* (i.e., outside lawful authority). This is the commonest type of judicial review.

Second, federal systems of government have a characteristic form of judicial review whereby courts are made responsible for enforcing the agreed-on division of functions between the central government and the component state or provincial governments. Such a division of functions is a necessary feature in any federal system, and by the process of judicial review the courts are made responsible for umpiring and enforcing the rules of the federal system. This power necessarily includes authority to declare invalid any state legislation or other state action that infringes on the constitutional authority of the central government or the other states in the federation. It would be extremely difficult to operate a federal system without such an umpire. As already noted, section 25 of the Judiciary Act of 1789 explicitly provided for Supreme Court review of cases decided in state courts where the constitutionality of state statutes was at issue. Justice Holmes once said:

> I do not think the United States would come to an end if we lost our power to declare an act of Congress void. I do think the Union would be imperilled if we could not make that declaration as to the laws of the several states. For one in my place sees how often a local policy prevails with those who are not trained to national views.[1]

The third type of judicial review is the power of the Supreme Court to declare acts of Congress unconstitutional. In more general terms, this is the review by courts over the acts of the legislative and executive departments of the same government. There is no superior-subordinate relationship as there is in the first two types of review. Here the courts, though coordinate parts of the government, nevertheless have the authority to declare actions of the other two branches invalid as contrary to the basic law. That explains why this system is often referred to as one of "judicial supremacy." It is judicial review in this third form that Americans customarily think of when the phrase is employed, for such power is enjoyed by American courts at both the federal and state levels.

It used to be customary to attribute the unique status of the Supreme Court, in comparison with the world's other high tribunals, to the Court's power of invalidating acts of Congress. To a certain extent this was true. No such authority resided in the highest courts of Britain or France. Switzerland, a federation that borrowed somewhat from American experience, deliberately rejected in 1848 the American pattern of judicial review and made the legislature the final interpreter of its constitution. The Canadian and Australian federations did give to their high courts authority to pass on the constitutionality of legislation; but their constitutions, lacking such broad protective standards as due process of law or equal protection of the laws, did not provide as much opportunity for judicial assertion of authority over constitutional interpretation as in the United States.

Within the present century, however, and particularly since World War II, a number of countries—including Argentina, Austria, India, Ireland, Italy, Japan, Norway, the Philippines, West Germany, and Yugoslavia—have established judicial tribunals with power to declare unconstitutional acts of coordinate legislative or executive branches. While the primary model for these developments has been the United States Supreme Court, the systems and the motivation for their adoption vary from country to country. The Japanese court was included in the postwar constitution drafted under General MacArthur. The Italians and Germans were influenced in part by the American example and in part by their experience with dictators. In Ireland and

---

[1]"Law and the Court," *Speeches* (Boston: Little, Brown, 1934), p. 102.

India judicial review was seen as a method of protecting ethnic minorities against majority rule.[2]

THE PREHISTORY OF JUDICIAL REVIEW

The theory on which the American practice of judicial review is based may be summarized as follows: that the written Constitution is a fundamental law, subject to change only by an extraordinary legislative process, and as such superior to common and statutory law; that the powers of the various departments of government are limited by the terms of the Constitution; and that judges are expected to enforce the provisions of the Constitution as the superior law and to refuse to enforce any legislative act or executive order in conflict therewith. What are the foundations of this theory in American thought and experience?

Foundations of Judicial Review

First there is the obvious influence of natural law, the belief that human conduct is guided by fundamental and immutable laws that have natural or divine origin and sanction. In English experience natural law was invoked first as a limitation on the king, and by Coke in the famous *Dr. Bonham's Case* (1610) against Parliament. "When an act of parliament is against common right or reason," said Coke, "the common law will control it and adjudge such act to be void." This view failed to establish itself in England, but in the American colonies conditions were more propitious. With few lawbooks, and with an increasing disrespect for English legal precedents, the colonists tended to fall back on the Bible or popular notions of natural law as their guides. Locke supplied the systematic statement of this position, concluding: "the fundamental law of Nature being the preservation of mankind, no human sanction can be good or valid against it."

Another factor was the confirmed practice in American experience of reducing the basic laws to writing. The Mayflower Compact of 1620, the Fundamental Orders of Connecticut in 1639, the charters granted to the colonies from 1620 to 1700—always the colonists sought to legitimize and to limit collective action by fundamental written instruments. But the provision of machinery for enforcing these fundamental laws was not given much attention. During the Colonial period there was review machinery of a sort in the powers

[2]For a comparative view of the work of constitutional courts in six countries, see Walter Murphy and Joseph Tanenhaus, *Comparative Constitutional Cases* (New York: St. Martin's Press, 1976); also Glendon Schubert and David J. Danelski (eds.), *Comparative Judicial Behavior* (New York: Oxford University Press, 1969); Edward McWhinney, *Judicial Review*, 4th ed. (Toronto: University of Toronto Press, 1969); Mauro Cappelletti, *Judicial Review in the Contemporary World* (Indianapolis: Bobbs-Merrill, 1971).

of disallowance exercised by the Privy Council in England over the acts of colonial legislatures. When the English yoke was thrown off, the initial Revolutionary enthusiasm saw the free popular legislatures as a self-sufficient guarantee against oppression of liberties. But it took only a little experience with all-powerful legislatures to demonstrate the abuses of unchecked authority, and at least three states experimented with special institutional arrangements to protect the fundamental law from encroachment.

Judicial Review in the Constitutional Convention

It is a never-ending puzzle why judicial review, which has become one of the outstanding features of the operation of the American Constitution, was not even mentioned in that document. What actually happened was that a group in the Constitutional Convention, led by Wilson and Madison, wanted to establish a council composed of the executive and a "convenient number" of the national judiciary, with a veto power over congressional legislation. This plan was defeated three times in the Convention. Several members objected that under this plan judges who would later have to decide on the validity of the law in a case would have prejudged the matter and that the separation of powers would be thus violated. But Madison on June 6 strongly defended the plan. The executive would need both control and support. Associating judges with him in his revisionary capacity would perform both functions and would also enable the judicial department "the better to defend itself against Legislative encroachments," Madison thought.

In the debate on the veto power, then, judicial review in this rather peculiar form was considered and rejected in favor of a purely executive veto. When the original plan failed, its sponsors proposed that the Supreme Court as a whole exercise revisionary powers over legislation. All bills would go both to the President and the Supreme Court, and either could object, whereupon the bill would need to be repassed by a two-thirds vote if either the President or a majority of the Court had objected, and by three-fourths if both had objected. This novel idea was defeated on August 15, three states to eight.

No further effort was made in the Convention to give the Supreme Court explicit revisionary powers over congressional legislation. This does not prove, of course, that the framers were opposed to judicial review as such. But the absence of explicit language did leave room for doubt, and controversy still persists as to their intentions. Charles A. Beard thought that his book, *The Supreme Court and the Constitution,* published in 1912, had settled what Felix Frankfurter in 1924 regarded as an "empty controversy."[3] Beard presented evidence that seventeen of the twenty-five men most influential in the Convention "declared, directly or indirectly, for judicial control." But in 1953

---

[3]Charles A. Beard, *The Supreme Court and the Constitution,* with an introduction by Alan F. Westin (Englewood Cliffs, N.J.: Prentice-Hall, 1962), pp. 1, 35.

William W. Crosskey concluded after a review of the same evidence that the Constitution had not intended to authorize general judicial review of acts of Congress,[4] and in 1958 Learned Hand took the equivocal position that judicial review was "not a logical deduction from the structure of the Constitution but only a practical condition upon its successful operation."[5]

The debates at the state ratifying conventions have been searched for statements favoring judicial review, particularly by members of the Convention, and some can be found—Marshall in Virginia, Wilson in Pennsylvania, Ellsworth in Connecticut. More attention has been given to Hamilton's clear presentation, in No. 78 of *The Federalist,* of the doctrine of a written constitution as a superior enactment, the preservation of which rests particularly with judges. A "limited constitution," he contended, "can be preserved in practice no other way than through the medium of courts of justice, whose duty it must be to declare all acts contrary to the manifest tenor of the Constitution void." Such authority does not "by any means suppose a superiority of the judicial to the legislative power." Hamilton concluded, "It only supposes that the power of the people is superior to both."

THE ESTABLISHMENT OF JUDICIAL REVIEW

With the passage of the Judiciary Act and the inauguration of the federal court system, the fate of judicial review was in the hands of the Supreme Court itself. As we have seen, its initial history did not suggest that it would be able to win a position of respect and power. When John Marshall was named Chief Justice of a Federalist Court in 1801, there were few cases awaiting adjudication, the Jeffersonians were about to assume control of the other two branches of government, and prospects for the Court were dim.

Yet within two years that Court, dominated by Marshall, had successfully asserted its authority to invalidate acts of Congress in one of the cleverest coups of American history. One week before he was to leave office, President Adams appointed forty-two new justices of the peace for the District of Columbia. The formal commissions of appointment had not been made out and delivered by Secretary of State John Marshall, who was holding the two positions simultaneously, when Jefferson became president on March 4, 1801, and he ordered his secretary of state, James Madison, not to deliver them.

Four of the frustrated appointees, headed by William Marbury, petitioned the Supreme Court for a writ of mandamus to compel Madison to deliver the commissions. Madison ignored a preliminary order issued by Mar-

---

[4]*Politics and the Constitution in the History of the United States* (Chicago: University of Chicago Press, 1953), Chapter 28.

[5]*The Bill of Rights* (Cambridge, Mass.: Harvard University Press, 1958). p. 15.

shall, and then Congress shut the Court down for a year by changing the dates of its sessions, to keep it from passing on the validity of the repeal of the Federalist Judiciary Act of 1801. Consequently Marbury's petition could not be acted on until 1803.

Marshall had a difficult problem to solve. He seemed to face two alternatives. He could order Madison to deliver the commissions, but it was certain Jefferson would countermand the order, and the Court would be exposed as powerless to enforce its order. Or he could avoid a test of strength with the executive by refusing to issue the writ, with the same result of advertising the Court's powerlessness. It is a measure of Marshall's genius that he escaped from this apparent dead end by manufacturing a third alternative, which enabled him to claim for the Court an infinitely greater power than Marbury had asked it to exercise, yet in a fashion that Jefferson could not possibly thwart.

This is how it was done. Marbury had applied for mandamus under section 13 of the Judiciary Act of 1789, which provided that "The Supreme Court . . . shall have power to issue . . . writs of mandamus, in cases warranted by the principles and usages of law, to any courts appointed, or persons holding office, under the authority of the United States." Marbury did not go first to a lower court. Under this statute he filed his petition directly with the Supreme Court. But Article III of the Constitution provides that the Supreme Court shall have original jurisdiction only in cases affecting ambassadors, ministers, and consuls and in cases where a state is a party. Marshall professed to believe that the statutory provision conflicted with the constitutional provision, and that Congress had attempted, contrary to the Constitution, to expand the original jurisdiction of the Supreme Court.

Of course, this was preposterous. Section 13 had been drawn by Oliver Ellsworth, later the third Chief Justice of the United States; it had been passed by the First Congress, which contained many ex-members of the Convention; and it had been actually enforced in 1794 by a Court that contained three ex-members of the Convention. The provision could be, and had been, interpreted in such a way as to raise no questions about adding to the Court's original jurisdiction. It could be taken to mean that the Court had power to issue the writ of mandamus whenever that remedy was appropriate in the disposition of cases properly brought in the Supreme Court, either on appeal or under its original jurisdiction. Thus in a case brought in the Court's original jurisdiction by a state, mandamus would be one of the available remedies. But such an interpretation would not have suited Marshall's purposes.

The proof of Marshall's intent is only too apparent in his opinion. If this was intended as a bona fide holding that the court lacked jurisdiction to hear the case, he should have made that ruling and then stopped. Jurisdiction is the first thing a court must establish, and if it is found lacking, then the court can do nothing but dismiss the case. Marshall, however, wanted to read Jefferson a lecture. Consequently the first question asked in his decision was whether Marbury had a right to the commission. He concluded that he did, and that Madison had wrongfully withheld it. Then he asked a second question—whether the laws of the country afforded Marbury a remedy for the right that Madison had violated. He said that they did. Only after this detour through some interesting political questions did Marshall come to the jurisdictional question as to whether Marbury was entitled to the remedy for which he had applied. And only then did Marshall announce his newly discovered conflict between section 13 and Article III.

Admiration for Marshall's skill is of course irrelevant to the basic question. Likewise we may pass over the ethical question presented by Marshall's deciding a case that arose out of his own negligence as secretary of state. The important matter is the logic of Marshall's demonstration that the Court must have the power to invalidate acts of Congress that it holds to be contrary to the Constitution. The case he makes is a strong one, admittedly profiting from Hamilton's argument in No. 78 of *The Federalist*. Marshall started from the proposition that the government of the United States as created by the Constitution is a limited government, and that "a legislative act, contrary to the constitution, is not law." Then what is the obligation of a court when it is asked to enforce such a statute? For Marshall the answer was obvious.

> If a law be in opposition to the constitution; if both the law and the constitution apply to a particular case, so that the court must either decide that case conformable to the law, disregarding the constitution, or conformable to the constitution, disregarding the law; the court must determine which of these conflicting rules governs the case; this is of the very essence of judicial duty.

After all, Marshall continued, the judicial power extends to cases arising "under the constitution." Is the Court to be forbidden to look into the Constitution when a case arises under it? Must it look only at the statute? Further, he noted that the judges take an oath to support the Constitution. It would be nothing less than immoral to compel them to participate as knowing instruments in the violation of the document they have sworn to support.

This argument has been ratified by time and by practice, and there is little point in quibbling with it. Of course the President also takes an oath to support the Constitution. Does not Marshall's argument then give him the right to refuse to enforce an act of Congress that he regards as unconstitutional? Equally questionable was the bland assumption by both Hamilton and Marshall that a judicial finding of repugnance between a statute and the Constitution was "equivalent to an objective contradiction in the order of nature and not a mere difference of opinion between two different guessers."[6] As Thomas Reed Powell says, "they both covered up this possibly question-begging difficulty by saying in somewhat different form that judges are expert

---

[6]Thomas Reed Powell, *Vagaries and Varieties in Constitutional Interpretation* (New York: Columbia University Press, 1956), p. 14.

specialists in knowing or finding the law.'' But we now know that constitutional interpretation is a matter of opinion, and that judicial expertise is no guarantee of correctness or wisdom.

Few now find such arguments against judicial review convincing. Yet there is a basic uneasiness tht will not die, and that occasionally boils up into bitter conflict, about the supremacy the Supreme Court has assumed in constitutional interpretation. There was, in fact, a less extreme position that the Court could have claimed for itself, that would nonetheless have enabled it to come up with the same disposition of the *Marbury* case. It could have claimed supremacy, not for its interpretations of the Constitution as a whole, but only over those portions of the Constitution pertaining to judicial organization and jurisdiction. Marbury's problem, of course, fell in this area. It could have been argued that the separation of powers principle required each branch to be the interpreter of its own constitutional authority. The judiciary would mark out its own area of constitutional power, but would intervene in the constitutional problems of the other two branches only when disputes arose between them. In *Marbury v. Madison,* however, ''coequality'' was rejected in favor of a policy of judicial supremacy.

This is not a place for a detailed history of the Supreme Court's subsequent use of its power to declare acts of Congress unconstitutional. After *Marbury,* no act of Congress was invalidated until the Missouri Compromise (already repealed) was voided by the disastrous *Dred Scott* decision in 1857. By contrast, from 1865 to 1979, 120 acts of Congress were held unconstitutional in whole or in part by the Supreme Court.[7] Thirteen of these came between 1934 and 1936, mostly involving New Deal recovery statutes. During the Warren Court years (1953-1969), judicial activism in support of civil liberties was largely responsible for 25 declarations of unconstitutionality, while the presumably less activist Burger Court from 1969 to 1979 struck down 21 federal statutes. As for state statutes and local ordinances, 848 were declared unconstitutional between 1789 and 1974.[8]

The Court-packing plan that President Roosevelt proposed in 1937 was by no means the first effort to limit the Supreme Court's powers over congressional legislation. One recurring proposal has been to require an extraordinary majority of the Court to invalidate legislation. In 1868, a bill passed the House that would have required a two-thirds vote of the Court for this purpose. In 1921 a constitutional amendment was proposed in Congress that would have required all but two justices to concur in a declaration of unconstitutionality. Such proposals were motivated by the five to four votes that had been the margin of decision in many important instances.

During the Progressive era in the early part of the twentieth century, the

[7]See Henry J. Abraham, *The Judicial Process,* 4th ed. (New York: Oxford University Press, 1980), p. 271; *The Constitution of the United States of America: Analysis and Interpretation,* Sen Doc. no. 82, 92nd Cong., 1973, pp. 1623-1785.

[8]*Ibid.,* Sen. Doc. no. 134, 93rd Cong., 1974, pp. S127-S135.

recall of judges was widely advocated and was actually provided for in some states. In 1912 the Progressive party platform advocated, not the recall of judges, but the recall of judicial decisions. LaFollette, in his bid for the Presidency in 1924, proposed an amendment authorizing Congress to reenact a law declared unconstitutional by the Supreme Court, thereby nullifying the decision. After the child labor law was held unconstitutional in 1918, Senator Owen presented a bill to reenact the law with a clause prohibiting the Supreme Court from invalidating it. No action was ever taken along any of these lines.

After his tremendous victory in the 1936 election, President Roosevelt felt strong enough to challenge the Court. As already noted, he chose the device of increasing the size of the Court, which had been juggled several times previously in American history for political purposes, but he presented his plan in a maladroit fashion. He made no reference to the constitutional crisis that had arisen out of the Supreme Court's dogged refusal to keep abreast of the times. Instead he painted a dubious picture of delay in federal court litigation, of the Supreme Court's heavy burden, and of the need for a "constant infusion of new blood." After one of the bitterest political battles in American history, the original plan was defeated in Congress.[9] Instead, a liberalized retirement bill was passed. Moreover, even before the final defeat of the Court-packing plan, the Supreme Court made a historic change of direction (often referred to as "the switch in time that saved nine"), which was confirmed by President Roosevelt's subsequent appointments to the Court.

The *Brown* decision in 1954 ushered in a period during which the Supreme Court was almost constantly in difficulties with some members of Congress and some sections of the populace, but again the institution of judicial review emerged unscathed. It should be obvious that the exercise of such power by the judiciary would not have been tolerated in a democratic government unless it had been wielded with a reasonable measure of judicial restraint and with some attention, as Mr. Dooley said, to the election returns. It therefore becomes appropriate to examine such systematic doctrines or practices as the Court has developed to limit its powers of judicial review.

JUDICIAL SELF-RESTRAINT: JUSTICIABLE QUESTIONS

There are always procedural techniques available to the Court by which it can avoid having to express an opinion on embarrassing or difficult issues. As already noted, the Court has almost complete control over its business through grant or refusal of writs of certiorari. Certiorari, moreover, is granted on the Court's own terms. In the famous 1951 Smith Act case involving prosecution

---

[9]See Leonard Baker, *Back to Back: The Duel Between FDR and the Supreme Court* (New York: Macmillan, 1967); Robert H. Jackson, *The Struggle for Judicial Supremacy* (New York: Knopf, 1941).

of the leaders of the American Communist party, *Dennis v. United States,* the court accepted the evidentiary findings of the court of appeals as final and limited its review to two relatively narrow constitutional issues. When the Court finally granted a full review of Smith Act convictions in a 1957 case, *Yates v. United States,* it came to much different conclusions from those it had reached in the *Dennis* case.

The all-too-familiar technique of the law's delay may also be utilized to rescue the Court from difficult situations, by postponing decisions until the heat has gone out of an issue The Court's castigation of Lincoln's trials of civilians before military tribunals during the Civil War was delivered from the safe vantage point of 1866, and martial law in Hawaii during World War II was voided in 1946. But these methods of judicial self-restraint have not been dignified by the kind or caliber of rationalizations to which we now turn.

Advisory Opinions

The Supreme Court is a court of law, and it has followed a fairly consistent policy of refusing to deal with issues unless they are presented as cases or controversies in the framework of a bona fide lawsuit. In application, this means that the federal courts will not issue advisory opinions indicating what the law would be on a hypothetical state of facts. President Washington in 1793, through his secretary of state, requested an advisory opinion from the Supreme Court regarding a proposed treaty, but the Court refused the opinion as beyond its competence to give.

If the Supreme Court did give advisory opinions, as supreme courts in several states are obligated to do on request of the governor or legislature, the Court would presumably not have the advantage of arguments by opposing counsel, nor would the opinions be binding should a genuine case or controversy subsequently come along raising the same issue. The granting of advisory opinions would almost certainly result in constant political embroilment and a substantial dissipation of the Court's influence and prestige.

The ban on advisory opinions is not a barrier to declaratory judgment actions, which are sometimes mistakenly confused with advisory opinions. In 1934 Congress passed the Federal Declaratory Judgment Act authorizing the federal courts to declare rights and other legal relations in cases of "actual controversy," and providing that "such declaration shall have the force and effect of a final judgment or decree and be reviewable as such."[10]

The declaratory judgment is a statutory, nontechnical method of securing a judicial ruling in cases of actual controversy, but without requiring the parties to put themselves in jeopardy by taking action based on their conflicting legal interpretations. No coercive order is normally issued in a declaratory

---

[10]The act was upheld in *Aetna Life Ins. Co. v. Haworth* (1937). For interesting discussions of declaratory judgment actions, see *Public Affairs Associates v. Rickover* (1962) and *Steffel v. Thompson* (1974).

judgment proceeding, for the assumption is that once the law has been declared the parties will act according to it. However, the judgment may be made the basis of further relief, if necessary, or quite commonly a petition for writ of injunction is joined with a declaratory judgment action.

"Friendly" Suits

From the principle that a lawsuit must pit against each other parties with adverse legal interests grows the practice in the federal courts of refusing to accept so-called "friendly suits." Obviously, if the interests of the opposing parties are actually not adverse, then motivation for bringing out all the relevant facts will be lacking, and the trial court will have no assurance that justice is being done. Particularly is this important when the constitutionality of a federal statute is being attacked, because both parties might actually be antagonistic to the statute.

Such a situation may be closely approached where a stockholder seeks to enjoin the corporation in which he owns stock from complying with an allegedly unconstitutional statute. Several significant pieces of constitutional litigation have occurred under these circumstances. For example, the federal income tax was declared unconstitutional in a suit brought by a common stockholder to enjoin the corporation's breach of trust by paying voluntarily a tax that was claimed to be illegal.[11]

When a stockholder of the Alabama Power Company sued to enjoin that company from carrying out its contract to sell a portion of its properties to the TVA, Justice Brandeis, speaking for four members of the Court, declared that the Court should decline to permit constitutional issues to be raised by the device of stockholders' suits.[12] That the government's case will at least be adequately presented in such controversies is now guaranteed by the provisions of the 1937 act requiring the United States to be made a party in any case where the constitutionality of an act of Congress is questioned.

Test Cases

Many suits are carefully planned and brought up to the Supreme Court as "test cases" to secure rulings on disputed constitutional issues. Organizations such as the American Civil Liberties Union and the National Association for the Advancement of Colored People devote much effort to finding good test cases involving constitutional principles on which they hope to draw a favorable ruling from the Supreme Court.

When a new and controversial federal statute is enacted and suits are begun challenging its constitutionality, the Department of Justice customarily

[11]*Pollock v. Farmers' Loan & Trust Co.* (1895). See also *Smith v. Kansas City Title & Trust Co.* (1921); *Carter v. Carter Coal Co.* (1936).

[12]*Ashwander v. Tennessee Valley Authority* (1936).

selects the case in which it feels the government has the strongest position to carry to the Supreme Court. Sometimes, of course, there is no choice. The case in which the Supreme Court declared the National Industrial Recovery Act unconstitutional, *Schechter Poultry Corp. v. United States* (1935), was, as Attorney General Jackson said, "far from ideal as a test case," but circumstances compelled the government to use it.[13]

Test cases must meet all the requirements of a valid case or controversy. If a case is too obviously "staged" simply for the purpose of drawing a court opinion, the Supreme Court may decline to accept it, as is demonstrated by the famous case of *Muskrat v. United States* (1911). In 1906 Congress authorized certain named Indians who had been given allotments of land to sue the United States in the Court of Claims in order to determine the validity of acts of Congress restricting alienation of Indian land and increasing the number of persons entitled to share in it. The attorney general was designated by the act to defend the case. The Supreme Court dismissed the suits when they were brought, on the ground that the United States had "no interest adverse to the claimants." The United States and the Indians were not in dispute as to their respective property rights. Instead, this was a "made-up" case, the object and purpose of which were "wholly comprised in the determination of the constitutional validity of certain acts of Congress." Thus Congress cannot through legislation create a case or controversy merely by stating an issue and by designating parties to present each side.

Standing to Sue

Not every person with the money to bring a lawsuit is entitled to litigate the legality or constitutionality of government action in the federal courts. In order to have standing to maintain such a suit, the individual must establish a sufficiency of interest in the controversy; and this involves satisfying the courts on two main points: (1) that the interest is peculiarly personal and not one shared with all other citizens generally; and (2) that the interest being defended is a legally protected interest, or right, which is immediately threatened by government action. In both these respects, however, the Supreme Court in recent years has tended to be less demanding.

The law of standing is generally thought to begin with *Frothingham v. Mellon* in 1923. Actually, some sixty years earlier the Court had stated that a plaintiff would not be heard "unless he shows that he has sustained, and is still sustaining, individual damage."[14] But the *Frothingham* case, though the word "standing" is nowhere mentioned, does mark the beginning of the Court's attention to the nature of the plaintiff's interest. Suit had been brought

[13]Robert H. Jackson, *The Struggle for Judicial Supremacy* (New York: Knopf, 1941), p. 113.

[14]*Mississippi & Missouri Railroad Co. v. Ward* (1863).

by a Mrs. Frothingham to enjoin the operation of a congressional statute providing grants to the states for programs to reduce maternal and infant mortality. She sought to sustain her standing in court by alleging that she was a taxpayer of the United States and that the effect of the appropriations authorized by this act would be to increase the burden of future taxation and thereby take her property without due process of law.

The Supreme Court unanimously denied her standing to bring the suit. Although taxpayers' suits are rather common in local and state courts, Justice Sutherland pointed out:

> . . . the relation of a taxpayer of the United States to the Federal Government is very different. His interest in the moneys of the Treasury—partly realized from taxation and partly from other sources—is shared with millions of others; is comparatively minute and indeterminable; and the effect upon future taxation, of any payment out of the funds, so remote, fluctuating and uncertain, that no basis is afforded for an appeal to the preventive powers of a court of equity.

The party who attacks the constitutionality of a federal statute, Sutherland continued, "must be able to show not only that the statute is invalid but that he has sustained . . . some direct injury as the result of its enforcement, and not merely that he suffers in some indefinite way in common with people generally."

Two years later, *Pierce v. Society of Sisters* (1925) met the "direct injury" test. Oregon adopted a constitutional amendment in 1922 requiring parents or guardians of children between the ages of eight and sixteen years to send them to a public school, and the failure to do so was a misdemeanor. A religious order that maintained a school got a court order restraining enforcement of the provision, though the direct effect of the act was on parents, not on schools. The Supreme Court affirmed, not only on the ground that the law would cause irreparable injury to the business and property of the religious group, but more importantly because the law "unreasonably interferes with the liberty of parents and guardians to direct the upbringing and education of children under their control." Thus the religious order was permitted to plead the rights of parents to strengthen its own somewhat less direct interest in the situation.[15]

Coleman v. Miller (1939) concerned a dispute as to whether the Kansas senate had legally ratified the child labor amendment and was filed by twenty members of the senate who challenged the right of the lieutenant governor to cast the tie-breaking vote, by virtue of which the amendment had been adopted.

---

[15]See also *Barrows v. Jackson* (1953), where a California property owner who had breached the obligations of a racially restrictive covenant forbidding sale of property to any but Caucasians was permitted to defend her action by invoking the constitutional rights of non-Caucasians, even though such persons were unidentified and not before the court or directly involved in the case in any way. In *Peters v. Kiff* (1972) the Court recognized the standing of a white man to challenge the exclusion of blacks from the grand jury that indicted him and the trial jury that convicted him.

The Court held that these senators "have a plain, direct and adequate interest in maintaining the effectiveness of their votes."[16]

Where a legal right or statutory authorization to sue cannot be demonstrated, judicial review is unavailable, no matter how real or obvious the damage done by government action. The Latin phrase is *damnum absque injuria*—that is, damage not recognized as a basis for judicial relief. *Alabama Power Co. v. Ickes* (1938) involved an attempt by a power company to enjoin the New Deal Public Works Administration from making grants to Alabama cities that would permit them to build municipal power systems competing with the established private company. The Supreme Court held that the company lacked standing to challenge the government's action, since it had no monopoly rights in the cities it served. "If its business be curtailed or destroyed by the operations of the municipalities, it will be by lawful competition from which no legal wrong results."[17]

Judicial review over entire areas of governmental action may be limited or entirely foreclosed by inability to establish that rights are involved. Government pensions and grants are normally on a privilege basis that does not subject them to judicial review. There is normally no protected interest in contracting with the government.[18] The original concept was that access to the mails was a privilege, but more recently certain rights to postal service have been recognized as justifying judicial review.[19]

In general, the trend has been in favor of increasing opportunities for judicial review and against technical concern about standing. Experience with arbitrary or unreviewable actions of federal administrative agencies led Congress to provide in the Administrative Procedure Act of 1946 that a person "suffering legal wrong because of agency action, or adversely affected or aggrieved within the meaning of a relevant statute, is entitled to judicial review thereof."[20]

The *Frothingham* decision, however, seemed to block the path toward judicial review of any congressional spending legislation. This barrier became of particular concern when Congress in 1965 was considering financial aid to elementary and secondary schools, including religious schools. Both advocates

---

[16]The plaintiffs in *Abington School District v. Schempp* (1963) had standing to raise the issue of Bible reading in the public schools because they sued in their capacity as students and parents of students "directly affected" by the laws and practices against which they complained.

[17]But in *Hardin v. Kentucky Utilities Co.* (1968), a private utility enjoying an almost complete monopoly of two markets was allowed to challenge the legality of a TVA plan to offer cheaper power in those areas.

[18]*Perkins v. Lukens Steel Co.* (1940).

[19]*Hannegan v. Esquire* (1946); *Lamont v. Postmaster General* (1965).

[20]For subsequent review of administrative agency decisions, see *Hardin v. Kentucky Utilities Co.* (1968) and *Association of Data Processing Service Organizations v. Camp* (1970); also "Judicial Review of Agency Action: The Unsettled Law of Standing," 69 MICHIGAN LAW REVIEW 540 (1971); Kenneth C. Davis, "The Liberalized Law of Standing," 37 UNIVERSITY OF CHICAGO LAW REVIEW 450 (1970).

and opponents of aid to parochial schools desired a Supreme Court ruling on its constitutionality but feared that the 1923 decision would tie the Court's hands. However, after passage of the act, the Court found in *Flast v. Cohen* (1968) that a taxpayer's suit could be brought to test the grants to religious schools, the reason being that here, unlike in *Frothingham,* the taxpayer was alleging violation of "specific constitutional limitations," namely, the First Amendment religion clauses.

In the *Flast* decision, Justice Harlan distinguished between the traditional "Hohfeldian" plaintiff, who sued to protect or assert his own personal rights, and the ideological or "non-Hohfeldian" plaintiff, who seeks to act "as surrogate for the population at large," and to vindicate "public rights." Clearly the old direct or special interest test had to be modified if non-Hohfeldian plaintiffs were to be granted standing.[21]

This issue was particularly pressing for the conservationists and ecologists of the 1960s and 1970s, who were protesting environmental damage over wide areas affecting great numbers of people. Organizations such as the Sierra Club were generally accorded standing in court, but in one important case, *Sierra Club v. Morton* (1972), the Supreme Court ruled that the club had failed to allege that its members would be affected by a proposed ski resort in a national forest and consequently that the club lacked standing to protest the development under the Administrative Procedure Act.

This ruling was largely neutralized, however, by *United States v. SCRAP* (1973) where the Court granted standing to a volunteer group challenging an Interstate Commerce Commission policy that handicapped recycling operations. Standing, the Court said, "is not confined to those who show economic harm," adding, "aesthetic and environmental well-being, like economic well-being, are important ingredients of the quality of life in our society, and the fact that particular environmental interests are shared by the many rather than the few does not make them less deserving of legal protection through the judicial process." Justice Douglas went further. In the *Sierra Club* case he proposed that a river should be recognized as a plaintiff to speak for "the ecological unit of life that is part of it."[22]

The general trend on the Burger Court, however, was to restore stricter standing tests for non-Hohfeldian plaintiffs. *Laird v. Tatum* (1972) rejected, by a vote of five to four, an effort to enjoin the Army from carrying on a program of surveillance of civilian political activities. The majority found that the plaintiffs had not sustained any direct injury and denied that the mere

[21]The phrase "Hohfeldian plaintiff" is that of Louis L. Jaffe and is derived from the work of the American legal scholar Wesley Newcomb Hohfeld, *Fundamental Legal Conceptions as Applied in Judicial Reasoning* (New Haven, Conn.: Yale University Press, 1946). See Louis L. Jaffe, "The Citizen as Litigant in Public Actions: The Non-Hohfeldian or Ideological Plaintiff," 116 UNIVERSITY OF PENNSYLVANIA LAW REVIEW 1033 (1968).

[22]See Christopher D. Stone, "Should Trees Have Standing?" 45 SOUTHERN CALIFORNIA LAW REVIEW 450 (1972).

existence of the Army's data-gathering system produced an unconstitutional "chilling effect" on the exercise of First Amendments rights.

A similar decision was *Schlesinger v. Reservists Committee to Stop the War* (1974), where a citizen group sought a judicial declaration that it was unconstitutional for members of Congress to hold commissions in the Armed Forces Reserves, the Court holding that the plaintiffs had suffered no concrete injury. Again, a taxpayer's suit, *United States v. Richardson* (1974), seeking to compel the secretary of the treasury to publish the budget of the Central Intelligence Agency, which is known only to a few key members of Congress, was rejected for lack of standing.

Again, *Warth v. Seldin* (1975) denied standing to organizations and individuals who sought to have the zoning ordinance of a Rochester suburb declared invalid because it excluded persons of low and moderate income from living in the town. The Court majority required the plaintiffs to show that they had "personally" been injured, not that injury had been suffered "by other, unidentified members of the class to which they belong and which they purport to represent".[23] Similarly, *Simon v. Eastern Kentucky Welfare Rights Organization* (1976) declared that indigents lacked standing to challenge the validity of federal tax regulations reducing the amount of free medical care hospitals must provide to obtain tax benefits conferred upon charities.

This rejectionist trend climaxed in *Valley Forge Christian College v. Americans United for Separation of Church and State* (1982), a five to four decision. Under statutory authorization for disposal of surplus property, the government had transferred an Army hospital to a religious college without payment. *Flast v. Cohen,* as just noted, had recognized the "special position" of the establishment clause in justifying court access; but the *Valley Forge* majority distinguished *Flast* on the ground that here there was no exercise of the taxing or spending power of Congress, nor did the plaintiffs identify any personal injuries suffered. Justice Brennan, dissenting, protested the use of the standing doctrine "to slam the courthouse door."[24]

Class Actions

A class action is a suit brought by one or more persons for themselves and on behalf "of all others similarly situated." The Federal Rules of Civil Procedure authorize class actions where a number of persons have a common

---

[23]But *Gladstone Realtors v. Village of Bellwood* (1979) upheld the right of a town and its residents to sue under the Fair Housing Act when real estate agents were illegally trying to tip the racial balance in an integrated neighborhood.

[24]See Gregory J. Rathjen and Harold J. Spaeth, "Access to the Federal Courts: An Analysis of Burger Court Policy Making," 23 AMERICAN JOURNAL OF POLITICAL SCIENCE 360 (1979). In *Los Angeles v. Lyons* (1983) the Burger Court ruled, five to four, that a man who had been subjected to a "choke hold" by police could sue the city for damages, but lacked standing to seek an injunction against this practice because there was no evidence that he might ever be choked again.

legal right and the group is "so numerous as to make it impractical to bring them all before the court." Before a class action can be prosecuted, the judge must determine that such a class exists and that the plaintiffs are members of the class.[25]

The purpose of the class action is to enable claims to be asserted by a large number of persons without formally bringing each person into court. The class action achieves economies of time, effort, and expense by the elimination of repetitious litigation and minimizes the possibility of inconsistent rulings involving common questions or related events.

The class suit has been widely employed by civil liberties, consumer, and environmental groups, and retaliatory legislation has been proposed in Congress to limit such suits. For example, President Nixon proposed in 1971 that consumer suits be allowed only after the Justice Department had successfully prosecuted merchants for deceptive practices. The Supreme Court has also taken some steps toward limiting class suits. *Zahn v. International Paper Co.* (1973) ruled that for a diversity suit to be maintained, every member of the class must have sustained $10,000 in damages. In *Eisen v. Carlisle & Jacquelin* (1974), brought on behalf of all odd-lot purchasers of stock on the New York Exchange over a four-year period, the Court held that the parties initiating a federal class action suit must notify, at their own expense, all other persons in the class.[26]

These decisions may reduce the number of class action suits brought in federal courts and the very large consumer-type suits, but they should have little impact on the smaller class actions that make up the majority of such suits. Likewise, the *Eisen* decision does not necessarily apply in states that permit class actions, of which California is the leader.

JUDICIAL SELF-RESTRAINT: SEPARATION OF POWERS

The Supreme Court operates constantly under the pressures imposed by the necessity of coexistence with its governmental colleagues in a separation of powers system. As a matter of prestige, it cannot allow itself to be put in a

---

[25]"Class Standing and the Class Representative," 94 HARVARD LAW REVIEW 1637 (1981). See "Developments in the Law: Class Actions," 89 HARVARD LAW REVIEW 1318 (1976).

[26]The Eisen rule does not apply to suits that seek only refunds or back pay. In the nation's largest class action consumer settlement, the Federal Department of Housing and Urban Development was ordered in 1974 to pay $60 million to 750,000 tenants for rent overcharges. In 1980 a federal judge accepted a class action suit by over 7,000 Vietnam veterans against the five chemical companies that had manufactured the chemical defoliant Agent Orange to which they had been exposed in Vietnam. But federal judges are showing more reluctance to recognize huge classes. In 1982 federal courts refused to accept suits by a nationwide class of women claiming injury by an intrauterine device, a class of 14 million tire owners seeking to sue a tire company, or all persons injured in a Kansas City hotel disaster (*The New York Times,* July 27, 1982).

position of subservience to the President or Congress, or to be made to look ineffective by handing down decrees that will not be enforced. But, by the same token, it seeks to reduce to a minimum the situations in which it seems to assert its superiority over Congress and the President. Because the judicial assumption of power to declare acts of Congress unconstitutional is its most striking claim of judicial superiority, the Supreme Court has sought in numerous ways to restrict its performance in this role.

In 1936, Justice Brandeis, concurring in *Ashwander v. Tennessee Valley Authority,* undertook to review the standards the Court had developed to avoid passing on constitutional questions. Among them were the following: (1) The Court will not anticipate a question of constitutional law in advance of the necessity of deciding it, nor is it the habit of the Court to decide questions of a constitutional nature unless absolutely necessary to a decision of the case. (2) The Court will not formulate a rule of constitutional law broader than is required by the precise facts to which it is to be applied. (3) The Court will not pass upon a constitutional question, although properly presented by the record, if there is also present some other ground upon which the case may be disposed of. Thus, if a case can be decided on either of two grounds, one involving a constitutional question, the other a question of statutory construction or general law, the Court will decide only the latter. (4) When the validity of an act of the Congress is drawn in question, and even if a serious doubt of constitutionality is raised, it is a cardinal principle that the Court will first ascertain whether a construction of the statute is fairly possible by which the question may be avoided. Illustrations of the application of these rules by the Court will be found in later chapters.

Turning to judicial-executive relations, respect for the President and a desire to avoid embarrassing clashes with executive authority have clearly been strong motivating factors in the Court's behavior. As Corwin says: "While the Court has sometimes rebuffed presidential pretensions, it has more often labored to rationalize them; but most of all it has sought on one pretext or other to keep its sickle out of this 'dread field.' " He goes on to point out that the tactical situation is such as to make successful challenge of the President somewhat more difficult than that of Congress, for "the Court can usually assert itself successfully against Congress by merely 'disallowing' its acts, [whereas] presidential exercises of power will generally have produced some change in the external world beyond ordinary judicial competence to efface."[27]

Marshall had been one of the first to recognize the judicial untouchability of the President operating in the executive field. So far as the President's "important political powers" were concerned, he said, the principle is that "in their exercise he is to use his own discretion, and is accountable only to his country in his political character, and to his own conscience." In

---

[27]Edward S. Corwin, *The President: Office and Powers,* 4th rev. ed. (New York: New York University Press, 1957), pp. 16, 25.

two important post-Civil War cases the Court ratified this doctrine and extended it to include even the President's duty to enforce the law. *Mississippi v. Johnson* (1867) was an action by Mississippi seeking to restrain President Andrew Johnson from enforcing certain Reconstruction acts on the ground of their alleged unconstitutionality. The state sought to minimize the seriousness of its request to the Court by contending that President Johnson in enforcing these laws was performing a "mere ministerial duty" requiring no exercise of discretion. The Court rejoined that the President's duty to see that the laws were faithfully executed was "purely executive and political," and went on:

> An attempt on the part of the judicial department of the government to enforce the performance of such duties by the President might be justly characterized, in the language of Chief Justice Marshall, as "an absurd and excessive extravagance." It is true that in the instance before us the interposition of the court is not sought to enforce action by the Executive under constitutional legislation, but to restrain such action under legislation alleged to be unconstitutional. But we are unable to perceive that this circumstance takes the case out of the general principles which forbid judicial interference with the exercise of Executive discretion.

A similar effort by Georgia to enjoin the secretary of war and the generals commanding the Georgia military district from enforcing the Reconstruction acts was likewise frustrated by the Court on the ground that they represented the executive authority of the government.[28] Judicial interposition in the President's conduct of foreign affairs is also generally forbidden to the Court by its own self-denying ordinances.[29]

Two major exceptions to the Supreme Court's policy of avoiding adjudication of presidential actions will be examined in Chapter 15. One is the famous *Steel Seizure* case in 1952, where the Court found President Truman's seizure of the steel mills to prevent a strike that would interfere with the flow of munitions to American troops in Korea to be unauthorized by statute and unjustified by inherent presidential powers. The second was *United States v. Nixon* (1974), involving the demand of the Watergate special prosecutor for the notorious White House tapes, where the Court gave priority to the obligation to provide a fair trial for the Watergate defendants over Nixon's claim of executive privilege.

The "Political Question" Doctrine

In a substantial number of instances, the Supreme Court has announced its refusal to decide a controversy because it involved a "political question."

---

[28]*Georgia v. Stanton* (1868).

[29]See the discussion in Chapter 16; also *Chicago & Southern Air Lines v. Waterman S. S. Corp.* (1948) and Rehnquist's opinion of *Goldwater v. Carter* (1979).

When this has occurred, considerations of potential conflict with the political branches of the government, such as have just been discussed, have usually been supplemented by professions of doubt as to judicial competence to handle the issues involved in particularly difficult enforcement problems. Significant statements of the political question doctrine as a limitation on judicial action have already been noted in *Luther v. Borden* (1849) and *Coleman v. Miller* (1939). Chief Justice Hughes said in the latter case that he would not attempt a definition of "the class of questions deemed to be political and not justiciable," but he did indicate that the two dominant considerations were "the appropriateness under our system of government of attributing finality to the action of the political departments, and also the lack of satisfactory criteria for a judicial determination."

As already noted, the political question doctrine was relied on by Justice Frankfurter in *Colegrove v. Green* (1946) as a rationalization for judicial refusal to correct population inequalities in congressional election districts. But Justice Brennan's opinion for the Court majority in *Baker v. Carr* (1962) limited the application of the doctrine to separation of powers situations. At present, then, the doctrine amounts to nothing more than a general self-imposed obligation on the Court to show appropriate deference to the President and Congress.

John P. Roche has attacked the political question doctrine as illogical and based on circular reasoning: "Political questions are matters not soluble by the judicial process; matters not soluble by the judicial process are political questions. As an early dictionary explained, violins are small cellos, and cellos are large violins."[30] It is Philippa Strum's opinion that while the political question doctrine is an "anachronism" on an activist Court, nevertheless it is likely to be "dusted off whenever the Court finds it necessary."[31]

Though not relying upon the political question doctrine, Jesse H. Choper has proposed an even more rationalized limitation on federal judicial involvement in separation of powers issues. In his view, federal courts should decline to decide all constitutional questions concerning the respective powers of Congress and the President.

The ultimate constitutional issues of whether executive action (or inaction) violates the prerogatives of Congress or whether legislative action (or inaction) transgresses the realm of the President should be held to be nonjusticiable; their final resolution to be remitted to the interplay of the national political process.[32]

[30]"Judicial Self-Restraint," 49 AMERICAN POLITICAL SCIENCE REVIEW 762–772 (1955).

[31]*The Supreme Court and "Political Questions": A Study in Judicial Evasion* (University: University of Alabama Press, 1974), p. 145. Justices Rehnquist and Powell debated the political question doctrine in *Goldwater v. Carter* (1979). See Chapter 16.

[32]Jesse H. Choper, *Judicial Review and the National Political Process* (Chicago: University of Chicago Press, 1980), p. 263.

Choper is concerned about the "fragile character" of judicial review and the possibility that the Supreme Court may exhaust its "institutional capital" by overuse of its powers. The courts should consequently allow the political process to settle the conflicts between the President and Congress and between the federal government and the states, leaving judicial review primarily to the protection of individual rights.

After the expansion of judicial review on the Warren Court, it was widely assumed that the Burger Court would be characterized by greater restraint and less innovation. Yet in 1972 the Burger Court held that capital punishment as then administered was unconstitutional, in 1973 it declared state criminal abortion laws invalid, and in 1974 its ruling in the Watergate tapes case made inevitable the first resignation of a President in American history. Subsequent terms have seen a continued high level of policy involvement.

While judicial activism has been much criticized, it is still generally assumed that the Supreme Court must be available to answer any constitutional question. Self-restraint counsels the Court to reach constitutional issues reluctantly and to be chary of disagreeing with legislatures or executives, whether national or state. But self-restraint is not the ultimate in judicial wisdom. The Court's primary obligation is not to avoid controversy. Its primary obligation is to bring all the judgment its members possess and the best wisdom that the times afford, to the interpretation of the basic rules propounded by the Constitution for the direction of a free society. The Supreme Court has a duty of self-restraint, but not to the point of denying to the nation the guidance on basic democratic problems that its unique situation equips it to provide.[33]

---

[33]Judicial activism is discussed from a variety of viewpoints in Stephen C. Halpern and Charles M. Lamb, eds., *Supreme Court Activism and Restraint* (Lexington, Mass.: Lexington Books, 1982).

9

Membership of Congress

The institutions and powers of the American Congress are provided for in the first article of the Constitution, which comprises in bulk somewhat over half the original document. The major considerations involved in the creation of a bicameral legislature have already been reviewed, as well as the principles that were to control the composition of the two houses. Our more detailed inquiry into the constitutional experience of Congress may begin with an examination of the provisions and practices relating to membership in the House of Representatives and Senate.

THE SENATE

The membership of the Senate, though not its size, is fixed by Article I, section 3, which provides for two senators from each state. Thus the size of the Senate is related directly to the number of states, and with the admission of new states it has grown from an original membership of twenty-six to its present one hundred. Article V guarantees that "no State, without its consent, shall be deprived of its equal suffrage in the Senate."

    The Constitution originally provided that senators would be chosen from each state by its legislature. This arrangement gave effect to the idea that the

Senate represented state governments rather than the people of the states. At first the legislatures were left entirely free to decide how they would select senators. In 1866, however, Congress did intervene to the extent of providing that if the two houses of a state legislature voting separately were unable to agree on a senator, they should meet in joint session and decide the matter by majority vote.

The movement for direct election of senators was motivated partly by the scandals and deadlocks that characterized legislative elections, and partly by the development of a more progressive tone in the country. Some states succeeded in taking the matter largely out of the hands of their legislatures by introducing a form of senatorial primary. Eventually the Seventeenth Amendment was adopted, becoming effective in 1913, and providing for the election of senators by direct popular vote.

APPORTIONMENT OF REPRESENTATIVES

Representation in the House is based on population. For this purpose Article I provided for an "enumeration," or census, to be made within three years after the first meeting of the Congress and to be repeated every ten years thereafter. In determining the basis for representation, all "free persons" and indentured servants were to be counted, plus "three-fifths of all other persons." This latter provision was a delicate method of referring to slaves, whom the slaveholding states wished to include in the electoral base, whereas the other states wanted them excluded, along with "Indians not taxed" (i.e., living in their tribal relationship). Until the first census was taken, Article I, section 2, alloted sixty-five seats to the respective states on the basis of a rough estimate of their populations. The number of representatives was not to exceed one for every 30,000 in the electoral base, but each state was to have at least one representative.

The only subsequent constitutional provision affecting representation in the House was made by the Fourteenth Amendment. The abolition of slavery by the Thirteenth Amendment knocked out the three-fifths compromise provision and automatically gave all blacks full weight for representation purposes. The Fourteenth Amendment recognized this change by language in section 2 apportioning representatives "among the several states according to their respective numbers, counting the whole number of persons in each State, excluding Indians not taxed."

Foreseeing the probable refusal to permit voting by blacks in the South, the Northern-dominated Congress provided in the same section for reduction in the representation of any state that denied to any of its adult male citizens the right to vote, except for participation in rebellion or other crime. In spite of long-continued and widespread denial of voting rights to blacks in Southern states, enforcement of this provision was never attempted, and it has been regarded as a dead letter in the Constitution.

The actual working out of the apportionment process depends not only upon the decennial census, but also upon subsequent adoption of a new apportionment plan that will give effect to the changes in the state population pattern. The Constitution provides no machinery for this purpose, but it is a task that obviously belongs to Congress. The general procedure was originally that Congress, within a year or two after the census results were available, would pass a reapportionment statute giving effect to the new population figures. Since no state ever liked to have its representation reduced, the total number of seats in the House was increased in every apportionment except one (1842), until it finally reached the figure of 435 under the 1911 statute.

Following the census of 1920, Congress for the first time found itself unable to agree on an apportionment plan, since the alternatives were either to reduce the representation of eleven states or again to incease the size of the House. This experience made it clear that there was no means of compelling Congress to perform its constitutional duty on apportionment. Finally in 1929 a permanent reapportionment statute was adopted for the 1930 census and all subsequent ones. This law freezes the size of the House at 435. After each census the Census Bureau prepares for the President a table showing the number of inhabitants of each state and the number of representatives to which each state would be entitled under two alternative methods of handling the population fractions left over after the state populations have been divided by the country-wide ratio. The President then transmits the information to Congress at the beginning of its next regular session. A reapportionment according to the method of computation employed in the previous apportionment then goes into effect unless within sixty days Congress itself enacts a different one.[1]

DISTRICTING FOR THE HOUSE

Fixing the number of representatives for each state is only the first part of the election process. It is still necessary to divide the states into election districts, unless the representatives are to be elected from the state at large, which was initially a fairly common practice. The districting responsibility is in general

---

[1]Following the 1980 census, charges were made of inaccuracy, particularly undercounting of minorities in the large cities. Federal judges in Detroit and New York ordered the Census Bureau to revise its figures to compensate for the alleged undercount in those cities, but the orders were reversed on appeal. Suits filed by Denver and Essex County, New Jersey, to compel the Census Bureau to disclose census data under the Freedom of Information Act were rejected by the Supreme Court in *Baldridge v. Shapiro* (1982). See "Demography and Distrust: Constitutional Issues of the Federal Census," 94 HARVARD LAW REVIEW 841 (1981). Apportionment standards are analyzed in Michel Balinski and H. Peyton Young, *Fair Representation: Meeting the Ideal of One Man, One Vote* (New Haven: Yale University Press, 1982).

left to the states, under the provision of Article I, section 4, that "the times, places and manner of holding elections for Senators and Representatives, shall be prescribed in each state by the legislature thereof."

However, the section goes on to provide that "the Congress may at any time by law make or alter such regulations." Under this authority Congress by the apportionment act of 1842 required every state entitled to more than one representative to be divided by its legislature into districts "composed of contiguous territory," each returning one member. The acts of 1901 and 1911 added a "compact" qualification for districts in an effort to limit the practice of gerrymandering.[2] But the 1929 act omitted any requirement for contiguous, compact, or even equal districts. In *Wood v. Broom* (1932) the Supreme Court held that this omission was intentional and had repealed the requirements of the previous laws. Consequently the Court could take no action to correct state redistricting acts setting up gerrymandered districts.

The Court initially held itself powerless also to remedy a state's failure to redistrict at all. The case of *Colegrove v. Green* (1946) presented the situation of Illinois, where the rural-dominated legislature refused after 1901 to revise the state's congressional districts because it would have been compelled to increase the proportion of seats going to Chicago. The Supreme Court refused to intervene on the ground that this was a matter for the "exclusive authority" of Congress. If the Supreme Court got involved it would, according to Justice Frankfurter, be entering a "political thicket." Moreover, the Court feared than any relief it could give would be negative; it could declare the existing system invalid, but could not draw new district lines, with the result that Illinois might be thrown into the forthcoming congressional elections, then only a few months away, with the necessity of electing all its House members at large.

This was a four to three decision, and the fourth vote for the majority was cast by Justice Rutledge, who did not agree with Frankfurter's general view that the courts had no responsibility over House districts, but who did favor judicial abstention in this case because he thought intervention just preceding the election would do more harm than good. The three dissenters— Justices Black, Douglas, and Murphy—contended that the failure to redistrict was "willful legislative discrimination" amounting to a denial of equal protection of the laws. Though judicial power to handle legislative districting issues was thus denied by only three members of the Court, the *Colegrove* decision was generally understood as establishing the principle of judicial nonintervention in legislative apportionments or electoral systems, and was cited as a precedent by the Court in refusing to review several subsequent state elec-

---

[2]Gerrymandering is the practice whereby the majority party in the state legislature draws district lines that will concentrate the strength of the opposition party into as few districts as possible and spread the strength of its own party over as many districts as possible. The usual result of gerrymandering is a number of odd-shaped districts.

tion cases.[3] But in 1960 the *Colegrove* rule came up for a new examination in *Gomillion v. Lightfoot,* an electoral-district controversy in which the Supreme Court did find that it could act. An Alabama state law had redefined the city boundaries of Tuskegee so as to place all but four or five of the city's black voters outside the city limits, without removing a single white voter or resident. The statute was unanimously declared unconstitutional by the Supreme Court.

While the *Gomillion* decision involved racial discrimination in violation of the Fifteenth Amendment, it helped to prepare the way for the more general attack on legislative malapportionment in *Baker v. Carr* (1962), already discussed in Chapter 4. In *Wesberry v. Sanders* (1964), Justice Black derived the principle of equal congressional districts from certain of Madison's statements at the Constitutional Convention and in *The Federalist,* and more specifically from the language in Article I about the choosing of representatives "by the people of the several States." It was the clear intention of the Convention, he asserted, to make "population . . . the basis of the House of Representatives." He summed up his position in this concluding paragraph:

> While it may not be possible to draw congressional districts with mathematical precision, that is no excuse for ignoring our Constitution's plain objective of making equal representation for equal numbers of people the fundamental goal for the House of Representatives. That is the high standard of justice and common sense which the Founders set for us.

Following *Wesberry,* the process of congressional redistricting went forward with remarkable speed. The principal problem has been gerrymandering with which, as already noted, the Court has seemed unable to deal.

TERMS

The two-year term for members of the House now seems fairly short, but it must be remembered that it was adopted at a time when democratic theory stressed the need for annual elections. In the Convention, Madison argued that a one-year term would be "almost consumed in preparing for and traveling to and from the seat of national business," and he favored a three-year term.

Proposals for extending the term to four years have often been made, most notably by President Johnson in 1966. Pointing to the accelerating volume of legislation, the increasingly complex problems, the longer sessions of Congress, and the increasing costs of campaigning, he urged a four-year term to attract better persons to the House, give them more time to develop an understanding of national problems, and free them from the pressures and costs of biennial campaigns.

[3]*South v. Peters* (1950); *MacDougall v. Green* (1948).

President Johnson's proposal called for representatives to be elected at the same time as the President, thus eliminating the midterm elections to the House that now provide some opportunity for public reaction to the administration in power. This feature was widely condemned even by those who favored the four-year term, and no action was taken.

The six-year term for senators is one of the major factors in the peculiar role that the Senate fills in the American system. Legally, the fact that only one-third of the seats fall vacant every two years gives the Senate the status of a "continuing body," compared with the House, which must reconstitute itself every two years.

QUALIFICATIONS

Article I lays down certain qualifications for senators and representatives as to age, citizenship, and residence. Senators must be thirty years of age, citizens of the United States for nine years, and inhabitants of the state from which they are elected. Representatives need be only twenty-five years old and citizens for seven years, but the residence requirement is the same. By custom representatives must reside not only in the state but in the district from which they are elected.

Members of Congress are disqualified for appointment to executive office by Article I, section 6, which provides: "No person holding any office under the United States, shall be a member of either house during his continuance in office." Thus to accept an executive appointment, members of Congress must resign their seats, and federal officials who are elected to Congress must resign their posts before they take their seats. Members of Congress, however, have been appointed on many occasions to represent the United States on international commissions and at diplomatic conferences. Such diplomatic assignments are not considered "offices" in the constitutional sense, being for specific, temporary purposes and carrying with them no extra compensation.[4]

A second disqualification affecting members of Congress is also stated in Article I, section 6: "No Senator or Representative shall, during the time for which he was elected, be appointed to any civil office under the authority of the United States, which shall have been created, or the emoluments whereof shall have been increased during such time." The purpose of this restriction seems to have been to prevent Congress from feathering the nests of its members by creating jobs to which they could be appointed, but it is a rather inept

---

[4]Many members of Congress hold commissions in the Armed Forces Reserves, and it has been objected that this biases them in passing on appropriations and other legislation for the military. In *Schlesinger v. Reservists Committee to Stop the War* (1974), a suit to have such membership ruled contrary to the incompatibility clause failed when the Supreme Court held that the plaintiffs lacked standing to raise the issue.

provision which has achieved no useful purpose on the few occasions it has been invoked.[5]

Each house is authorized by Article I, section, 5, to "be the judge of the elections, returns and qualifications of its own members."[6] The "qualifications," it has been established by *Powell v. McCormack* (1969), are those stated in the Constitution. In the Convention, Madison opposed a suggestion that Congress itself should have the power to set qualifications for its members, fearing it might be used by a stronger legislative faction to keep out "partizans of a weaker faction." In *The Federalist,* No. 60, Hamilton wrote that the qualifications of legislators were fixed by the Constitution, "and are unalterable by the legislature."

However, on several occasions both houses have in effect enforced additional qualifications by refusing to seat duly elected members who met the constitutional qualifications. The Test Oath Act of 1862 imposed as a qualification on all members of Congress (as well as other federal officials) the taking of an oath that they had not participated in rebellion against the United States.

Individual congressmen have been disqualified on several grounds. The House refused to seat a Utah polygamist in 1900. Victor L. Berger of Wisconsin, a Socialist, was refused his seat by the House in 1919 because of his conviction under the Espionage Act for opposing the war. His constituents reelected him, and he was again denied his seat. Before his election for a third time, his conviction was reversed by the Supreme Court, and the House then seated him. In the late 1920s the Senate refused to seat Frank L. Smith of Illinois and William S. Vare of Pennsylvania because of scandals in connection with their campaign funds.

In 1967 Adam Clayton Powell, black congressman from New York and then the most influential member of his race in a public position, was denied his seat in Congress. There was a judgment of criminal contempt outstanding against him, and his conduct as chairman of the House Education and Labor Committee had been bizarre and irregular. He than ran in a special election to fill the vacancy and was reelected with 86 percent of the vote. He also filed suit for an injunction ordering the House to seat him. Though he lost in the two lower courts, the Supreme Court in *Powell v. McCormack* (1969) ruled that the House had no power to deny a seat to a duly elected member who met the constitutional qualifications for the office. Previous instances of exclusion were held to have been unconstitutional. Congressional interest in pre-

---

[5]See *Ex parte Levitt* (1937).

[6]In *Roudebush v. Hartke* (1972), the Supreme Court held that this provision did not prohibit Indiana from conducting a recount of the 1970 election ballots for U.S. senator. After seven months of failure to decide which candidate had been elected to the Senate from New Hampshire in 1974, the Senate finally gave up the effort and declared the seat vacant, to be filled by a special election. See "The Power of a House of Congress to Judge the Qualifications of Its Members," 81 HARVARD LAW REVIEW 673 (1968).

serving its integrity, the Court said, could be safeguarded by censure or expulsion.[7]

EXPULSION AND CENSURE

Members of Congress are not subject to impeachment, not being regarded as "civil officers" of the United States. The Constitution does provide, however, that each house may expel its members by a two-thirds vote, or punish them for "disorderly behavior." Congress is the sole judge of the reasons for expulsion. The offense need not be indictable. In 1797 the Senate expelled William Blount for conduct that was not performed in his official capacity or during a session of the Senate or at the seat of government. The Supreme Court has recorded in a dictum its understanding that the expulsion power "extends to all cases where the offence is such as in the judgment of the Senate is inconsistent with the trust and duty of a member."[8]

When the Southern states seceded in 1861, their senators were not expelled. The Senate simply noted that the seats had "become vacant." However, two Missouri senators were subsequently expelled for acts against the Union. Formal censure proceedings have been brought against only four of its members in Senate history. Senator Joseph McCarthy was censured in 1954 for conduct "contrary to Senatorial traditions." In 1967 Senator Thomas J. Dodd was censured for conduct in connection with use of campaign funds, tending "to bring the Senate into dishonor and disrepute." In 1978 Rep. Charles D. Diggs, Jr., was convicted of padding his office payroll and accepting kickbacks. He subsequently accepted censure on condition that a House investigation be dropped—only the second instance of House censure in this century.

In 1978 and 1979 the FBI set up the so-called Abscam operation, which involved offering money to officials in return for legislative assistance to a fictitious wealthy Arab. Six members of the House and one senator accepted the money and were subsequently convicted. Senator Harrison A. Williams resigned from the Senate to avoid expulsion. Two convicted members of the House resigned, one was expelled, and three were defeated for reelection.[9]

---

[7] In *Bond v. Floyd* (1966), the Supreme Court ruled that the Georgia legislature had violated the First Amendment rights of Julian Bond by twice denying him the seat to which he had been elected because he had made public statements opposing the war in Vietnam and the draft.

[8] *In re Chapman* (1897).

[9] The procedure employed by the FBI in "targeting" certain members of Congress and offering them the opportunity to commit a crime was criticized as "entrapment." See Bennett L. Gershman, "Abscam, the Judiciary, and the Ethics of Entrapment," 91 *Yale Law Journal* 1565 (1982). However, the Supreme Court in *Lederer v. United States* (1983) refused to hear appeals of four convicted legislators. A Senate committee absolved the FBI of political persecution but criticized it for mismanaging the case (*The New York Times*, December 17, 1982).

THE FILLING OF VACANCIES

Vacancies may occur in either house of Congress by death, resignation, expulsion, or the acceptance of a disqualifying office. For senators, who were originally chosen by state legislatures, section 3 of Article 1 authorized temporary state executive appointments to fill vacancies occurring during recesses of the legislature. The Seventeenth Amendment superseded this provision with a general authorization to state governors to call a special election, but the amendment also provided "that the legislature of any state may empower the executive thereof to make temporary appointments until the people fill the vacancies by election as the legislature may direct."

In practice almost all states have authorized their governors to proceed on this basis. The result is that Senate vacancies are usually filled immediately by an appointee who serves until the next general election in his or her state, at which time a senator is elected for the remainder of the original term.

So far as the House is concerned, Article I, section 2, makes the following provision for special elections: "When vacancies happen in the representation from any state, the executive authority thereof shall issue writs of election to fill such vacancies." However, rather than incur the expense of a special election to fill out a term that may have only a few months to run, twenty-two states fill vacancies by some form of appointment process, and fourteen of those states give political parties control over the selection of a new legislator. Puerto Rico also had such a law, allowing a vacancy to be filled by the party of the legislator who previously held the seat. The Supreme Court upheld the Puerto Rico law in *Rodriguez v. Popular Democratic Party* (1982) against the contention that it violated the one-person, one-vote principle.

PRIVILEGES AND IMMUNITIES OF MEMBERS

Article I, section 6, provides in part: "The Senators and Representatives . . . shall in all cases, except treason, felony and breach of the peace, be privileged from arrest during their attendance at the session of their respective houses, and in going to and returning from the same; and for any speech or debate in either house, they shall not be questioned in any other place." Immunity from arrest during sessions of the legislature was one of the protections asserted by the English Parliament in its struggle with the Crown, and embodied in the English Bill of Rights. It is of comparatively minor significance in the American Constitution. The phrase, "treason, felony or breach of the peace" has been interpreted by the Court as withdrawing all criminal offenses from the scope of the privilege.[10] Thus the only area left for its operation is arrests

---

[10]*Williamson v. United States* (1908).

in civil suits, which were common when the Constitution was adopted, but are now seldom made. The immunity does not apply to service of process in either civil or criminal cases.[11]

Much more important is the freedom of speech guaranteed to members of Congress by the provision that they should not be questioned "in any other place" for any speech or debate.[12] The purpose of such legislative immunity is to prevent intimidation of legislators by the executive or holding them accountable before a possibly hostile judiciary. While legislators may abuse their freedom, the constitutional theory is that the public interest will be best served if they are free to criticize, investigate, or take unpopular positions. As Justice Frankfurter said in *Tenney v. Brandhove* (1951): "Legislators are immune from deterrents to the uninhibited discharge of their legislative duty, not for their private indulgence but for the public good. One must not expect uncommon courage even in legislators."

The "speech or debate" clause means that members of Congress cannot be sued for libel or slander or in any other way held legally accountable for statements made in their official capacity except by the House or Senate. Not only words spoken on the floor of Congress but written reports, resolutions offered, the act of voting, and all things "generally done in a session of the House by one of its members in relation to the business before it" are covered. This was the ruling in *Kilbourn v. Thompson* (1881), where the Court held that members of the House were not liable to suit for false imprisonment because they had instituted legislative proceedings as a result of which the plaintiff was arrested.

Gravel v. United States (1972) interpreted legislative "business" rather strictly, however. In an effort to give wider circulation to the classified Pentagon papers released by Daniel Ellsberg in 1971, Senator Gravel read portions of the papers into the record at a committee session and then arranged with a private firm for their publication. A federal grand jury sought to determine whether any violation of federal law had occurred and demanded Gravel's testimony as to how he secured the papers, which the Senator resisted as an infringement of his legislative immunity. He lost in the Supreme Court, the majority holding that private publication of the papers "was in no way essential to the deliberations of the House" and that Gravel's arrangements with the press "were not part and parcel of the legislative process." The dissenters thought this was "a far too narrow view of the legislative function" and that it was part of a legislator's duty "to inform the public about matters affecting the administration of government."

Legislative immunity may or may not extend to legislative aides or others who carry out legislative purposes. In *Gravel,* the Court held that for the pur-

[11]*Maryland v. United States* (1981) upheld a law exempting members of Congress from paying income taxes to the state where they live while attending sessions of Congress.

[12]Legislative immunity was extended to members of state legislatures in *Tenney v. Brandhove* (1951).

pose of construing the privilege, the Senator and his aide were to be "treated as one." But in *Dombrowski v. Eastland* (1967), the Court ruled that counsel for a Senate committee could be sued for conspiring to violate the civil rights of a group of activists, even though the senator who headed the committee could not be sued. The Court said that the immunity doctrine "is less absolute, although applicable, when applied to officers or employees of a legislative body, rather than to legislators themselves." To the same effect was *Doe v. McMillan* (1973), which held that no action could be taken against members of a congressional committee and its staff who prepared and issued a report containing libelous statements about named District of Columbia school-children; but the Court warned that the Government Printing Office or legislative personnel "who participate in distributions of actionable material beyond the reasonable bounds of the legislative task, enjoy no Speech or Debate Clause immunity." Likewise the theory of the *Powell* decision was that while members of the House could not be sued, action could be brought against employees of the House.

In two cases the Supreme Court has considered the relationship of the speech or debate clause to criminal prosecutions of members of Congress. In *United States v. Johnson* (1966), a congressman had made a speech on the floor of the House in return for payment by private interests, and was convicted of conspiring with these interests to defraud the United States. The government contended that the "speech or debate" clause forbade only prosecutions based on the content of a speech, such as libel actions, but not those founded on the antecedent unlawful conduct of accepting a bribe. However, the Supreme Court held unanimously that the purpose of the clause, growing as it did out of the long struggle of Parliament for independence from the king and his courts, was to protect legislators from "intimidation by the executive and accountability before a possibly hostile judiciary," and that consequently any judicial inquiry into the motivation of a congressman's speech was in violation of the Constitution.

But in *United States v. Brewster* (1972), the Court interpreted the *Johnson* ruling narrowly to cover only "legislative acts or the motivation for legislative acts." Brewster was charged with accepting a bribe to influence his vote on postal rate legislation. The Court majority concluded that taking a bribe "is not a legislative act," and the ruling was supported by broad policy statements about not immunizing members of Congress from criminal prosecution. The minority contended that immunity extends not only to a legislator's vote but "precludes all extracongressional scrutiny as to how and why he cast . . . his vote in a certain way." The constitutional intention, said Justice Brennan, was that members of Congress should be accountable "solely to a member's own House and never to the executive or judiciary."

Judicial interpretation of the speech and debate clause has continued to cause difficulties. In *Eastland v. U.S. Servicemen's Fund* (1975), the Court broadly construed the exemption to forbid judicial interference with congressional subpoenas that were "within the sphere of legitimate legislative activity." *United States v. Helstoski* (1979) ruled that prosecutors could not introduce any evidence of past legislative activities in the criminal trial of a present or former member of Congress.[13] But *Hutchinson v. Proxmire* (1979) held that the speech and debate clause does not protect against libel suits arising out of congressional press releases, newsletters, or telephone calls to executive agencies.[14]

---

[13]"Evidentiary Implications of the Speech or Debate Clause," 88 YALE LAW JOURNAL 1280 (1979).

[14]The speech or debate clause does not protect state legislators from federal prosecution; *United States v. Gillock* (1980). *Davis v. Passman* (1979) held that a suit by a congressional staff member alleging sex discrimination stated a proper cause of action, but expressed no opinion on whether the legislator's action was shielded by the speech or debate clause.

10

Legislative Powers and Procedure

The first words in the Constitution, following the Preamble, are: "All legislative powers herein granted shall be vested in a Congress of the United States." These grants cover a remarkable variety of powers. The strictly legislative or "lawmaking" role of Congress is exercised by the passing of statutes, which are of four general types: (1) public laws that formulate authoritative rules of conduct, substantive or procedural, applicable generally to all classes of persons or events specified in the statute; (2) private acts which apply to named individuals, usually for the purpose of adjusting claims against the government; (3) revenue acts that provide the government's funds; and (4) appropriation acts that make revenues available for expenditure for specified purposes.

In addition to its lawmaking role, Congress has a number of other functions. Its role in proposing amendments to the Constitution—what may be called its *constituent* power—has already been examined. The *electoral* functions that fall to the House and Senate if no candidate for the Presidency or vice-presidency secures a majority in the electoral college, and their joint role in canvassing the electoral vote, will be treated in connection with the discussion of the President, as will also the *executive* authority of the Senate in consenting to the ratification of treaties and giving advice and consent to appointments.

This chapter will discuss the general constitutional principles that have been developed and applied in determining the existence and extent of legislative power as well as the congressional impeachment power, the contempt power, the power to investigate, and the power of administrative supervision, concluding with a brief account of constitutional provisions as to legislative procedure.

PRINCIPLES OF LEGISLATIVE POWER

As the legislative organ of a government of delegated powers, Congress must be able to support any exercise of legislative authority as both authorized and not forbidden by the Constitution. There are two types of authorizations in Article I, section 8. The first seventeen clauses specifically enumerate a series of powers ranging all the way from punishment of counterfeiting to the declaration of war. Then clause 18 is a general authorization "to make all laws which shall be necessary and proper for carrying into execution the foregoing powers, and all other powers vested by this Constitution in the government of the United States, or in any department or officer thereof."

The relationship of this last clause, referred to in the ratification debates as "the sweeping clause," to the enumerated powers preceding it quickly became the subject of controversy between Federalists and Jeffersonians, between broad and strict constructionists. The issue was joined over Hamilton's plan for a national bank, as presented to the First Congress. There was no authorization in the Constitution for Congress to create a bank; in fact, the Convention had specifically refused to grant to Congress even a restricted power to create corporations. On President Washington's invitation, Hamilton and Jefferson submitted their respective views on whether he should sign the bill; they are classical expositions of divergent theories of constitutional interpretation.

Jefferson emphasized the "necessary" in the necessary and proper clause. Since all the enumerated powers could be carried out without a bank, it was not necessary and consequently not authorized. Hamilton, on the other hand, argued that the powers granted to Congress included the right to employ "all the *means* requisite and fairly applicable to the attainment of the *ends* of such power," unless they were specifically forbidden or immoral or contrary to the "essential ends of political society."

The Hamiltonian theory of a broad and liberal interpretation of congressional powers was successful in persuading Washington to sign the bank bill, and it has generally predominated in subsequent constitutional development. In 1819 Marshall gave the definitive statement of this view in the great case of *McCulloch v. Maryland*. Congressional authority to create a bank (the second Bank of the United States, incorporated by statute in 1816) was again the issue. Marshall found implied congressional power to establish a bank in its expressly granted powers to collect taxes, to borrow money, to regulate commerce, to declare and conduct a war; for "it may with great reason be contended, that a government, entrusted with such ample powers, on the due execution of which the happiness and prosperity of the nation so vitally depends, must also be entrusted with ample means for their execution." A corporation was such a means. "It is never the end for which other powers are exercised."

Marshall analyzed the necessary and proper clause at length. He rejected the strict Jeffersonian interpretation, which "would abridge, and almost annihilate this useful and necessary right of the legislature to select the means." His final, and famous, conclusion was:

> Let the end be legitimate, let it be within the scope of the constitution, and all means which are appropriate, which are plainly adapted to that end, which are not prohibited, but consistent with the letter and spirit of the constitution, are constitutional.

Perhaps the principal doctrinal challenge of a general character that federal legislative power has had to meet since *McCulloch v. Maryland* is dual federalism, already discussed in Chapter 4. Decisively rejected in *Darby Lumber,* dual federalism experienced a surprising revival in *National League of Cities v. Usery* (1976), which held that state sovereignty forbids congressional regulation of wages and hours of state and municipal employees. While *Usery* contradicted forty years of Supreme Court rulings, it corresponded to the constitutional views of the Reagan administration.

Notice should also be taken of a view that is at the opposite extreme from dual federalism. This is the theory put forward by James Wilson of Pennsylvania during the Convention period that "whenever an object occurs, to the direction of which no particular state is competent, the management of it must, of necessity, belong to the United States in Congress assembled."[1] This contention of sovereign and inherent power in Congress was repeated by counsel in the case of *Kansas v. Colorado* (1907). The steps in the argument were that complete legislative power must be vested either in the state or national governments; that the states are limited to internal affairs; and that "consequently all powers which are national in their scope must be found vested in Congress." The Court rejected this position as in violation of the Tenth Amendment, and held that powers of a national character not delegated to Congress were "reserved to the people of the United States."

In constitutional theory, then, Congress does not derive its authority from any doctrine of sovereign and inherent power. Delegation by the Constitution is the source of federal legislative authority. However, as the subsequent discussion of the commerce power in particular will indicate, Wilson's assertion

---

[1]James De Witt Andrews, *Works of James Wilson* (Chicago: Callaghan and Company, 1896), I: 558.

that Congress must have the power required to deal with national problems has gradually been accepted; and a broad doctrine of implied power, based on the necessary and proper clause, has been a supplemental source of great significance in equipping Congress with authority commensurate with its responsibilities.

DELEGATION OF LEGISLATIVE POWER

There is a Latin saw, *delegata potestas non potest delegari,* which may be translated as meaning that delegated power cannot be redelegated. The Supreme Court accepts this prohibition as applied to Congress. And yet delegation of legislative power is an absolute necessity of practical government and has been practiced from almost the beginning of the Republic. The Supreme Court has recognized this need. Chief Justice Taft once said that the extent and character of permissible delegation "must be fixed according to common sense and the inherent necessities of the governmental co-ordination."[2] The Court has thus been placed in a dilemma, which it has been able to resolve only by tortuous explanations and legal fictions that what is delegation in fact is not delegation in law.

The reasons why Congress must indulge in extensive delegation of legislative power are well known. The legislative machinery is ponderous. Members of Congress may succeed well enough in the task of formulating general policies, but lack the time and expert information needed to prescribe the specific methods for carrying out those policies. Moreover, a piece of legislation once enacted is extremely hard to amend, whereas the problems with which the legislation aims to deal may be constantly changing. These legislative limitations have become increasingly obvious with the expansion of governmental intervention into the regulation of the economy, and in emergency or wartime periods the pressure on Congress to authorize broad delegations of its powers to the executive is especially great. Finally, Congress sometimes uses the delegation technique when it realizes that a problem exists, but is uncertain how to handle it. By delegation the "hot potato" can be passed on to other hands.

Marshall was the first to rationalize a legislative delegation. In *Wayman v. Southard* (1825) he distinguished "important subjects, which must be entirely regulated by the legislature itself, from those of less interest, in which a general provision may be made, and power given to those who are to act under such general provisions to fill up the details." This suggestion that delegation may be employed only in dealing with less important subjects has proved completely untenable. On the other hand, the legal fiction that dele-

---

[2]*J. W. Hampton, Jr., & Co. v. United States* (1928). For a general discussion see Sotirios A. Barber, *The Constitution and the Delegation of Congressional Power* (Chicago: University of Chicago Press, 1975).

gation is merely a "filling up the details" of a statute has been a perennially useful one. In *United States v. Grimaud* (1911) the Court was confronted with a statute authorizing the secretary of agriculture to make rules and regulations with respect to grazing on national forest reservations, which it upheld on the ground that it was "impracticable" for Congress itself to adopt such regulations, covering as they did "local conditions."

Marshall's conception of "filling up the details" of course demands that there be an announced general legislative plan into which the details fit. Consequently the Court has consistently demanded that Congress supply standards to guide and control the acts of delegatees. But the Court has normally been willing to accept rather broad and general standards as meeting constitutional requirements—such as the standard that the Interstate Commerce Commission shall fix rates that are "just and reasonable"[3] or the standard that the Federal Communications Commission shall grant licenses to radio stations when it is in the "public convenience, interest or necessity" to do so.[4]

A special type of delegation is that made in so-called "contingent legislation." Here the delegation is not of power to make rules or fill in details; it is delegation of authority to determine facts or make predictions that are to have the effect of suspending legislation or, alternatively, of bringing it into effect. For example, the McKinley tariff of 1890 authorized the admission of certain articles free of duty but added that if a foreign country producing any of these commodities should impose upon American products duties found by the President to be "reciprocally unequal and unreasonable," then the President would have power to suspend the duty-free status of the foreign commodities, and duties set out in the act would become payable. The Supreme Court upheld this delegation in *Field v. Clark* (1892), declaring that the President's role was not that of a legislator but "mere agent of the lawmaking department to ascertain and declare the event upon which its expressed will was to take effect."[5]

Judicial acceptance of delegation was suspended for a brief period during the New Deal. In *Panama Refining Company v. Ryan* (1935), the Court invalidated a statute giving the President authority to exclude from interstate commerce oil produced in excess of state regulations. *Schechter Corp. v. United States* (1935) held that the National Industrial Recovery Act had gone too far in giving the President authority to promulgate codes of fair competition. One year later, in *Carter v. Carter Coal Co.* (1936), the Guffey Coal Act was invalidated, partly because it was held to delegate legislative power to set up a code of mandatory regulations for the coal industry. This time the delegation was doubly condemned since it was not even to government officials but to representatives of the coal industry.

[3]Upheld in *Interstate Commerce Commission v. Illinois Central R.R. Co.* (1910).
[4]Upheld in *Federal Radio Commission v. Nelson Brothers* (1933).
[5]See also *J. W. Hampton, Jr. & Co. v. United States* (1928).

No subsequent statutes have been invalidated on delegation grounds, though there have been numerous opportunities to do so.[6] The broad delegations of the Economic Stabilization Act of 1970, described by Arthur S. Miller as an "economic Gulf of Tonkin resolution" and under which Nixon ordered the wage-price freeze in 1971, never got to the Supreme Court.[7] The Bank Secrecy Act of 1970 requiring banks to maintain whatever reports and records the secretary of the treasury believed to be possessed of a "high degree of usefulness" in furthering criminal, tax, or regulatory investigations was upheld by the Court in *California Bankers Association v. Shultz* (1974). In *Dames & Moore v. Regan* (1981) the Court held that the International Emergency Economic Powers Act of 1977 delegated authority to President Carter broad enough to encompass his agreement with Iran on freeing the American hostages.[8]

THE IMPEACHMENT POWER

Congress functions in a quasi-judicial capacity in the process of impeachment, which is governed by Article II, section 4, providing a means of removing from office "the President, Vice-President and all civil officers of the United States" on conviction of "treason, bribery, or other high crimes and misdemeanors." Under Article I, the House of Representatives has "the sole power of impeachment." It exercises this power by passing, by majority vote, "articles of impeachment," which perform the function of an indictment.[9]

[6]Agricultural regulatory statutes were upheld in *Currin v. Wallace* (1939), *United States v. Rock Royal Co-op* (1939), and *Hood & Sons v. United States* (1939). The Fair Labor Standards Act was cleared in *Opp Cotton Mills v. Administrator of Wage and Hour Division* (1941). Wartime price and rent controls were upheld in *Yakus v. United States* (1944) and *Bowles v. Willingham* (1944). The Renegotiation Act of 1942 authorizing Department of Defense officials to renegotiate war contracts to avoid excessive profits was approved in *Lichter v. United States* (1948). A 1948 statute making not only present but also future state laws applicable to federal enclaves within states was accepted in *United States v. Sharpnack* (1958).

[7]In *Federal Energy Administration v. Algonquin SNG, Inc.* (1976), the Supreme Court held that the Trade Expansion Act of 1962, on the authority of which Presidents Nixon and Ford imposed license fees on imported oil for national security reasons, justified their actions and did not unconstitutionally delegate legislative power. In *National Cable Television Assn. V. United States* (1974), the Supreme Court, applying the principles of the *Schechter* and *Hampton* cases, construed narrowly a statutory grant of power to the FCC to impose fees for its services in order to avoid a delegation issue.

[8]For a principled attack on delegation by Congress, see Theodore J. Lowi, *The End of Liberalism* (New York: W. W. Norton & Co., Inc., 1969), Chapter 5.

[9]See Raoul Berger, *Impeachment; The Constitutional Problems* (Cambridge, Mass.: Harvard University Press, 1973); Charles L. Black, Jr., *Impeachment: A Handbook* (New Haven: Yale University Press, 1974); House Committee on the Judiciary, 93rd Cong., 1st sess., *Impeachment: Selected Materials* (Washington: Government Printing Office, 1973); "The Scope of the Power to Impeach," 84 YALE LAW JOURNAL 1316 (1975); John R. Labovitz, *Presidential Impeachment* (New Haven, Conn.: Yale University Press, 1978).

The Senate is given "the sole power to try all impeachments." At the trial the House acts as the prosecutor through an appointed committee of managers, and the Senate sits as a court. Its presiding officer is the vice-president, unless the impeachment proceedings involve the President, in which case the Chief Justice of the United States presides. This arrangement is specified by the Constitution in order to remove the vice-president from a situation where his own interests would be so directly involved. Though the Senate is under no obligation to follow all the technical rules of judicial procedure, it accords to the accused the principal rights provided in a law court, including benefit of counsel and compulsory process for obtaining witnesses. The Constitution requires a two-thirds vote of the senators present for conviction.

Impeachment is not applicable to military and naval officers, who are not "civil officers." Members of Congress likewise may not be subjected to impeachment. Though "civil," they are not "officers," for Article I, section 6, provides that "no person holding any office under the United States, shall be a member of either house during his continuance in office."

Impeachment actions have been brought against ten federal judges, four of whom were convicted, and two members of the executive branch. President Andrew Johnson in 1868 and Secretary of War Belknap in 1876. Neither was convicted. Belknap sought to evade trial by resigning his office, but the Senate heard the case anyway, thus establishing the proposition that a civil officer can be impeached after he has left office. In such a case the penalty of "removal from office" which the Constitution specifies as a possible judgment would be impossible, but the other stated penalty of "disqualification to hold and enjoy any office of honor, trust or profit under the United States" could of course still be applied. The Constitution forbids any punishment other than these two for an officer convicted on impeachment, but such a conviction is no bar to subsequent prosecution in the regular courts for any wrongful acts. Prosecution under these conditions would not constitute double jeopardy.

The failure of the Senate, by one vote, to convict Andrew Johnson, and the vindictive partisanship responsible for his impeachment, were generally thought to have so discredited the impeachment device as to preclude its future use against a President. Consequently, as the possible implication of Richard Nixon in the Watergate scandals began to emerge in early 1973, initial suggestions of impeachment were not taken seriously. But the sensational televised hearings conducted by the Senate Committee on Watergate, chaired by Senator Sam Ervin; the revelation that White House conversations had been taped; the firing by the President of Special Prosecutor Archibald Cox; and all the other shattering events of that period resulted in the undertaking of an impeachment inquiry by the House Judiciary Committee, culminating in public hearings in July, 1974.

Two major constitutional issues were raised by these proceedings. First was the meaning of "high crimes and misdemeanors." The phrase, which originated in English parliamentary impeachment practice, is subject to three possible interpretations. One is that offered by Gerald Ford when he was urging the impeachment of Justice Douglas in 1970:

> . . . an impeachable offense is whatever a majority of the House of Representatives considers it to be at a given moment in history; conviction results from whatever offense or offenses two-thirds of the other body considers to be sufficiently serious to require removal of the accused from office.[10]

The second position goes to the other extreme. It asserts that impeachment is limited to serious, indictable crimes. As President Nixon's attorneys argued in their presentation to the House Judiciary Committee: "Not only do the words inherently require a criminal offense, but one of a very serious nature, committed in one's governmental capacity."

The third position, which falls between the other two, is that violation of a criminal statute is not a prerequisite for impeachment so long as the offense is a serious one. The staff lawyers for the Judiciary Committee concluded:

> To confine impeachable conduct to indictable offenses may well be to set a standard so restrictive as not to reach conduct that might adversely affect the system of government. Some of the most grievous offenses against our constitutional form of government may not entail violations of the criminal law.

These issues were debated at length during the Nixon impeachment proceedings. The phrase "high crimes and misdemeanors" was shown clearly to have covered more than indictable offenses in English parliamentary practice. But the President's counsel contended that the broader English practice was a "seventeenth-century aberration . . . used as a weapon by Parliament to gain absolute political supremacy at the expense of the rule of law," an aberration that the framers had rejected.

The debates on impeachment at the Constitutional Convention and in the state ratifying conventions were minutely examined. It was noted that when "maladministration" was suggested as a ground for impeachment, Madison rejected it, saying that "so vague a term will be equivalent to a tenure during the pleasure of the Senate." On the other hand, Madison said that the President must be removable for "negligence or perfidy." Edward Rutledge regarded "abuse of trust" as impeachable. Prior American experience with impeachment was also examined. Judge Halsted L. Ritter had been convicted for bringing "his court into scandal and disrepute," hardly indictable offenses.

The majority of the House Judiciary Committee adopted the middle position, which was also clearly the view of the majority of the scholarly community. A minority on the Judiciary Committee, however, insisted that an

---

[10]Irving Brant, *Impeachment: Trials and Errors* (New York: Knopf, 1972), pp. 5–6.

indictable criminal offense must be proved; as the saying went, they insisted on finding a "smoking gun" at the scene of the crime.

With this division on the committee, it voted three articles of impeachment. The first, charging obstruction of justice by the President in the Watergate coverup, was adopted by a vote of twenty-seven to eleven, with six Republicans joining the twenty-one Democrats. The second alleged abuse of presidential power by misuse of the FBI, CIA, and other government agencies; it was adopted by a vote of twenty-eight to ten. The third, charging Nixon with contempt of Congress by refusing to obey the committee's subpoenas, was more narrowly passed by twenty-one to seventeen. The committee refused to approve two additional articles dealing with Nixon's taxes and the secret bombing of Cambodia.

Eventually the "smoking gun" was supplied by Nixon himself when on August 5, 1974, under pressure of the Supreme Court's unanimous opinion in *United States v. Nixon,* he released transcripts of tapes revealing that he had taken command of the coverup only six days after the Watergate break-in, and that he had kept this information from his staff and his counsel. With this damning evidence, the ten Republicans who had supported the President in the votes on all three articles came over to accept the obstruction of justice charge.

A second constitutional issue involved in the Nixon impeachment was whether there was any limit on the investigative powers of the House Judiciary Committee when conducting an impeachment inquiry. The argument for the committee was that the impeachment power of Congress is an intentional breach in the separation of powers principle, and that consequently Congress is the sole judge of what evidence is relevant and can compel its production by the executive. The President's position was that preservation of the integrity of the presidency required that he decide what evidence was relevant to the investigation, and in fact he refused to obey subpoenas for tapes demanded by the committee. However, the committee was able to secure some tapes that had been submitted to Judge Sirica; and on April 30, 1974, Nixon released to the public edited versions of a number of tapes.

The committee chose not to go to court in an attempt to secure additional tapes or to seek to hold the President in contempt for his refusal. Instead, as just noted, the refusal to honor the committee's subpoenas was made the basis for the third article of impeachment.

Finally, notice should be taken of Raoul Berger's contention that conviction by the Senate on impeachment would be subject to review by the Supreme Court.[11] The constitutional and practical objections to such review are so obvious as to make the proposition, as Charles L. Black said, an "absurdity."[12]

[11]Op. cit., Chapter 3.
[12]Op. cit., p. 54.

THE LEGISLATIVE CONTEMPT POWER

The power of the English Parliament to punish for contempt of its authority, developed in the centuries of struggle with the Crown, was so firmly established as an inherent legislative power that the framers thought it unnecessary to write it into the Constitution. Contempt proceedings may be brought for such offenses as disturbances in the legislative chamber,[13] for bribing members of Congress, or—most often—for refusing to testify before committees of Congress under subpoena.[14]

Either house can issue its own process, enforceable by its sergeant-at-arms, to cause the arrest and imprisonment of any person found to be in contempt of its authority. There need be no participation by the courts in this procedure. However, legislative imprisonment according to *Anderson v. Dunn* (1821) may not be extended beyond the session of the body in which the contempt occurred. Experience with legislative judgments of contempt showed that these proceedings tended to be lengthy and irregular, and the absence of the procedural protections of the law courts was generally disapproved.

Consequently, Congress passed an act in 1857 providing that any person refusing to appear before a committee or to answer questions pertinent to an inquiry should, in addition to existing pains and penalties, be deemed guilty of a misdemeanor and be subject to indictment and punishment. In operation this statute requires the following steps: First, the committee before which the alleged contempt occurred must recommend a contempt citation to the parent body, which must vote the citation. The congressional action is then transmitted to the United States attorney, who presents the matter to a federal grand jury. If an indictment is voted, the case is then tried in a federal district court, with appeal to the court of appeals and, if certiorari is granted, to the Supreme Court.

The 1857 act did not preclude the House or Senate from continuing to punish contempts directly, and in fact summary proceedings were common through the nineteenth century. As late as 1934 the Senate convicted a witness of contempt and sentenced him to ten days in jail.[15] Such convictions could be reviewed on habeas corpus, but obviously judicial proceedings under the

---

[13]*Groppi v. Leslie* (1972).

[14]Administrative officers of the government are not immune from the legislative contempt power. Contempt citations for refusal to turn over subpoenaed material against Secretary of State Henry Kissinger in 1975 and Secretary of the Interior James G. Watt in 1982 were narrowly averted. In 1974 G. Gordon Liddy, former Nixon aide, already in prison for Watergate involvement, was convicted of contempt for refusal to testify before a House committee. In 1983 the House voted to hold Anne Gorsuch, head of the Environmental Protection Agency, in contempt for refusal, as directed by the President, to turn over agency documents demanded by a House committee. The Department of Justice took the extraordinary position that it was not obligated to file the contempt suit but could make its own judgment as to whether the House committee was entitled to the documents. A federal judge rejected this contention, but ultimately a compromise was arranged and the contempt charge was dropped.

[15]Carl Beck, *Contempt of Congress* (New Orleans, La.: Hauser Press, 1959), p. 213.

1857 act provide much more satisfactory judicial protection of the rights of witnesses. Congress has now completely abandoned any use of its summary procedures.[16]

THE INVESTIGATORY POWER

One of the most significant legislative powers is not even mentioned in the Constitution. The power to investigate is an implied power, supplementary to the power to legislate, to appropriate, to pass on the elections and returns of members, and so on. It is an extremely broad power because the need of Congress for information is broad, but at the same time it is not free from constitutional limitations.[17]

The Supreme Court was initially inclined to construe the investigatory power rather narrowly. In *Kilbourn v. Thompson* (1881), three limiting principles were laid down: inquiries could not invade areas constitutionally reserved to the courts or the executive; they must deal with subjects on which Congress could validly legislate; and the resolutions setting up the investigations must suggest a congressional interest in legislating on that subject.

By 1927, however, the Court's attitude was much different. *McGrain v. Daugherty* arose out of a Senate inquiry into the connection of the Department of Justice with the Teapot Dome scandal. The brother of the attorney general sought to avoid testifying on the ground that the Senate was exceeding its proper legislative powers, but the Court disagreed. Granting that Congress had no "general power to inquire into private affairs," here the Senate was looking into the administration of the Department of Justice. Clearly this was a subject on which Congress could legislate and on which information would be useful.

Under this broad "proper legislative purpose" test, what constitutional limits remain on the power of legislative investigation? First, a witness is protected by the ban on self-incrimination in the Fifth Amendment. If he or she "takes the Fifth," claiming that the evidence being requested would tend to be incriminating, the witness can safely decline to answer further questions and is protected from possible prosecution for contempt. While a witness is

---

[16]The Ethics in Government Act of 1978 authorizes the Senate to enforce its subpoenas by securing a court order granting immunity and compelling the witness to testify on pain of imprisonment for contempt.

[17]On congressional investigations, see M. Nelson McGeary, *The Development of Congressional Investigative Power* (New York: Columbia University Press, 1940); "Congressional Investigations: A Symposium," 18 UNIVERSITY OF CHICAGO LAW REVIEW 421 (1951); William F. Buckley, ed., *The Committee and Its Critics* (Chicago: Henry Regnery Company, 1962); Walter Goodman, *The Committee: The Extraordinary Career of the House Committee on Un-American Activities* (New York: Farrar, Straus & Giroux, 1968); James Hamilton, *The Power to Probe: A Study of Congressional Investigations* (New York: Random House, 1976); Louis Fisher, *The Constitution Between Friends* (New York: St. Martin's Press, 1978), pp. 140-150.

not admitted to have conclusive power to decide that the answer to a question will tend to be incriminating, on the other hand the witness cannot be forced to reveal the reason for keeping silent; for if it were truly incriminating, then the constitutional protection would have been breached. Consequently a committee chairman must necessarily allow great latitude in permitting the witness to judge the consequences of answering a question.

The principal problem with a Fifth Amendment claim, of course, is that it almost invariably does great damage to the reputation of the claimant and may also be the basis for punitive actions of various kinds. Persons in both public and private employment have lost their jobs as a result of refusing to testify before congressional committees, and Senator Joseph McCarthy pilloried those appearing before his committee as "Fifth Amendment Communists."[18]

Two other defenses were recognized in *McGrain v. Daugherty*—a witness may refuse to answer when the committee is exceeding the bounds of its authorization[19] and when the questions are too vague or not pertinent to the matter under inquiry. A witness who refuses to answer on these grounds runs a considerable risk of being successfully prosecuted for contempt.

The First Amendment was offered as a defense for the first time by witnesses appearing before the House Committee on Un-American Activities in the 1940s. They contended that the committee was attempting by forced exposure of their views and activities to abridge their freedom of speech and association and to punish them for their opinions. This claim met with no success in the courts until 1957 when, in *Watkins v. United States,* Chief Justice Warren did recognize the relevancy of the First Amendment, saying, "Abuses of the investigative process may imperceptibly lead to abridgement of protected freedoms." He warned that "there is no congressional power to expose for the sake of exposure." However, he drew back from actually attributing such motives to committee members, and the Court's ruling did not rest on First Amendment grounds. It simply held that the authorization given to the Un-American Activities Committee by the House was unconstitutionally broad.[20]

The *Watkins* decision brought the Court under severe criticism, and various retaliatory measures were proposed in Congress.[21] Two years later the Court retreated from that ruling. *Barenblatt v. United States* (1959) involved a college professor who refused to answer questions by the Un-American Ac-

---

[18]See *Slochower v. Board of Education* (1956), *Lerner v. Casey* (1958), *Beilan v. Board of Education* (1958), and *Nelson v. County of Los Angeles* (1960).

[19]See *United States v. Rumely* (1953), and *Deutch v. United States* (1961).

[20]Similarly, in *Sweezy v. New Hampshire* (1957), the Court ruled that a state investigation directed to find "subversive persons" was invalid because of absence of legislative control over the investigation.

[21]See C. Herman Pritchett, *Congress versus the Supreme Court: 1957–1960* (Minneapolis: University of Minnesota Press, 1961), pp. 45–48.

tivities Committee about his alleged membership in the Communist party. In a five to four decision, Justice Harlan now ruled that the committee's mandate was not too vague. The "persuasive gloss of legislative history" showed that the House meant the committee to have "pervasive authority to investigate Communist activities." As for the First Amendment, Harlan agreed that "in a different context" the committee's tactics would raise constitutional issues "of the gravest character." But the Communist party was not "an ordinary political party." Congress had found its goal to be overthrow of the government by force and violence. Since self-preservation is "the ultimate value of any society," the balance between the competing private and public issues at stake had to be struck in favor of public needs.

Justice Black wrote the principal dissent in *Barenblatt.* He attacked Harlan's balancing principle, saying it simply gave Congress and the Court the right to ignore the First Amendment. Even if balancing was a proper method of determining the meaning of the First Amendment, Black thought it had been done badly here. Harlan had balanced the right of the government to preserve itself against Barenblatt's right not to talk. What should have been thrown into the scale was the interest of society, of the people as a whole "in being able to join organizations, advocate causes and make political 'mistakes' without later being subjected to governmental penalties for having dared to think for themselves." On the other side of the scale, the congressional interest was vastly overstated as "self-preservation," with no mention that the legislative power to make laws affecting speech and association is limited.

Black also denied that the committee had a "proper legislative purpose." The history of the committee had demonstrated that its "chief aim, purpose and practice" was the illegal one of trying witnesses and punishing them "by humiliation and public shame." He added: "The Court today fails to see what is here for all to see—that exposure and punishment is the aim of this Committee and the reason for its existence."[22]

The Supreme Court went even beyond *Barenblatt* in two 1961 decisions, *Wilkinson v. United States* and *Braden v. United States.* Wilkinson had gone to Atlanta to organize opposition sentiment against the Un-American Activities Committee, which was holding hearings there, and was subpoenaed to appear before the committee within one hour after he arrived in the city. Braden had circulated a petition asking the House not to permit the committee to conduct hearings in the South. He was required to go from Rhode Island to Atlanta for questioning about the petition. A five-judge majority supported the inquiry in both cases, Justice Stewart holding that *Barenblatt* had settled the major issues of congressional authorization and First Amendment relevance.

[22]On the same day as *Barenblatt,* the Court ruled in *Uphaus v. Wyman* (1959) that the director of a summer camp could be forced to supply the names of all guests at the camp over a two-year period to the New Hampshire attorney general, who had been authorized by the state legislature to find out whether there were any "subversive persons" in the state.

It thus appeared that the Court had recognized a practically unlimited power of congressional inquiry; but in fact, due partly to changes in the Court's membership, *Braden* and *Wilkinson* marked the end of an era. The Court now began to reverse almost every contempt conviction that came before it. These reversals were accomplished for the most part without challenging the scope of investigatory power or querying the motives of the investigators. They were achieved primarily by strict judicial enforcement of the rules on pertinency, authorization, and procedure plus strict observance of the constitutional standards governing criminal prosecutions.[23]

The Court did invoke the First Amendment in *Gibson v. Florida Legislative Investigation Committee* (1963), involving a state rather than a congressional committee. An officer of the NAACP had been ordered to appear before a legislative committee that wanted to find out whether any members of the association were Communists. Gibson's refusal to bring membership records with him to the hearing was upheld by the Court, on the ground that the state had failed to demonstrate the existence of any substantial relationship between the NAACP and subversive activities that would justify an invasion of its rights to privacy of association.[24]

The tangled case of *Stamler v. Willis* (1966, 1969) raised the interesting possibility that a congressional committee could be enjoined from conducting an investigation. In one of its typical proceedings, the Un-American Activities Committee subpoenaed Dr. Jeremiah Stamler for a hearing in Chicago. He declined to answer questions and filed suit to enjoin the hearing on a variety of constitutional grounds, which the court of appeals decided were substantial enough to require trial. In retaliation, the committee started contempt proceedings against Stamler. These two cases, inextricably bound together, moved up and down in the courts until 1973, when the government agreed to drop the contempt proceeding if Stamler would drop his civil suit.[25] This left unreversed the court of appeals holding that a witness called before a congressional committee could counterattack and bring suit questioning the legality of a committee operating in areas affecting First Amendment rights.

Two years later, however, the Supreme Court acted to counter this tactic. The Senate Judiciary Subcommittee on Internal Security, contending that an organization that operated coffeehouses near military bases and helped fi-

---

[23]Examples are *Deutch v. United States* (1961), *Yellin v. United States* (1963), *Russell v. United States* (1962), *Slagle v. Ohio* (1961), and *Gojack v. United States* (1966). An exception was *Hutcheson v. United States* (1962), where the Court upheld the contempt conviction of a labor union official.

[24]In *DeGregory v. Attorney General of New Hampshire* (1966), an inquiry of the same type as those involved in *Sweezy* and *Uphaus* was, like *Gibson,* held to have been justified by no "compelling state interest." The record was found to be "devoid of any evidence that there is any Communist movement in New Hampshire."

[25]Thomas P. Sullivan, Chester M. Kamin, and Arthur M. Sussman, "The Case against HUAC: The *Stamler* Litigation," 11 HARVARD CIVIL RIGHTS-CIVIL LIBERTIES LAW REVIEW 243 (1976).

nance underground newspapers was a subversive threat to the morale of the Armed Forces, subpoenaed its bank records. Since the subpoena was served on the bank, the organization could not contest its validity by defying it and so sought an injunction against the subcommittee, alleging that exposure of the identity of its contributors would dry up donations and violate the organization's First Amendment rights. The Court in *Eastland v. U.S. Servicemen's Fund* (1975), with only Douglas dissenting, ruled that the speech and debate clause forbade judicial interference with congressional subpoenas that were within the sphere of legitimate legislative activity.

By turning contempt-of-Congress prosecutions over to the federal courts, Congress has conceded that judges are to fix the constitutional limits of the investigatory power. Federal judges may naturally feel under some pressure, in handling such cases, to construe the investigatory power rather broadly and to defer to the congressional judgment as to what information is needed for the proper performance of legislative tasks. But the two houses of Congress, precisely because they have turned responsibility for contempt judgments over to the courts, tend to take less responsibility for supervising the work of their committees. When Congress itself tried contempts, the tendency was to consider the circumstances of committee action rather carefully, and often the parent body refused to support a committee contention that a contempt charge was warranted. But now that the courts make the final decision, committee requests for a contempt citation tend to be approved automatically.[26]

The congressional investigatory power has sometimes been shamefully abused, as by the house Committee on Un-American Activities[27] and Senator Joseph McCarthy. But, responsibly used, the power to investigate is a vital safeguard against both governmental and private wrongdoing, as was so forcefully demonstrated by the Senate Select Committee on Watergate in 1973 and the House Judiciary Committee impeachment investigation in 1974.

ADMINISTRATIVE SUPERVISION AND BUDGET PROCEDURES

The Constitution is not as clear as it might be in allocating responsibility for direction and control of the federal adminstrative establishment. To be sure,

---

[26]From 1950 to 1965 the House approved every one of the 129 contempt citations requested by the Un-American Activities Committee. Only 9 of these citations resulted in final conviction. (*The New York Times,* February 8, 1966). One of the rare instances when the House rejected a committee's contempt recommendation occurred in 1971, when the House Commerce Committee sought to hold the Columbia Broadcasting System in contempt for refusing to cooperate in its investigation of the CBS documentary *The Selling of the Pentagon.* The House voted down the citation by a vote of 226 to 181.

[27]The House Committee on Un-American Activities was abolished in 1974 and its duties and staff transferred to the House Judiciary Committee. In 1969 its name had been changed to the House Committee on Internal Security.

the President has the power to require the opinion in writing of the heads of departments on any subject relating to the duties of their offices, and he has the tremendous leverage that comes with the power to appoint. However, Congress also has a powerful constitutional basis from which to assert supervisory authority. The Senate's advice and consent must be secured for all important appointments. By its legislative authority, Congress can set up, abolish, or modify agencies, offices, and activities. Through its power to appropriate, it controls the nature and extent of administrative programs. Through the power to investigate, it can expose and embarrass officials or operations that are legislatively disapproved.

With these potentialities, it is not surprising that Congress and the President have often been in conflict as to their respective powers of supervision over the federal establishment. But the single-headed Presidency is in an incomparably better position to direct, supervise, and control the administrative branch than is the multitudinous Congress. Experience has been so clear on this point as to convince even Congress, which has gone far toward yielding to the executive two important functions that definitely belong to the legislature—control of finances and departmental organization.

The Budget and Accounting Act of 1921 established the principle and practice of the executive budget, under which the President is responsible for formulating and presenting to Congress a complete and detailed expenditure plan for the following fiscal year. Congress retains authority, in adopting the annual appropriations acts, to modify the executive budget in any way it sees fit. But as a practical matter, the congressional appropriations committees can give only a limited review to expenditure proposals totaling around 700 billion dollars annually.

A congressional appropriation has generally been regarded by the executive as merely an authorization to spend. Consequently Presidents have on numerous occasions, when Congress had appropriated funds for purposes or in amounts they did not approve, placed part of the appropriation in "reserves" or "impounded" some or all of the funds. Minor controversies between the two branches resulted, but it was not until President Nixon undertook to impound appropriated funds on a massive scale that the issue reached constitutional proportions. He not only made deep cuts in many domestic programs but even terminated congressionally approved operations by a total impoundment of their appropriations. The usual targets were appropriations for highway construction, housing, control of water pollution, and other environmental programs, and the usual justification was the need to hold down expenditures to control inflation. Intended recipients of these grants quickly took the administration to court and were generally successful in the lower courts.[28] Likewise, the first case to get to the Supreme Court, *Train v.*

---

[28]See "Impoundment of Funds," 86 HARVARD LAW REVIEW 1505 (1973); "Protecting the Fisc: Executive Impoundment and Congressional Power," 82 YALE LAW JOURNAL 1636 (1973); Louis Fisher, *Presidential Spending Power* (Princeton, N.J.: Princeton University Press, 1975), Chapters 7 and 8.

City of New York (1975), held that an appropriation act which specified that certain sums "shall be allotted" did not permit the administration to withhold any of these funds, even though elsewhere in the act the authorization was for sums "not to exceed" the specified amounts.

Congress, seeing in presidential impoundment a denial of its power to spend, make laws, and override vetoes, undertook to develop legislation that would drastically reduce the opportunity for presidential intervention. At the same time Congress recognized that its own slipshod fiscal practices, which never required appropriations to be considered in relation to anticipated revenues, had furnished the President with justification for his actions. Consequently a serious effort was made to reform congressional budget procedures, which resulted in the Congressional Budget and Impoundment Control Act of 1974. Briefly, the act creates budget committees in each house to oversee expenditures and revenues and establishes the Congressional Budget Office to give Congress the type of expertise now available to the President through the Office of Management and Budget. The act also provides procedures by which Congress can force the President to spend funds he has impounded.[29]

In 1981 President Reagan made an entirely unanticipated use of the new congressional machinery. The 1974 act had created a "reconciliation" mechanism by which Congress could alter existing programs to meet the goals set in its budget resolutions. Under pressure of the President and his director of the Office of Management and Budget, reconciliation was used by Republican congressional leaders in both houses as a vehicle to consolidate all budget cuts in one package, providing detailed instructions to the appropriations committees as to where and how much they should cut. A final conference committee involving more than 250 House and Senate conferees worked out the most comprehensive package of budget cuts in history, affecting hundreds of federal programs. The reconciliation procedure was used again in 1982, but met greater resistance, and in 1983 the President had to resort to veto threats as he lost control of the budget in the Democratic House and to a considerable degree in the Republican Senate.[30]

As for organization of the federal establishment, Congress has by a series of reorganization acts authorized the President to prepare reorganization plans for submission to Congress. These plans go into effect automatically unless vetoed by one or both houses of Congress within a specified time period, the provisions for veto varying somewhat in the different statutes. Numerous reorganization plans have been put into effect in this fashion, perhaps the most

[29]The President may propose to defer spending to a later time, and such action stands unless overturned by a resolution in either house of Congress. But if the President proposes to rescind the funds entirely, both the House and Senate must approve the action within forty-five days. If either chamber fails to approve, the President must release the funds at the end of the forty-five days. The *Chadha* decision may invalidate this provision.

[30]Article I, section 7, requires that "All bills for raising revenue shall originate in the House of Representatives." But the 1982 Tax Act originated in the Senate and the House did not consider it but sent it directly to conference. Nineteen members of Congress sued to invalidate the tax increase on that ground (*The New York Times,* November 20, 1982).

important being those establishing the Executive Office of the President in 1939; the Department of Health, Education, and Welfare in 1953; and the Office of Management and Budget in 1970. However, the Departments of Transportation (1976), Energy (1977), and Education (1979) were created directly by acts of Congress. President Reagan proposed abolishing both the Energy and Education Departments.

THE LEGISLATIVE VETO

The legislative veto, invented for use with reorganization plans, proved increasingly attractive to Congress as a device for controlling acts of the President and administrative regulations.[31] The Lend-Lease Act of 1941 contained a congressional veto provision, and during World War II Congress adopted the veto to check on the broad war-making power it had delegated to the administration. From 1932 to 1975 almost two hundred statutes carried some form of provision for the congressional veto; and during the Carter administration more than fifty statutes were passed with provisions allowing one or both houses, or a congressional committee, to approve or disapprove executive branch action. In 1982 the Senate passed a bill allowing a two-house veto, without presidential review, of most regulations issued by executive and independent agencies.

Every President since Hoover has contended that the legislative veto is an unconstitutional infringement on executive power, and President Carter announced in 1978 that he would not feel bound by congressional vetoes. As a candidate President Reagan supported the legislative veto, but after election his attorney general indicated he would consider legislative vetoes unconstitutional if they intruded on the presidential power to manage the executive branch.

The question was finally resolved in favor of the executive in *Immigration and Naturalization Service v. Chadha* (1983). At issue was a section of the Immigration and Nationality Act that allows a single house of Congress to overturn certain decisions made by the Service. In this instance an administrative decision to suspend deportation of an alien, approved by the attorney general, had been vetoed by the House of Representatives. In a six to one ruling, Chief Justice Burger held that the veto was essentially "legislative" in purpose and effect, and consequently was required by Article I to be made by both houses of Congress and presented to the President for approval or dis-

---

[31]On the legislative veto, see Joseph P. Harris, *Congressional Control of Administration* (Washington, D.C.: Brookings Institution, 1964); Harold H. Bruff and Ernest Gellhorn, "Congressional Control of Administrative Regulation: A Study of Legislative Vetoes," 90 HARVARD LAW REVIEW 1369 (1977); Louis Fisher, *The Constitution Between Friends* (New York: St. Martin's Press, 1978), pp. 99–108; Murray Dry, "The Congressional Veto and the Constitutional Separation of Powers," in Joseph M. Bissette and Jeffrey Tulis, eds., *The Presidency in the Constitutional Order* (Baton Rouge: Louisiana State University Press, 1981), pp. 195–233.

approval. Justice White, the lone dissenter, upheld the legislative veto, considering it "an important if not indispensable political invention" for securing the accountability of the executive and independent agencies. Justices Powell and Rehnquist would have decided the case on other grounds and did not reach the legislative veto issue.

The *Chadha* case was the Court's most far-reaching statement on executive-legislative relations in a century, and it impacted on more laws than the Court has struck down in its entire history. The War Powers Act was one of the most important statutes affected. Although immediate effect of the decision was, of course, to remove important limits on executive or administrative action, it was likely to stimulate Congress to provide other checks or to be more cautious in granting statutory powers to the executive.

Supplementing the legislative veto, individual members of Congress have increasingly resorted to the courts to challenge the validity of executive action and policies. In spite of barriers imposed by the issue of standing and the political question doctrine, a number of such suits have been heard, at least in the lower federal courts. Examples are *Holtzman v. Schlesinger* (1973), seeking to enjoin military action in Cambodia; *Kennedy v. Sampson* (1974), testing the presidential pocket veto; and *Environmental Protection Agency v. Mink* (1973), seeking information about proposed atomic underground explosions in Alaska.[32]

LEGISLATIVE PROCEDURE

The constitutional provisions governing legislative procedure require little explication. Article I, section 4, provides that "the Congress shall assemble at least once in every year, and such meeting shall be on the first Monday in December, unless they shall by law appoint a different day." Since by law each Congress terminated on March 4 of the odd years, the "lame duck" session beginning in December of the even years was automatically limited to about three months. This circumstance encouraged legislative filibustering— that is, the deliberate consumption of time in debate in order to prevent the adoption of legislation. Another objection to this time schedule was that congressmen elected in November of the even years did not normally begin service until the next December, thirteen months later. In the meantime, congressmen who had been defeated in November returned to Washington in December and sat in Congress until March 4. The term "lame duck" was applied to these congressmen who, repudiated at the polls, continued to represent their constituents through an entire congressional session. Lame duck Congresses were finally terminated when the Twentieth Amendment, sponsored by Senator Norris, was adopted in 1933. Under its provisions the terms of senators

---

[32]See "Congressional Access to the Federal Courts," 90 HARVARD LAW REVIEW 1632 (1977).

and representatives end at noon on January 3, and the two regular sessions of each Congress begin on that date.[33]

The President is authorized by Article III, section 3, to call "both houses or either of them" into special session. He may indicate in his call the reasons for bringing them into special session, but Congress is in no way limited thereby as to the subjects it can take up.

The presiding officer of the House is its Speaker. The majority party selects its candidate in caucus, and then supports him unanimously when the vote is taken. Unlike the Speaker in the English House of Commons, who must preserve strict impartiality, the American Speaker continues to be a partisan and is in fact the most powerful member of his party in the House. He has a vote and may on occasions take the floor to participate in debate.

The Senate has for its presiding officer the vice-president. When serving in this capacity the vice-president's title is President of the Senate. He has no vote except in case of a tie (Art. I, sec. 3). Giving the vice-president this function in the Senate is a clear defiance of the principle of separation of powers, but the framers apparently concluded that this was the only way to give the vice-president a useful occupation. The Constitution authorizes the Senate to choose a president pro tempore, to preside in the absence of the vice-president, "or when he shall exercise the office of President of the United States." As in the House, the majority party caucuses to agree on the president pro tempore, who is typically chosen on grounds of seniority.

The rules of the Senate guarantee unlimited debate, but in 1917 a rule was adopted permitting cloture to be imposed by a two-thirds vote of senators present and voting (sixty-seven if all senators were present). On that basis, cloture was imposed only seventeen times between 1917 and 1975. Repeated efforts of liberals to modify the cloture rule finally achieved a qualified success in 1975, by modification of the rule to require only sixty votes to limit debate. When cloture is voted, thereafter debate is limited to one hour for each senator. Experience soon proved that filibustering could be continued after cloture by time-consuming quorum calls and roll-call votes on minor amendments. In 1979 postcloture debate was limited to one hundred hours. But the chance to offer amendments is almost endless, and procedural matters, such as roll-calls, do not count against the time limit.

[33]However, after the 1982 election President Reagan called the Ninety-seventh Congress back into session, in which defeated members of Congress participated.

11

Taxation and Fiscal Powers

The broadest constitutional grant of fiscal authority to Congress is that in Article I, section 8, clause 1: "The Congress shall have power to lay and collect taxes, duties, imposts and excises, to pay the debts and provide for the common defence and general welfare of the United States."[1] The possession of adequate sources of revenue and broad authority to use public funds for public purposes are essential conditions for carrying on an effective government. Consequently the first rule for judicial review of tax statutes is that a heavy burden of proof lies on anyone who would challenge any congressional exercise of fiscal power. In almost every decision touching the constitutionality of federal taxation, the Supreme Court has stressed the breadth of congressional power and the limits of its own reviewing powers. "The power to tax involves the power to destroy," said Marshall in *McCulloch v. Maryland* (1819). The authorization of the Constitution "reaches every subject,"[2] it embraces "every conceivable power of taxation."[3] If the authority to tax is ex-

---

[1]The four terms used to describe governmental levies are broad enough to cover any known form of taxation. "Duties" and "imposts" are interchangeable terms describing customs dues levied on goods imported from foreign countries; "excises" refer to internal revenue taxes on the manufacture, sale, use, or transfer of property within the United States.

[2]*License Tax Cases* (1867).

[3]*Brushaber v. Union Pacific R. R.* (1916).

ercised oppressively, "the responsibility of the legislature is not to the courts, but to the people by whom its members are elected."[4] Yet in spite of such statements, the fiscal powers of Congress are not unlimited, and judicial review has a role to play here as elsewhere. The Constitution includes certain specific limitations on the taxing power, and to the interpretation of these restraints we turn first.

SPECIFIC LIMITATIONS ON THE TAXING POWER

Direct Taxation

Article I, section 9, states the following prohibition: "No capitation, or other direct, tax shall be laid, unless in proportion to the census or enumeration herein before directed to be taken." But what is a "direct" tax? When this provision was under discussion in the Constitutional Convention, King asked precisely this question, and according to Madison's notes, "No one answered." The Supreme Court was first called on to give an answer in *Hylton v. United States* (1976), when a tax on carriages was attacked as a direct tax, and consequently as one that had to be apportioned among the states on the basis of population. The Court unanimously upheld the tax as indirect and thus constitutional. The only taxes that the judges thought must clearly be regarded as direct were capitation and land taxes.

During the Civil War, Congress for the first time resorted to income taxation as a source of federal revenue, with no provision for apportionment. The Supreme Court upheld the law in *Springer v. United States* (1881) on the ground that an income tax was not a direct tax. Congress thus had every reason to be confident of its authority when in 1894 it levied a tax of 2 percent on incomes in excess of $4,000. This statute was a great victory for the progressive forces of the country, and a sectional triumph for the South and West over the industrial Northeast, where persons with such incomes were mostly located. Before the Supreme Court the tax was depicted as a "Communist march" against the rights of property, and the Court was told that it had never heard nor would ever hear a case more important than this.

The Court handed down two decisions in *Pollock v. Farmers' Loan & Trust Co.* (1895). In the first it ruled that, since taxes on real estate are direct taxes, taxes on the income or rents from real estate must similarly be considered direct. The decision also invalidated taxation of income from municipal bonds. However, the Court had been evenly divided, with one member absent because of illness, on the main issue as to whether taxes on the income from stocks and bonds were also to be regarded as direct. In the second decision the Court, by a vote of five to four, ruled that such taxation was direct, and went on to hold the entire tax invalid, thus reversing the law of the preceding

---

[4]*Veazie Bank v. Fenno* (1869).

hundred years. This surrender of the Court to entrenched wealth, in the same year that it refused to apply the Sherman Act against the sugar trust[5] and upheld the conviction of Eugene V. Debs for violating an injunction during the Pullman strike,[6] earned the Court a popular reputation as a tool of special privilege that was not dispelled for forty years.[7]

A campaign to "repeal" the Court's decision by adoption of a constitutional amendment got under way immediately, and was finally successful in 1913. The Sixteenth Amendment provides: "The Congress shall have power to lay and collect taxes on incomes, from whatever source derived, without apportionment among the several States, and without regard to any census or enumeration." Congress quickly took advantage of the amendment to pass an income tax law, which now provides the principal revenue source for the federal government.

The authorization to tax incomes "from whatever source derived" has been interpreted, in spite of its breadth, as subject to certain limitations. The Court in *Eisner v. Macomber* (1920) held that stock dividends could not be treated as taxable income. Stock dividends were not "income" but capital, and consequently still fell under the apportionment rule. In spite of vigorous subsequent attacks on *Eisner v. Macomber,* the principle of the decision has been maintained, though sometimes narrowed in application.

The Uniformity Requirement

After the affirmative grant of power in the first part of Article I, section 8, clause I, the clause concludes with this proviso: "But all duties, imposts and excises shall be uniform throughout the United States." Since all direct taxes must be apportioned among the states on the basis of population, it follows that only indirect taxes can be subject to the rule of uniformity. This requirement simply means that the thing or activity taxed must be taxed at the same rate throughout the United States. It is "geographical" uniformity that is demanded, the Court ruled in upholding the inheritance tax in *Knowlton v. Moore* (1900).[8]

Taxes on Exports

Article I, section 9, clause 5, provides: "No tax or duty shall be laid on articles exported from any state." This provision was demanded by the agrar-

---

[5]*United States v. E. C. Knight Co.* (1895).

[6]*In Re Debs* (1895).

[7]Perhaps not unaffected by the storm it had aroused, the Court refused to use the *Pollock* precedent to invalidate other questioned taxes. An inheritance tax was upheld as an excise in *Knowlton v. Moore* (1900); and in *Flint v. Stone Tracy Co.* (1911), the Court approved a 1909 statute levying a 1 percent tax on the net income of corporations.

[8]The 1979 windfall profits tax on decontrolled crude oil did not violate the uniformity requirement because of exemption of Alaska oilfields from the tax; *United States v. Ptasynski* (1983). See also *Florida v. Mellon* (1927).

ian states to ensure that the national government could not interfere with export of their surplus agricultural products.[9]

Not every tax bearing on exports is forbidden by this clause. A tax levied directly on the articles exported or on the right to export them is, of course, covered. So are stamp taxes on foreign bills of lading that evidence the exports, and stamp taxes on marine insurance policies covering the exports. But a tax on the income of a domestic corporation engaged in the export business is not an export tax. Nor is a general tax laid on all property equally, including goods intended for export, unconstitutional if it is not levied on goods in the actual course of exportation or because of their intended exportation.

TAXATION FOR NONREVENUE PURPOSES

In addition to these specifically stated limits on the federal taxing power, the Supreme Court has found certain implied restrictions that derive from the inherent nature of the federal system. One major constitutional issue has grown out of congressional efforts to use the taxing power for purposes that are primarily regulatory, and that result in the raising of comparatively little revenue, or sometimes none at all. Does this mixture of motives invalidate a tax statute? Must the taxing power be limited to revenue purposes only? The Supreme Court has not thought so, except in a very few instances and under quite unusual circumstances.

The protective tariff is a clear case of using taxation for goals other than the raising of revenue. The first tariff law was passed in 1789, but the Supreme Court had no occasion to pass on the constitutionality of this form of taxation until 1928. Then, in *J. W. Hampton, Jr., & Co. v. United States,* the Court was able to cite in its support some 140 years of practice and the fact that it does bring in revenue. "So long as the motive of Congress and the effect of its legislative action are to secure revenue for the benefit of the general government, the existence of other motives in the selection of the subjects of taxes can not invalidate Congressional action," wrote Chief Justice Taft.

Other regulatory or prohibitory taxes have come before the Court with less impressive genealogy but have been no less firmly upheld. Two types of rationalization can be distinguished in the Court's approach to these problems. The first sustains the questioned tax on the ground that the taxing power is being employed to help enforce another of the federal government's specifically granted powers. In this posture the constitutional case for the tax is strengthened by its auxiliary relationship to an admittedly valid federal purpose. Thus in *Veazie Bank v. Fenno* (1869), the Court upheld a 10 percent tax on state bank notes, the admitted purpose of which was to drive them out of

---

[9]Conversely, the states, by Art. I, sec. 10, clause 2, are forbidden, without the consent of Congress, to lay imposts or duties on imports or exports, except what may be absolutely necessary to enforce their inspection laws.

existence and leave the field to the notes of the newly authorized national banks. The Court regarded this tax as justified by congressional interest in a sound and uniform currency.[10]

Regulatory or prohibitory taxes have also been upheld, however, even when there was no relationship to other powers of Congress, and where they had to stand or fall on their own merits. In this situation the Supreme Court's reasoning has typically stressed the impropriety of any judicial questioning of the motives of Congress. The classic case is *McCray v. United States* (1904), which involved an act of Congress levying a tax of 10 cents per pound on oleomargarine artificially colored yellow to look like butter, and only ¼ cent per pound on uncolored margarine. There could be no doubt that the statute was adopted at the behest of the dairy industry to handicap the sale of a competitive product. But the Court denied that "the motives or purposes of Congress are open to judicial inquiry in considering the power of that body" to enact legislation. The statute was on its face an excise tax, and so it followed that it was within the power of Congress.

The principle of the *McCray* case was again endorsed in *United States v. Doremus* (1919), where Congress used a small tax requirement to compel the registration of persons engaged in the narcotics trade; but four justices dissented on the ground that the statute was a bold attempt to exercise police power reserved to the states.

The *Doremus* minority position won control of the Court three years later in *Bailey v. Drexel Furniture Co.* (1922), also known as the *Child Labor Tax Case*. This decision invalidated the Federal Child Labor Tax Act, passed in 1919 to replace the 1916 Child Labor Act based on the commerce clause, which the Supreme Court had held unconstitutional in *Hammer v. Dagenhart* (1918). The clumsily drafted 1919 law levied a tax of 10 percent on the annual net profits of businesses which at any time during the year employed children in violation of the standards prescribed in the act. The Court, while denying that it had any right or desire to inquire into congressional motives, concluded that this "so-called tax" revealed on its face that it was not a revenue measure, but rather a penalty to regulate child labor. Similarly in *United States v. Constantine* (1935), a grossly disproportional federal excise tax, amounting to $1,000, imposed only on retail liquor dealers carrying on business in violation of local law, was declared unconstitutional.

It is not easy for the Court to arrive at such conclusions, for they necessarily involve a finding that Congress has been guilty of improper motives and has used a constitutional subterfuge to accomplish ends that the Constitution forbids. Moreover, the contention that the taxing power of Congress is limited by the regulatory powers reserved to the states by the Tenth Amendment derives from the same dual federalism reasoning embodied in the dis-

---

[10]Other decisions made on similar reasoning were the *Head Money Cases* (1884) and *Sunshine Anthracite Coal Co. v. Adkins* (1940).

credited case of *Hammer v. Dagenhart* (1918). Although the Court abandoned dual federalism in interpreting the federal commerce power and specifically overruled *Hammer v. Dagenhart* in *United States v. Darby Lumber Co.* (1941), some members of the Court illogically continued to apply the doctrine against the federal taxing power.

The principal case is *United States v. Kahriger* (1953), where the Court upheld the challenged tax but both majority and minority used dual federalism reasoning. Following the Kefauver nationwide investigation into gambling and racketeering in 1950, Congress levied a tax on persons engaged in the business of accepting wagers and required that they register with the Collector of Internal Revenue. One of the charges against the tax was that it infringed on the police powers of the states. Justice Reed for the majority thought this was a relevant issue and noted that the legislative history indicated a congressional motive to suppress gambling, but finally upheld the statute on the ground that the Court could intervene only if there were provisions in the act "extraneous to any tax need." Justice Frankfurter's dissent, condemning the tax by a rationale straight out of *Hammer v. Dagenhart,* argued that "when oblique use is made of the taxing power as to matters which substantively are not within the powers delegated to Congress, the Court cannot shut its eyes to what is obviously, because designedly, an attempt to control conduct which the Constitution left to the responsibility of the States, merely because Congress wrapped the legislation in the verbal cellophane of a revenue measure."[11]

Justices Black and Douglas dissented in *Kahriger* on the ground that requiring a person to register and confess that he was engaged in the illegal business of gambling amounted to self-incrimination contrary to the Fifth Amendment. Justice Reed sought to counter the rather obvious logic of this position by contending that the privilege against self-incrimination "has relation only to past acts," whereas the wagering tax was assessed on "the business of wagering in the future." Fifteen years later, in *Marchetti v. United States* (1968) and *Grosso v. United States* (1968), the Court with only one dissent overruled *Kahriger* and voided the tax on self-incrimination grounds.[12]

INTERGOVERNMENTAL TAX IMMUNITY

A second major implied limitation on congressional power to tax is the immunity to federal taxation of state governments, their property, and activities. This immunity rule rests on no specific language of the Constitution. Rather

[11]See also *Sonzinsky v. United States* (1937), where the Court upheld a license tax on manufacturers of, or dealers in, firearms likely to be used in criminal activities, such as sawed-off shotguns and machine guns, but only because the tax was not attended by any "offensive regulation."

[12]Similarly, taxes on unregistered firearms and a marijuana transfer tax were held to violate the Fifth Amendment in *Haynes v. United States* (1968) and *Leary v. United States* (1969).

it is a judicially constructed doctrine, based on certain assumptions by the Supreme Court about the conditions for successful operation of a federal system.

The immunity doctrine was first developed by the Supreme Court, in the famous case of *McCulloch v. Maryland* (1819), to protect *federal* activities from *state* taxation. The Bank of the United States, incorporated by Congress in 1816, had a branch in Maryland. The bank was politically unpopular; and in 1818 the state legislature imposed a tax on all banks in the state not chartered by the state legislature, which McCulloch, cashier of the branch bank, refused to pay. Marshall upheld the bank's position. After a notable argument demonstrating the power of Congress to incorporate the bank, which is discussed in Chapter 10, he went on to consider the state's claim to taxing power. The ruling principle, he began, is "that the constitution and the laws made in pursuance thereof are supreme; that they control the constitution and laws of the respective States, and cannot be controlled by them." From this axiom Marshall deduced three corollaries: "1. That a power to create implies a power to preserve. 2. That a power to destroy, if wielded by a different hand, is hostile to, and incompatible with, these powers to create and to preserve. 3. That where this repugnancy exists, that authority which is supreme must control, not yield, to that over which it is supreme." Since the power to tax is, in Marshall's words, "the power to destroy," it followed that the Maryland tax was unconstitutional.[13]

State immunity from federal taxation was first asserted by the Court in *Collector v. Day* (1871), where the salary of a Massachusetts judge was declared to be immune from the Civil War federal income tax. Justice Nelson grounded the Court's holding directly on the *McCulloch* and *Dobbins* precedents, saying: "If the means and instrumentalities employed by [the federal] government to carry into operation the powers granted to it are, necessarily, and, for the sake of self-preservation, exempt from taxation by the States, why are not those of the States depending upon their reserved powers, for like reasons, equally exempt from Federal taxation?"

Only Justice Bradley pointed to the obvious flaw in this reasoning. State taxation of the instruments of the federal government is a very different thing from federal taxation of the instruments of a state government. State taxation "involves an interference with the powers of a government in which other States and their citizens are equally interested with the State which imposes the taxation." But when Congress levies a tax affecting the states, every state has a voice in the decision through its representatives, and so the states are actually consenting to their own taxation. There is thus a political check on possible abuse of the federal taxing power against the states, whereas a state

---

[13]The *McCulloch* principle was followed in *Osborn v. Bank of the United States* (1824). *Weston v. Charleston* (1829), and *Dobbins v. Erie County* (1842), the latter case holding that a state had no power to tax the office, or the emoluments of the office, of a federal officer.

legislature is subject to no such sense of restraint in levying a tax whose incidence is nationwide.

The doctrine of *Collector v. Day* was continued and enlarged in *Pollock v. Farmers' Loan & Trust Co.* (1895), which exempted from federal taxation state and local bonds and the interest therefrom. Then, in the 1920s, a conservative Court carried the immunity doctrine to ridiculous extremes. In *Gillespie v. Oklahoma* (1922) a state tax applied to income accruing to the lessee of some Indian oil lands was held invalid by a five to four vote, the majority reasoning that the lessee was an instrumentality of the United States used by the government "in carrying out duties to the Indians." Another five to four decision in *Panhandle Oil Co. v. Mississippi* (1928) invalidated a state gasoline tax collected on gasoline sold to the federal government. Still another five to four decision, *Long v. Rockwood* (1928), held it unconstitutional for a state to tax royalties received from a patent granted by the United States, on the theory that taxing royalties from federal patents would interfere with federal efforts to promote science and invention.

The Court returned to more sober views in the 1930s. The extensions of the immunity principle had rested on the thinnest kind of a Court majority, and represented an extreme view of what constituted a "burden" on government operations. The basis for reversing these decisions had been laid by the dissenting opinions that Justice Holmes and Brandeis, later joined by Stone, had written. It was Holmes who effectively disposed of Marshall's dictum when he rejoined in his *Panhandle* dissent: "The power to tax is not the power to destroy while this Court sits." Holmes left the Court in 1932, and Brandeis early in 1939, so that the major task of translating the minority view of the preceding decade into the majority position of the Roosevelt Court fell to Stone. He had consistently argued that immunity from intergovernmental taxation was not to be supported by merely theoretical conceptions of interference with the functions of government. He demanded that any burdens alleged to result be proved by economic data.

Fox Film Corporation v. Doyal (1932) overruled *Long v. Rockwood,* decided only four years earlier. *Helvering v. Mountain Producers Corporation* (1983) overruled *Gillespie v. Oklahoma,* restoring the right to tax oil company income from leased school lands. Next, the long-standing reciprocal exemption of state and federal employees from taxation on their income fell. *Helvering v. Gerhardt* (1938) ruled that immunity from federal taxation should not be allowed beyond that vitally necessary for the continued existence of the states. A nondiscriminatory tax on the net income of state employees, concluded Justice Stone for the Court, could not possibly obstruct the performance of state functions.[14]

---

[14]Immunity of federal employees from state taxation was denied in *Graves v. O'Keefe* (1939). The decision specifically overruled *Collector v. Day.*

State activities not considered essential to the preservation of state government had never enjoyed tax immunity. The Court had first ruled to this effect in *South Carolina v. United States* (1905), where a state-owned liquor monopoly had been held subject to federal internal revenue taxes. This position was restated in *New York v. United States* (1946), upholding federal taxation on the sale of mineral water bottled by the state of New York at Saratoga Springs.

The immunity doctrine is thus no longer a substantial limitation on the congressional taxing power. Of course Congress cannot levy a property tax on a state capitol building, or a stamp tax on writs served by state courts, or any other tax that falls directly on an essential state activity. But of the taxes thus prohibited, the only one of practical importance is the tax on income from state and municipal bonds.[15] Even here, it seems not unlikely that the Court would support Congress if it ever took the initiative in subjecting income from these bonds to the federal income tax.

The same principles now confine federal exemption from state taxation to the "possessions, institutions, and activities of the Federal Government itself."[16] When a state tax falls on a party who is in contractual relationship with the government, the tax is valid, even if it is clear that the tax will be passed on to the government or proportionately increase its costs.[17]

More difficult problems arise when a private party is utilizing government property in manufacture of materials for the government, as often happens on defense contracts. The general distinction here is that the state may not levy a *property* tax on such property, even though it is in private hands and the tax is to be collected from the private taxpayer,[18] but that it may levy a *privilege* tax on the activities of such persons, even though these activities involve the use of government property, and the value or amount of such property is the partial or exclusive basis for measurement of the tax.[19]

---

[15]See *Commissioner of Internal Revenue v. Shamberg's Estate* (1945).

[16]*United States v. Allegheny County* (1944). In *Department of Employment v. United States* (1966) the Court held that the American Red Cross is an instrumentality of the United States, for purposes of immunity from state taxation, and that Congress had not waived that immunity. In *United States v. Tax Commission of Mississippi* (1975), the Court held unconstitutional a tax regulation that operated by means of a suppliers' markup to require military installations in Mississippi to pay the equivalent of a state sales tax on liquor sold by the installation.

[17]See *Alabama v. King & Boozer* (1941) and *James v. Dravo Contracting Co.* (1937). *United States v. New Mexico* (1982) held that a contractor managing government atomic laboratories and meeting costs by payment from federal funds was subject to the state gross receipts tax. But states may not extend the sales tax to equipment leased to the federal government; *California State Board of Equalization v. United States* (1982).

[18]*United States v. Allegheny County* (1944).

[19]*United States and Borg Warner Corp. v. City of Detroit* (1958); *United States v. Township of Muskegon* (1958); *City of Detroit v. Murray Corp.* (1958).

THE POWER TO SPEND

Revenues are raised by taxation in order to be spent for public purposes. What are the constitutional limitations on the spending power? The basic principle of legislative control over the purse, established by the British Parliament after a long struggle with the Crown, is safeguarded by the provision in Article I, section 9, that "No money shall be drawn from the Treasury, but in consequence of appropriations made by law."[20] But are there any constitutional limits upon the purposes for which Congress may appropriate federal funds? Clearly Congress can spend money to achieve any of the purposes delegated to it by the Constitution, such as regulating commerce among the states or taking the census. But can reliance also be placed upon the rather enigmatic language of the taxing clause, which speaks of paying the debts and providing for "the common defence and general welfare"?

Spending and the General Welfare

On occasions it has been urged that the general welfare clause is an independent grant of legislative power to the federal government, quite unrelated to the preceding clause of the same sentence which deals with taxation. In other words, this argument treats the comma after "excises" as though it were a semicolon (as in fact it was up until practically the end of the Constitutional Convention). This position has never been authoritatively accepted. Story contended in his *Commentaries* that adoption of this view would have the tremendous result of transforming the federal government from one of delegated powers into one "of general and unlimited powers."

Rejection of this independent status for the general welfare clause leaves it with what can be called a "purposive" function. However, two purposive theories have been put forward, identified with Madison and Hamilton. Madison asserted that the phrase, "common defence and general welfare," was nothing more than a summary of all the specifically enumerated powers in the subsequent clauses of Article I, section 8. In No. 41 of *The Federalist* he wrote: "Nothing is more natural nor common, than first to use a general phrase, and then to explain and qualify it by a recital of particulars." So Congress could spend only for the express functions stated elsewhere in the Constitution. Hamilton, on the other hand, contended that the general welfare clause conferred a power separate and distinct from the enumerated powers, and that Congress consequently had a substantive power to tax and to appropriate, limited only by the requirement of furthering the general welfare of the United States.

The case of *United States v. Butler* (1936) gave the Court an opportunity to settle the argument that Madison and Hamilton had begun. The Agricul-

---

[20]See "The CIA's Secret Funding and the Constitution," 84 YALE LAW JOURNAL 608 (1975).

tural Adjustment Act of 1933 provided for federal payments to farmers who would cooperate in the government's program of price stabilization through production control. The money paid the farmers was to come from processing taxes on agricultural commodities which were authorized by the same statute. Butler challenged the tax, not as a tax (for it was clearly legal) but as a means of providing money for a program of agricultural production control, which he alleged to be an unconstitutional invasion of the powers of the states—in short, "as a step in an unauthorized plan." The Court ratified this stratagem by ruling that the tax and the spending were in fact "parts of a single scheme."

In *Butler* the Court decided that Hamilton was right: the general welfare clause meant that congressional power to spend was "not limited by the direct grants of legislative power found in the Constitution." The only limitation was that taxing and spending, in order to meet the general welfare standard, would have to be on "matters of national, as distinguished from local, welfare."

This was an important victory for the spending power, but the Court immediately proceeded to make it a hollow one by transferring the argument to an entirely new issue. Whether the spending was for national rather than local welfare was of no importance, Justice Roberts concluded for the *Butler* majority, since, as a statutory plan to regulate and control agricultural production, the act invaded the reserved rights of the states and was consequently invalid under the Tenth Amendment. Congress could not "under the pretext of the exertion of powers which are granted" seek to accomplish "a prohibited end."

The *Butler* decision was little more than a nine-day wonder. As a barrier to federal agricultural regulation it was soon bypassed as the type of program it condemned was reenacted by Congress under the commerce power and upheld by a more cooperative Court in *Mulford v. Smith* (1939) and *Wickard v. Filburn* (1942). As a general threat to the spending power, it was dispelled in 1937 when the Court upheld the tax provisions of the Social Security Act. *Steward Machine Co. v. Davis* involved the unemployment compensation section of the act, which provided for a federal payroll tax on employers of a certain percentage of the wages they paid to employees. The proceeds of the tax went into the general federal treasury. If employers paid state taxes into an unemployment fund set up under a satisfactory state law, they could credit such payments against the federal tax up to 90 percent.

The Court denied by a five to four vote that these tax provisions were an attempt to coerce the states or to invade their reserved powers. The states were given, true enough, a compelling inducement to provide unemployment compensation; but the Court viewed this not as coercion but as freedom to adopt such social legislation without putting the employers of some states at a disadvantage compared with employers in other states without unemployment compensation.

A second decision on the same day, *Helvering v. Davis,* sustained the

Social Security Act system of old-age benefits. The argument on this head had been that the taxing power was being used to benefit a particular class of persons, but the Court believed Congress might reasonably conclude that provision for old-age security would promote the general welfare. The discretion to make such decisions "belongs to Congress, unless the choice is clearly wrong, a display of arbitrary power, not an exercise of judgment."

In *Buckley v. Valeo* (1976) the *Butler* and *Helvering* cases were called upon to legitimate the system of public financing for presidential election campaigns set up by the Federal Election Campaign Act of 1974. Rebutting the argument that public funding was contrary to the general welfare, the Court said that appellants were mistakenly treating the general welfare clause "as a limitation upon congressional power," whereas it is "a grant of power, the scope of which is quite expansive, particularly in view of the enlargement of power by the Necessary and Proper Clause. . . . It is for Congress to decide which expenditures will promote the general welfare."

BORROWING AND MONETARY POWERS

Clauses 2 and 5 of Article I, section 8, give Congress power "to borrow money on the credit of the United States" and "to coin money, regulate the value thereof, and of foreign coin." These authorizations have figured incidentally in several constitutional episodes already discussed. Thus, the holding in *McCulloch v. Maryland* (1819) that Congress had the implied power to establish a national bank drew authority in part from clause 5, as did *Veazie Bank v. Fenno* (1869) in upholding federal power to tax state bank notes out of existence. However, there are two major crises in American history in which the interpretation of these powers was directly and importantly at issue. The first led up to and was resolved by the *Legal Tender Cases* (1871), the second by the *Gold Clause Cases* (1935).

In Chapter 1 it was pointed out how important the currency problem was in the minds of the members of the Constitutional Convention. Their dislike for "cheap money" led them to prohibit states from coining money, emitting bills of credit, or making anything but gold and silver coin legal tender in payment of debts. Their distrust of paper money even led them to strike out an authorization to Congress to "emit bills of credit" that was included in the original draft of the borrowing clause. However, they did not go so far as to forbid the federal government to issue paper money, and in fact the existence of this power was assumed to be included within the borrowing power as soon as the government began operations.

In connection with the financing of the Civil War, Congress went further and made "greenbacks" (i.e., bills of credit) legal tender at face value in the payment of debts between private individuals. In *Hepburn v. Griswold* (1870) the Court by a vote of four to three held the legal tender acts unconstitutional in so far as they required the acceptance of greenbacks in fulfillment of contracts made before the acts were passed, and ruled that creditors would be deprived of due process if compelled to accept depreciated paper money in payment of such debts.

The *Hepburn* holding, if maintained, would have had a tremendous impact, for the nation's economy had adjusted to the use of greenbacks, and many debtors would have been ruined if required to repay their borrowings in hard money. So the popular pressure for reconsideration was very great. On the day the decision was announced, President Grant sent the nominations of two new justices to the Senate. With their votes, the *Hepburn* decision was overruled five to four in the *Legal Tender Cases* (1871).[21]

The new majority held that a congressional power could be implied from a group of expressly granted powers, and by lumping together the war power, borrowing power, and power to coin money, the Court found adequate support for the legal tender legislation. As for taking of property without due process, the revised view was that a loss due to the legal tender provision was no more a legal deprivation of property than a loss due to changes in the purchasing power of money. In spite of this emphasis on the war power, *Juilliard v. Greenman* (1884) upheld legal tender notes in peacetime. The new amalgam of powers that it cited in support included those to lay taxes, pay debts, borrow money, coin money, and regulate the value of money.

Though the Supreme Court in the *Legal Tender Cases* held that creditors who had merely specified for payment in "lawful money" had to accept legal tender at face value, in *Trebilcock v. Wilson* (1872) it added that Congress had not intended to, and possibly could not constitutionally, require creditors who had specified for payment in gold dollars to accept greenbacks at face value. After this decision many creditors insisted on "gold clauses" (i.e., language requiring payment in gold dollars) in bonds, and by 1933 almost all public and private bonds contained such clauses.

The *Gold Clause Cases* (1935) grew out of legislative and executive action in 1933 reducing the gold content of the dollar, with the intention of cheapening money, raising prices, and rescuing agriculture and industry from depression. As elements in the devaluation program, gold payments by the Treasury were suspended, and persons owning gold or gold certificates were required to turn them in to the Treasury in exchange for other currency. Provisions in both private contracts and government bonds for payment in gold were abrogated.

This program of course led to a flurry of litigation. The leading decision came in *Norman v. Baltimore & Ohio Railroad Co.* (1935). The holder of a railroad bond promising payment of interest in gold coin of the United States demanded his interest in gold or in an increased number of devalued dollars equal in gold content to the dollars promised before devaluation. By a five to

---

[21]*Knox v. Lee* and *Parker v. Davis*.

four vote the Court denied this claim. The contract was interpreted as requiring the payment of money, not the delivery of gold bullion. Congress has broad powers of control over the monetary system, and these powers cannot be frustrated by contracts between private parties creating vested rights outside the scope of congressional control. Finally, the Court thought Congress might reasonably conclude that abrogation of the gold clauses in private contracts was an appropriate means of carrying out this revised monetary policy. Justice McReynolds, expressing his dissent, blurted out to the packed courtroom: "As for the Constitution, it does not seem too much to say that it is gone."[22]

Whether Congress could abrogate the gold clause in the government's own contracts was another matter. *Perry v. United States* (1935) concerned a government bond issued in 1918 which promised that the principal and interest would be paid in United States gold coin "of the present standard of value." By a vote of eight to one the Court held that the obligation incurred in exercise of the power to borrow money must be given preference over the government's power to regulate the value of money, and consequently that the promise to pay in gold coin could not be abrogated. However, five justices ruled that the person bringing the suit could recover only for actual losses as a result of the government's action, and since there had been none in this case, he was not entitled to sue. Justice Stone in a separate opinion pointed to the Court's dilemma in undertaking to suggest that

> . . . the exercise of the sovereign power to borrow money on credit . . . may nevertheless preclude or impede the exercise of another sovereign power, to regulate the value of money; or to suggest that although there is and can be no present cause of action upon the repudiated gold clause, its obligation is nevertheless, in some manner and to some extent, not stated, superior to the power to regulate the currency which we now hold to be superior to the obligation of the bonds.

Congress proceeded to ensure that these dilemmas would cause the Court no further trouble by passing a statute denying consent to sue the government on these grounds.

---

[22]For an account of the extraordinary measures which President Roosevelt was prepared to take in case the Court had not upheld the government in the *Gold Clause Cases,* see William E. Leuchtenberg, "The Origins of Franklin D. Roosevelt's 'Court-Packing' Plan," in Philip B. Kurland, ed., *The Supreme Court Review: 1966* (Chicago: University of Chicago Press, 1966), pp. 352–54.

12

The Commerce Power

The commerce clause has a classic, but deceptive, simplicity. "The Congress shall have power," says Article I, section 8, clause 3, "to regulate commerce with foreign nations, and among the several states, and with the Indian tribes." With this sparse formula the drafters of the Constitution placed in the hands of the federal government a power, the absence of which in the central government under the Articles of Confederation had been largely responsible for the decision to frame a new Constitution.

The language, be it noted, is in terms of a positive grant of power to Congress. The commerce clause does not say what power to "regulate commerce," if any, is left to the states. Nor is any definition attempted of the key words in the clause. As much as any part of the Constitution, this clause has derived its meaning from experience.

Congress undertook the regulation of foreign commerce immediately, but it was quite slow in testing the extent of its constitutional power over commerce among the states. It was not until the adoption of the Interstate Commerce Act in 1887 that the federal government really entered the domestic regulatory field. Consequently, during the first century of the nation's history the commerce clause problems that the Supreme Court was asked to decide grew for the most part out of *state* regulation challenged as infringing the constitutionally protected but largely unexercised power of Congress to regulate commerce among the states.

GIBBONS v. OGDEN

The first case in which the commerce clause figured before the Supreme Court was *Gibbons v. Ogden* (1824), one of the landmarks in American constitutional law. It has been customary to credit Marshall with deciding this case in accordance with his own strongly nationalistic views. Actually, his assertion of federal power was less broad and forthright than it might have been. Marshall could write clearly enough when he wanted to, but as Frankfurter says, this opinion "was either unconsciously or calculatedly confused."[1]

Robert Fulton, the inventor, and Robert R. Livingston had been granted an exclusive right by the State of New York to navigate its waters by steamboat. Ogden had a license from them to engage in navigation. Gibbons, on the other hand, was seeking to operate steamboats between New York and New Jersey under a license granted to him by the federal government. Ogden sought to enjoin Gibbons from using vessels within New York waters, to which Gibbons responded that his boats, being licensed under an act of Congress, could not be excluded by any state law. For our present purposes the important part of the Supreme Court's ruling is Marshall's discussion of the character and extent of the congressional power to regulate commerce.

Daniel Webster, appearing before the Supreme Court as counsel for Gibbons, argued for the broadest possible scope of federal power. The authority of Congress to regulate commerce, he contended, "was complete and entire." It went as far as the concept of commerce went, and "in such an age as this, no words embraced a wider field than commercial regulation. Almost all the business and intercourse of life may be connected, incidentally more or less, with commercial regulations." Naturally, in Webster's view, commerce included navigation. Opposing counsel, on the other hand, would limit commerce "to traffic, to buying and selling, or the interchange of commodities," and would exclude navigation from its scope.

Marshall agreed with Webster about navigation being necessarily a part of commerce:

> Commerce, undoubtedly, is traffic, but it is something more: it is intercourse. It describes the commercial intercourse between nations, and parts of nations, in all its branches. . . . The power over commerce, including navigation, was one of the primary objects for which the people of America adopted their government.

[1]Felix Frankfurter, *The Commerce Clause under Marshall, Taney and Waite* (Chapel Hill, N.C.: University of North Carolina Press, 1937), p. 17. William W. Crosskey refers to "the somewhat confusing verbiage" of Marshall's opinion; *Politics and the Constitution in the History of the United States* (Chicago: University of Chicago Press, 1953), p. 266.

But Marshall failed to claim for Congress the "complete and entire" power over commerce for which Webster had contended. He did seem to start out in that direction. Congressional power over commerce with foreign nations, he said, was admittedly complete. It comprehended "every species of commercial intercourse between the United States and foreign nations." Moreover, "commerce, as the word is used in the constitution, is a unit, every part of which is indicated by the term."

Now, since commerce is a unit, and since as applied to foreign nations it covers all commercial intercourse, does it not carry the same meaning when applied to commerce "among the several states"? The word "among," continued Marshall, "means intermingled with. A thing which is among others, is intermingled with them. Commerce among the States, cannot stop at the external boundary line of each State, but may be introduced into the interior." Then, having laid the basis for claiming complete federal power to regulate commerce, Marshall drew back.

> It is not intended to say that these words comprehend that commerce which is completely internal, which is carried on between man and man in a State, or between different parts of the same State, and which does not extend to or affect other States. Such a power would be inconvenient, and is certainly unnecessary.

Note that Marshall does not say that such a power was not intended or made possible by the Constitution. He says only that it would be "inconvenient" and "unnecessary" for Congress to exercise such power. Then he adds, in what is the most significant single sentence of the decision: "Comprehensive as the word 'among' is, it may very properly be restricted to that commerce which concerns more States than one." He gives several reasons for this limitation, but the most important is this:

> The genius and character of the whole government seem to be, that its action is to be applied to all the external concerns of the nation, and to those internal concerns which affect the States generally; but not to those which are completely within a particular State, which do not affect other States, and with which it is not necessary to interfere, for the purpose of executing some of the general powers of the government.

Consequently, "the completely internal commerce of a State . . . may be considered as reserved for the State itself."

This whole discussion was largely unnecessary to the actual decision in *Gibbons v. Ogden,* which turned on the Court's finding of a conflict between the state and federal statutes. In these circumstances, "the acts of New York must yield to the law of congress," Marshall said. Breaking up the steamboat monopoly was a popular action, but the long-range constitutional importance of the ruling lay in Marshall's rejection of Webster's case for a complete federal power to regulate commerce, and his establishment of a divided authority over commerce, which has been the source of some of the most perplexing problems in American constitutional law.

Subsequently this distinction came to be referred to as that between "interstate" and "intrastate" commerce, and the test for distinguishing between the two categories was whether commerce crossed a state line or not. Marshall, however, did not use these two labels, and his conception of commerce "which concerns more States than one" was considerably more sophisticated. He felt compelled to concede that the "completely internal commerce of a State" was not within federal power, yet he defined such commerce as that which did not "extend to or affect other States"—certainly not the same thing as saying it is commerce that does not cross a state line.

Marshall's subtle distinctions, however, were soon lost in hard and fast dichotomies. Justice McLean, who thought he was expounding Marshall's views, said in *The Passenger Cases* (1849): "All commercial action within the limits of a State, and which does not extend to any other State or foreign country, is exclusively under state regulation." Chief Justice Taney, whose goals were definitely not those of Marshall, claimed to be stating Marshall doctrine in *The License Cases* (1847) when he spoke of "internal or domestic commerce, which belongs to the States, and over which congress can exercise no control."

INTERSTATE AND INTRASTATE COMMERCE

So it came about that Marshall, who had a unitary conception of commerce, by his decision in *Gibbons v. Ogden* laid the basis for splitting commerce among the states into two parts, designated by two terms that he never used. The power of Congress to regulate commerce among the states was assumed to be correctly stated as the power to regulate *interstate* commerce.

Interstate Commerce

Under this approach, the crossing of a state line is the basic justification for federal regulatory authority. Whatever moves across state lines—goods, commodities, persons, intelligence, or whatever—comes within the ambit of congressional power. The breadth of definition that Marshall claimed for "commerce" has been maintained and even expanded. For he qualified "intercourse" by the preceding word "commercial," whereas subsequent decisions of the Supreme Court have made it clear that there need be no actual commercial character to an interstate movement to bring it under the commerce power. The people who cross an interstate bridge "may be as truly said to be engaged in commerce as if they were shipping cargoes of merchandise from New York to Liverpool."[2] In *Caminetti v. United States* (1917), the Mann

---

[2]*Covington Bridge Co. v. Kentucky* (1894).

Act, which is based on the commerce power, was held to apply to the transportation of a woman across state lines for immoral purposes, even though no commercial motive was present.

Of course, the major transportation industries offer the classic type of interstate commerce. Congressional power over navigation was settled by the *Gibbons* case, and there was no constitutional doubt as to the power of Congress to pass the Interstate Commerce Act for the regulation of the railroads in 1887. In the *Pipe Line Cases* (1914), the Court upheld federal authority to regulate the transportation of oil and gas in pipelines from state to state, even though the pipelines were not common carriers and transported only the oil and gas of their owners. Regulation of the trucking industry was asserted by the Motor Carrier Act of 1935. Interstate movement of electric power came under federal control in the Federal Power Act of 1935, and the Natural Gas Act of 1938 provided for much the same powers in that field.

What is sent across state lines need not be tangible. Federal control over the interstate transmission of intelligence by telegraph was asserted by the Court in 1878, when it said that the powers of the commerce clause "are not confined to the instrumentalities of commerce, or the postal service known or in use when the Constitution was adopted, but they keep pace with the progress of the country, and adapt themselves to the new developments of time and circumstances."[3] Federal control over radio transmission, provided for in 1927 by the Federal Radio Act, was upheld in 1933, Chief Justice Hughes saying: "No state lines divide the radio waves, and national regulation is not only appropriate but essential to the efficient use of radio facilities."[4]

An activity that does not itself involve movement across state lines may be regarded as interstate commerce because of the use of the instrumentalities of such commerce. The classic case is that of the correspondence schools, which are interstate commerce because of their necessitous reliance on the United States mails.[5] Regulation of public utility holding companies under the federal act of 1935 was upheld on the ground that their subsidiaries usually operate on an interstate basis, and that the services the holding company performs for its subsidiaries involve continuous and extensive use of the mails and other facilities of interstate commerce.[6]

In all these decisions the Court has emphasized the unity of interstate transportation. An interstate journey cannot be broken up into the component parts that occur within each state. As Marshall said, "Commerce among the States cannot stop at the external boundary line of each State." In *Wabash Railway Co. v. Illinois* (1886), the Court struck down a state claim to regulate the charges for that portion of an interstate journey which took place within

[3]*Pensacola Telegraph Co. v. Western Union Telegraph Co.* (1878).
[4]*Federal Radio Commission v. Nelson Bros.* (1933).
[5]*International Text Book Co. v. Pigg* (1910).
[6]*Electric Bond & Share Co. v. S.E.C.* (1938).

the state. "Whatever may be the instrumentalities by which this transportation [from New York to Illinois] is effected, it is but one voyage."

Intrastate Commerce

All this emphasis upon the crossing of a state line as the basic test for commerce logically led to the conclusion that what did not cross a state line was not interstate commerce. Marshall himself appeared to lay the foundation for this position by one of the many dicta propounded in *Gibbons v. Ogden.* Speaking of the right of states to enforce inspection laws for the purpose of improving "the quality of articles produced by the labor of a country," he said that these laws "act upon the subject before it becomes an article . . . of commerce among the States." Thus he appeared to divide into two separate, self-contained processes the production of articles and their transportation in commerce. This artificial distinction, which seems inconsistent with his basic conception of the unity of commerce, was developed by later justices into a limitation of tremendous importance on the completeness of the federal commerce power. In application it worked two ways. First, it helped to *uphold state* regulation or taxation as applied to commercial interests that were claiming immunity from state control on the ground that interstate commerce was involved. Second, it helped to *defeat federal* regulation by limiting congressional power; and this second effect became more significant after 1890 as Congress began to use its regulatory powers for the first time in a significant fashion.

An illustration of the first category is supplied by *Kidd v. Pearson* (1888), involving a state prohibition law that forbade the manufacture of alcohol for sale outside the state. This law was upheld on the ground of the clear distinction between manufacturing and commerce. Manufacture is the fashioning of raw materials into a changed form for use. Commerce is buying and selling and the transportation incidental thereto. If the regulation of commerce included regulation of all manufactures that were intended to be the subject of commercial transactions, the Court said, then "Congress would be invested, to the exclusion of the States, with the power to regulate . . . every branch of human industry."

As an example of the second category, consider what the production-distribution distinction did to the enforcement of the Sherman Act. In *United States v. E. C. Knight Co.* (1895) this statute was held inapplicable to a sugar monopoly that had acquired nearly complete control of the manufacture of refined sugar within the United States. The reason was simple. "Commerce succeeds to manufacture, and is not a part of it." Commerce among the states does not begin until goods "commence their final movement from the State of their origin to that of their destination." The monopolistic acts here charged "related exclusively to the acquisition of the Philadelphia refineries and the business of sugar refining in Pennsylvania, and bore no direct relation to commerce between the States.'' In other decisions the Court applied the same principle to mining,[7] lumbering,[8] fishing, farming, oil production,[9] and generation of hydroelectric power.[10]

The Beginning of Interstate Commerce

This separation between production and distribution has enormous practical consequences. If the Congress cannot regulate production, and the states cannot burden interstate distribution, it becomes vital to determine just where one process stops and the other begins. In general, the rule is that interstate commerce begins when goods are delivered to a common carrier for transit outside the state, or when they actually start a continuous journey between two states. The local movement of goods preparatory to their delivery to a common carrier is not part of the interstate journey. After the continuous interstate journey has begun, temporary interruptions in the course of transportation do not legally break the continuity of the journey.[11]

The Ending of Interstate Commerce

Determination of the point at which an interstate journey ends and state authority resumes is an equally important problem. Marshall dealt with such an issue in the second commerce case that his Court decided, *Brown v. Maryland* (1827). In this case the goods involved were imports from abroad into Maryland, and that state sought to levy a license tax on the importer. Article I, section 10, forbids the states to lay duties on imports, and Marshall, searching for a practical rule on the subject, held that imported goods retained their character as imports as long as they remained unsold in the original package. The "original package" doctrine has continued to be used as a judicial rule of thumb. So far as interstate (as opposed to foreign) commerce is concerned, its effect is to forbid states to exert their police power on goods shipped in from other states while remaining in the original packages, unsold, unbroken, and unused. Stated positively, this doctrine protects the first sale of goods within the state while in the original package. Since the original package has this important protective character, it is not surprising that numerous controversies have arisen as to just what the original package is in different circumstances.[12]

---

[7]*United Mine Workers v. Coronado Coal Co.* (1922); *Oliver Iron Mining Co. v. Lord* (1923).

[8]*Coe v. Errol* (1886).

[9]*Champlin Refining Co. v. Corporation Commission* (1932).

[10]*Utah Power and Light v. Pfost* (1932).

[11]*Coe v. Errol* (1886).

[12]*Austin v. Tennessee* (1900); *Cook v. Marshall County* (1905).

THE POWER TO "REGULATE"

Although the federal power to regulate commerce is thus not a "complete" power, wherever the power does exist it is "plenary." Consequently the breadth of regulatory power that Congress may exercise within its recognized scope of authority has seldom been successfully questioned. Efforts to read restrictive interpretations into the word "regulate" have almost uniformly failed. Regulation, the Court has said, means not only protection and promotion, but also restriction and even prohibition.

The railroad field was the first in which Congress really tested the extent of its regulatory authority. The Interstate Commerce Act of 1887, setting up a regulatory commission with rather limited powers, was upheld by the Court in *Interstate Commerce Commission v. Brimson* (1894) as a necessary and proper means of enforcing congressional authority. In 1916 Congress took what then seemed the rather extreme step of providing in the Adamson Act for the eight-hour day and specifying wage and overtime rates on the railroads. The Court by a bare five to four margin approved the statute in *Wilson v. New* (1917) as necessary to prevent the interruption of commerce by a nationwide strike. The even more drastic plan for recapture of excess rail earnings in the Transportation Act of 1920 was upheld by the Court in 1924.[13]

The Commerce Power as a National Police Power

A severe test of congressional power over commerce was presented when Congress began, around the turn of the century, to explore the possibilities of using the commerce clause as a kind of national police power. An act of 1895 made it unlawful to transport lottery tickets into a state from another state or a foreign country. By a five to four vote the law was upheld in *Champion v. Ames* (1903). Harlan's opinion overruled the objection that regulation did not extend to complete prohibition and accepted the prevention of harm to the public morals as an appropriate goal of the commerce power, without any showing of effect on the safety or efficiency of commerce. The states were free to take action against intrastate traffic in lottery tickets. Why then could not Congres provide that "commerce shall not be polluted by the carrying of lottery tickets from one State to another"? The Court was clearly aware that if Congress could not prohibit the interstate traffic in lottery tickets, a no-man's-land would be created where neither federal nor state regulation could enter.

On the authority of *The Lottery Case,* the Supreme Court upheld the Food and Drug Act of 1906, which prohibited the introduction of impure foods and drugs into the states by means of interstate commerce.[14] The Mann

---

[13]*Dayton-Goose Creek R. Co. v. United States* (1924).
[14]*Hipolite Egg Co. v. United States* (1911).

Act (1910), forbidding the transportation of women in interstate commerce for the purpose of prostitution and debauchery, was upheld in 1913 on the basis of these precedents.[15] "Of course it will be said that women are not articles of merchandise," the Court wrote, "but this does not affect the analogy of the cases." The applicable principle was the simple one "that Congress has power over transportation 'among the several States'; that the power is complete in itself; and that Congress, as an incident to it, may adopt not only means necessary but convenient to its exercise, and the means may have the quality of police regulations."

The Child Labor Decision

This technique of closing the channels of interstate commerce, which had been uniformly successful in meeting constitutional tests, was then applied by Congress in the Federal Child Labor Act of 1916. This statute prohibited transportation in interstate commerce of the products of factories, mines, or quarries where children under the age of fourteen had been permitted to work more than eight hours a day or six days a week or at nights. In the historic case of *Hammer v. Dagenhart* (1918) the statute was declared unconstitutional by a five to four vote.[16]

The power to regulate commerce, said Justice Day for the majority, is the power "to control the means by which commerce is carried on," not the right "to forbid commerce from moving." To establish the correctness of this view the Court, of course, had somehow to deal with the contrary precedents just reviewed. Instead of overruling them, Day labored to explain that lottery tickets, impure food, and prostitutes are harmful in and of themselves, whereas goods produced by child labor "are of themselves harmless." In the case of the harmful categories, their regulation in interstate commerce could only be satisfactorily achieved by banning their movement altogether. But with harmless commodities, prohibition of their interstate movement by Congress was unconstitutional. This astounding argument was fittingly answered by Justice Holmes in his dissent.

> The notion that prohibition is any less prohibition when applied to things now thought evil I do not understand. But if there is any matter upon which civilized countries have agreed . . . it is the evil of premature and excessive child labor. I should have thought that if we were to introduce our own moral conceptions where in my opinion they do not belong, this was preëminently a case for upholding the exercise of all its powers by the United States.

[15]*Hoke v. United States* (1913).

[16]For an interesting account of the development of this case, see Stephen B. Wood, *Constitutional Politics in the Progressive Era: Child Labor and the Law* (Chicago: University of Chicago Press, 1968).

The more reputable part of Day's argument rested on the well-established doctrine that manufacturing, mining, and the like are intrastate commerce, subject to local regulation. In this statute Congress professed to observe the distinction between production and distribution and in form regulated only the latter. But in fact, Day said, the aim was "to standardize the ages at which children may be employed in mining and manufacturing within the States." Congress cannot use *its* admitted powers to oust the states from the exercise of *their* admitted powers. "The grant of authority over a purely federal matter was not intended to destroy the local power always existing and carefully reserved to the States in the Tenth Amendment to the Constitution."

This is a classic statement of the doctrine of dual federalism—that the powers delegated to the national government are nevertheless limited by the reserved powers of the states. When this view had been pressed upon the Court in *The Lottery Case,* Harlan had rejected it in positive fashion: "If it be said that the act of 1895 is inconsistent with the Tenth Amendment, reserving to the States respectively or to the people the powers not delegated to the United States, the answer is that the power to regulate commerce among the States has been expressly delegated to Congress."

Holmes subjected Day's logic to more extensive analysis in his *Hammer* dissent. Certainly what Congress had done—forbidding the transportation of goods in interstate commerce—was within the power expressly given to Congress by the commerce clause, if considered only as to its immediate effects. If it was to be declared unconstitutional, it would have to be because of its possible reaction upon the conduct of the states—in this case, because of its effect upon their freedom to permit child labor. "But if an act is within the powers specifically conferred upon Congress, it seems to me that it is not made any less constitutional because of the indirect effects that it may have, however obvious it may be that it will have those effects, and that we are not at liberty upon such grounds to hold it void."

Holmes went on to point out how often the exercise of a federal power limited state freedom. For example, federal taxation of state bank notes had driven them out of circulation. But his main emphasis was upon the admitted right of Congress to regulate interstate commerce. When states seek to send their products across a state line, "they are no longer within their rights. If there were no Constitution and no Congress their power to cross the line would depend upon their neighbors. Under the Constitution such commerce belongs not to the States but to Congress to regulate."

Obviously Holmes was right, but the majority view in *Hammer v. Dagenhart* remained at least in theory the official interpretation until the decision was overruled in 1941. Influential as it may have been, it was never anything but an exception to the general rule, which as stated by Harlan in *The Lottery Case* is that the power to regulate commerce "is plenary, is complete in itself, and is subject to no limitations except such as may be found in the Constitution." It was the general rule, not the exception, that the Court followed in upholding the power of Congress over interstate commerce in stolen motor vehicles in 1925[17] and kidnapped persons in 1936.[18]

THE CONCEPT OF "EFFECT UPON COMMERCE"

In spite of this emphasis on transportation across state lines as the basis for congressional power over commerce, other doctrinal developments on the Supreme Court laid the basis for the twentieth-century growth of the commerce power. This expansion came about primarily by application of the concept of "effect upon commerce." Under this doctrine, Congress could regulate not only commercial activities where state lines were crossed, but also activities which *affected* interstate commerce.

As all else in this field, the effect doctrine traces back to Marshall's opinion in the *Gibbons* case. There he said, in spelling out the area of commercial regulation remaining in the hands of the states under the commerce clause, that "it is not intended to say that these words comprehend that commerce . . . which does not extend to or affect other States." When the double negative is eliminated, this is an affirmation that Congress *can* regulate commerce within a state that affects other states.

By 1900 it was clear that congressional power over commerce would have to be freed from its exclusively "interstate" connotations if substantial expansion of congressional power over the industrial and commercial life of the country was to occur. Marshall's effect doctrine was available for this purpose. Of course, "effect" is a vague word; it may be useful if we endeavor to classify various types of situations where activities of a geographically intrastate character have such obvious impact on commerce among the states as to make application of the effect doctrine reasonable.

Effect through Intermingling

First we may note that it is possible for intrastate commerce to be physically so intermingled or intertwined with interstate commerce that the two cannot practically be divided for regulatory purposes; under these circumstances interstate commerce can simply not be regulated without also regulating intrastate commerce. A good example of this situation is supplied by *Southern Railway Co. v. United States* (1911). The case arose when the company hauled on its interstate railroad in *intrastate* traffic three cars not equipped with safety couplers as required by the federal Safety Appliance Act.

---

[17]*Brooks v. United States* (1952).

[18]*Gooch v. United States* (1936). The federal Travel Act of 1970, which makes criminal the use of facilities of interstate commerce for carrying on illegal activities such as gambling, was upheld in *Erlenbaugh v. United States* (1972) as applied against persons who shipped racing "scratch sheets" from Chicago into Indiana by train. But see *Rewis v. United States* (1971).

The statute specifically applied, not only to equipment used in interstate commerce, but also to cars "used in connection therewith." The Court approved this assertion of federal control over railroad cars that did not themselves cross state lines, saying: "This is so, not because Congress possesses any power to regulate intrastate commerce as such, but because its power to regulate interstate commerce is plenary and consequently may be exerted to secure the safety of the persons and property transported therein and of those who are employed in such transportation, no matter what may be the source of the dangers which threaten it."

"Stream of Commerce"

A second situation is the so-called "stream of commerce." The case commonly regarded as the fount of this notion was *Swift & Co. v. United States* (1905). Chicago stockyards firms had been charged with conspiracy in restraint of trade, and they objected that the purchase and sale of cattle in Chicago was not commerce among the states. Justice Holmes replied for the Court:

> Commerce among the States is not a technical legal conception, but a practical one, drawn from the course of business. When cattle are sent for sale from a place in one State, with the expectation that they will end their transit, after purchase, in another, and when in effect they do so, with only the interruption necessary to find a purchaser at the stock yards, and when this is a typical, constantly recurring course, the current thus existing is a current of commerce among the States, and the purchase of the cattle is a part and incident of such commerce.

By similar reasoning, Chief Justice Taft upheld federal regulation of stockyards in *Stafford v. Wallace* (1922) and grain exchanges in *Chicago Board of Trade v. Olsen* (1923).[19]

The Shreveport Doctrine

Still a third type of situation in which the effect of local commerce on interstate commerce has achieved constitutional significance is illustrated by the famous *Shreveport Rate Case* (1914). The situation was that Shreveport, Louisiana, competed with Houston and Dallas, Texas, for the trade of the intervening Texas territory. Interstate rates from Shreveport to Texas cities, regulated by the ICC, were higher than the intrastate rates fixed by the Texas Railroad Commission from Dallas and Houston to the same cities for comparable distances. Thus Shreveport was placed at a competitive disadvantage because of the interstate character of its commerce into Texas. The ICC agreed that it could not permit interstate traffic to be thus burdened, and issued an

---

[19]For recent illustrations of "stream of commerce" reasoning, see *Allenberg Cotton Company, Inc. v. Pittman* (1974), and *Maryland v. Louisiana* (1981).

order requiring Texas *intrastate* rates from Dallas and Houston to be equalized with the interstate rates from Shreveport into Texas.

Justice Hughes wrote a strong opinion for the Court upholding federal power to exercise such control over intrastate commerce. The commerce power of Congress is "complete and paramount. . . . It is of the essence to this power that, where it exists, it dominates. Interstate trade was not left to be destroyed or impeded by the rivalries of local governments." Congress was given power by the commerce clause to see "that the agencies of interstate commerce shall not be used in such manner as to cripple, retard or destroy it." Consequently,

> Wherever the interstate and intrastate transactions of carriers are so related that the government of the one involves the control of the other, it is Congress, and not the State, that is entitled to prescribe the final and dominant rule, for otherwise Congress would be denied the exercise of its constitutional authority and the State, and not the Nation, would be supreme within the national field.

Direct versus Indirect Effect

These various rationalizations of federal control might appear to open the way for complete exclusion of state regulation, and an achievement of that completeness of the federal commerce power for which Webster had argued in the *Gibbons* case. The Supreme Court, however, did not mean to go so far as that, and consequently there runs through all these cases an insistence by the Court that it is holding back something from the completeness of federal power. It is not *any* effect on commerce, however minimal, which justifies congressional control over intrastate activities. The Court tried a variety of semantic devices in the 1920s and 1930s in an attempt to indicate what kinds of effects justify federal control and what do not—the relation must be "close," the effect must be "substantial"—but the test most often suggested as a standard for judicial review of congressional action was "directness" as opposed to "indirectness" of effect.

The Court first began to talk in terms of direct and indirect effects in the early antitrust cases. Thus in the *Sugar Trust Case* (1895) the Court held that the chance "trade or commerce might be indirectly affected" by a sugar company merger was not enough to entitle the government to a Sherman Act decree. At this point the Court's dogma was that sale of a product was incidental to its production, and could never affect commerce other than incidentally or indirectly. But as time went on the Court became less sure on this point. In Holmes's opinion in the *Swift* case, sales became an element in an interstate stream, an integral part of an entire interstate movement. Chief Justice Taft in the *Chicago Board of Trade* case went even further in defining the kind of effect that justified federal control as "whatever amounts to more or less constant practice, and threatens to obstruct or unduly to burden the freedom of interstate commerce."

Clearly the direct-indirect test was a slippery one, with which different courts could get different results. Where Congress or its agent, the ICC, had definitely claimed an area of intrastate commerce under the effect doctrine, the Court tended to acquiesce. As Taft said in the *Chicago Board of Trade* case, "It is primarily for Congress to consider and decide the fact of the danger [to commerce] and meet it. This court will certainly not substitute its judgment for that of Congress in such a matter unless the relation of the subject to interstate commerce and its effect upon it are clearly non-existent."

But where the statute was a general one, like the Sherman Act, then the Court had to satisfy itself, as an original proposition, that the facts of the particular case demonstrated not merely the *existence,* but the *directness* of the effects upon commerce. In the three decades following the *Swift* decision in 1905, a predominantly conservative Court did find such directness in most of the important controversies, thus expanding the federal commerce power. The result of this expansion was not only to justify federal regulation of business, but also to permit the Court to strike at labor unions and their practices under federal law.

Early applications of the Sherman Act against labor organizations, as in the *Danbury Hatters Case,*[20] led Congress to attempt to exempt labor unions from its scope by section 6 of the Clayton Act (1914). However, the Court substantially interpreted this provision out of existence, and found directness of effect on commerce in such intrastate labor actions as a violent strike by the United Mine Workers against a coal company[21] and a secondary boycott by the stonecutters' union in the *Bedford Cut Stone* case of 1927.[22]

This was the status of the law and the Court's holdings when the National Recovery Administration legislation came up for judicial review in the famous case of *Schechter Poultry Corp. v. United States* (1935). The NRA was a major reliance of the New Deal in its attack on the Depression. Under the statute, codes of fair practice had been adopted for most of the industries of the country, large and small, fixing minimum wages and maximum hours, and regulating unfair or destructive competitive practices. President Roosevelt's high hopes for the NRA as a kind of partnership between capital and labor had not been fulfilled, and it was near collapse by the time the Supreme Court mercifully administered the *coup de grâce* in 1935. Our concern, however, is with the constitutional theory of the decision.

The statute's assertion of federal control was over transactions "in or affecting interstate or foreign commerce." The Schechter Corporation was a Brooklyn slaughterhouse operator that purchased live poultry in New York or Philadelphia, trucked it to the Brooklyn plant, slaughtered it, and then sold

[20]*Loewe v. Lawlor* (1908).

[21]*Coronado Coal Co. v. United Mine Workers* (1925).

[22]*Bedford Cut Stone Co. v. Journeymen Stone Cutters' Assn.* (1927). See also *Local 167 I.B.T. v. United States* (1934).

it to local retail dealers in Brooklyn. The live poultry code did not concern transportation or the practices of commission men. It dealt with hours and wages in the slaughterhouse and the company's local selling practices. Chief Justice Hughes for a unanimous Court held that these activities of the Schechter Corporation were not "transactions in interstate commerce."

Consequently the Schechter Corporation could be brought under the NRA only by one of the several "effect" notions. Would the "stream of commerce" doctrine apply? The Court said no. "So far as the poultry here in question is concerned, the flow in interstate commerce had ceased." Was there a direct effect upon interstate commerce that would justify the regulation? Again the answer was negative. Any effects present were indirect. The distinction between direct and indirect effects, Hughes said, "is clear in principle," but he impliedly admitted that he could not state it by falling back on illustration from individual cases the Court had decided in the past. What he was clear about, however, was that "the distinction between direct and indirect effects of intrastate transactions upon interstate commerce must be recognized as a fundamental one, essential to the maintenance of our constitutional system. Otherwise . . . there would be virtually no limit to the federal power and for all practical purposes we should have a completely centralized government." And he added, after mentioning the government's contention that such centralized powers were necessary to meet the economic emergency in the country: "It is not the province of the Court to consider the economic advantages or disadvantages of such a centralized system. It is sufficient to say that the Federal Constitution does not provide for it."

One year later a sharply divided Court did a reprise on this theme in *Carter v. Carter Coal Co.* (1936), which invalidated the coal industry codes set up under the Bituminous Coal Conservation Act of 1935. This time it fell to Justice Sutherland to write the opinion, and he dared to do what Hughes had been unwilling to attempt in the *Schechter* case—namely, to define the difference between a direct and an indirect effect on commerce.

> The word "direct" implies that the activity or condition invoked or blamed shall operate proximately—not mediately, remotely, or collaterally—to produce the effect. It connotes the absence of an efficient intervening agency or condition. And the extent of the effect bears no logical relation to its character. The distinction between a direct and an indirect effect turns, not upon the magnitude of either the cause or the effect, but entirely upon the manner in which the effect has been brought about. If the production by one man of a single ton of coal intended for interstate sale and shipment . . . affects interstate commerce indirectly, the effect does not become direct by multiplying the tonnage, or increasing the number of men employed, or adding to the expense or complexities of the business, or by all combined.

Sutherland then went on to underline the application of these principles to the current problem:

Much stress is put upon the evils which come from the struggle between employers and employees over the matter of wages, working conditions, the right of collective bargaining, etc., and the resulting strikes, curtailment and irregularity of production and effect on prices; and it is insisted that interstate commerce is *greatly* affected thereby. But . . . the conclusive answer is that the evils are all local evils over which the federal government has no legislative control. The relation of employer and employee is a local relation. . . . And the controversies and evils, which it is the object of the act to regulate and minimize, are local controversies and evils affecting local work undertaken to accomplish that local result. Such effect as they may have upon commerce, however extensive it may be, is secondary and indirect. An increase in the greatness of the effect adds to its importance. It does not alter its character.

This opinion was the dead end of the directness-indirectness dogma. It illuminated as by a flash of lightening a judicial dream world of logical abstractions, where there was no difference between one ton of coal and a million tons of coal, where considerations of degree were not cognizable by the law. Production was local. A production crisis in every part of the country simultaneously could never add up to a national problem with which Congress could deal; it could never have anything other than an indirect effect on commerce.

Sutherland sought to demonstrate that this fantastic result was required by the precedents. But the effect doctrine had been proved to be flexible enough to accommodate earlier legislative efforts to deal with intrastate commercial activities. "A survey of the cases," said Cardozo, dissenting along with Brandeis and Stone, "shows that the words [direct and indirect] have been interpreted with suppleness of adaption and flexibility of meaning." He was thinking of Holmes in the *Swift* case, Hughes in the *Shreveport* holding, Taft in *Chicago Board of Trade v. Olsen.* These were pragmatic and realistic appraisals of the federal commerce power which expose Sutherland's elaborate conceptualism in the *Carter* case as absurdly irrelevant to the issues before the country. The commerce power, Cardozo summed up, should be "as broad as the need that evokes it."

THE COMMERCE POWER AFTER 1937

Neither the Court nor the country could live with the doctrine of *Carter v. Carter Coal Co.* Within a year the standard stated by Justice Cardozo in dissent there became the majority view of the Court. The vehicle for this return to reality was *National Labor Relations Board v. Jones & Laughlin Corp.* (1937), involving the constitutionality of the National Labor Relations Act. This case was decided some two months after President Roosevelt had sent his Court-packing plan to Congress, while the Court was still the center of violent political controversy. The decision, which saw Chief Justice Hughes and Justice Roberts joining the liberal trio of Brandeis, Cardozo, and Stone in upholding the statute, was widely regarded as the Court's contribution toward restoration of peaceful relations by acceptance of the New Deal.

The Wagner Act

The National Labor Relations Act, popularly known as the Wagner Act, aimed to protect the right of employees to organize into labor unions and to bargain collectively with their employers. The statute defined certain types of interference with these rights as unfair labor practices and set up the NLRB with authority to compel employers to cease and desist from such practices. There was widespread employer resistance to the statute, and obviously it could not be applied to production industries if the *Schechter* and *Carter* view of the commerce clause was correct.

The key jurisdictional provision in the Wagner Act was that empowering the NLRB to forbid any person from engaging in any unfair labor practice "affecting commerce." The Jones & Laughlin Company was one of the nation's major steel producers, with integrated operations in several states. The particular unfair labor acts charged in this case took place in one of the company's Pennsylvania plants, and the constitutional question was whether these practices had a sufficient effect upon commerce to justify congressional control. Chief Justice Hughes said:

> In view of respondent's far-flung activities, it is idle to say that the effect would be indirect or remote. It is obvious that it would be immediate and might be catastrophic. We are asked to shut our eyes to the plainest facts of our national life and to deal with the question of direct and indirect effects in an intellectual vacuum.

This, of course, was precisely what Sutherland had done in the *Carter* opinion. Hughes continued:

> When industries organize themselves on a national scale, making their relation to interstate commerce the dominant factor in their activities, how can it be maintained that their industrial labor relations constitute a forbidden field into which Congress may not enter when it is necessary to protect interstate commerce from the paralyzing consequences of industrial war?

The stress that the Hughes opinion placed on the importance and nationally integrated character of the steel industry certainly suggested that these factors were important in justifying the Court's decision. But on the same day the Court also upheld the application of the Wagner Act to a trailer manufacturer[23] and to a small manufacturer of men's clothing[24] on the authority of the *Jones & Laughlin* decision. Apparently a business did not after

---

[23]*NLRB v. Fruehauf Trailer Co.* (1937).
[24]*NLRB v. Friedman–Harry Marks Clothing Co.* (1937).

all need to be one whose interruption by strike would be "catastrophic" in order to justify coverage by the statute.

For a couple of years after the *Jones & Laughlin* decision, there was a flurry of cases searching for loopholes in its doctrine, but none was found.[25] After 1939 cases testing the constitutional coverage of the NLRB largely disappeared from the Supreme Court's docket. The board did continue to run into an occasional unfavorable decision in the federal courts of appeals, but it appeared to be almost literally true that in no labor relations case over which the NLRB was willing to claim jurisdiction as affecting commerce would the Supreme Court deny the validity of the claim. Indeed, the NLRB eventually undertook voluntarily to limit its own jurisdiction, setting up categories of cases which it could have legitimately handled but which it announced it would not accept.

An occasional exception was caused by a conflict between the commerce power and another constitutional provision. In *McCulloch v. Sociedad Nacional de Marineros de Honduras* (1963), involving the Board's assertion of jurisdiction over foreign seamen, the Court rejected the board's claim as threatening the responsibility of the executive for relations with foreign nations. In *NLRB v. Catholic Bishop of Chicago* (1979) the Court denied the board's jurisdiction over lay faculty members in Catholic high schools. Finding in the legislative history of the Wagner act no clear "affirmative intention" that the act should apply to religious schools, the Court majority declined to construe the statute in a way that would raise sensitive First Amendment religion issues.[26]

The Fair Labor Standards Act

As the Wagner Act furnished the occasion for bringing down the *Schechter* and *Carter* decisions, it fell to another labor statute, the Fair Labor Standards Act, to demolish *Hammer v. Dagenhart*. This 1938 statute, also called the Wages and Hours Act, was the last major piece of New Deal legislation adopted. The formula it employed was similar to that of the 1916 federal child labor law, Congress making it unlawful to ship in interstate commerce goods produced in violation of the wage and hour standards set by the act. The

[25]See *Consolidated Edison Co. v. NLRB* (1938); *Santa Cruz Fruit Packing Co. v. NLRB* (1938); *NLRB v. Fainblatt* (1939). Later cases upholding a broad interpretation of NLRB authority are *Polish Alliance v. Labor Board* (1944); *Guss v. Utah Labor Board* (1957); and *NLRB v. Reliance Fuel Oil Corp.* (1963).

[26]In *Associated Press v. NLRB* (1937) the Court had rejected the contention of the news agency that the First Amendment gave it exemption from the Wagner Act. *NLRB v. Yeshiva University* (1980) raised no constitutional issue, but simply the question whether the bargaining unit approved by the NLRB was too broad. The Court concluded that it was, viewing professors as in fact university managers or supervisors rather than employees. See Arthur M. Sussman, "University Governance through a Rose-Colored Lens," in Philip B. Kurland and Gerhard Casper, eds., *The Supreme Court Review: 1980* (Chicago: University of Chicago Press, 1981), pp. 27–55.

coverage of the act was not as broad as that of the Wagner Act. Where that statute had applied to unfair labor practices "affecting commerce," the Fair Labor Standards Act was made applicable to employees "engaged in commerce or in the production of goods for commerce."

The basic decision upholding the constitutionality of this act was *United States v. Darby Lumber Co.,* announced unanimously by the Court in 1941. As Justice Stone said, there would have been little need for any extended discussion of the constitutional issue, since Congress was asserting its clear power over the movement of goods across state lines, if it had not been for *Hammer v. Dagenhart.* Stone's attention was consequently devoted primarily to disposing of that derelict on the stream of the law.

> In that case it was held by a bare majority of the Court over the powerful and now classic dissent of Mr. Justice Holmes . . . that Congress was without power to exclude the products of child labor from interstate commerce. The reasoning and conclusion of the Court's opinion there cannot be reconciled with the conclusion which we have reached, that the power of Congress under the Commerce Clause is plenary to exclude any article from interstate commerce subject only to the specific prohibitions of the Constitution.
>
> *Hammer v. Dagenhart* has not been followed. The distinction on which the decision was rested that Congressional power to prohibit interstate commerce is limited to articles which in themselves have some harmful or deleterious property—a distinction which was novel when made and unsupported by any provision of the Constitution—has long since been abandoned. . . .
>
> The conclusion is inescapable that *Hammer v. Dagenhart* was a departure from the principles which have prevailed in the interpretation of the Commerce Clause both before and since the decision and that such vitality, as a precedent, as it then had has long since been exhausted. It should be and now is overruled.

The *Darby* decision, clear-cut as it was, did not suffice to settle the jurisdictional questions under the Fair Labor Statndards Act in the definitive fashion that the *Jones & Laughlin* decision had achieved for the Wagner Act. Two reasons account for the continuing stream of wage and hour cases after 1941. First, the absence of any administrative tribunal like the ICC or the NLRB to perform enforcement functions under the act withheld from the courts, in Frankfurter's words, "the benefit of a prior judgment, on vexing and ambiguous facts, by an expert administrative agency."[27]

Second is the fact that Congress in enacting the statute did not see fit to exhaust its constitutional power over commerce. By failing to make the Wages and Hours Act applicable to all employment "affecting commerce," Congress prevented the Court from using the Wagner or Sherman Act precedents. In FLSA cases it had to be established to the satisfaction of the courts in each instance that the employees involved were engaged "in commerce" or "in the production of goods for commerce."

[27] *10 East 40th Street v. Callus* (1945).

Application of these statutory standards required the drawing of some rather fine lines. Since type of work done by the employee, and not the nature of the employer's business, determines coverage, it was possible for an employer to have some workers who were covered and others who were not. Thus an examination of the nature of the duties of individual employees and their relation to interstate commerce or the production of goods for commerce was usually required to settle a disputed case. The original act specified that "an employee shall be deemed to have been engaged in the production of goods if such an employee was engaged . . . in any process or occupation necessary to the production thereof, in any State." Because the Court tended to interpret this language as authorizing a fairly broad coverage of fringe workers,[28] Congress in 1949 amended the statute to apply only to workers "directly essential" to production. In 1961 another amendment expanded the act's coverage to every employee "in an enterprise engaged in commerce or in the production of goods for commerce," thus liquidating the necessity to distinguish among employees in the same enterprise.[29] The amendment included as "enterprises" hospitals and schools, whether public or private, a provision upheld in *Maryland v. Wirtz* (1968) against charges that such use of the commerce clause violated state sovereignty. In *Fry v. United States* (1975) the Court ruled that claims of state sovereignty did not protect state employees from federal wage controls under the Economic Stabilization Act of 1970.

But one year later, an unexpected five to four decision, *National League of Cities v. Usery* (1976), overruled *Wirtz* and distinguished *Fry.* For the Court, Justice Rehnquist held that federal wage and hour requirements for state and municipal employees, enacted by Congress in 1974, were unconstitutional. The decision was based on the long-abandoned *Hammer v. Dagenhart* theory that the commerce power is limited by state "sovereignty" and the reserved powers guaranteed to the "States as States." Rehnquist wrote:

> There are attributes of sovereignty attaching to every state government which may not be impaired by Congress, not because Congress may lack an affirmative grant of legislative authority to reach the matter but because the Constitution prohibits it from exercising the authority in that manner.

He thought that if Congress could determine wage and hour standards for state employees, "there would be little left of the state's separate and independent existence." This ruling, which Brennan called "mischievous," marked the first time the Court had struck down major congressional economic legislation since the judicial attack on the New Deal in the 1930s.

[28]See *Kirschbaum v. Walling* (1942); *Borden Co. v. Borella* (1945); *Martino v. Michigan Window Cleaning Co.* (1946).

[29]The amendment also provided that any company doing an annual business in excess of $1 million was engaged in interstate commerce for purposes of the act.

National League of Cities generated a tremendous volume of constitutional commentary, much of it unfavorable, concentrating on the uncertainties raised by the ruling.[30] Exactly what were the "functions essential to the separate and independent existence of the state" that could not be abrogated by the federal government? Did this limitation on the commerce power also apply to the congressional spending power and to section 5 of the Fourteenth Amendment?

A substantial volume of litigation was also generated, some forty-two cases growing out of *Usery* being filed by 1978. But subsequent experience has shown the actual effect of the decision to be minimal. The Court interpreted the *Usery* doctrine narrowly in the important case of *Hodel v. Virginia Surface Mining and Reclamation Assn.* (1981). Here Virginia coal producers had challenged the federal law covering surface mining on steep slopes, arguing that the statute was actually concerned with regulating the use of private lands, a traditional state function, rather than with the interstate commerce effects of destructive surface coal mining. A federal district court, relying on *Usery,* had declared the law unconstitutional.

But Justice Marshall for a unanimous Court concluded that the doctrine of *National League of Cities* was irrelevant here. Its application would require a threefold finding: (1) that the challenged statute regulated the "States as States"; (2) that the federal regulation covered matters that are indubitably "attributes of state sovereignty"; and (3) that state compliance would directly impair state ability to "structure integral operations in areas of traditional functions." The first of these requirements was not satisfied in *Hodel.* The federal law did not regulate the "States as States"; it governed only the activities of private coal operators. Congress had simply displaced state regulation of private activities affecting interstate commerce. Since the first requirement of *Usery* was not met, Marshall found it unnecessary to apply the other two doctrines.

Usery was again rejected in *Equal Employment Opportunity Commission v. Wyoming* (1983), involving a federal law making it illegal for employers to discriminate on the basis of age against persons between 40 and 70 years of age. Wyoming had forced a game warden to retire at age 55. A federal judge, relying on *Usery,* ruled that applying federal law to the states violated the Tenth Amendment and infringed on their sovereign authority over their own employees. But by a five to four vote (Blackmun reversing his *Usery* position) the Court held the federal law applicable to states and local governments. Stevens suggested that *Usery* should be put in the category of cases

[30]See Frank I. Michelman, "States' Rights and States' Roles," 86 YALE LAW JOURNAL 1165 (1977); Laurence H. Tribe, "Unraveling *National League of Cities:* The New Federalism and Affirmative Rights to Essential Government Services," 90 HARVARD LAW REVIEW 1065 (1977); Jeff Powell, "The Compleat Jeffersonian: Justice Rehnquist and Federalism," 91 YALE LAW JOURNAL 1317 (1982).

"whose subsequent rejection is now universally regarded as proper," and that congressional power to regulate the terms and conditions of employment throughout the economy should be fully recognized.[31]

Agricultural Regulation

The initial New Deal effort to handle the farm problem by invoking the federal taxing power was defeated by the Court in *United States v. Butler*. Congress soon found a stopgap after *Butler* in soil conservation, for which farm payments similar to those of the unconstitutional production control program were available. As a more permanent approach, Congress turned to marketing controls. The Agricultural Marketing Act of 1937, under which milk marketing agreements were set up to control prices in the major milksheds of the country, was held constitutional by the Court in two 1939 decisions involving the New York and Boston areas. The Court said that since most of the milk under agreements moved in interstate commerce and the intrastate milk was inextricably mixed with interstate milk, the regulation of prices of all milk in these markets was a valid exercise of the commerce power.[32]

The Agricultural Adjustment Act of 1938 utilized a new control device, marketing quotas. In 1939 such quotas on tobacco marketing were upheld by the Court in *Mulford v. Smith*. The Court emphasized that the statute did not purport to limit production but merely to control the sales of tobacco in interstate commerce so as to prevent the flow of commerce from causing harm. But how tenuous a relationship to interstate commerce the Court was willing to accept was dramatically demonstrated in *Wickard v. Filburn* (1942). Here a farmer raising twenty-three acres of wheat, none of it intended for interstate commerce since all was to be consumed on the farm or fed to stock, was held to have such an effect on interstate commerce as to be liable to the marketing penalties imposed by the act of 1938.

As Justice Jackson recognized, the Court, in spite of the "great latitude" permitted to the commerce power in its post-1937 decisions, had not yet held that production might be regulated "where no part of the product is intended for interstate commerce or intermingled with the subjects thereof." Now in *Wickard v. Filburn* it was prepared to do so, and Jackson's justification of this result is the highwater mark of commerce clause expansionism. The guiding principle is that "even if appellee's activity be local and though it may not be regarded as commerce, it may still, whatever its nature, be reached by Congress if it exerts a substantial economic effect on interstate commerce, and this

---

[31]The same four-judge minority (Rehnquist, Burger, Powell and O'Connor) had held in *Federal Energy Regulatory Commission v. Mississippi* (1982) that a federal law requiring state utility regulators to encourage energy conservation violated the Tenth Amendment.

[32]*United States v. Rock Royal Cooperative* (1939); *Hood & Sons v. United States* (1939). See also *United States v. Wrightwood Dairy Co.* (1942).

irrespective of whether such effect is what might at some earlier time have been defined as 'direct' or 'indirect.' "[33]

Navigable Streams and Federal Power Projects

Another important area of congressional interest concerns navigable waters and the hydroelectric power derived from them. Here the basic decision is *United States v. Appalachian Electric Power Co.* (1940). The Federal Water Power Act of 1920 made it unlawful to construct a dam for water power development in a navigable water of the United States without first securing a license from the Federal Power Commission. This license controls service, rates, and profits of the licensee, and provides for recapture of the project by the government after fifty years on payment of the net investment therein.

In the *Appalachian* case the contention was that the New River in West Virginia was not navigable, and that even if it were, the government had no right to impose the conditions set forth in the license, since most of them had nothing to do with navigation or its protection. The Court held that the New River was navigable and announced a revised test of navigability that greatly increased federal authority. The Court also held that the government's power over navigable waters was not restricted to control relating to navigation. The power being exercised was the commerce power, of which navigation is only a part. "Flood protection, watershed development, recovery of the cost of improvements through utilization of power are likewise parts of commerce control. . . . Navigable waters are subject to national planning and control in the broad regulation of commerce granted the Federal Government."

Of course the federal government may itself build dams in navigable streams under its commerce power. Attempts to question the legitimacy of and the motives behind the construction of federal multiple-purpose dams where power generation was an important factor have uniformly failed. The Boulder Canyon Project Act of 1928 was upheld in *Arizona v. California* (1931). The constitutionality of the TVA power-development program was supported by a federal trial court in 1938 against an attack by eighteen private power companies, but the Supreme Court found it unnecessary to pass on the constitutional issue, holding that the utilities had suffered no legal injury from TVA activities and consequently had no ground for bringing the suit.[34]

The Sherman Act

The breadth of the commerce clause has also been demonstrated in Sherman Act prosecutions. In 1942 the Department of Justice secured indictments

---

[33]The constitutionality of the Wholesome Meat Act of 1967, providing for federal regulation of meat plants selling intrastate, was never questioned.

[34]*Tennessee Electric Power Co. v. T.V.A.* (1939). See also *Oklahoma ex rel. Phillips v. Guy Atkinson Co.* (1941).

against an underwriters' association that represented a membership of nearly 200 fire insurance companies, charging conspiracy to fix rates and monopolize trade and commerce. This prosecution challenged a famous Supreme Court decision dating back to 1869, *Paul v. Virginia,* which had held that the writing of insurance was a local activity, not interstate commerce. "These contracts are not articles of commerce in any proper meaning of the word," the Court said. The effect of the decision was to uphold a state law requiring insurance companies not incorporated in the state to secure a license and deposit bonds with the state treasurer before doing business in the state.

On the basis of this decision, the insurance business developed into one of gigantic proportions in the nation while retaining constitutionally its local status. But in *United States v. South-Eastern Underwriters Assn.* (1944), the Supreme Court terminated this anomalous situation. Justice Black, speaking for a four-judge majority, started by noting that *Paul v. Virginia* and all the other precedents holding insurance business not to be commerce were cases where the validity of state statutes had been at issue, and the question had been the extent to which the commerce clause might automatically deprive states of the power to regulate insurance. It was in these circumstances that the Court had consistently upheld state regulatory authority. The *South-Eastern* case was the first in which the Court had been asked to pass on the applicability of a federal statute to companies doing an interstate insurance business.

Coming at the problem from this angle, an entirely different line of precedents became applicable. All the cases in which the transportation or movement across state lines of lottery tickets, stolen automobiles, kidnapped persons, and the like had been held to be interstate commerce and subject to federal regulation were the controlling authorities. If activities of these variegated sorts were interstate commerce, then Black felt that "it would indeed be difficult now to hold that no activities of any insurance company can ever constitute interstate commerce." Although a contract of insurance might not in itself be interstate commerce, the entire transaction of which it is a part is a chain of events crossing state boundaries. "No commercial enterprise of any kind which conducts its activities across state lines has been held to be wholly beyond the regulatory power of Congress under the Commerce Clause. We cannot make an exception of the business of insurance."

After this decision Congress passed a statute permitting the states to regulate and tax the insurance business, and exempted it from any federal statutes, with the exception of the Sherman Act and three others. The Supreme Court upheld the statute in *Prudential Insurance Co. v. Benjamin* (1946) and *Robertson v. California* (1946).[35]

In *Goldfarb v. Virginia State Bar* (1975), the Court held that minimum fee schedules for legal services relating to residential real estate transactions,

---

[35]This exemption was applied in *Western & Southern Life Insurance Co. v. Board of Equalization* (1981) to justify a California tax on out-of-state insurance companies doing business in the state.

published and enforced by the organized bar, constituted price fixing in violation of the Sherman Act. Interstate commerce was sufficiently affected for Sherman Act purposes in that significant amounts of funds for financing purchases of homes came from outside the state.

Organized baseball had enjoyed a wholly illogical exemption from the Sherman Act since 1922.[36] In *Flood v. Kuhn* (1972), the Court again upheld the "reserve clause," under which the club first signing a player has continuing and exclusive right to his services.[37] The Court conceded that baseball was obviously interstate commerce but ruled that the exemption it had long enjoyed from the Sherman Act was an "established aberration" in which Congress had acquiesced and which Congress, not the Court, would have to correct. Congress did nothing, but in 1975 the baseball owners and players themselves entered into long and complicated negotiations that one year later resulted in a contract limiting the reserve system and enabling a player to become a free agent after six years of major league service.

THE COMMERCE POWER AND CRIME

The commerce power has often been relied on to support federal legislation and action against criminal activities of various sorts. Earlier examples are the ban on interstate transportation of stolen automobiles, sustained by the Court in *Brooks v. United States* (1925) and the Federal Kidnapping Act, upheld in *Gooch v. United States* (1936).

Federal jurisdiction in these statutes derived basically from the crossing of state lines, but either in the statutory language or as applied by the courts, the "effect" doctrine was often invoked. A 1951 statute prohibiting the shipment of gambling machines in interstate commerce included registration and reporting requirements applicable to all manufacturers and dealers, with no necessary relation to interstate commerce. In *United States v. Five Gambling Devices* (1953), the Court construed this requirement narrowly in order to avoid the issue of constitutionality.

More recent Court decisions on federal jurisdiction have gone both ways. In the Consumer Credit Protection Act of 1968, Congress struck at "loan-sharking"—i.e., the use by organized crime of extortionate means to collect payments on loans. In *Perez v. United States* (1971), the Court sustained a conviction under this act for a transaction that had taken place entirely within one state. Justice Douglas contended that legislative hearings had established a relation between local loan sharks and interstate crime, but Justice Stewart, dissenting, thought that loan-sharking was a "wholly local activity."

---

[36]*Federal Baseball Club v. National League* (1922); *Toolson v. New York Yankees* (1953).

[37]Other sports do not enjoy this exemption. See *United States v. International Boxing Club* (1955); *Radovich v. National Football League* (1957).

The Federal Travel Act of 1970 prohibits interstate travel in furtherance of certain criminal activities. In *Erlenbaugh v. United States* (1972) it was applied against persons who shipped racing "scratch sheets" from Chicago into Indiana by train. However, *Rewis v. United States* (1971) held that operators of a lottery near a state line were not responsible if out-of-state customers patronized their establishment.

The Omnibus Crime Control and Safe Streets Act of 1968 makes it illegal for any person convicted of a felony to receive or transport any firearm "in interstate commerce or affecting commerce." In *United States v. Bass* (1971) the Court reversed a conviction where there had been no showing that the firearms were commerce-related. But *Scarborough v. United States* (1977) upheld a conviction where the government showed only that the firearms had once moved in commerce, but made no attempt to prove the defendant had obtained them after his felony conviction.

The Commerce Clause and Civil Rights

In a 1946 decision sustaining the "death sentence" provision of the Public Utility Holding Company Act, the Supreme Court said: "The federal commerce power is as broad as the economic needs of the nation."[38] Recent experience has shown that it is also as broad as the social needs. In the Civil Rights Act of 1964 Congress undertook to ban racial discrimination in public accommodations throughout the country. The constitutional foundations for the statute were the commerce clause and the equal protection clause. However, in *Heart of Atlanta Motel, Inc. v. United States* (1964) and *Katzenbach v. McClung* (1964), the Supreme Court found the commerce clause alone fully adequate to support the statute.

The act applied to three classes of business establishments: inns, hotels, and motels; restaurants and cafeterias; and theaters and motion picture houses—if their operations "affect commerce." The act defined what it meant by affecting commerce. Any inn, motel, or other establishment that provides lodging to transient guests affects commerce per se. Restaurants and cafeterias affect commerce if they serve interstate travelers or if a substantial portion of the food they serve or products they sell have "moved in commerce." Motion picture houses and theaters affect commerce if they customarily present films or performances that "move in commerce."

The two 1964 test cases were brought by an Atlanta motel and a Birmingham restaurant. The Court, noting that it was applying principles "first formulated by Chief Justice Marshall in *Gibbons v. Ogden*," unanimously upheld the act as applied to both. Only two questions need be asked, said Justice Clark for the Court: did Congress have a rational basis for finding

---

[38] *American Power & Light Co. v. SEC* (1946). The "death sentence" was a statutory requirement that holding companies be simplified and reorganized, and their operations limited to those of an integrated public utility system.

that racial discrimination by places of public accommodation affected commerce; and were the means it selected to eliminate that evil reasonable and appropriate? The answer to both was in the affirmative. The fact that Congress was using the commerce power to legislate against "moral wrongs" was irrelevant so far as the constitutional foundation for the enactment was concerned.[39]

The commerce-based Civil Rights Act of 1964 also provided in Title VII against discrimination in employment and created the Equal Employment Opportunity Commission. The Equal Pay Act of 1963 forbade discrimination in compensation on the basis of sex. The Civil Rights Act of 1968 in Title VIII prohibited discrimination on the basis of race, color, religion, or national origin in the sale or rental of housing.

In the 1968 Civil Rights Act, Congress demonstrated that the commerce power could be employed to restrain as well as to protect civil rights. Reacting to the 1967 riots in the cities and the apparent connection with the disturbances of traveling radicals and "black power" agitators, Congress attached a rider to the 1968 statute making it a federal crime to use the facilities of interstate commerce or to cross state lines for the purpose of inciting a riot or violence.

[39]The statute was successfully invoked in *Daniel v. Paul* (1969) against a segregated amusement park in Arkansas that claimed to be a private club but sold "memberships" for 25 cents. The Court held that the act applied because the "club" advertised for patronage from an audience that the management knew included interstate travelers and because the food served moved in interstate commerce. See generally Paul R. Benson, Jr., *The Supreme Court and the Commerce Clause, 1937–1970* (New York: Dunnellen, 1971).

13

The Commerce Power
and the States

In the Republic's early years, Congress, which admittedly possessed regulatory power over commerce among the states, generally failed to exercise it or used it very incompletely. The states, on the other hand, were continually adopting legislation that, intentionally or not, touched interstate commerce. It then became the duty of the Supreme Court to decide whether the Constitution left room for the states to exercise those controls, or whether regulatory power belonged exclusively to Congress. The Court has wrestled with these issues for two centuries, and no end is in sight.

THE EXCLUSIVENESS ISSUE

Whether and to what extent the commerce power is an exclusive power of Congress was a major focus of Marshall's three discussions concerning the commerce clause. In *Gibbons v. Ogden* (1824) New York State had clearly undertaken to assert authority over interstate navigation using New York waters. In *Brown v. Maryland* (1827) the state had levied a rather heavy license tax on importers of foreign articles and had forbidden them to sell the goods they imported until they paid the tax. In *Willson v. Black-Bird Creek Marsh Co.* (1829) a dam built across a navigable creek under authority of a Delaware law had been broken by a vessel. When the owners of the dam brought an action of trespass against the owner of the vessel, he defended on the ground that the creek was a navigable highway that had been unlawfully obstructed by the dam.

After Marshall, problems of similar character came before the Taney Court. In *The License Cases* (1847) liquor purchased in one state was sold in another state without the vendor's obtaining the license required by law in the state of sale. *The Passenger Cases* (1849) arose when New York and Massachusetts imposed on masters of ships coming into the state from foreign ports a tax for each passenger aboard, the proceeds of which were used to defray the costs of examining passengers for contagious diseases and to maintain a hospital for those found to be diseased.

The Concurrent Power Theory

Judicial discussion in this series of cases developed several theories of exclusiveness in federal-state relations under the commerce clause. The first may be called *the theory of concurrent power.* According to this view no field of regulation was exclusively reserved to Congress by the commerce clause. Both Congress and the states had authority to range over the entire field of commerce. The only limitation on state power to regulate commerce was the supremacy clause of Article VI—that is, a federal statute would definitely displace any conflicting state statute. In the absence of such conflicting legislation, the states would be free to go as far as they liked.

This argument was made on behalf of the state in *Gibbons v. Ogden.* It was contended that the state had the regulatory power prior to the adoption of the Constitution, and that it was retained by the Tenth Amendment. The affirmative grant of regulatory power to Congress did not oust the states, "unless in its own nature . . . the continued exercise of it by the former possessor is inconsistent with the grant," which was alleged not to be the case here. To support the concurrent theory, the analogy of the taxing power was used. The Constitution gives Congress power to lay and collect taxes, but this grant clearly does not interfere with the exercise of the same power by the states. Why does not the same situation prevail with respect to the commerce power?

Marshall met this argument head on and refuted it. The commerce and taxing powers are similar neither in their terms nor their nature.

> The power of taxation . . . is a power which, in its own nature, is capable of residing in, and being exercised by, different authorities at the same time. . . . When, then, each government exercises the power of taxation, neither is exercising the power of the other. But, when a State proceeds to regulate commerce with foreign nations, or among the several States, it is exercising the very power that is granted to Congress, and is doing the very thing which Congress is authorized to do.

The Dormant Power Theory

At the opposite pole from the concurrent power doctrine was the so-called *dormant power theory*. Where the former gave maximum range to state authority, the latter reduced state power to a minimum. Stated succinctly, the dormant view was that the grant of commerce power to Congress, even though unexercised by Congress, necessarily prevented the states from regulating commerce and invalidated any regulations which impinged on commerce.

Justice Johnson's concurring opinion in *Gibbons v. Ogden* forthrightly adopted this view; New York's action in granting a monopoly affecting interstate commerce was invalid whether or not there was conflicting legislation by Congress, he contended. But Marshall avoided taking a position on the issue. In discussing state power, he said, "we may dismiss . . . the inquiry, whether it is surrendered by the mere grant to congress, or is retained until congress shall exercise the power. We may dismiss that inquiry because it has been exercised, and the regulations which congress deemed it proper to make, are now in full operation." In the *Black-Bird* case there was, in Marshall's view, no conflicting federal act (though actually Willson's vessel was licensed under the same federal statute as Gibbons's boat had been), but again Marshall avoided deciding that the state act authorizing damming of a navigable creek was "repugnant to the power to regulate commerce in its dormant state" by holding that the state power being used was the police power rather than the commerce power.

Thus the dormant power theory won no explicit official endorsement from the Court, but at the same time it was not definitively rejected, as the concurrent notion had been. So it continued to figure in Supreme Court discussions. It was avowed by part of the Court in *The License Cases* (1847), where the justices were so badly split that no opinion for the Court was possible. Two years later in *The Passenger Cases* (1849), the dormant power theory finally achieved a victory as the Court held state taxing power to have been abridged "by mere affirmative grants of power to the general government." This was Taney's characterization of the opinion, and naturally he protested it, saying: "I cannot foresee to what it may lead." Actually it led nowhere, for in another three years the concept of the "dormant" commerce clause as an absolute bar to state regulation of commerce was abandoned by every member of the Court except one in the great case of *Cooley v. Port Wardens of Philadelphia* (1852). Before we get to that point, however, we must trace the fortunes of still another unsuccessful doctrine of the period.

The Mutual Exclusiveness Theory

This third theory is that of *mutual exclusiveness*. The defeat of the concurrent doctrine in the *Gibbons* case had established that there must be some degree of exclusiveness in the congressional commerce power, some areas of regulation from which the states were excluded. The question was, how much exclusiveness, and how was it to be determined? One possible answer was that the field of commercial regulation was divided into two parts by a definite line. On one side of the line the federal government could regulate; the other side belonged to the states; each had to keep out of the other's territory. Their powers, in short, were mutually exclusive.

Marshall seemed in the *Gibbons* case to mark off a sphere of regulation belonging exclusively to the states. He referred there to "that immense mass of legislation, which embraces everything within the territory of a State, not surrendered to a general government." Becoming more specific, he alleged that "inspection laws, quarantine laws, health laws of every description, as well as laws for regulating the internal commerce of a state, and those which respect turnpike roads, ferries, etc., are component parts of this mass. No direct general power over these objects is granted to congress; and, consequently, they remain subject to state legislation."

Similarly, though he did not state it so clearly, Marshall appeared to argue that Congress had exclusive jurisdiction over its sphere, and thus neither the state nor the nation could exercise the powers of the other. But then he very cleverly recaptured for the federal government much of the authority that he had appeared to give away to the states. "It is obvious," he says, "that the government of the Union, in the exercise of its express powers . . . may use means that may also be employed by a State, in the exercise of its acknowledged powers." In other words, to regulate commerce among the states it may be necessary to regulate commerce within a state. Thus he grafted onto his talk about mutually exclusive state and national powers what Crosskey calls the "doctrine of inevitable concurrency as to the means of their execution."[1] But of course this confusion made no difference, because Marshall decided the case on the quite different ground of collision between a state and a federal act.

This strange performance may make some sense if we note that mutual exclusiveness was Jeffersonian doctrine, put forward to protect state claims in opposition to federal power. Marshall may have felt that he could best restrain this view by appearing to accept it while at the same time smothering its impact in a welter of words. In the *Black-Bird* case he continued his apparent tactics of mollification of states' rights sentiment without yielding up the substance of federal power. State authorization of the dams was justified, Marshall said, by "the circumstances of the case." The legislative aims were the draining of swamps, with consequent improvement of health and enhancement of property values. Thus it was action taken under the state's police power, not a regulation of commerce, that was involved, and there was no need to avow or disavow mutual exclusiveness. It was not until the *Cooley* discussion in 1852 that the Court definitely rejected mutual exclusiveness, its

[1] W. W. Crosskey, *Politics and the Constitution in the History of the United States* (Chicago: University of Chicago Press, 1953), p. 695.

support by that time having dwindled, as in the case of the dormant power theory, to one member of the Court.

The Selective Exclusiveness Theory

The winner in this doctrinal conflict was the theory of *selective exclusiveness*. Interestingly enough, this was precisely the view Webster had urged on the Court in his original *Gibbons* argument. His contention there was "that the power of Congress to regulate commerce was complete and entire, and, to a certain extent, necessarily exclusive." By this he meant that some, but not all, areas of commercial regulation were absolutely foreclosed to the states by the constitutional grant of power to Congress. Who would decide in which areas Congress had exclusive power? Presumably that would fall to the Supreme Court. Marshall knew that if he agreed with Webster, he would have to claim for the Court a breadth of discretionary power that was bound to be unpopular with the Jeffersonians. It was perhaps for this reason that he failed to adopt straightforwardly Webster's doctrine of selective exclusiveness, but sought to achieve much the same result by the devious route of mutual exclusiveness plus inevitable concurrency in means of execution.

In any case, Webster was finally vindicated by *Cooley v. Port Wardens of Philadelphia* (1852). A state act of 1803 provided that ships in the port of Philadelphia arriving from or bound to any foreign port must engage a local pilot. Failure to do so would result in a fine equal to half the cost of pilotage, payable to the board of wardens of the port to the use of a fund for superannuated pilots and their dependents. By an act of 1789 Congress had in effect adopted all then-existing state harbor regulations and provided that pilots should continue to be regulated in conformity "with such laws as the States may respectively hereafter enact for the purpose, until further legislative provision shall be made by Congress."

Justice Curtis, writing the Court's opinion, was confronted first of all with the necessity of finally deciding one way or the other on the dormant power theory. For if the mere grant of the commercial power to Congress *ipso facto* deprived the states of all power to regulate pilots, then Congress could not confer on the states the power thus to legislate, and the act of 1789 would be void. So the Court had to start from first principles.

> The grant of commercial power to congress does not contain any terms which expressly exclude the States from exercising an authority over its subject-matter. If they are excluded, it must be because the nature of the power, thus granted to congress, requires that a similar authority should not exist in the States. . . . But when the nature of a power like this is spoken of . . . it must be intended to refer to the subjects of that power, and to say they are of such a nature as to require exclusive legislation by congress.

Thus Curtis shifted gears from the theoretical problem of the "nature" of the commerce power to the pragmatic examination of the "subjects" of that power. In this real world Curtis's first observation was that the subjects of regulation are "exceedingly various" and "quite unlike in their nature." Such heterogeneity of subjects quickly led Curtis to conclude that the rules by which they were regulated must be similarly adaptable. Whereas "some imperatively demand . . . a single uniform rule, operating equally on the commerce of the United States in every port," others "as imperatively demand . . . that diversity, which alone can meet the local necessities."

This analysis clearly doomed the dormant power theory, and Curtis wrote its epitaph in these words: "It is the opinion of a majority of the court that the mere grant to congress of the power to regulate commerce, did not deprive the States of power to regulate pilots." Instead, Curtis accepted the principle of selective exclusiveness as the Court's rule for the future, in these two pregnant sentences:

> Either absolutely to affirm, or deny that the nature of this power requires exclusive legislation by congress, is to lose sight of the nature of the subjects of this power, and to assert concerning all of them, what is really applicable but to a part. Whatever subjects of this power are in their nature national, or admit only of one uniform system, or plan of regulation, may justly be said to be of such a nature as to require exclusive legislation by congress.

Subjects lacking in these characteristics, by the same token, were not within the exclusive power of Congress. Pilotage laws, Curtis concluded, were in this latter category.

> The Act of 1789 contains a clear and authoritative declaration by the first congress, that the nature of this subject is such, that until congress should find it necessary to exert its power, it should be left to the legislation of the States; that it is local and not national; that it is likely to be best provided for, not by one system, or plan of regulation, but by as many as the legislative discretion of the several States should deem applicable to the local peculiarities of the ports within their limits.

The *Cooley* decision marks the end of the formative period for constitutional theory on federal-state relations under the commerce clause. From this period certain basic principles emerged. First, the commerce clause, by its own force and effect, gave Congress exclusive power to regulate certain kinds of commerce and voided any state infringement on those areas.[2]

Second, the rule developed by the Court conceded that there were areas where commerce among the states or with foreign nations might constitutionally be regulated by the states. Marshall had sought to leave room for such state action by giving it another name—regulation of a "police" character. This was sheer quibbling, which Taney properly exposed in *The License Cases*.

---

[2]For this reason it is still possible to speak of the "dormant commerce clause." See Julian N. Eule, "Laying the Dormant Commerce Clause to Rest," 91 YALE LAW JOURNAL 425 (1982).

Third, in the determination of this question of constitutional power, the Supreme Court was to be an active participant. True, the grant of regulatory power is to Congress. But Congress gives its attention to commerce only sporadically, whereas the Court is continuously on tap. For well over a century since *Cooley* it has consistently performed the role of umpire, enforcing the laws of Congress against conflicting state laws, invalidating state statutes discriminating against commerce, and determining whether the states are entering fields belonging to the national government under the Constitution.

STATE REGULATION AND COMMERCE

Thomas Reed Powell used to say that he could easily state the principles of the commerce clause in three sentences: "Congress may regulate interstate commerce. The states may also regulate interstate commerce, but not too much. How much is too much is beyond the scope of this statement."[3] The Supreme Court cannot evade the question of "how much is too much" that easily. In fact, this is precisely the issue it has faced in literally hundreds of cases since *Cooley* was decided.

In these federal-state commercial controversies, the decisions are complicated and often seem contradictory. It is hard to derive understandable principles out of the welter of factual situations with which the Court has dealt. Admittedly the issues are complex, but it must be frankly recognized that part of the confusion results from the fact that the judicial decisions have reflected, in Justice Rutledge's words, "not logic alone, but large choices of policy, affected . . . by evolving experience of federalism."[4]

It is easy to say that the conflict has been between a nationalism as represented by Marshall and the states' rights interests that Taney symbolized. But these labels do little toward promoting an understanding of judicial motivation over the years. Nearly all the members of the Court have been nationalists in the sense that they knew the economic history of the Confederation and were resolved to prevent fractionalization of American commerce or the setting up of trade barriers around each state.

But a nationalist view on the question of state regulation of commerce may be motivated, not by concern for an unobstructed national market, but by a laissez-faire hostility toward business regulation or taxation in general. If these motives are involved, then there may be a liberal-conservative tinge to the decisions, and the judicial lineups may seem somewhat confused. In the preceding chapter, the liberal position was that of justifying a broad extent of federal power under the commerce clause, as against conservative restrictions on federal regulatory authority. But in these federal-state conflicts, the

[3]Thomas Reed Powell, *Vagaries and Varieties in Constitutional Interpretation* (New York: Columbia University Press, 1956), p. ix.

[4]*Prudential Insurance Co. v. Benjamin* (1946).

liberal doctrine has called for limiting the inhibitions that the federal commerce clause imposes on the states, while the conservative has emphasized federal power as a limitation on state regulation or taxation.

Take the case of *Di Santo v. Pennsylvania* (1927). Pennsylvania required that persons selling steamship tickets to or from foreign countries had to be licensed. Filing of a bond was involved, and a showing that the person was actually an agent for steamship companies. The law was plainly designed to prevent fraud on the public, but the Court majority struck it down as a regulation of foreign commerce, over the dissent of Holmes, Brandeis, and Stone. It is fairly clear that the decision did not register an intent to protect commerce, but simply distaste for all business regulation. In *California v. Thompson* (1941) a liberalized Court overruled the *Di Santo* decision, and in numerous other cases made it evident that its dominant motive was to clear the channels for a reasonable amount of state regulation or revenue.

State Regulation in the Absence of Federal Legislation

Turning to the cases, it is helpful to divide them into two categories. First we may consider those in which state legislation impinging on commerce among the states is challenged and there is no conflicting federal legislation. Here the alleged conflict is directly with the "dormant" commerce clause, and the court must decide whether state regulation is consistent with the area of free trade carved out by the Constitution itself.

In such situations the Court may conclude that the state regulation is either valid or invalid. A holding of validity will be basically on the grounds developed by Curtis in the *Cooley* decision—namely, that the problem is essentially a local one in which there is no necessity for a uniform national rule. The case of *Bob-Lo Excursion Co. v. Michigan* (1948) well illustrates this situation. The Michigan civil rights act had been invoked against a Detroit amusement park company that operated an excursion steamer to an island on the Canadian side of the Detroit River. The company had refused to transport a black girl to the island, and in court the defense was that the state law could have no applicability to foreign commerce. The Supreme Court majority, however, held that this commerce was only technically foreign, and was in fact "highly local," the island being "economically and socially, though not politically, an amusement adjunct of the city of Detroit." Moreover, there was nothing in the Michigan law "out of harmony, much less inconsistent, with our federal policy in the regulation of commerce between the two countries." The Court concluded: "It is difficult to imagine what national interest or policy, whether of securing uniformity in regulating commerce, affecting relations with foreign nations or otherwise, could reasonably be found to be adversely affected by applying Michigan's statute to these facts or to outweigh her interest in doing so."

Commonly associated with the assertion that the situation is essentially local is the supporting rationalization that the state law constitutes no burden on commerce. Even where a law does have some clearly burdening effects, it may still be rescued by showing that the burden falls uniformly on the commerce affected without discrimination in favor of any group or locality. An interesting example of this position is found in *South Carolina Highway Department v. Barnwell Brothers* (1938).

South Carolina law prohibited on the highways of that state motor trucks and trailers wider than 90 inches and heavier than 20,000 pounds. These limits were substantially stricter than those in adjacent states, so that trucks meeting legal requirements elsewhere might not be able to operate in South Carolina. A general federal statute regulated interstate trucks, but it did not cover size and weight. In these circumstances the Court permitted the state law to stand. The "essentially local" requirement of the *Cooley* case was met. "Few subjects of state regulation," said Justice Stone, "are so peculiarly of local concern as is the use of state highways." Certainly the statute imposed a burden on commerce, but it fell on all truckers equally. If there had been any evidence that the state was seeking to favor its own citizens, the result would probably have been different.[5]

When the Court majority tips the scale in the other direction, and state legislation is invalidated, the discussion usually still follows the line of the *Cooley* case, but the answers are different. The Court finds that in the particular situation, unless a national, uniform rule is enforced, the burden on commerce will be too serious to be borne. And it may make a difference, as just suggested, if it appears that the burden is purposeful and deliberate. Again, the best way of getting a sense of the argument is to give examples.

In *Southern Pacific Co. v. Arizona* (1945), Arizona had passed a train-length law prohibiting operation within the state of trains more than fourteen passenger cars or seventy freight cars in length. The statute was justified as a safety measure, the hazards to trainmen from "slack action" being allegedly greater on longer trains. The railroad brotherhoods who sponsored the legislation were also perhaps not unmindful of the fact that it would create more jobs. The Court majority concluded that the claims for increased safety were slight and dubious, and were outweighed by the "national interest in keeping

---

[5]A New Mexico newspaper and radio station were enjoined from accepting or publishing within the state a Texas optometrist's advertising, under a state law forbidding price advertising on eyeglasses. The Court in *Head v. New Mexico Board of Examiners* (1963) upheld the statute as a valid exercise of the police power and not discriminatory against interstate commerce or operating to disrupt its uniformity. *Exxon Corp. v. Governor of Maryland* (1978) upheld a law prohibiting producers or refiners of petroleum products from operating retail service stations in Maryland. There was no discrimination since Maryland's entire gasoline supply came from outside the state; and it did not prohibit the flow of interstate goods, place added costs on them, or distinguish between in-state and out-of-state companies in the retail market.

An executive order issued by Boston's mayor restricting public works contracts to companies that agreed to fill at least half the jobs with Boston residents was not an unconstitutional burden on interstate commerce; *White v. Massachusetts Council* (1983).

interstate commerce free from interferences which seriously impede it and subject it to local regulation which does not have a uniform effect on the interstate train journey which it interrupts." If there was to be regulation of train lengths, the Court indicated that it would have to come from Congress, since national uniformity was "practically indispensable to the operation of an efficient and economical national railway system." There might seem to be some conflict between this decision and *Barnwell Brothers,* but the Court explained that states have a much more extensive control over their highways than over interstate railroads.

State legislative control over state highways does have its limits, however. In *Morgan v. Virginia* (1946) the law requiring the separation of passengers by race on all motor carriers within the state was invalidated so far as it affected buses in interstate travel. Having just asserted in the *Southern Pacific* case that states had unusual powers of control over motor vehicle traffic, the Court now had to make clear that this point had no particular relevance to the present case. The important thing was whether an undue burden would result from permitting local rules to govern seating in interstate buses. The Court held that there would be real disturbances to the comfort of passengers and their freedom of choice in selecting accommodations. "It seems clear to us that seating arrangements for the different races in interstate motor travel require a single, uniform rule to promote and protect national travel."[6]

Bibb v. Navajo Freight Lines (1959) saw the Court strike down an Illinois statute requiring plastic contour rear-fender mudguards on trucks operating in the state, and making the conventional mudflap, which is legal in forty-five states, illegal in Illinois. The Court regarded this as a nondiscriminatory but nevertheless unconstitutionally severe burden on commerce.[7]

In *Raymond Motor Transportation v. Rice* (1978) Wisconsin's regulations barring operation of sixty-five-foot double trucks on state highways were unanimously declared unconstitutional as placing a substantial burden on interstate commerce and making only the most speculative contribution to highway safety. Then the same ban came up from Iowa in *Kassell v. Consolidated Freightways Corp.* (1981). The Court majority gave the same answer, but this time there was more dispute. Seven justices, though divided four to three, still agreed that Iowa had not proved the danger of sixty-five-foot doubles; but Brennan and Marshall, as Black had done in *Southern Pacific,* condemned the majority for second-guessing the Iowa legislature and joined in nullifying

---

[6]In *Colorado Anti-Discrimination Commission v. Continental Air Lines* (1963) an airline was charged with violation of the state antidiscrimination act because of refusal to hire a black pilot. The airline contended that the *Morgan* case required interstate carriers to be free from diverse state regulations in the field of racial discrimination. But the Supreme Court held that there was no such need for uniform regulation in this situation, and that the act imposed no undue burden on the airline.

[7]*Great Atlantic & Pacific Tea Co. v. Cottrell* (1976) held that Mississippi could not bar Louisiana milk satisfying Mississippi health standards simply because Louisiana had not signed a reciprocity agreement with Mississippi.

the law only because Iowa officials had admitted the "protectionist" purpose of the law—namely, to shunt interstate traffic from Iowa roads into other states.[8]

It is hard, however, for the justices to avoid balancing or divining the legitimacy of state purposes against allegations of burdens on commerce.In *Hunt v. Washington State Apple Advertising Commission* (1977) the Court held that North Carolina, which grows apples, was burdening and discriminating against the sale of Washington apples in North Carolina by its labeling requirements. New Jersey's quite understandable effort to bar out-of-state garbage from being dumped in New Jersey was nevertheless held discrimination against commerce in *Philadelphia v. New Jersey* (1978). In two 1983 holdings, *Don't Waste Washington Legal Defense Foundation v. Washington* and *Hartigan v. General Electric,* the Court let stand decisions holding that states may not prevent out-of-state nuclear waste from being transported or stored within their borders. But *Pacific Gas & Electric Co. v. State Energy Commission* (1983) ruled that states may block new nuclear power plants until the federal government has approved a means for disposing of nuclear waste.

Restrictions may involve outgoing as well as incoming commerce. States may endeavor to retain certain resources for the benefit of their own citizens, but these are still trade barriers. *New England Power Co. v. New Hampshire* (1982) held that a state cannot prohibit the sale to other states of power produced by utilities within the state. An Oklahoma law forbidding the transport or shipping of minnows for sale outside the state was struck down in *Hughes v. Oklahoma* (1979). Arizona's requirement that all cantaloupes grown in the state be packed and crated in the state, defended as intended to protect the reputation of Arizona growers, was overruled in *Pike v. Bruce Church* (1970).[9]

Where the burden takes the form of a complete obstruction to commerce, then the case against the state regulation involved is very strong indeed. In *Edwards v. California* (1941) the Court held unconstitutional a California statute making it a misdemeanor for anyone knowingly to bring or assist in bringing into the state a nonresident "indigent" person.

State Power Where Federal Legislation Exists

Now we turn to situations where Congress has adopted legislation regulating interstate commerce, with which state action is alleged to conflict. The Court's problem in these cases is simpler: to decide whether Congress has completely occupied the field, or whether it has left some room for nonconflicting state legislation. There is likely, nevertheless, to be opportunity for considerable differences of opinion even here, since legislative intent is often difficult to appraise.

[8]A 1983 law raising the federal gasoline tax also opened thousands of miles of U.S. highways to doubles, causing outright defiance by some states (*New York Times,* April 11, May 20, 1983).

[9]But *White v. Massachusetts Council* (1983) upheld an order by Boston's mayor requiring at least half of the workers on each city-funded construction project to be Boston residents.

An interesting group of cases concerns those in which state labor laws have been seen to be in conflict with the national labor relations acts. Many of the cases have gone against the states, on the ground that Congress had preempted the field by its regulatory legislation. An important decision was *Hill v. Florida* (1945), where a state statute providing for compulsory licensing of labor union business agents was held to conflict with the purposes of the Wagner Act. State laws interfering with the right to strike, in public utilities as well as in private businesses, have been invalidated.[10]

Similarly, states have been forbidden to enjoin peaceful picketing[11] or to award damages therefor.[12] Relief, by damages or otherwise, has been denied for unfair labor practices.[13] State antitrust laws cannot be used to prevent the effectuation of collective bargaining agreements,[14] or to enjoin a strike as a restraint of trade.[15] Since the Railway Labor Act expressly sanctions union shop agreements, a state right-to-work law cannot be invoked to abrogate such agreements.[16] In general, states have not been permitted to duplicate remedies provided by federal legislation.[17]

An important decision *upholding* state power against federal preemption claims in the labor field was *Allen-Bradley Local v. Wisconsin Employment Relations Board* (1942), in which the Court held that federal legislation was not intended to impair a state's powers to punish or in some instances to prevent offensive conduct relating to "such traditionally local matters as public safety and order and the use of streets and highways." In this case state action was approved against mass picketing, threats of physical violence against workers, and obstruction of access to a plant by strikers.[18]

Another significant decision favorable to the states was *DeVeau v. Braisted* (1960). The New York–New Jersey waterfront compact, dealing with labor racketeering in New York Harbor, and state legislation implementing it, disqualified felons from holding office in waterfront labor organizations. The Supreme Court held that congressional consent to the compact eliminated any ground for the contention that such regulations conflicted with federal labor

---

[10]*United Transportation Union v. Long Island R. R.* (1982); *Motor Coach Employees v. Missouri* (1963); *International Union v. O'Brien* (1950).

[11]*Garner v. Teamsters Union* (1953).

[12]*San Diego Unions v. Garmon* (1957, 1959).

[13]*Guss v. Utah Labor Board* (1957).

[14]*Teamsters Union v. Oliver* (1959).

[15]*Weber v. Anheuser-Busch, Inc.* (1955).

[16]*Railway Employees Department v. Hanson* (1956)

[17]*Garner v. Teamsters Union* (1953).

[18]See also *United Automobile Workers v. Wisconsin Employment Relations Board* (1956). In *Brotherhood of Locomotive Engineers v. Chicago R. I. & P. R. Co.* (1966) an Arkansas "full crew" law was upheld against the charge that a 1963 act of Congress had preempted the field. But *Jackson Transit Authority v. Amalgamated Transit Union* (1982) held that the Urban Mass Transportation Act of 1964 did not strip the states of their traditional control over labor relations involving local governments and unions.

legislation, though a minority believed the situation to be indistinguishable from *Hill v. Florida*.

This issue of federal preemption and federal-state statutory conflict has been faced in many fields other than labor relations.[19] An interesting case from another area is *Huron Portland Cement Co. v. Detroit* (1960), where the Court upheld a conviction for violation of Detroit's smoke-abatement ordinance by a vessel in the Detroit harbor, even though the ship was operating in interstate commerce and its boiler met the standards of federal legislation.

Congressional Legitimization of State Regulations

There has been a notable line of cases upholding the right of Congress to legitimize state trade barriers where the motivation had general public approval. This technique was first employed to assist states that wished to prohibit the sale of intoxicating liquor. In 1890 the Court ruled in *Leisy v. Hardin* that Iowa could not, "in the absence of congressional permission to do so," prevent the first sale in the original package of liquor brought into the state. Within a few months Congress reacted to this decision by passing the Wilson Act rendering intoxicating liquor upon arrival in a state or territory "subject to the operation and effect of the laws of such state or territory enacted in the exercise of its police powers, to the same extent as though such . . . liquors had been produced in such state or territory, and . . . not . . . exempt therefrom by reason of being introduced therein in original packages or otherwise." The Court promptly sustained the validity of this legislation in *In re Rahrer* (1891), saying: "No reason is perceived why, if Congress chooses to provide that certain designated subjects of interstate commerce shall be governed by a rule which divests them of that character at an earlier period of time than would otherwise be the case, it is not within its competency to do so."

Congress then went further and passed the Webb-Kenyon Act of 1913 over the veto of President Taft, whose attorney general told him it was unconstitutional. This statute prohibited the shipment of liquor into any state where it was intended to be used in violation of state law. Thus it had the effect of divesting liquor of the protection of its interstate character even before it had begun to move in commerce and before it had come into the state where its illegal use was intended. The Supreme Court upheld the law, saying it was but an extension of the principle of the Wilson Act, for the purpose of "making it impossible for one State to violate the prohibitions of the laws of another through the channels of interstate commerce."[20] The substance and

---

[19]See the discussion of *Pennsylvania v. Nelson* (1956), and the preemption controversy to which it gave rise in Congress, in Chapter 4. In *Railroad Transfer Service v. Chicago* (1967), involving a transfer service for passengers and baggage between Chicago railroad stations, the Court held that the Interstate Commerce Act had preempted the field and invalidated attempts by the city to require the service to secure a license that gave the city a veto power over its operations.

[20]*Clark Distilling Co. v. Western Maryland R. Co.* (1917).

much of the exact language of the Webb-Kenyon Act were subsequently written into the Twenty-first Amendment. "Since that amendment," said Justice Brandeis in 1939, "the right of a State to prohibit or regulate the importation of intoxicating liquor is not limited by the commerce clause."[21]

STATE TAXATION AND THE IMPORTS-EXPORTS CLAUSE

State taxation of commerce presents special problems not met in the preceding discussion of state regulation. For one thing, another provision of the Constitution is here called into play as a supplement to the commerce clause, the imports-exports clause of Article I, section 10. This clause reads, in part: "No state shall, without the consent of Congress, lay any imposts or duties on imports or exports, except what may be absolutely necessary for executing its inspection laws." Another differentiating factor is that, as we saw earlier in this chapter, the taxing power is admittedly a concurrent power, whereas the commerce power is not.

Both the imports-exports clause and the commerce clause were first applied to a state effort to tax foreign commerce in the famous case of *Brown v. Maryland* (1827). Here a state act required importers of foreign articles to have a license in order to be able to sell these goods. The state contended that this was an occupational tax, not a tax on imports, but Marshall pierced through this verbiage. "No goods would be imported if none could be sold." However, he recognized that freedom of imports from taxation could not be a perpetual immunity. At some point imports must become assimilated into the general mass of property in a state and subject to state taxation. Marshall suggested the "original package" doctrine for determining when this point was reached:

> It is sufficient for the present to say, generally, that when the importer has so acted upon the thing imported, that is has become incorporated and mixed up with the mass of property in the country, it has, perhaps, lost its distinctive character as an import, and has become subject to the taxing power of the State; but while remaining the property of the importer, in his warehouse, in the original form or package in which it was imported, a tax upon it is too plainly a duty on imports to escape the prohibition in the constitution.

Although Marshall was rather tentative in putting forth the original package doctrine, it proved to have great survival value. For 132 years, as Justice Frankfurter said in 1959, the Court followed the doctrine "without a

---

[21]*Finch Co. v. McKittrick* (1939). These legislative techniques for divesting liquor of its character as interstate commerce were almost exactly repeated in dealing with the products of convict labor. See *Whitfield v. Ohio* (1936) and *Kentucky Whip & Collar Co. v. Illinois Central R. R. Co.* (1937). Congressional legitimation of state regulation of the insurance business was discussed in the preceding chapter.

single deviation." Indeed, in *Hooven & Allison Co. v. Evatt* (1945) the Court apparently extended its principle to apply not only to imports for sale, but also to imports for the importer's own use or consumption.

There never was any logical reason, however, to grant imports original package protection from nondiscriminatory state taxes. The original purpose of the imports clause was to prevent discrimination against foreign goods, and to bar taxes that would benefit states through which imports first passed at the expense of interior states of final destination and use. In *Michelin Tire Co. v. Wages* (1976) the Court finally saw this point and upheld state taxation on all imports, provided such taxes were imposed equally on all goods, foreign and domestic, and were not levied on goods still in transit. Decisions to the contrary, going back to *Low v. Austin* (1872), were overruled.

The Twenty-first Amendment, which leaves the states completely unconfined by traditional commerce clause limitations when they restrict the importation of intoxicating liquors for distribution or consumption within their borders, does not repeal the imports-exports clause. Consequently the states are still forbidden to tax liquor imports while in the original package.[22] Similarly, states may not prohibit the sale of untaxed liquor to airline passengers leaving on overseas flights, for delivery to them on arrival at their foreign destination.[23]

STATE TAXATION AND COMMERCE

The Supreme Court has examined the impact of state taxes on interstate commerce in a staggering number of cases, but from the decisions two general principles emerge more or less clearly. First, the Court has generally been resolved that state tax power shall not be used to discriminate against interstate commerce. Second, it has been equally certain that the status of interstate commerce should not be used to permit business operations to escape paying a fair share of local tax burdens. Application of these conflicting principles has been most difficult, partly because of the impossibility of being certain about the final incidence of the disputed taxes.

Implementing the first principle is the rule that property cannot be taxed while it is actually in interstate transit.[24] When interstate transit has terminated, the goods become immediately taxable and the original package gives no protection.[25] However, a tax that falls with intentional discriminatory incidence on goods originating outside the state is unconstitutional.[26]

[22]*Department of Revenue v. James B. Beam Distilling Co.* (1964).

[23]*Hostetter v. Idlewild Bon Voyage Liquor Corp.* (1964).

[24]*State Freight Tax Case* (1873). But it may be difficult to determine when interstate transit actually begins: *Coe v. Errol* (1886).

[25]*Woodruff v. Parham* (1869); *Sonneborn Bros. v. Cureton* (1923).

[26]*Welton v. Missouri* (1876).

Robbins v. Shelby County Taxing District (1887) ruled that, when delivery of goods was made from outside the state in consequence of a contract of sale entered into within the state, state taxes could not constitutionally be levied.[27] But states have largely plugged this tax loophole by "use" taxes, levied at the same rate as state sales taxes, imposed on the use of goods purchased outside the state.[28]

Discrimination is also evident when local business is given a commercial advantage over interstate commerce. Thus *Boston Stock Exchange v. State Tax Commission* (1977) held a New York stock transfer tax unconstitutional because it imposed a greater tax liability on out-of-state orders than on in-state sales. In *Maryland v. Louisiana* (1981) the Court struck down a tax imposed by Louisiana on offshore gas piped into the state, 98 percent of which went on to other states. Local users of gas were protected from paying the tax by various tax credits. Similarly, *Arizona Public Service Co. v. Snead* (1982) ruled that the state could not tax electricity exported from the state more heavily than that sold within the state.

A state cannot refuse to permit an out-of-state corporation to do business in the state, but taxing the privilege of doing business is more complicated. Where a state does both an intrastate and interstate business, the state can of course levy a privilege tax on the doing of the intrastate business.[29] *Spector Motor Service v. O'Connor* (1951) struck down a privilege tax on a corporation doing only an interstate business, but subsequent rulings have upheld a franchise tax if it is merely the "just equivalent" of other taxes,[30] and *Spector* was overruled by *Complete Auto Transit v. Brady* (1977).[31]

Where concerns do both local and interstate business, with their property being employed in both types of commerce, various apportionment formulas have been used, which the Supreme Court has approved provided the result was a fair measure for the protection provided by the state.[32] Apportioned taxes based on corporate net income have generally been regarded as not a burden on interstate commerce,[33] but state taxes on corporate gross receipts are more questionable, making possible burdensome "multiple taxation" by

[27]This rule was followed in *McLeod v. Dilworth* (1944), *Freeman v. Hewit* (1946), and *Nippert v. City of Richmond* (1946).

[28]Upheld in *Henneford v. Silas Mason Co.* (1937). For problems in the collection of use taxes, see *Nelson v. Sears, Roebuck & Co.* (1941), *General Trading Co. v. State Tax Cmsn.* (1944), *Miller Bros. v. Maryland* (1954), and *National Bellas Hess, Inc. v. Illinois* (1967).

[29]*Pacific Telephone & Telegraph Co. Tax Cmsn.* (1936).

[30]*Railway Express Agency v. Virginia* (1959); *Colonial Pipeline Co. v. Traigle* (1975).

[31]In accord, *Department of Revenue of Washington v. Assn. of Washington Stevedoring Companies* (1978), and *Exxon Corp. v. Wisconsin Department of Revenue* (1980). But these rules do not apply to foreign commerce. *Japan Line v. County of Los Angeles* (1979) held that the commerce clause bars states and localities from taxing foreign property used exclusively in international commerce.

[32]*Western Union Tel. Co. v. Massachusetts* (1888); *Pullman's Palace Car Co. v. Pennsylvania* (1891).

[33]*Northwestern States Portland Cement Co. v. Minnesota* (1959).

all the states in which the corporation did business.[34] However, in *General Motors Corp. v. Washington* (1964), a tax measured by gross wholesale sales of motor vehicles and parts in the state, even though unapportioned, was upheld on the ground that taxable local business was so mingled with interstate business that the state was justified in attributing all sales in Washington to its local activity.[35]

The apportionment principle, originating largely in connection with railroad transportation, has not been so directly applicable to navigation and air transport. For vessels the general rule is that they are taxable only at their home port, unless they have acquired actual situs in another state by continuous employment there, and this rule prevents multiple taxation.[36] However, in 1949 the apportionment principle was successfully applied by Louisiana to a barge line operating on the Mississippi.[37] Minnesota was able to utilize a version of the home port theory in winning the Court's approval for a personal property tax on the entire air fleet of Northwest Airlines, a Minnesota corporation, even though only a fraction of the fleet was in the state on tax day.[38]

Taxation of motor vehicles has largely avoided apportionment problems. Every truck entering a state can be charged a toll for its use of state highways, and the only question is whether the tax is within reasonable bounds. Since the basic decision in *Hendrick v. Maryland* (1915) comparatively few taxes on motor vehicles have been declared invalid on commerce grounds.[39] A "use and service charge" of $1 for all passengers enplaning at the Evansville, Indiana, airport was upheld by the Court in 1972 as a reasonable charge to help defray the costs of airport construction and maintenance and so not a burden on commerce "in the constitutional sense."[40]

In *Complete Auto Transit v. Brady* (1977) the Court generalized from over a century of experience a "four-prong" test for the validity of state taxation, based on the "practical effect" of the tax: whether it (1) "is applied to

---

[34]*Joseph v. Carter & Weekes Stevedoring Co.* (1947).

[35]*Joseph v. Carter & Weekes* was overruled by *Department of Revenue of Washington v. Assn. of Washington Stevedoring Companies* (1978), and *Moorman Mfg. Co. v. Bair* (1978) held that the commerce clause did not prohibit any overlap in the computation of taxable income by several states.

[36]*Gloucester Ferry Co. v. Pennsylvania* (1885); *Old Dominion S. S. Co. v. Virginia* (1905).

[37]*Ott v. Mississippi Barge Line Co.* (1949).

[38]*Northwest Airlines v. Minnesota* (1944). In *Northwestern States Portland Cement Co. v. Minnesota* (1959) the Court held there was no showing that an apportionment formula imposed "a burden upon interstate commerce in a constitutional sense."

[39]Examples of taxes upheld are *Aero Mayflower Transit Co. v. Georgia Public Service Cmsn.* (1935), *Dixie Ohio Express v. State Revenue Cmsn.* (1939), and *Capitol Greyhound Lines v. Brice* (1950). Taxes were held unacceptable in *Interstate Transit v. Lindsey* (1931) and *Ingels v. Morf* (1937).

[40]*Evansville-Vanderburgh Airport Authority District v. Delta Airlines* (1972).

an activity with a substantial nexus in the taxing State, (2) is fairly apportioned, (3) does not discriminate against interstate commerce, and (4) is fairly related to the services provided by the State." It was this fourth prong on which the Court impaled itself in *Commonwealth Edison Co. v. Montana* (1981).

That state, possessing 50 percent of the nation's low-sulfur coal reserves, had levied a 30 percent severance tax on all coal mined in the state, a tax that by 1981 was supplying 20 percent of the state's total revenue. Was this tax "fairly related" to the services provided by the state, or was it an "OPEC-like revenue maximization" at the expense of the rest of the nation? For the Court majority Justice Marshall held that this was "essentially a matter for legislative, not judicial, resolution." Three dissenting justices protested that this tactic "emasculates the fourth prong," and though White concurred with the majority, he feared that the decision might prove "an intolerable and unacceptable burden on commerce."

The *Commonwealth Edison* ruling is consistent with the Court's tendency since the 1930s to avoid, if at all possible, striking down state tax measures on constitutional grounds.[41] Perhaps the initial cause was the desperate financial situation of the states during the Depression, when the Court felt under some compulsion to approve the new taxes developed to save the states from bankruptcy. Another factor was the uncertainty of some justices as to the validity of their credentials as tax umpires. Around 1940 Justices Black and Douglas, joined for a time by Frankfurter, revived the Taney doctrine that the responsibility of enforcing the commerce clause involves so much discretion that it belongs more appropriately to Congress[42]—a position renewed by Marshall in *Commonwealth Edison*. But the basic constitutional position is still that stated by Frankfurter in *Freeman v. Hewitt* (1946): "The Commerce Clause was not merely an authorization to Congress to enact laws for the protection and encouragement of commerce among the States, but by its own force created an area of trade free from interference by the States." To which the Court added in *Boston Stock Exchange v. State Tax Commission* (1977):

[41]In *Cory v. White* (1982), involving the competing claims of California and Texas to tax the Howard Hughes estate, the Court ruled that multiple taxation on the basis of domicile does not offend the Constitution.

[42]See Taney's dissent in *Pennsylvania v. Wheeling Bridge Co.* (1852); the dissent of Black, Douglas, and Frankfurter in *McCarroll v. Dixie Greyhound Lines* (1940); and Black's concurring opinion in *Northwest Airlines v. Minnesota* (1944).

After the decision in *Northwestern States Portland Cement Co.,* upholding the right of a state to impose a net income tax on the purely interstate business of a foreign corporation, Congress entered this field for the first time and passed a statute limiting the powers of states to tax the net income of interstate corporations. Subsequent congressional efforts to legislate on multiple state taxation were unsuccessful; but in 1966 seven states drafted the Multistate Tax Compact for this purpose, and other states subsequently joined. See *U. S. Steel Corp. v. Multistate Tax Commission* (1978).

The Commerce Clause does not, however, eclipse the reserved "power of the States to tax for the support of their own governments" . . . or for other purposes . . . ; rather, the Clause is a limit on State power. Defining that limit has been the continuing task of this Court. . . .

But the Court admitted:

This case-by-case approach has left "much room for controversy and confusion and little in the way of precise guides to the States in the exercise of their indispensable power of taxation."

14
Qualification and Election
of the President

The creation of the Presidency of the United States by the Constitutional Convention was political invention of a very high order. While there can have been in 1787 no conception of the powerful and multifaceted office that history and practice were to make of the Presidency, the basis was laid for this development by the bold decisions of the Founders.

Their duality of views on the presidential office has already been noted. On one side was the preference for an executive that would be nothing more than an institution for carrying the will of the legislature into effect, with an incumbent appointed by and accountable to the legislature. On the other side was the strong-executive faction, which wanted a single-headed office independent of the legislature. As the Convention deliberated, the key decisions increasingly favored the latter view.

In the controversy over ratification of the Constitution, fear of these strong executive powers was one of the motives most widely exploited by opponents of the new charter. Hamilton in No. 67 of *The Federalist* ridiculed the efforts that had been made to present the office as possessed of practically royal prerogatives. As for the unity of the executive, he contended that far from being a danger, it made the institution more susceptible of popular surveillance and control, while at the same time guaranteeing energy in the office, "a leading character in the definition of good government."

What the "energy" of George Washington and his successors has made of the office cannot be recounted here. Our concern is the much narrower one of examining the basis that the specific provisions of Article II, as judicially interpreted, have provided for the presidential office, and the authority that these provisions have conferred, or the limits they have imposed, upon presidential power. Thus confined, much of the flesh and blood of the Presidency is outside the scope of our consideration. For the Supreme Court has only infrequently been called on to resolve the constitutional issues of the Presidency. Where executive action has impinged on private rights, or occasionally in cases of conflict between the President and Congress, judicial intervention to define the constitutional situation has been successfully invoked. But over the broad political reaches of presidential power the judicial influence has been minor. In the area of the present chapter, which deals with the qualifications and electoral arrangements for the Presidency, judicial interpretation has seldom been important.

QUALIFICATIONS

The Constitution provides that "No person except a natural born citizen, or a citizen of the United States, at the time of the adoption of this Constitution, shall be eligible to the office of President." The clause making eligible persons who were citizens of the United States at the time of the adoption of the Constitution was of only temporary significance, but it was necessary since every adult in the United States in 1787, who had been born in this country, had been born a British subject.

Every person born in the United States and subject to its jurisdiction is a citizen and, of course, a natural-born citizen. Persons born abroad and acquiring citizenship by the process of naturalization are thus excluded from eligibility to the Presidency. But persons born abroad to American citizen parents are considered natural-born American citizens.[1]

The other qualifications of the President as stated in Article II are the age of thirty-five years, and residence for fourteen years within the United States. Although these are the only constitutional qualifications that must be met for eligibility to the Presidency, in effect Congress has added to them by providing that persons convicted of various federal crimes shall, in addition to other penalties, be incapable of holding office under the United States.

[1]Congress so provided by Act of March 26, 1790, 1 Stat. 415.

PRESIDENTIAL ELECTION
AND THE CONSTITUTION

The Original Plan

The constitutional solution of the problem of presidential selection was to provide that each state should "appoint, in such manner as the legislature thereof may direct, a number of electors, equal to the whole number of Senators and Representatives to which the State may be entitled in the Congress." That the electors should not be holders of federal office was guaranteed by the further provision that "no Senator or Representative, or person holding an office of trust or profit under the United States, shall be appointed an elector."

The choosing of the President was thus to be in the hands of a selected group of citizens in each state, equal in number to that state's congressional delegation. But the resemblance to Congress went no further. Instead of assembling in the capital, the electors were to "meet in their respective States, and vote by ballot for two persons, of whom one at least shall not be an inhabitant of the same State with themselves." The results of the vote were to be transmitted to the president of the Senate, who would open the sealed certificates in the presence of both houses, and the votes would then be counted. The person with the greatest number of votes was to be the President, provided he had a majority of the whole number of electors. If two candidates were tied, and both had more than a majority, the House was immediately to choose between them. If no candidate had a majority, then the House would choose from the five highest on the list. In either event the House was to vote by states, "the representation from each State having one vote," with a majority required to elect. After the choice of the President, the person having the next greatest number of votes was to be vice-president, and in the event of a tie, the Senate was to choose between the contenders.

The intention of the framers as to the role of the electors was not entirely clear. Hamilton thought the electors could freely choose candidates for President on the basis of their own judgment and experience, but others have argued that the electoral plan was a step toward, not away from, popular election and that the electors were to be bound by pledges they had given in securing appointment.[2] In any case, the unanimity of agreement on Washington prevented any difficulties arising in the first two elections.

With the development of political parties, the electoral plan was immediately in trouble. The result of the 1796 balloting was to give the Presi-

---

[2]Lucius Wilmerding, Jr., *The Electoral College* (New Brunswick, N.J.: Rutgers University Press, 1958), pp. 19-22.

dency and vice-presidency to different parties, with John Adams and Thomas Jefferson ranking first and second in the electoral voting.

This was a minor defect, however, compared with the result in 1800. Jefferson and Aaron Burr, as the Republican candidates for President and vice-president, were both named by each Republican elector, so that a tie resulted. Everyone understood that Jefferson was the Presidential choice, but the tie threw the election into the House, voting by states. It took prolonged balloting before the House finally elected Jefferson in February, 1801.

Problems under the Twelfth Amendment

This experience exposed a constitutional defect so serious that immediate repair was needed. Consequently the Twelfth Amendment was adopted in 1804, and it still controls the electoral process. It made the following changes: (1) the electors were to ballot separately for President and vice-president; (2) if no candidate for President received a majority, the House, voting as before by states, was to choose "from the persons having the highest numbers not exceeding three on the list"; (3) the vice-president also had to receive a majority of the electoral votes, and if no one achieved a majority, the Senate was to choose between the two highest candidates; (4) if the choice of President fell to the House, and it had not made a choice by March 4, the vice-president was to act as President; and (5) it was specifically provided that no person constitutionally ineligible to the office of President should be eligible to that of vice-president.

This was an improvement, but the election of 1824 showed how unsatisfactory was the alternative of selection by the House. The breakdown of the congressional caucus in that election caused votes to be cast for a number of candidates, the three highest being Andrew Jackson with ninety-nine, John Quincy Adams, eighty-four, and William H. Crawford, forty-one. Henry Clay, Speaker of the House and one of the defeated candidates, swung the vote to Adams, to the vast outrage of the Jackson forces, who claimed that the House was morally bound to select the candidate with the highest electoral vote. The subsequent development of a mature two-party system kept futher electoral difficulties from arising until 1876.

The Hayes-Tilden election controversy was an incredibly tangled affair. The truth seems to be that the Democrats stole the election in the first place, and the Republicans then stole it back. There was no doubt that Tilden, the Democratic candidate, had a popular majority. He was conceded 184 electoral votes, one less than a majority, and Hayes had 165, while 20 were in dispute. Disagreement centered on Louisiana, South Carolina, and Florida, from which rival sets of returns had been sent in amid charges of fraud and violence, and Oregon, where one elector was in dispute. A majority of the Senate was Republican and a majority of the House was Democratic. If the president of the

Senate decided which votes to count, Hayes would win, whereas if the election was thrown into the House, Tilden would be elected.

The Twelfth Amendment provides that the president of the Senate should open the certificates, but does not say who should do the counting or decide what votes to count. With the two houses hopelessly deadlocked, a completely extraconstitutional compromise was eventually enacted at the end of January, 1877. A fifteen-man Electoral Commission was created, composed of five members of the house (three Democrats and two Republicans), five Senators (three Republicans and two Democrats), and five members of the Supreme Court. Four of the justices were designated in the act by reference to their judicial circuits, and they were evenly divided as to parties. The fifth justice, chosen by these four, was Joseph P. Bradley of new Jersey, a Republican, whose vote gave the Republicans an eight to seven margin on each of the issues before the Commission, electing Hayes by a vote of 185 to 184.

Thus was the country rescued from the consequences of a faulty electoral system by a device entirely unknown to the Constitution. In 1887 Congress by statute provided that any dispute over appointment of electors was to be conclusively settled by the state itself, provided it did so at least six days before the time for the meeting of the electors. If a state failed to perform this function and its electoral vote remained in dispute, it would not be counted unless both houses of Congress agreed. So the 1876 dilemma need not be reenacted, and no subsequent presidential election has posed the threat of comparable breakdown in electoral machinery. But certain basic characteristics of the electoral college system remain as perennial subjects of controversy.

ELECTORAL COLLEGE PROBLEMS

Distortion of the Popular vote

The first objection to the electoral college system is the disproportion it usually yields between the electoral vote and the popular vote. The electoral college margin of the winning candidate is typically much greater than his majority in the popular vote. This does no real harm, of course, and may even have some psychological value when it results in giving a clear electoral college majority to a candidate who secured only a plurality in the popular vote.[3]

[3]On electoral college problems and proposals for reform, see Neal Peirce, *The People's President* (New York: Simon & Schuster, 1967); James David Barber, ed., *Choosing the President* (Englewood Cliffs, N.J.: Prentice-Hall, 1974); Lawrence D. Longley and Alan G. Braun, *The Politics of Electoral College Reform* (New Haven, Conn.: Yale University Press, 1972); Wallace S. Sayre and Judith H. Parris, *Voting for President* (Washington, D.C.: Brookings Institution, 1970); Judith Best, *The Case against Direct Election of the President* (Ithaca, N.Y.: Cornell University Press, 1975); Nelson W. Polsby and Aaron Wildavsky, *Presidential Elections,* 4th ed. (New York: Scribner's, 1975).

But electoral college distortion can also have the opposite consequence of deflating a popular vote majority or plurality into an electoral vote minority. In three presidential elections—1824, 1876, and 1888—the winning candidate did not lead in the popular vote. However, in two of these three cases, it is hardly fair to blame the electoral system for the perversion of the popular mandate. In 1824 this responsibility rests on the House for failing to select the popular favorite, Jackson, and similarly in 1876 it was the Electoral Commission which made the decisions that kept Tilden out of office. Thus the 1888 experience, when Harrison was elected with 100,000 fewer popular votes than Cleveland, is the only bona fide case of the electoral college yielding a minority president. Nevertheless, it may well be argued that even one case is one too many, and that the mere existence of such a possibility is a grave defect in an electoral system.[4]

The Unit Vote

Actually, the major reason for this potentiality of electoral miscarriage is not a constitutionally required feature of the electoral system. The primary cause of distortion is the practice (which, with minor exceptions, all states have followed for well over a century) of each state casting its electoral votes as a unit for the candidate securing a majority or plurality of the popular votes in that state, rather than using some plan of proportional division of the electors.

The Constitution does not control the manner in which the states shall "appoint" their electors, and a great variety of means have been employed. In the first three presidential elections, choice of electors by the state legislatures was the usual method. Thereafter popular election became the rule, and at first several states used the district plan, which meant that a state's electoral vote could be divided among the candidates. By 1832, however, all states had abandoned the district plan, and it has since been employed only rarely. With the statewide general ticket system of choosing electors, it is virtually impossible for a split result to occur. No state is likely to abandon the present plan on its own initiative, for a proportional division of its vote while other states retained the block principle would minimize its electoral college importance.

The unit-vote system makes each of the big states, where the parties are

---

[4]In 1976 the switch of only 9,246 popular votes in Ohio and Hawaii could have changed enough electoral votes to elect Gerald Ford, even though Carter led by 1.7 million votes nationwide.

A 1978 task force of the Twentieth Century Fund proposed a so-called bonus plan that would guarantee election of the popular vote winner while retaining the electoral college. It called for a bonus of 102 votes (two for each state plus the District of Columbia) to be awarded to the candidate receiving the most popular votes nationwide, on top of his electoral college total. The bonus plan would have assured the election of the popular vote winner in every election in U.S. history.

usually rather evenly balanced, a glittering jackpot. The parties must give major attention to capturing votes in the large states, where the potential payoff is so great, while largely disregarding the smaller states. The candidates are usually selected from the large states, and the parties must direct their appeals to the interests of their urban and industrial residents. Moreover, with the entire electoral vote of each large state subject to determination by the margin of a few thousand votes, bad weather, fraud, appeals to minority groups, and other fortuitous circumstances may detemine the choice of President.

Another effect of the unit-vote system is that it prevents voters who supported the losing candidate in each state from having any impact on the electoral result. Though a candidate may secure only 51 percent of the popular votes, he is awarded the entire electoral vote of the state, and those who opposed him are in effect coerced by the system into supporting him. In 1966 the state of Delaware filed an unusual suit with the Supreme Court in its original jurisdiction, contending that the unit-voting system abridged the political rights of individuals by canceling each state's minority votes, gave the large states a favored position, created the possibility of minority Presidents, and in general guaranteed distortion and debasement in the electoral process. The Supreme Court dismissed the suit.[5]

Other Distorting Factors

The unit system of casting electoral votes is not the only cause of the typical lack of correspondence between the electoral and popular results. There is in addition the overweighting of the electoral vote of the less populous states, which results from giving each state, large or small, two electoral votes on the basis of its two Senators.

A further factor in causing skewed electoral results is the varying rate of voter turnout in the states. In the South, where the real contests until recently were decided in the Democratic primaries, the final elections tended to be routine, attracting relatively few voters. The past disfranchisement of black voters in the area also contributed to low turnout, so that in general each electoral vote case by a Southern state represented only a fraction of the voters per electoral vote elsewhere.

Finally, shifts in population and varying rates of population growth among the states between census periods cause additional disproportion between popular and electoral votes. In the election of 1980 each state still cast the number of electoral votes it had been awarded under the census of 1970. Thus New York had forty-one electoral votes in the 1980 election, whereas her population as shown by the 1980 census would have entitled the state to only thirty-six votes.

[5]*Delaware v. New York* (1966).

The Status of Electors

A second disturbing feature of the present system is the status of the electors. Successful operation of the electoral college system requires that the electors regard themselves as automatons, whose sole function is to cast an electoral vote for the candidates of their party. General acceptance of the automatic character of the electors' function is reflected in the fact that their names do not even appear on the ballot in most states. However, in some elections there have been organized efforts in certain Southern states to claim for electors the freedom of choice that presumably was theirs in the original constitutional theory. In part this freedom has been asserted by individual electors. But it has also been claimed by state legislatures that have provided for unpledged slates of electors, under no instructions from the electorate and completely free to vote their own choices in the electoral college.

In 1948 a Democratic elector from Tennessee, who was also on the slate of electors for the States' Rights Dixiecrats, cast his electoral vote for Thurmond instead of Truman. In 1956 one of Alabama's Democratic electors refused to support Stevenson and cast his vote for an Alabama circuit judge.

In 1960 several slates of electors unpledged to any candidate were on state ballots. Georgia's twelve Democratic electors were not pledged to support Kennedy, and only five of Alabama's eleven Democratic electors were so pledged. In Mississippi there were two sets of Democratic electors, one unpledged, while in Louisiana the States' Rights party's electors were unpledged. In the actual balloting the six unpledged Alabama electors and all eight Mississippi electors voted for Senator Harry F. Byrd of Virginia. So did one of the Republican electors from Oklahoma, Henry D. Irwin. After Kennedy's narrow victory at the polls, Irwin and an Alabama attorney made contact with all the victorious electors of both parties urging them to withhold their electoral votes or to vote for a third candidate, in the hope that Kennedy would be deprived of his electoral vote majority and the election be thrown into the House. But the plan failed, and no elector except Irwin violated his pledge. There was one defection in each of the 1968 and 1972 elections.[6]

Election by the House

A third feature of the present system that is almost universally condemned is the choice of a President by the House, voting by states, in the event that no candidate receives a majority of the electoral vote. Since the Twelfth Amendment has been in effect, this has happened only once, in 1824, and it yielded a result in conflict with the voters' choice. Much more serious results are possible if the experience is ever repeated, as it very nearly was in 1948. Had Truman lost Ohio and California—and his combined majority in

---

[6]An Alabama statute requiring electors to vote for the nominees of their party was upheld by the Supreme Court in *Ray v. Blair* (1952).

these two states was 25,472 out of 6,700,000 votes cast—the election would have been thrown into the House, because of the success of the third-party candidate in four states.

In the House as constituted on January 3, 1949, twenty-one state delegations had a Democratic majority, twenty had a Republican majority, three were evenly divided, and four represented states carried by the States' Rights ticket. It is hard to overestimate the turmoil that would have been involved in getting twenty-five of these delegations to agree on Truman, Dewey, or Thurmond in the short period from January 3 to noon of January 20, the hour when the new President's term was to begin. If no President had been selected by that time, then the vice-president, chosen from between Alben Barkley and Earl Warren by the Senate, which had fifty-four Democrats, would have begun to act as President.

Again, in 1960 a shift of only a few thousand votes in key states carried by Kennedy with narrow margins would have left him, as well as Nixon, without an electoral college majority and enabled the Byrd electors to throw the choice of president into the House. In 1968, for the first time in history, there was a complete slate of electors for three candidates in every state. George Wallace hoped to throw the election into the House, but though he received 9.9 million votes (13.5 percent) and though there was a difference of only 500,000 votes between Nixon and Humphrey, the luck of the electoral college translated Nixon's 43.4 percent of the popular vote into 56 percent (302 votes) of the electoral total.

In 1980 there were also three national slates, and again the possibility of the election being thrown into the House was raised. But John Anderson, though receiving 7 percent of the popular vote, carried no states, and Reagan's popular majority of 50.7 percent and victory in forty-four states gave him 489 electoral votes to Carter's 49.[7]

PROPOSALS FOR ELECTORAL REFORM

Reform of the electoral college system has been perennially discussed, but the difficulty of taking action has always been the absence of a consensus on an alternative. A principal reason for this inability to agree on any change in the electoral arrangements is that, in spite of the defects pointed out above, many persons feel, with considerable justification, that the present system has worked reasonably well. It has met crises successfully. No President has had to be chosen by the House since 1824. No President has been elected with fewer popular votes than his opponent since 1888. The method has been a strong source of support for the two-party system by handicapping the development

[7]For a horrendous view of what might have happened, see Laurence H. Tribe and Thomas M. Rollins, "Deadlock: What Happens If Nobody Wins," 246 ATLANTIC 49 (1980).

of third parties. Although twelve men who received less that 50 percent of the popular vote have been elected President,[8] only three were supported by less than 45 percent of the electorate—Lincoln with 39.79 percent in 1860, Wilson with 41.85 percent in 1912, and Nixon with 43.4 percent in 1968.

Defenders of the present system admit, of course, that the casting of electoral votes by state units gives predominant campaign importance to the large states, the large cities, and key minority groups in the large cities. But their response is that it is appropriate for urban influences to control in electing the President because state legislatures and the U.S. Senate are overweighted in representation of rural areas and the small states. Thus one imbalance tends to correct the other.

The Proportional-Vote Plan

The proportional-vote was originally referred to as the Lodge-Gossett amendment after its two initial sponsors. This plan would give candidates for the Presidency such proportion of the electoral vote in each state as the candidate received of the total vote cast for the Presidency in that state, percentages being figured to three places beyond the decimal point. This plan would make the relation between the electoral and popular vote exactly proportional, but would not correct the distortions arising from the small-state advantage in electoral votes, differences in the rate of turnout, or census lag in dividing electoral votes among the states.

Fears have been expressed that the proportional electoral count might encourage the formation of third parties or a whole group of splinter parties. The present block system has been a barrier to the success of third parties, for unless they can get the top vote in one or more states, they get no credit at all for their popular votes in the electoral college. But under a proportional system of recording the vote, all votes cast are given effect and the chances of a party with a mere plurality vote winning the Presidency are increased. For this reason the Lodge-Gossett plan, when before the Senate in 1950, was revised by addition of the Lucas amendment, requiring a 40 percent plurality in the electoral vote to elect a President. If no candidate had such a proportion, the election would be thrown into Congress, the House and Senate, sitting jointly, to elect the President from the top two candidates.

In addition to reflecting more accurately the popular strength of the candidates, the proportional plan would retain the importance of the states in the electoral process, and would encourage turnout and the growth of the second party in previously one-party states, since every vote cast would be given effect in the count. Objections to the plan, in addition to its possible encouragement of splinter parties, are that the large states would lose their present com-

---

[8]This figure would be increased to fifteen by adding the three Presidents—Adams (1824), Hayes (1876), and Harrison (1888)—who were elected despite the fact that they had fewer popular votes than their opponents.

manding position, while the small states would not give up their advantage of two electoral votes regardless of size, and that it would still be possible for a candidate to be elected President with fewer popular votes than his opponent.

The District-Vote Plan

The district plan, originally sponsored by Senator Mundt, would require electors to be chosen by districts, using either the existing congressional districts or the same number of districts drawn specifically for presidential elections. The two electoral votes awarded to each state by reason of its Senate seats would of course continue to be subject to statewide election. Unlike the proportional plan, which dispenses with electors, the district plan would retain the position of elector, and the candidate for elector receiving a plurality of the votes in his district would be elected. If no candidate achieved a majority in the electoral vote, the President would be chosen from among the highest three candidates by the senators and representatives sitting jointly and voting as individuals.

The arguments for the district plan are that it would eliminate the electoral distortions and emphasis on the large states that result from the unit-vote plan; that by using congressional districts it would give exactly the same kind of representative quality to the electoral vote as is found in Congress; and that, unlike the proportional plan, it would discourage third parties because they would have to carry individual congressional districts in order to have any electoral impact.

Against the district plan the arguments are that it is preferable to have different bases for the election of President and members of Congress; that the temptation to gerrymander congressional districts would be too great to control, since gerrymandering would now pay off twice, in both congressional and presidential elections; that many states would continue to vote as a unit, since the winning party is often dominant in the entire state; and that rural and one-party states would be advantaged at the expense of urban areas.

Direct Election

The simplest and most direct plan for electing the President would be to abandon the electoral college system entirely, ignore state lines, and throw all the voters of the nation into a single electorate for choice of the President. The case for this method is very strong. The votes of all individuals would be equal. Since all votes count in the national total, political activity would be encouraged in all areas, including previously one-party states.

The direct nationwide vote is the most democratic system. The President, as the only elected national official (along with the vice-president), should be chosen by the nation and responsible to it. Only direct election can guarantee that the person elected President will be the one with more popular votes than any other candidate. Under the unit, proportional, or district plan it is possible for a candidate to lose in the popular vote and win in the electoral vote; all three systems are lotteries where the relation between the popular and electoral votes is subject to chance.

Direct election would of course eliminate the electoral vote advantage now enjoyed by the small states, and for this reason it was long assumed that a constitutional amendment abolishing the electoral vote system could never secure ratification by three-fourths of the states. But in fact the small-state advantage has been more than offset by the advantage the unit system gives to the large states. Increasingly it has become evident that the only practicable way to remedy these inequities is to abandon the states as electoral areas.

Direct election would create some problems calling for decision. An absolute majority of the popular votes could hardly be required for election; as already noted, fifteen past Presidents polled less than 50 percent of the vote. On the other hand, if a plurality is sufficient to elect, this might encourage splinter parties to enter candidates and fragment the national vote. A President who took office on the basis of a 30 percent plurality would be in a very weak position to exercise national leadership.

But if 40 percent or some other minimum plurality is adopted, provision must be made for the eventuality that no candidate may achieve that minimum. There are two possibilities. One is a runoff election limited to the top two candidates. The other is election by Congress, with members of both houses sitting jointly and voting as individuals. The first is democratic but expensive and a complete novelty at the national level. The second is less democratic but simpler and sanctioned by past practice. Opponents of the direct election plan argue that it would eliminate critical leverage for metropolitan areas underrepresented elsewhere in the political system, that it would undermine the two-party system, and that it would weaken the presidential mandate as splinter party candidates eroded the winner's electoral base.

After Wallace's third-party threat to the electoral system in 1968, interest in the direct election alternative increased sharply. In 1969 a constitutional amendment sponsored by Senator Birch Bayh and supported by President Nixon passed the House by a vote of 339 to 70. However, it failed in the Senate in 1970 when two efforts to stop a filibuster were defeated. In 1977 President Carter renewed the direct election proposal, and Senator Bayh reintroduced his constitutional amendment, which was narrowly approved by the Senate Judiciary Committee, but got no further. A 1980 Gallup poll showed overwhelming popular support for direct election: 67 percent for to 19 percent against.

TERM AND TENURE

The decision of the Convention for a four-year term was based in large part on the delegates' preference for presidential reeligibility. When Washington declined a third term, he did so for reasons of personal convenience. But when Jefferson announced in 1807 that he would withdraw after two terms, he stressed Washington's example and raised the issue to one of principle, arguing that indefinite reeligibility would undermine the elective system and turn the Presidency into a life tenure post. The subsequent examples of Madison, Monroe, and Jackson gave the two-term tradition almost unassailable validity.

The first concerted attack on the two-term tradition came in 1876 from a group of Republican politicians who wanted Grant to run for a third term, but the resistance was overwhelming. In 1908 Theodore Roosevelt, having served three and a half years of McKinley's term and one term in his own right, stated that "the wise custom which limits the President to two terms regards the substance and not the form," and stated flatly that "under no circumstances will I be a candidate for or accept another nomination." However, by 1912 he had changed his mind, and unsuccessfully sought a third term. Calvin Coolidge found himself in somewhat the same position in 1928, but he never definitely stated his view on the application of the two-term tradition in his case, merely announcing that he did not "choose to run for President in 1928."

Thus it was left for Franklin Roosevelt definitely to breach the tradition in 1940, when the electorate concluded that maintenance of the two-term limit was less important than retaining his experienced leadership in a world at war. Election for a precedent-shattering fourth term was quickly followed by Roosevelt's death on April 12, 1945.

The tragic denouement of this experiment with unlimited reeligibility, combined with pent-up Republican frustration over four successive defeats by the same candidate, quickly produced a move for writing the two-term rule into the Constitution. When the Republicans won control of the Eightieth Congress they immediately pushed through such an amendment, which was ratified in 1951. The Twenty-second Amendment provides that no person shall be elected to the office of President more than twice, and that no person who has held the office of President, or acted as President, for more than two years of a term to which some other person was elected President, shall be elected more than once. This provision would have made Theodore Roosevelt ineligible in 1912 and Coolidge in 1928, but not Johnson in 1968.

In support of the two-term limit, it can be argued that the physical toll of eight years in the Presidency under present conditions is all that any person can safely endure and that it is desirable to have an automatic limit on presidential ambitions. On the other hand, this provision forecloses the possibility of retaining an experienced President for a third term in times of emergency, and it may substantially weaken the authority of the President in the closing years of the second term. During the Carter administration, some support developed for a single six-year presidential term, the argument being that with reelection foreclosed, the President could concentrate on promoting the public interest without considering the impact on his electoral fortunes. A Gallup poll rejected the proposal, only 32 percent favoring it.

SUCCESSION

Apart from the expiration of his term, the President's tenure in office may be terminated by resignation, impeachment, inability to perform his duties, or death. Eight Presidents have died in office, and there have been three instances when substantial doubt existed about the ability of the President to perform his duties. Andrew Johnson was impeached but not convicted, while Richard Nixon averted impeachment and certain conviction by resigning.

The Status of the Vice-President

The constitutional provision for these contingencies is found in Article II, section I, as follows: "In case of the removal of the President from office, or of his death, resignation, or inability to discharge the powers and duties of the said office, the same shall devolve on the Vice-President." Another relevant provision is in the Twelfth Amendment, which requires that the vice-president have the same qualifications as the President.

The vagueness of the constitutional language on succession has been the cause of much controversy. What is it that devolves upon the vice-president when the President dies, resigns, or is impeached? Is it the "office" of President, or only the "powers and duties" of the office? Was it intended that the vice-president become President, or that he simply "act" as President until a new President was elected?

An excellent case can be made for the latter alternative, both on the basis of the language of the Constitution and on what is known about the intention of the framers from other evidence. Certainly the drafters intended that only an acting President be installed under the circumstances described in the latter part of the same paragraph, which provides: "And the Congress may by law provide for the case of removal, death, resignation or inability, both of the President and Vice-President, declaring what officer shall then act as President." The point is then driven home by the rest of the paragraph: "And such officer shall act accordingly, until the disability be removed, or a President shall be elected." There is also the language of the Twelfth Amendment, which prescribes what shall be done if no candidate secures the requisite majority of votes in the electoral college or the House: "Then the Vice-President shall act as President, as in the case of the death or other constitutional disability of the President."

There was no need to construe the constitutional language on succession until 1841, when President Harrison died after only one month in office. It therefore fell to Vice-President John Tyler to establish the practice in this all-important respect. Tyler was on his Virginia farm when Harrison died on April 4, and the cabinet sent him a notice of the fact, addressing him as vice-president. Tyler took the oath prescribed by the Constitution on April 6, but the certificate of the judge who administered the oath noted that Tyler deemed himself "qualified to perform the duties and exercise the powers and offices of President . . . without any other oath" than the one he had taken as vice-president. He nevertheless took the presidential oath, since "doubts may arise, and for greater caution."

This statement of Tyler's would indicate that he initially thought of himself as an acting President, and his cabinet appears to have taken the same position. However, on April 9 Tyler issued an "inaugural address" in which he spoke of himself as having been called "to the high office of President of this Confederacy." The claim was not accepted without controversy. John Quincy Adams recorded in his diary on April 16 his view that Tyler's position was "in direct violation both of the grammar and context of the Constitution." When Congress met on May 31, the customary resolutions were proposed informing the President that Congress was ready to proceed to business. Amendments were offered in both houses to strike out the word "President" and insert instead "Vice-President, now exercising the office of President," but they were defeated. Thus the institution of acting President was strangled at birth.

The Twentieth Amendment terminated any possible doubt on this matter by providing, in section 3: "If, at the time fixed for the beginning of the term of the President, the President elect shall have died, the Vice-President elect shall become President." The Twenty-fifth Amendment added: "In case of the removal of the President from office or of his death or resignation, the Vice-President shall become President."

Succession Beyond the Vice-President

The Constitution authorizes Congress to declare what "officer shall . . . act as President" in case neither the President nor vice-president is living or able to serve. Congress acted on this authorization in 1792, by passing a statute that provided for the succession first of the president pro tempore of the Senate and then of the Speaker of the House. It was not contemplated that these officials would have much time in office, however, for the statute required immediate steps to be taken for choosing a successor through the electoral college, who would be elected for a full four-year term. If any President had ever been elected under this statute, the synchronization of presidential elections with congressional would of course have been destroyed. But the act of 1792 never had to be utilized.

In 1886 Congress adopted a different theory of presidential succession, providing that the heads of the seven cabinet departments then existing, beginning with the secretary of state, should constitute the line of succession after the vice-president. This act repealed the 1792 provision requiring immediate election of a new President, but it substituted therefor a direction to the acting President to assemble Congress within twenty days if it were not in session, thus apparently intending to give Congress a chance to arrange for election of a President if it should see fit to do so.

Thus the law stood when Harry Truman became President to serve out the last three years and nine months of Franklin Roosevelt's fourth term. Truman was disturbed by the fact that during this long period when there would be no vice-president, succession would go to the man whom he named as secretary of state. He felt that it was undemocratic for him to be in a position to name his successor, and in a special message to Congress on June 19, 1945, he urged revision of the 1886 law to place the Speaker of the House and the president pro tempore of the Senate ahead of the cabinet in the line of succession. The Republican Eightieth Congress adopted these proposals in the Presidential Succession Act of 1947.

Under this statute the Speaker of the House, upon resigning as Speaker and as a member of the House, is to act as President when a successor to the Presidency is needed and there is no vice-president. If there is no Speaker, or if he fails to qualify, the President pro tempore of the Senate, upon resigning his post and his Senate seat, is to act as President. In either event the acting President is to serve for the remainder of the current presidential term, unless he is filling in because the President elect or vice-president elect had failed to qualify or the President was temporarily disabled; in such a situation his status would terminate if and when the President did qualify or the disability was removed. Cabinet officers follow in the line of succession according to the seniority of their departments.[9] A Cabinet officer must resign his departmental headship on taking the presidential oath of office, but his occupancy of the office would last only until there was a Speaker or President pro tempore available to succeed him. The statute clearly states that the title of all successors taking presidential office under the act will be "Acting President."

The act of 1947 was a bad piece of legislation.[10] Placing the Speaker and President pro tempore ahead of the secretary of state and other cabinet members was ill-advised, considering that secretaries of state have tended to be men of greater stature, ability, and prominence than the heads of the two houses of Congress. Moreover, having the succession pass to congressional officers

---

[9]The order of departments is as follows: State, Treasury, Defense, Attorney General, Post Office, Interior, Agriculture, Commerce, and Labor. The newest cabinet departments, all created since 1947—Health, Education, and Welfare (now Health and Human Services); Housing and Urban Development; Transportation; Energy; and Education—are not included in the line of succession.

[10]See Joseph E. Kallenbach, "The New Presidential Succession Act," 41 AMERICAN POLITICAL SCIENCE REVIEW 931 (1947).

opens the way for transfer of party control over the Presidency if either house of Congress is controlled by the party that lost the last presidential election. Finally, since the Speaker or President pro tempore serves out the remainder of the four-year term after taking office, even though the congressional term to which he was elected may have expired in the meantime, there is the possibility of a new kind of lame duck President.

The constitutional flaws in the statute are equally serious, running counter as it does to the theory of separation of powers. The Constitution requires that the person named by Congress as a successor must be an "officer" of the United States. It also declares that no person holding "any office under the United States" is eligible to a seat in Congress. Consequently a member of Congress cannot be an "officer of the United States," and so is ineligible to act as President. The act of 1792 was clearly unconstitutional, because it provided that the acting President was to retain his seat in Congress and his post as President pro tempore or Speaker. The 1947 act chose the other horn of the dilemma, requiring the Speaker or President pro tempore to resign his legislative post and seat *before* becoming acting President. But it is only as they hold these posts that they are entitled to act as President. Thus the 1947 act seems also to be clearly contrary to the Constitution.

The Twenty-fifth Amendment

In 1965 Congress sought to solve the succession problem by insuring that the vice-presidency would never be vacant for long. The Twenty-fifth Amendment, ratified in 1967, provides in section 2 that "whenever there is a vacancy in the office of the Vice-President, the President shall nominate a Vice-President who shall take office upon confirmation by a majority vote of both houses of Congress."

The amendment was widely praised, but the first occasion for its use revealed entirely unanticipated difficulties. In 1973 Vice-President Spiro Agnew pleaded no contest to charges of income tax evasion and resigned. Nixon then named Gerald Ford, House minority leader, as vice-president; he took office on December 6, 1973, after confirmation by bipartisan votes of 387 to 35 in the House and 92 to 3 in the Senate. Nine months later, Nixon, facing certain impeachment and conviction, also resigned, making Ford President. Ford, in turn, selected Nelson Rockefeller as vice-president, but a long delay in his confirmation left the nation for four months without a vice-president.

Thus the Twenty-fifth Amendment not only failed to prevent a vacancy in the vice-presidency but, much more important, produced the astounding result of placing in office both a President and a vice-president neither of whom had been elected to those posts. President Ford, moreover, owed his selection to his discredited predecessor.

This experience led to consideration of alternative methods of filling vice-presidential vacancies, and there were even serious suggestions that the office be abolished.[11] Vice-presidential nominees have usually been hurriedly selected at party conventions for reasons of political balance rather than competence. The office is an awkward one, with no duties except to preside over the Senate unless the President wishes to find other work for the vice-president to do. If the office were abolished, a vacancy in the Presidency could be filled temporarily by the Speaker of the House or the secretary of state as Acting President while a special election was held.

PRESIDENTIAL INABILITY

The Constitution takes account of the President's possible "inability to discharge the powers and duties of the said office," and, as in the case of death or removal, the vice-president is directed to take over. However, unlike death or removal, inability may be only a temporary condition that can pass away and leave the President as fit as ever to continue his duties. If the original constitutional intention that the vice-president would be only an acting President under all contingencies had come to fruition, there would be little difficulty in the vice-president's filling in temporarily for a disabled President. But the fact that the office of acting President is unknown to our history in other eventualities has resulted in some doubt as to its applicability in cases of inability.[12]

Four American Presidents have suffered serious disability during their terms of office. President Garfield was shot on July 2, 1881, and lingered on until his death on September 19. During this period he was able to perform only one official act, the signing of an extradition paper. A majority of Garfield's cabinet believed that any performance of presidential functions by Vice-President Arthur would automatically oust Garfield from the Presidency, on the theory that there could not be two Presidents at the same time. Consequently Arthur took no action.

On September 26, 1919, President Wilson suffered a collapse and was disabled for many weeks. For over three months he saw no one except his wife and the doctors. Mrs. Wilson gave him such state papers as she thought he could handle; others were referred by her to cabinet members. Secretary of State Lansing, at the onset of the President's illness, tried to secure support for having Vice-President Marshall take over Wilson's powers and duties, but was unsuccessful. Then Lansing took the initiative in calling several cabinet meetings. When Wilson heard of this, he regarded it as an assumption of Presidential authority, and requested Lansing's resignation.[13]

[11]Arthur Schlesinger, Jr., "Is the Vice-Presidency Necessary?" 233 ATLANTIC 37 (May 1974); and "On the Presidential Succession," 89 POLITICAL SCIENCE QUARTERLY 475 (1974).

[12]See generally John D. Feerick, *From Failing Hands: The Story of Presidential Succession* (New York: Fordham University Press, 1965).

[13]See Richard Hansen, *The Year We Had No President* (Lincoln: University of Nebraska Press, 1962); Gene Smith, *When the Cheering Stopped* (New York: Morrow, 1964).

President Eisenhower had three serious illnesses in a little over two years. He had organized the Presidency for the first time on the staff principle with which he was familiar from his military experience, with substantial delegations of authority that kept many of the normal concerns of his predecessors from coming to his attention. He had moreover made greater use of his vice-president than had been customary in the past. During Eisenhower's convalescences the role of the vice-president was somewhat expanded, including the chairing of cabinet meetings and sessions of the National Security Council, but the primary responsibility for keeping the wheels turning was assumed by the White House staff, headed by Sherman Adams.

The attempted assassination of President Reagan on March 30, 1981, at a time when Vice-President Bush was in Texas, caused a temporary flurry of concern about the line of succession, which was compounded by Secretary of State Haig's televised claim from the White House that he was "in charge." But the President's surprisingly prompt recovery and his well-organized White House staff prevented any serious issue of disability from arising.

Each of these emergencies created a temporary power vacuum and aroused concern about constitutional unpreparedness for handling situations of such great potential danger. Each emergency could have been eased by having the vice-president become acting President for a temporary period. This did not occur, a principal reason being uncertainty as to the effect this assumption of responsibility would have on the status of the disabled President.

In the absence of any legislation or constitutional consensus on this problem, President Eisenhower wisely took the initiative and in March, 1958, made public an agreement he had reached with Vice-President Nixon concerning a possible future inability. This agreement called for the vice-president to serve as "acting President, exercising the powers and duties of the office until the inability had ended." Then the President "would resume the full exercise of the powers and duties of the office." President Kennedy entered into a similar agreement with Vice-President Johnson in 1961, as did President Johnson with Vice-President Humphrey in 1965.

Section 3 of the Twenty-fifth Amendment gave constitutional recognition to the Eisenhower-Nixon type of arrangement by providing that the President, if unable to discharge the powers and duties of his office, could transfer them to "the Vice-President as Acting President" by filing a written declaration of inability with the president of the Senate and the Speaker of the House. The President could resume his powers and duties by a written declaration to the same two officers.

The most difficult problem that the drafters of the Twenty-fifth Amendment foresaw was the possibility that the President might suffer a mental illness and not recognize his inability.[14] Stripping a President of his office against

---

[14]Questions have been raised concerning the mental stability of President Nixon during the period prior to his resignation. See Theodore H. White, *Breach of Faith: The Fall of Richard Nixon* (New York: Atheneum, 1975): Bob Woodward and Carl Bernstein, *The Final Days* (New York: Simon & Schuster, 1976).

his will is a grave prospect, yet the need for such action could arise. Section 4 consequently provided a formula which it was hoped would protect all interests in such a crisis. The vice-president and a majority of the cabinet "or such other body as Congress may by law provide" were authorized to declare the President unable to serve by written notice to the heads of the two houses of Congress, and on the filing of such a declaration the vice-president would become Acting President.

The President could resume his powers by written notice to the two houses that the inability had ceased to exist. However, if the vice-president and a majority of the cabinet (or other designated body) within four days thereafter notified Congress that in their opinion the President had not recovered from his disability, then Congress would have to decide the issue. It would assemble within forty-eight hours and reach a decision within twenty-one days. If two-thirds of both houses voted that the President was unable to discharge his duties, the vice-president would continue as acting President. Otherwise the President would resume his office.[15]

The process of nominating presidential candidates has not been considered in this chapter, since it is not controlled by constitutional provisions. But the Federal Election Campaign Act of 1974, providing for public financing of major party nominating conventions and primary and general election campaigns, did present constitutional issues. In *Buckley v. Valeo* (1976) the Supreme Court upheld public funding as a use of public money to facilitate and enlarge public discussion and participation in the electoral process. The major statutory provisions—full funding for the two major parties, only partial funding for minor parties, limitation of new-party candidates to postelection funds, and denial of funds to parties receiving less than 5 percent of the vote— were all upheld by the Court as not unjustifiably restrictive of minority political interests. Justice Rehnquist, dissenting, thought that this preference for the major parties had enshrined them "in a permanently preferred position" and violated the Fifth and First Amendments.[16]

---

[15]During the last weeks of Nixon's presidency, when he faced impeachment and the government seemed to be coming to a standstill, there were some suggestions that he "take the Twenty-fifth" and step aside temporarily, allowing Vice-President Ford to serve as acting-President until Nixon's status was determined. Obviously the Twenty-fifth Amendment was not intended for this kind of situation. According to charges by Laurence Barrett and William Safire, after President Reagan was shot, White House aides took action to block any implementation of the Twenty-fifth Amendment procedure for determining whether the President was disabled (*New York Times,* June 6, 1983).

[16]However, in *Anderson v. Celebrezze* (1983) the Court protected the position of third-party candidates by striking down an Ohio requirement that independent candidates for the presidency must file by March for the November election.

15

Executive Powers in General

In turning to a general discussion of presidential authority, it is particularly important to recall the limitations of this volume. It is not a constitutional history. It is not a compendium of governmental practice under the Constitution. Thus, in discussing the subject of executive powers under the Constitution there can be no thought of undertaking any detailed account, either chronological or analytical, of the development of the theory or practice of executive power. Our concern is the more limited one of focusing attention on the problems of interpretation and controversy to which the constitutional language pertaining to executive power has given rise. For reasons having to do with the separation of powers, already noted, the courts have usually been reluctant to intervene in controversies over executive power. Nevertheless, there have been opportunities for some strikingly important expressions of judicial opinion on these problems.

THE PRESIDENT AND LAWMAKING

We begin with the paradox that some of the President's most important executive powers are legislative. They are legislative in the sense that the Constitution gives him a role to play in relation to Congress as an institution and in relation to its adoption of legislation.

First, the President has certain functions in connection with the convening and adjourning of Congress. The regular annual sessions of Congress are stipulated by the Constitution, but the President is authorized by Article II, section 3, "on extraordinary occasions, [to] convene both houses, or either of them," in special session, a power that has often been exercised. He has the power to adjourn Congress, but only in case the two houses disagree with respect to the time of adjournment, an eventuality which has never occurred.

Again, the President has an important role as the initiator of legislative programs, based on the following language from Article II, section 3: "He shall from time to time give to the Congress information of the state of the Union, and recommend to their consideration such measures as he shall judge necessary and expedient." Accordingly, a "State of the Union" message is submitted to Congress by the President, usually in person, at the beginning of each regular session, followed by the annual budget message plus special messages from time to time. Executive influence on formulation of the legislative program, of course, does not stop here. The policy leadership of the administration is continuously manifested by the preparation of draft bills, testimony before congressional committees by department heads and other officials of the executive branch, and use of the President's vast powers as party leader and manipulator of public opinion. Strenuous use of these powers enabled President Reagan in effect to take over the taxing and spending authority of Congress in 1981.

Approval of Legislation

The role of the President in the final approval of legislation is carefully safeguarded by the Constitution. Under Article I, section 7, "every bill" and "every order, resolution, or vote to which the concurrence of the Senate and House of Representatives may be necessary" must be presented to the President for approval or disapproval. There are only three exceptions to this general rule of presidential participation. First, the requirement is by its terms not applicable to actions affecting only a single house, such as adopting rules of procedure, appointing officers and employees, establishing special committees, or passing resolutions not purporting to have any legislative effect. Second, as already noted in Chapter 2, the President does not participate formally in the process of proposing amendments to the Constitution.

Third, joint action of the two houses in the form of concurrent resolutions are customarily not submitted to the President. They are used, for example, in correcting errors in bills after they have been adopted, setting up joint committees of the two houses, or fixing the time of adjournment. But increasingly they have been used by Congress for essentially lawmaking purposes, as in withdrawing authority previously granted to the executive by statute or vetoing administrative actions.[1] As so used, the concurrent resolution

or legislative veto is a violation of the President's right under Article I to participate in the legislative process, as the Supreme Court held in *Immigration and Naturalization Service v. Chadha* (1983). That case, as previously noted, involved a one-house veto of administrative action, but the broad holding invalidated the concurrent resolution or legislative veto as provided for in some 200 statutes.

Executive Veto Power

The President's power to veto legislation is referred to as a "qualified" or "suspensive" veto, since it can be overridden by a two-thirds vote of both houses. Nevertheless, it is scarcely possible to overestimate the contribution that the veto power makes to executive authority. The number of times the President exercises the veto is of course no index to its importance. The mere existence of the power is a constant factor in congressional thinking, and legislative planning is generally circumscribed by realization of the necessity of producing measures that the President will be willing to sign.

Thinking and practice with respect to use of the veto power have varied greatly during our history. The first six Presidents usually vetoed bills only on the ground that they were unconstitutional or technically defective. Jackson was the first President to adopt a policy of vetoing bills simply because he considered them objectionable in aim and content, but even so he vetoed only twelve bills in eight years. Only fifty-one vetoes were recorded up to the Civil War.

Eight Presidents—the most recent being Garfield—never vetoed a single measure. Grover Cleveland and Franklin Roosevelt, on the other hand, used the veto 584 and 635 times, respectively. No presidential veto was overridden until Tyler's administration, and it still occurs very infrequently. Even Franklin Roosevelt, who originated more than one-third of all the vetoes in American history up to that time, was reversed only nine times. Eisenhower, with 181 vetoes, was overridden only twice. Neither Kennedy nor Johnson was overriden. Five of Nixon's 43 vetoes were overridden, and 12 of Ford's 66. Only one significant Reagan veto of a total of 11 was overridden in his first two years.

If the President decides to veto a bill, he returns it unsigned within ten days to the house in which it originated, accompanying it with a statement of his objections. The veto stands unless, with a quorum present, it is overridden

[1]For example, the Lend-Lease Act of 1941 delegated certain temporary powers to the President, the expiration date being June 30, 1943. However, the act provided that the powers would lapse earlier if Congress should pass a concurrent resolution declaring that they were "no longer necessary to promote the defense of the United States." See a defense of the constitutionality of the provision in Edward S. Corwin, *The President: Office and Powers, 1787–1957,* 4th rev. ed. (New York: New York University Press, 1957), pp. 129–130; and President Roosevelt's objection in Robert H. Jackson, "A Presidential Legal Opinion," 66 HARVARD LAW REVIEW 1353 (1953). See also D. W. Buckwalter, "The Congressional Concurrent Resolution: A Search for Foreign Policy Influence," 14 MIDWEST JOURNAL OF POLITICAL SCIENCE 434 (1970).

by a two-thirds vote in each house. On the question of a repassage of the bill, the way each member votes must be recorded, which imparts a greater sense of responsibility to the action.

The President can permit a bill to become law without his signature by failing to return it with his signature within ten days after he has received it. This procedure is used when the President does not approve of a bill, but feels it impossible or impolitic to veto it. However, in these circumstances the bill will become law only if Congress is still in session after the ten days have expired. If Congress adjourns within the ten-day period, the bill does not become law, and is said to have been given a "pocket veto." A pocket veto is an absolute veto, since the adjournment of Congress prevents any attempt at repassage of the bill.[2]

The President must by practice accept or reject a bill *in toto*; he has no "item veto." Thus there is a temptation for Congress to attach legislation that the President is known to oppose, as a rider to some vitally important bill. Numerous proposals to give the President an item veto, primarily with respect to appropriations measures, have uniformly failed.[3]

THEORIES OF EXECUTIVE POWER

When we turn from the President as participant in lawmaking to the President as operating head of the executive branch, the first relevant constitutional provision is the initial sentence of Article II: "The executive power shall be vested in a President of the United States of America." There has been considerable disagreement as to whether these words comprise a grant of power or are a mere designation of office. If the latter view is taken, then the executive power must be defined by the more or less specific authorizations to the President found elsewhere in Article II, such as the power to grant pardons, to receive ambassadors, to make appointments, or to take care that the laws be faithfully executed.

But is there any reason for concluding that this more restrictive view of executive powers is the correct or preferable one? The main argument against the broader concept is based on a supposed logical difficulty. Why, it is said,

---

[2]Adjournment of the first session of a Congress amounts to "adjournment" for purposes of the pocket veto, the Supreme Court held in *The Pocket Veto Case* (1929). But Nixon's effort to use the pocket veto during a five-day Christmas recess in 1970 was invalidated in *Kennedy v. Sampson* (1973), and when this decision was upheld by the Court of Appeals for the District of Columbia, the Justice Department decided not to appeal. However, in 1974 President Ford announced that on the advice of the attorney general he reserved the right to use the pocket veto during congressional recesses, a position he abandoned in 1976.

[3]Nixon's effort to achieve the purposes of the item veto by use of the impounding power is discussed in Chapter 10. See also Jong R. Lee, "Presidential Vetoes from Washington to Nixon," 37 JOURNAL OF POLITICS 522 (1975).

should Article II start out with a general grant of executive power and then be followed by more specific grants? Chief Justice Taft sought to dispose of this query by explaining that the specific grants lend emphasis "where emphasis was regarded as appropriate."[4] On the basis of extensive research into eighteenth-century practices and terminology, Crosskey concludes that draftsmanship of that period typically made use of "a general proposition followed by an incomplete enumeration of particulars, or things which, arguably, are particulars, included within the antecedent general expression."[5]

But perhaps the best reason for regarding the initial sentence of Article II as a grant of power is that only by this method is the President equipped with the broad authority that the chief executive of a state must have. The prime characteristic of executive power is that it is "residual." The executive is always in session, always available to fill in gaps and meet emergencies. In contrast, as Locke says, "the lawmaking power is not always in being, and is usually too numerous and so too slow for the dispatch requisite to execution."[6]

If further support is needed for the position that the "executive power" phrase is a broad grant of power, it can be found in an action of the First Congress, commonly referred to as the "decision of 1789." In setting up the new department of foreign affairs, the House fell into a debate as to how the secretary of the department would be removed. Some members thought the Senate's consent would be necessary, just as in appointment, and others said Congress could provide any arrangement for removal it saw fit under the necessary and proper clause. The language actually put into the statute, "whenever the said principal officer shall be removed from office by the President," reflected the majority conclusion that the President already had the right of removal on the basis of his "executive power" under the Constitution.

The only other language approaching the executive power provision in breadth of authorization is the sentence in Article II, section 3: "He shall take care that the laws be faithfully executed." Although this is a notably broad grant of power, it also served the limiting function of emphasizing the American notion of the executive as subordinate to the law, in contrast with the wide prerogative powers of the English executive.

For a satisfactory indication of how these two general grants of executive power have been interpreted and what they have meant in practice, nothing less than a history of the Presidency would be adequate. But fortunately for our purposes, an understanding of the two principal contrasting interpretations of executive power can be supplied by two Presidents, Theodore Roosevelt and William H. Taft. Roosevelt wrote his activist personality and

[4] *Myers v. United States* (1926).

[5] W. W. Crosskey, *Politics and the Constitution in the History of the United States* (Chicago: University of Chicago Press, 1953), p. 379.

[6] John Locke, *Of Civil Government,* book 2, chapter 14.

expansive attitude into constitutional law with his "stewardship" conception of the presidential office. His theory was

> . . . that the executive power was limited only by specific restrictions and pro-hibitions appearing in the Constitution or imposed by the Congress under its Constitutional powers. . . . I declined to adopt the view that what was imper-atively necessary for the Nation could not be done by the President unless he could find some specific authorization to do it. My belief was that it was not only his right but his duty to do anything that the needs of the Nation demanded unless such action was forbidden by the Constitution or by the laws.[7]

Taft found this position incompatible with his more sedentary view of the Presidency. In lectures that he gave in 1916 after his Presidential term, he said:

> The true view of the Executive functions is, as I conceive it, that the President can exercise no power which cannot be fairly and reasonably traced to some specific grant of power or justly implied and included within such express grant as proper and necessary to its exercise. Such specific grant must be either in the Federal Constitution or in an act of Congress passed in pursuance thereof. There is no undefined residuum of power which he can exercise because it seems to him to be in the public interest.[8]

The issue that emerges here, then, is whether the President must always be able to cite a law of the United States or a specific constitutional author-ization in support of his actions, or whether the broad "executive power" with which he is vested justifies any actions he conceives as being in the public interest, so long as there is no conflict with existing legislation or constitutional provisions. Locke put this issue in its classical form. Pointing to the relative characteristics of executive and legislature already quoted, he concluded that the executive must always be equipped with discretionary and prerogative powers.

> For the legislators not being able to foresee and provide by laws for all that may be useful to the community, the executor of the laws, having the power in his hands, has by the common law of Nature a right to make use of it for the good of the society, in many cases where the municipal law has given no direction, till the legislative can conveniently be assembled to provide for it. Many things there are which the law can by no means provide for, and those must necessarily be left to the discretion of him that has the executive power in his hands, to be ordered by him as the public good and advantage shall require; nay, it is fit that the laws themselves should in some cases give way to the executive power, or rather to this fundamental law of Nature and government—viz., that, as much as may be, all the members of the society are to be preserved.

[7]Theodore Roosevelt, *Autobiography* (New York: Macmillan, 1913), pp. 388–389.

[8]William Howard Taft, *Our Chief Magistrate and His Powers* (New York: Columbia University Press, 1916), pp. 139–40.

The Supreme Court found it necessary to take a position on this issue in *In re Neagle* (1890), and it lined up with Locke. The *Neagle* case grew out of a highly bizarre set of facts. Supreme Court Justice Stephen J. Field, whose judicial circuit included California, had had his life threatened by a disappointed litigant named Terry, and the attorney general assigned a United States marshal to protect Field while riding the circuit in that state. When Terry appeared about to make a physical attack on Field, the marshal, Neagle, killed him. There was some local feeling favorable to Terry, and Neagle was arrested and held by state authorities on a charge of murder. The United States sought Neagle's release on habeas corpus under a provision of the federal statutes making the writ available to one "in custody for an act done or omitted in pursuance of a law of the United States."

The problem was that Congress had enacted no *law* authorizing the President or the attorney general to assign marshals as bodyguards to federal justices. But the Supreme Court did not propose to interpret "law" so narrowly. "In the view we take of the Constitution . . . any obligation fairly and properly inferrible from that instrument, or any duty of the marshal to be derived from the general scope of his duties under the laws of the United States, is a 'law,' within the meaning of this phrase."

It would be unthinkable, said the Court, which admittedly had a more than academic interest in the matter, for a sovereign government to have "within the domain of its powers no means of protecting . . . judges" in the discharge of their duties. The power must exist somewhere, and the only question is where. The legislature could pass a law, but it had not done so. Then, in language practically paraphrasing Locke, the Court turned to the President, whom it found admirably equipped for performing such a function, through his cabinet, his appointees, his executive departments, his control over the armed forces, through all those who "aid him in the performance of the great duties of his office, and represent him in a thousand acts."

There is "a peace of the United States," the Court went on, and by necessity and design the President is the principal conservator of that peace. The President's duty to see that the laws are faithfully executed is consequently not "limited to the enforcement of acts of Congress . . . according to their *express terms*" but includes also "the rights, duties and obligations growing out of the Constitution itself, our international relations, and all the protection implied by the nature of the government under the Constitution." Thus the duty assigned to the marshal in this affair was properly considered to arise "under the authority of the law of the United States."

This broad interpretation of the laws, which the President was obliged faithfully to execute, was underlined five years later in the case of *In re Debs*. As already noted, President Cleveland sent troops to Chicago to deal with a railway strike and had his attorney general secure a federal court injunction against the strikers. There was no explicit statutory basis for the injunction, but the Supreme Court sustained it on the broad ground that: "Every government, entrusted, by the very terms of its being, with powers and duties to be exercised and discharged for the general welfare, has a right to apply to its own courts for any proper assistance in the exercise of the one and the discharge of the other." Here again the theme was that the right of self-preservation must belong to a government, whether claimed by statute or not, and that the executive was constitutionally entitled to act in such cases.

In contrast to these strong supports for the doctrine of inherent or implied presidential powers stands the 1952 decision in the famous *Steel Seizure Case (Youngstown Sheet and Tube Co. v. Sawyer)*. A few hours before a nationwide steel strike was to begin on April 9, 1952, President Truman issued an executive order directing the secretary of commerce to take possession of and operate the steel mills of the country. The President based his action on a contention that the work stoppage would jeopardize national defense, particularly in Korea. The next morning he sent a message to Congress reporting his action, and a second message on April 21. The steel companies obeyed the secretary's orders under protest, and brought suit for injunction against him in the District of Columbia district court. On April 30, Judge Pine granted a preliminary injunction restraining the secretary from continuing the seizure. The case went to the Supreme Court with almost unprecedented speed; and on June 2, the Court held by a six to three vote that the President had exceeded his constitutional powers.

Chief Justice Vinson's opinion for the three dissenters was in the spirit of the *Neagle* and *Debs* cases. His theory of the President's seizure was that its purpose was "to faithfully execute the laws by acting in an emergency to maintain the status quo, thereby preventing collapse of the legislative programs [military procurement and anti-inflation] until Congress could act." Admittedly there was no statutory authorization for the seizure in the Taft-Hartley Act, which Congress had passed in 1947 to deal with nationwide strikes. But Vinson regarded the constitutional grant of "executive power" to the President, and his constitutional responsibility to execute the laws, as providing inherent power for such presidential action. His reading of the Constitution and his interpretation of the purpose of the Founders was that "the Presidency was deliberately fashioned as an office of power and independence." His illustrations ran all the way from Washington's vigorous suppression of the Whiskey Rebellion, Jefferson's initiative in the Louisiana Purchase, and Lincoln's wholly unauthorized Emancipation Proclamation, down to President Roosevelt's World War II nonstatutory seizures of aircraft and industrial plants.

Judge Pine's decision in the district court had challenged such an interpretation of executive powers under the Constitution. He denied that the President had any "inherent" powers not traceable to an express grant in the Constitution. As his sole authority for this position, he cited the passage from Taft's book already quoted. Judge Pine dismissed Roosevelt's stewardship theory as one that does not "comport with our recognized theory of government." The numerous instances in American history where Presidents have acted on a theory of inherent powers he dismissed as "repetitive, unchallenged, illegal acts."

Judge Pine's action in enjoining the steel seizure was upheld by the Supreme Court, but his denial of inherent powers to the President was not ratified by the Court. Only Black and Douglas approved the Pine position that the President was limited to expressly granted powers. Like Judge Pine, they took up dogmatic positions based on a hard-and-fast interpretation of the separation of powers. Black disposed of the entire controversy in thirteen paragraphs, and his argument was on such a plane of lofty moral and constitutional generalities that he did not bother to cite a single Supreme Court decision bearing on the substantive issue. But the other majority justices did not accept this separation of powers dogma. Frankfurter specifically attached a paragraph to Black's opinion for the Court in order to warn that "the considerations relevant to the legal enforcement of the principle of separation of powers seem to me more complicated and flexible than may appear from what Mr. Justice Black has written."

Consequently we must turn away from Black and Douglas to the other four majority justices in search for the real doctrine of the steel decision. All four of their opinions recognize that American constitutional law is a pragmatic affair. Jackson, for example, stressed the folly of any rigorous notions about strict separation of the branches of government. Successful operation of our system requires a combination of "separateness" with "interdependence," "autonomy" with "reciprocity." He thought that "presidential powers are not fixed but fluctuate, depending upon their disjunction or conjunction with those of Congress." He believed that when the President "takes measures incompatible with the expressed or implied will of Congress, his power is at its lowest ebb," and because he was convinced that the President had done that here, he found the action unconstitutional.

Frankfurter likewise approached the problem as a matter of balancing the equities in this particular instance between the two democratic branches of the government, to both of which the Supreme Court owed deference. Examination of congressional actions pertaining to use of presidential seizure powers from 1916 to the passage of the Taft-Hartley Act convinced Frankfurter that Congress had "deemed seizure so drastic a power as to require it to be carefully circumscribed whenever the President was vested with this extraordinary authority." When considering the Taft-Hartley bill, Frankfurter went on, Congress gave considered attention to the seizure device and on "a balance of considerations . . . chose not to lodge this power in the President." It is true that Congress did not write into the act a statutory prohibition on presidential seizure, but it "expressed its will to withhold this power from the President as though it had said so in so many words."

In *New York Times Co. v. United States* (1971), involving the government's attempt to enjoin the press from publishing the so-called Pentagon

Papers,[9] the court likewise rejected, by a vote of six to three, a presidential claim to inherent power to protect national defense secrets that was unsupported by statutory authorization. But two of the majority justices, Stewart and White, were willing to grant the existence of a "sovereign prerogative" power to protect the confidentiality of materials related to the national defense and only voted against the President because they could not say that disclosure of the Pentagon Papers would "surely result in direct, immediate, and irreparable damage to our Nation or its people." Another majority justice, Marshall, stressed that, as in the *Steel Seizure* case, Congress had refused to adopt legislation that would have given the President the power he sought here. Speaking for the three dissenters, Harlan would have granted the President's inherent power to act, subject only to a judicial determination that the issue lay within "the proper compass of the President's foreign relations power" and a determination by the secretary of state or secretary of defense that "disclosure of the subject matter would irreparably impair the national security."

Presidential power, though not necessarily inherent power, was upheld by a unanimous Court in *Dames & Moore* v. *Regan* (1981). The case involved President Carter's agreement with Iran that secured the release of fifty-two American hostages early in 1981. The agreement cancelled all attachments against Iranian assets in the United States, and transferred from U.S. courts to an international tribunal all legal claims by American firms against Iran. The Court concluded that the 1977 Emergency Economic Powers Act explicitly gave the President authority to void attachments against Iranian assets. As for the transfer of legal claims out of the country, the Court found no statutory authorization, but held that Congress had "implicitly" approved of Carter's action by a long-standing pattern of acquiescence in presidential settlement of claims disputes with other nations. Should any firms be dissatisfied with their treatment by the international tribunal, the Court volunteered that they could sue the United States in the Court of Claims.

THE POWER OF APPOINTMENT

Basic to executive authority is the President's power to appoint the officials of the administration. Article II, section 2, provides:

> [The President] shall nominate, and by and with the advice and consent of the Senate, shall appoint ambassadors, other public ministers and consuls, judges of the Supreme Court, and all other officers of the United States, whose appointments are not herein otherwise provided for, and which shall be established

---

[9]A forty-seven-volume classified study made by direction of the secretary of defense as to how the United States became involved in the Vietnam War, which was made available to the press by Daniel Ellsberg. See Neil Sheehan et al., *The Pentagon Papers* (New York: Bantam, 1971).

by law; but the Congress may by law vest the appointment of such inferior officers, as they think proper, in the President alone, in the courts of law, or in the heads of departments.

This language establishes four different methods of appointment—by the President with Senate confirmation, by the President alone, by the courts of law, and by the heads of departments. Congress has no appointment power, except, under Article I, to choose its own officers.[10] Nevertheless, Congress is involved very deeply in the process of appointment, as the following discussion will indicate.[11]

Qualifications and Disqualifications

In creating offices, Congress can specify the qualifications to be possessed by appointees to those offices. Familiar statutory requirements relate to citizenship, residence, age, political affiliation, professional attainments, and so on. Congress has even provided on occasion that presidential appointments shall be made from among a small number of persons named by others. Thus an act of 1920 required that the Railroad Labor Board consist of three men to be appointed from six nominees by employees, and three to be chosen from six nominees by carriers. The civil service system is, of course, a general limitation on the executive appointment power.

Senatorial Confirmation

The requirement that appointments by the executive shall be subject to approval by the upper house of the legislature is peculiar to the United States, and to the several countries of Central and South America that have used the American Constitution as a model. The Senate's advice and consent is given by a majority of a quorum. The distinction between "officers" who need Senate confirmation and "inferior officers" who do not is entirely in the discretion of Congress. The Constitution apparently assumes that these two categories will cover the field, but in extraconstitutional practice a third and very numerous category, "employees," is recognized, who may be appointed by officers whose status is lower than that of department head.[12]

When the framers of the Constitution spoke of the Senate's "advice" on nominations, they apparently were thinking of collective advice by the Senate acting as a kind of council for the President. But the Senate has never

---

[10]In *Buckley v. Valeo* (1976) the Court held that the six members of the Federal Election Commission, four of whom were appointed by Congress, were "officers of the United States" and consequently must be appointed by the President.

[11]G. Calvin Mackenzie, *The Politics of Presidential Appointments* (New York: Free Press, 1981).

[12]Joseph P. Harris, *The Advice and Consent of the Senate* (Berkeley: University of California Press, 1953).

functioned as such a council, and it is obviously impractical for it to offer advice on appointments in any collective fashion. However, advice is given by individual senators, which is made very effective by the practice of "senatorial courtesy." A nomination to a federal office within a state, on which the senator or senators of that state from the President's party have not been consulted, will almost invariably be refused confirmation if the aggrieved senator chooses to make an appeal to his colleagues. Where the appointment is to an office in Washington, it is normal procedure to consult with the senator of the state from which the appointee comes, but if this is not done the rule of senatorial courtesy is less likely to be applied when confirmation is requested. If the Senate does refuse confirmation for a high-level appointment, it is usually for broad policy reasons, not because the rule of senatorial courtesy has been ignored.

Recess Appointments

Article II, section 2, clause 3, provides: "The President shall have power to fill up all vacancies that may happen during the recess of the Senate, by granting commissions which shall expire at the end of their next session." The word "happen" does not mean that the vacancy must have actually developed while the Senate was in recess. A vacancy occurring during a Senate session, which for any reason remains unfilled by the end of the session, can be filled by a recess appointment. This, plus the fact that a recess appointee can serve throughout the next session of the Senate, opens up the possibility of the President's using recess appointments to keep in office persons whom the Senate would refuse to confirm, and this has occasionally happened. In fact, President Jefferson appears to have kept Robert Smith as his secretary of the navy for four years without Senate confirmation by this device. President Reagan, hostile to the Legal Services Corporation, made recess appointments to its board of like-minded persons to avoid Senate rejection of the nominees. In retaliation, Congress forbade any funding cuts by a board not confirmed by the Senate.

THE POWER OF REMOVAL

Surprisingly, the Constitution makes no express provision for the removal of federal officials except through the process of impeachment, which is an unwieldy and quite impractical device, useful only on extraordinary occasions. This gap has been filled by executive practice, legislative provisions, and judicial interpretation.

Two principal constitutional issues have arisen in connection with removals. First, is removal solely an executive function, or can the Senate claim a share in removing officials who were appointed subject to Senate confirmation? Hamilton in No. 77 of *The Federalist* expressed the opinion that the consent of the Senate "would be necessary to displace as well as to appoint." But the First Congress, faced with this issue in setting up the Department of State, acted on the theory, as we have already seen, that the President alone possessed the removal power.

In fact Congress tacitly recognized the existence of an unrestrained presidential removal power from 1789 to 1867, and it developed into one of his most effective instruments for control of the executive branch. In 1867, however, Congress passed the Tenure of Office Act, which forbade the removal by the President of department heads without consent of the Senate. President Andrew Johnson's attempt to remove his secretary of war in violation of this act was one of the charges in his impeachment. Following Johnson's term the act was modified, and it was completely repealed in 1887 without ever having been the subject of constitutional test.

Meanwhile, however, Congress had passed in 1876 a law providing that postmasters of the first, second, and third class, appointed for four-year terms, should be subject to removal by the President "by and with the advice and consent of the Senate." The Supreme Court finally had occasion to rule on this law in 1926, in the famous case of *Myers* v. *United States.* President Wilson removed Myers, a first-class postmaster in Portland, Oregon, in 1920 before his four-year term was up, without seeking Senate consent. Myers brought suit in the Court of Claims for his salary for the balance of his four-year term, but the Supreme Court held by a vote of six to three that the law of 1876 was unconstitutional.

Chief Justice Taft's opinion for the Court was one of the longest and most elaborate in its history. First, he relied upon the "decision of 1789," and the subsequent practice of untrammeled removal power. The Tenure of Office Act of 1867 he dismissed as a temporary divergence from legislative policy resulting from partisan controversy. Second, and more importantly, he derived the principle of the removal power directly from the Constitution, specifically from the grant of "executive power" and "faithful execution of the laws" clause. Obviously, said the Chief Justice, the President "alone and unaided could not execute the laws. He must execute them by the assistance of subordinates." It follows that "in the absence of any express limitation respecting removals, that as his selection of administrative officers is essential to the execution of the laws by him, so must be his power of removing those for whom he cannot continue to be responsible."

Chief Justice Taft went on to develop this argument in language that seemed to be illumined by his own experience in the presidential office. He said:

> When a nomination is made, it may be presumed that the Senate is, or may become, as well advised as to the fitness of the nominee as the President, but in the nature of things the defects in ability or intelligence or loyalty in the administration of the laws of one who has served as an officer under the President, are facts as to which the President, or his trusted subordinates, must be better

informed than the Senate, and the power to remove him may, therefore, be regarded as confined, for very sound and practical reasons, to the governmental authority which has administrative control.

Indeed, there is an imperative need for the President to be able to remove his immediate subordinates, to whom the President delegates exercise of his discretion and discharge of his political duties. Since there is nothing in the Constitution that would permit a distinction between these officials and those engaged in more normal duties, Taft concluded that an unrestricted power to remove attaches to all positions filled by the President.

The Taft opinion failed to convince three members of the Court, including Holmes and Brandeis. Holmes thought the arguments based on constitutional grants of executive power were "spider's webs inadequate to control the dominant facts." However, the Taft decision was sound law because it was sound politics and sound administration in equating the powers of the President with his responsibilities. Where the opinion was unsound was in its attempt to decide more than the case called for. Taft veered off from considerations applicable to a postmastership into dicta about executive officials not in a position of direct responsibility to the President, saying:

> There may be duties of a quasi-judicial character imposed on executive officers and members of executive tribunals whose decisions after hearing affect interests of individuals, the discharge of which the President can not in a particular case properly influence or control. But even in such a case he may consider the decision after its rendition as a reason for removing the officer, on the ground that the discretion regularly entrusted to that officer by statute has not been on the whole intelligently or wisely exercised. Otherwise he does not discharge his own constitutional duty of seeing that the laws be faithfully executed.

This dictum challenged the statutory basis on which Congress had established the Interstate Commerce Commission in 1887, the Federal Trade Commission in 1914, and the Federal Tariff Commission in 1916. To be sure, the statutes setting up these agencies did not require Senate concurrence in removals, but the commissioners were in each case made removable by the President "for inefficiency, neglect of duty, or malfeasance in office," and the clear implication of this statutory language was that the President was forbidden to remove on any other ground. A restriction of a different sort was placed in the Budget and Accounting Act of 1921, making the comptroller general subject to removal (aside from impeachment) only by joint resolution of Congress and then only after a hearing that established incapacity, inefficiency, neglect of duty or malfeasance, or conduct involving moral turpitude.

Such legislation raised the second major issue concerning the removal power. Granting that removal is solely an executive function, can the exercise of this executive power be regulated by law? The *Myers* decision was correctly interpreted by Congress as challenging the validity of any restrictions on the President's removal power. Consequently as new quasi-judicial commissions or regulatory agencies were set up, no such restrictive language was inserted in their statutes.[13]

A test of Taft's dictum was inevitable, and it took the form of *Humphrey's Executor v. United States* (1935). Humphrey, first appointed to the Federal Trade Commission by President Coolidge, was reappointed by President Hoover in 1931 for a seven-year term. His views were not in accord with the philosophy of the New Deal, and President Roosevelt in 1933 requested Humphrey's resignation, saying: "I do not feel that your mind and my mind go along together on either the policies or the administering of the Federal Trade Commission, and, frankly, I think it is best for the people of this country that I should have a full confidence." When the resignation was not forthcoming, the President removed him. Humphrey died shortly afterwards but his executor brought suit in the Court of Claims for his salary from the time of removal until his death.

The Supreme Court ruled unanimously that this action had exceeded the President's authority. In view of the fact that the removal was based squarely on Chief Justice Taft's dictum in the *Myers* case, it was, of course, necessary for Justice Sutherland, who wrote the *Humphrey* decision, to disavow the Taft theory. This he did by pointing out that the officer involved in the *Myers* case, a postmaster, was "restricted to the performance of executive functions," and rather lowly ones at that. In contrast, Humphrey was a member of "an administrative body created by Congress to carry into effect legislative policies embodied in the statute," performing its duties "without executive leave." In fact, Sutherland continued, a Federal Trade Commissioner "occupies no place in the executive department and . . . exercises no part of the executive power vested by the Constitution in the President." The Federal Trade Commission is a "quasi-legislative or quasi-judicial" agency, which Congress intended to discharge its duties "independently of executive control." Forbidding the President to remove its commissioners except for cause is a legitimate way of implementing that policy, "for it is quite evident that one who holds his office only during the pleasure of another, cannot be depended upon to maintain an attitude of independence against the latter's will."

Sutherland challenged not only the dicta of Taft's opinion, but also its basic constitutional theory. He ignored Taft's interpretation of the executive power clause as a grant of authority. He appeared to whittle down presidential power to two categories. First, there were the prerogatives explicitly granted to the President in the Constitution. The impact of the "decision of 1789," Sutherland said, was limited to this category, since it concerned the secretary of state, an officer who was "purely executive . . . responsible to the President, and to him alone, in a very definite sense." The second category of presidential responsibility was for those officials who exercised only nondiscretionary

[13]The statutes setting up the Federal Power Commission, reorganized in 1930, and the Federal Communications Commission and the Securities and Exchange Commission, both created in 1934, lack any limitation on the President's removal power.

or ministerial powers, such as postmasters. Apart from these two classes of officials, it appeared that Congress was free to impose such limitations as it chose upon the removal power. Congress reacted immediately to the *Humphrey* decision by writing into the National Labor Relations Act, then in the process of enactment, the most stringent provision it had yet applied to a regulatory commission: "Any member of the board may be removed by the President, upon notice and hearing, for neglect of duty or malfeasance in office, but for no other cause."

Arthur E. Morgan attempted unsuccessfully to use the *Humphrey* decision to invalidate his removal as chairman of the TVA by President Roosevelt in 1938.[14] But in 1958 the Court applied and extended the *Humphrey* doctrine in *Wiener* v. *United States.* Wiener was removed from the War Claims Commission by President Eisenhower to make way for a deserving Republican. Though the statute erecting the commission had placed no limitation on the President's right to remove its members, the Court held that from the quasi-judicial nature of the agency it could be assumed that "Congress did not wish to have hang over the commission the Damocles' sword of removal by the President for no reason other than that he preferred to have on that Commission men of his own choosing." Under the *Wiener* decision, then, the President's power of removal, which normally can be exercised at his discretion, may be exercised on quasi-judicial agencies only for cause, regardless of whether Congress has so provided.[15]

The legislation establishing the federal civil service system and providing certain protections for the tenure of government employees is, of course, a valid limitation on the executive power of removal. Similarly, a legislative requirement for the removal of civil servants engaging in political activities has twice been held constitutional by the Supreme Court.[16]

EXECUTIVE PRIVILEGE

The Presidency of Richard Nixon brought to a head some long-standing concerns about the awesome power of the executive office and the lack of means for enforcing presidential responsibility. Since Franklin Roosevelt, the presidential office had burgeoned at the expense of Congress, and it had become

[14]*Morgan v. TVA* (1941). See C. Herman Pritchett, *The Tennessee Valley Authority: A Study in Public Administration* (Chapel Hill, N.C.: University of North Carolina Press, 1943), pp. 203–216.

[15]President Reagan's 1983 removal of three members of the Commission on Civil Rights was questioned on this ground (*The New York Times,* June 1, 1983).

[16]*United Public Workers v. Mitchell* (1947); *U.S. Civil Service Commission* v. *National Assn. of Letter Carriers* (1973). The removal of federal employees on loyalty-security grounds, carried out after 1947 under executive orders issued by Presidents Truman and Eisenhower, is discussed in C. Herman Pritchett, *Constitutional Civil Liberties* (Englewood Cliffs, N.J.: Prentice-Hall, 1981), Chapter 6.

accepted doctrine that a powerful President was required to deal with national problems. But Nixon went beyond previous Presidents in several important respects, particularly in the degree to which he centralized power in the White House and in his attitude of distrust and near-contempt for Congress.

The Watergate scandals destroyed Nixon's "imperial Presidency" and provoked an unprecedented examination of the constitutional position of the office.[17] Separation of powers problems that previously had been only subjects for speculation by constitutional scholars suddenly erupted in newspaper headlines and TV commentaries. One major issue was the validity of the claim of "executive privilege" which Nixon had earlier put forth to justify refusal to respond to congressional requests for information and which he now raised in denying White House tapes and other records demanded by the congressional investigating committees, the Watergate special prosecutor, and judges in several Watergate cases. His position was that executive privilege had been asserted by all Presidents going back to Washington, that his discussions with members of the White House staff were protected by the necessity of confidentiality, and that the principle of separation of powers guarantees each of the branches of government the right to defend itself against incursions by the other branches.

While it is true that earlier Presidents had on occasion refused to submit information requested by Congress, the instances were considerably fewer than Nixon claimed, while the phrase "executive privilege" and the defense of confidentiality dated back only to the Eisenhower administration.[18] As the Senate Watergate Committee began operations in 1973, Nixon forbade any of his White House aides to testify before it, a position from which he quickly withdrew under pressure, and in fact the Ervin Committee did hear testimony from all relevant White House aides.

Nixon also refused to submit White House tapes subpoenaed by both the Senate Committee and the House Judiciary Committee in its impeachment inquiry. However, the Watergate special prosecutor, Archibald Cox, went to court in his demand that the tapes be made available to the Watergate grand jury and was upheld by Judge John Sirica. Recognizing that there was some need to protect presidential confidentiality, Sirica indicated that he would himself review the subpoenaed materials to screen out any matter where executive privilege was validly invoked, and that he would then pass the rest on to the grand jury. Sirica's ruling was upheld by the Court of Appeals for the District

---

[17]See Arthur M. Schlesinger, Jr., *The Imperial Presidency* (Boston: Houghton Mifflin Company, 1973); Frederick C. Mosher et al., *Watergate: Implications for Responsible Government* (New York: Basic Books, Inc., 1974); Rexford G. Tugwell and Thomas E. Cronin, eds., *The Presidency Reappraised* (New York: Praeger Publishers, 1977); Philip B. Kurland, *Watergate and the Constitution* (Chicago: University of Chicago Press, 1978).

[18]See Raoul Berger, *Executive Privilege: A Constitutional Myth* (Cambridge, Mass.: Harvard University Press, 1974); also "Executive Privilege and Congressional Inquiry," 12 UCLA LAW REVIEW 1044, 1364 (1965). For a critique of Berger's rejection of all executive privilege claims, see Ralph K. Winter, Jr., "The Seedlings for the Forest," 83 YALE LAW JOURNAL 1730 (1974).

of Columbia in *Nixon v. Sirica* (1973), and Nixon then complied without carrying an appeal to the Supreme Court.

The Supreme Court's turn to speak on executive privilege came in 1974. In preparation for the major Watergate coverup trial, special prosecutor Leon Jaworski,[19] subpoenaed some sixty-four tapes. Judge Sirica ordered compliance, and his decision was upheld by the Supreme Court in *United States v. Nixon* (1974).[20] The Court unanimously denied the President's right to make a final, unreviewable claim of executive privilege.

> Neither the doctrine of separation of powers, nor the need for confidentiality of high-level communications, without more, can sustain an absolute, unqualified, presidential privilege of immunity from judicial process under all circumstances.

The Court did grant that there was a limited executive privilege with a constitutional base—mentioning particularly the need to protect military, diplomatic, or sensitive national security secrets—and assured that the courts would recognize claims of confidentiality related to the President's ability to discharge his constitutional powers effectively.[21] But no national security claims were involved here. There was only "the generalized assertion of privilege," which "must be considered in light of our historic commitment to the rule of law" and "must yield to the demonstrated specific need for evidence in a pending criminal trial."

PRESIDENTIAL IMMUNITIES

President Nixon's involvement in the Watergate coverup raised other legal issues concerning presidential immunities. As just noted, subpoenas were up-

---

[19]Jaworski had succeeded Archibald Cox after the "Saturday night massacre," when Attorney General Elliott Richardson and Assistant Attorney General William Ruckelshaus resigned rather than carry out Nixon's order to fire Cox, who was then removed by Solicitor General Robert H. Bork as acting attorney general. See J. Anthony Lukas, *Nightmare* (New York: Viking, 1976).

[20]For comment see Paul A. Freund, "On Presidential Privilege," 88 HARVARD LAW REVIEW 13 (1974); Kurland, op. cit., Chapter 3. All the documents in the case are collected in Leon Friedman, ed., *United States v. Nixon: The President before the Supreme Court* (New York: Chelsea House Publishers, 1974).

[21]The Court was criticized by some for this admission, since it was the first time the Court had ever explicitly recognized the legitimacy of a claim of executive privilege. In *United States v. Reynolds* (1953), a suit under the Tort Claims Act arising from the death of three civilians in a military plane crash, the government contended that executive department heads had power to withhold any documents from judicial view if they deemed it in the public interest to do so. The Court found it unnecessary to accept this position, deciding *Reynolds* on a narrower ground. Philip Kurland criticized executive privilege as "a tool for the preclusion of legislative oversight, which is the only real check on abuse of executive power." To counter the Court's concession in *Nixon,* he argued that Congress should provide a statutory definition of the doctrine and a strict assertion of the conditions under which the privilege could be claimed by Presidents (*Los Angeles Times,* June 22, 1975). See also "Symposium: *United States v. Nixon,*" 22 UCLA LAW REVIEW 1 (1974). In 1983 President Reagan made a questionable claim of executive privilege in refusing to permit Environmental Protection Agency documents, unrelated to the executive office, to be turned over to a congressional committee.

held against Nixon in two cases. There had been some doubt whether the President was subject to subpoena because of the obvious enforcement problem if he chose to resist. The principal precedent was Chief Justice Marshall's subpoena to President Jefferson in the 1807 treason trial of Aaron Burr. While Marshall's opinion clearly rejected the contention that the President was immune from subpoena, the later developments in the case were somewhat confused and the subpoena was not actually enforced.[22]

In *Mississippi v. Johnson* (1867), the Supreme Court declined to issue an injunction against the President, pointing out that if he refused obedience, the Court would be "without power to enforce its process." When Judge Sirica subpoenaed Nixon's tapes for use of the Watergate grand jury, he considered it immaterial "that the court has not the physical power to enforce its order to the President." He simply relied on "the good faith of the executive branch." In fact, Nixon did yield to both subpoenas, though prior to the Supreme Court's decision in *United States v. Nixon* his counsel had refused to give assurance that Nixon would obey a Supreme Court order. It was generally agreed that if such resistance had occurred, it would have been cause for immediate impeachment.

A second issue raised by Watergate was whether a President is subject to criminal indictment while in office. The Watergate grand jury was convinced by the evidence it received that Nixon had participated in the coverup, and it wished to indict him along with the other principals. It was dissuaded, however, by Jaworski, who—taking it upon himself to decide this constitutional question—told the grand jury that the President was constitutionally protected against indictment.[23] Consequently, Nixon was merely named as an "unindicted co-conspirator" by the grand jury. In accepting the case of *United States v. Nixon,* the Supreme Court agreed to consider whether an incumbent President can be named in this manner; but after consideration, the justices ruled that the issue was irrelevant and so failed to express an opinion on it.

The Constitution makes it clear that after a President leaves office he can be prosecuted for criminal acts performed in office, even if he has already been convicted on impeachment for those acts (Art. I, sec. 3). Nixon faced the prospect of various legal actions following his resignation. A proposal that Congress grant him immunity from criminal prosecution was dropped, and in any event it could have had no binding effect. President Ford's pardon foreclosed any federal criminal prosecutions.

Civil prosecutions remained a possibility, and two suits were brought against Nixon after he left the White House. The first arose out of the wiretapping of some seventeen White House aides and journalists at Nixon's or-

---

[22]*United States v. Burr* (1807). See Raoul Berger, "The President, Congress, and the Courts—Subpoenaing the President: Jefferson v. Marshall in the Burr Case," 83 YALE LAW JOURNAL 1111 (1974).

[23]For the opposing view that a president can be criminally prosecuted while in office, see Raoul Berger, "The President, Congress, and the Courts—Must Impeachment Precede Indictment?" 83 YALE LAW JOURNAL 1111, 1123 (1974).

ders in an effort to find out who was leaking government foreign policy plans to the press. Wiretaps were placed on the home phone of Morton Halperin, a National Security Council employee, and maintained for many months after he left his government job. Halperin brought a civil suit for damages against Nixon, Henry Kissinger, and eight other officials for violation of his Fourth Amendment rights and Title III of the Omnibus Crime Control Act. The Court of Appeals for the District of Columbia in *Halperin v. Kissinger* (1979) ruled that Nixon had only a qualified immunity and that he, along with Kissinger, Mitchell, and Haldeman, were subject to suit. On appeal, *Kissinger v. Halperin* (1981), the Supreme Court divided four to four leaving Nixon subject to suit.

In the meantime, another suit had been progressing through the courts, brought by a former air force official, A. Ernest Fitzgerald, whom Nixon had ordered fired after he publicly criticized military cost overruns. Fitzgerald was successful in the lower courts, but in *Nixon v. Fitzgerald* (1982) the Supreme Court, dividing five to four, held the President absolutely immune from civil damages for his official acts "in the absence of explicit affirmative action by Congress." The Court considered this immunity "a functionally mandated incident of the President's unique office."

Justice White, dissenting, charged that this ruling would permit the President "deliberately to inflict injury on others by conduct that he knows violates the law." However, two White House aides also named in Fitzgerald's suit were held to have only a qualified immunity and they remained subject to suit.[24] The *Fitzgerald* ruling of course terminated Halperin's case against Nixon, but left Kissinger, Mitchell, and Haldeman still vulnerable.

PRESIDENTIAL PAPERS

Another issue concerns the ownership of presidential papers and records. Past practice has proceeded on the assumption that Presidents own their papers and take them with them when they leave the White House.[25] However, because of the circumstances under which Nixon left office and the relevance of his tapes and papers to ongoing criminal investigations, Congress passed the

---

[24]*Harlow v. Fitzgerald* (1982).

[25]It should be realized that this practice developed when the Presidency was practically a personal office, with only a few assistants and secretaries. Since 1939, when the Executive Office of the President was established, the Presidency has become institutionalized. There were fourteen staff agencies in the Nixon White House, 36 special assistants, and 3,400 executive employees in all. The explosion in "presidential" papers is indicated by the following data: Hoover, in one term, accumulated a million pages; Roosevelt, in three terms, 10.5 million pages; Eisenhower, in two terms, 11 million pages; Kennedy, in less than one term, 13 million; Johnson, in one and one-half terms, 17 million; and Nixon, in one and one-half terms, 42 million pages. The notion that these papers are the personal property of the President obviously requires rethinking (*The New York Times*, September 10, 1975).

Presidential Recordings and Materials Preservation Act of 1974, which required the General Services Administration to issue protective regulations for the Nixon materials. They were to be screened, the purely private papers returned to Nixon, and the balance made available to the public.

In *Nixon v. Administrator of General Services* (1977) the Court upheld the act by a vote of seven to two, rejecting contentions that the separation of powers, executive privilege, and Nixon's privacy and First Amendment rights had been invaded. Whether the act, which referred to Nixon by name, constituted a bill of attainder (i.e., legislative punishment) was discussed at length by Justice Brennan, who concluded for the Court that the statute had not been motivated by a "congressional determination of [Nixon's] blameworthiness and a desire to punish him." Justice Stevens concurred on the ground that Nixon "constituted a legitimate class of one," differing from all other presidents in resigning office under unique circumstances and accepting a pardon for offenses committed while in office. For this reason, Congress was justified in enacting "special legislation directed only at one former President."[26]

THE POWER TO PARDON

Article II, section 2, provides that the President "shall have power to grant reprieves and pardons for offenses against the United States, except in cases of impeachment." A pardon is usually thought of as an act of grace to correct a conviction or sentence that seems mistaken, harsh, or disproportionate to the crime. However, American Presidents have on numerous occasions used the pardoning power to grant amnesty to an entire group.[27] Congress also has the power to grant amnesties; it has done so in remitting penalties incurred under national statutes[28] and by providing immunity from prosecution for persons testifying before courts or congressional investigating committees.[29] However, Congress cannot interfere with the President's right to issue amnesties.[30]

The effect of a pardon is to grant exemption from the punishment the law inflicts for a crime. Since imprisonment and fine are the normal punishments, a pardon frees a convicted criminal from serving any uncompleted term of imprisonment and from paying any unpaid fine. Loss of certain civil and political rights is often an additional penalty for conviction of crime. Since a

[26]Chief Justice Burger, dissenting, charged that the decision was "a grave repudiation of nearly 200 years of judicial precedent and historical practice." Rehnquist colorfully suggested that the ruling "countenances the power of any future Congress to seize the official papers of an out-going President as he leaves the inaugural stand."

[27]Upheld in *Armstrong v. Unites States* (1872).

[28]*The Laura* (1885).

[29]*Brown v. Walker* (1896).

[30]*United States v. Klein* (1872).

pardon will restore these rights, one may still be sought on behalf of persons who have completed their sentences and paid their fines.

In *Ex parte Garland* (1867) the Supreme Court ruled that the result of a pardon is to wipe out completely all effects of the conviction for crime, Justice Field stating: "When the pardon is full, it releases the punishment and blots out of existence the guilt, so that in the eye of the law the offender is as innocent as if he had never committed the offence."[31]

Marshall early stated the rule that a pardon must be accepted to be valid,[32] which was followed in *Burdick v. United States* (1915). President Wilson had offered a full pardon for all offenses against the United States to one Burdick, whose testimony was wanted by a federal grand jury. Burdick, however, refused to accept the pardon, and the Supreme Court unanimously backed him.[33]

The only directly stated limitation on the President's pardoning power is that it does not apply to cases of impeachment, thus preventing the President from undoing the effect of such legislative punishment. A conviction for criminal contempt of court can be pardoned; but civil contempt actions, whose purpose is to enforce the rights of litigants, cannot be frustrated by a pardon.

The validity of a "conditional" pardon was upheld in *Schick v. Reed* (1974).[34] On review of a soldier's murder conviction and death sentence imposed by court-martial, President Eisenhower had commuted the sentence to life imprisonment, with the condition that the prisoner would never be eligible for parole. Marshall, dissenting, contended that the Court's 1972 ruling in *Furman v. Georgia* declaring capital punishment unconstitutional had voided the original sentence, leaving simple life imprisonment with eligibility for parole as the only legal alternative. He also contended that the President could not use his pardoning power to create unauthorized punishments.

President Ford's pardon of Richard Nixon, to whom Ford owed his office, was the most controversial in American history. To avert certain impeachment and conviction, Nixon had resigned effective August 9, 1974. By so doing he retained pension rights and other perquisites extended by law to ex-Presidents, which he would have forfeited had he been convicted on impeachment. The impeachment proceedings were thereby aborted, the Judiciary Committee simply submitting a final report to the House. Actually the impeachment proceedings could have been continued even after the resignation and in spite of the pardon, since the pardoning power does not apply to cases of impeachment.

Ford's pardon of Nixon, which had been negotiated secretly without consultation with any responsible political figures and announced on Septem-

---

[31] But see *Carlesi v. New York* (1914) for a limitation on this principle.

[32] *United States v. Wilson* (1833).

[33] But see *Chapman v. Scott* (1925) and *Biddle v. Perovich* (1927).

[34] A precedent was *Ex parte Wells* (1855). The *Schick* decision also presumably upheld the commutation granted by President Nixon in 1971 to James Hoffa, former head of the Teamsters Union, with the condition that he was barred from engaging in Teamster activities until 1980.

ber 8 with bombshell effects, raised several constitutional questions. First, it was alleged that the pardon violated the spirit of the constitutional ban on pardons in cases of impeachment. More significant was the challenge to the timing and scope of the pardon. Ford granted "a full, free and absolute pardon unto Richard Nixon for all offenses against the United States which he, Richard Nixon, has committed or may have committed or taken part in during the period from January 20, 1969 through August 9, 1974."

On September 8 Nixon had not been impeached by Congress or indicted for any crime, though he had been named as an unindicted co-conspirator in the Watergate coverup case. Since Nixon had admitted no criminal acts, it appeared that Ford had made an executive finding of guilt in referring to crimes that Nixon "has committed." Also, the pardon guaranteed Nixon absolute immunity from federal criminal prosecution at a time when possible criminal acts on his part were still actively under investigation.

It is true that at the Constitutional Convention language proposing that pardons could be granted only "after conviction" was rejected on the ground that "pardon before conviction might be necessary in order to obtain the testimony of accomplices." Moreover, in *Ex parte Garland* (1867), a closely divided Court held that the pardoning power "may be exercised at any time after . . . commission [of the offense], either before legal proceedings are taken, or during their pendency, or after conviction and judgment." However, this statement was dictum; and since the Court speaks of "offenses," it can be argued that until there has been a confession or at least an indictment, there is no "offense" and thus no power to pardon.

The public reaction to the Nixon pardon was highly unfavorable and, together with the revelation that Nixon had considered the possibility of pardoning himself and his Watergate associates before resigning, led to proposals for a constitutional amendment that would bar pardons prior to conviction.[35]

---

[35]As one of his first acts in office, President Carter issued a pardon to all draft evaders of the Vietnam War—some 10,000. In 1981 President Reagan pardoned two former FBI officials who had been found guilty in 1980 for authorizing illegal searches of antiwar activists in 1973, saying they had not acted "with criminal intent." A presidential pardon does not reverse a jury verdict of guilt.

16

Control of Foreign Relations

The doctrine of "political questions," we noted in Chapter 8, is available for the Supreme Court's use when an issue of private right that it is asked to decide turns on considerations largely outside judicial competence or authority. It is significant that the political questions doctrine has been perhaps most often invoked by the Court to avoid decisions relating to the conduct of American foreign relations. An early instance was *Foster v. Neilson* (1829), where the Court refused to rule on the location of the boundary between Spain and the United States in 1804 because this was "more a political than a legal question," and one on which the courts must accept the decisions of the "political departments."

The development of constitutional principles in the foreign relations field is thus more properly traced through the medium of diplomatic history than constitutional law, and the present chapter will be accordingly of limited scope. The Supreme Court has nevertheless on several occasions stated principles of primary importance in the guidance and rationalization of American practice in the field of foreign relations.[1] Of course the federal courts administer general international law in so far as it is applicable in cases coming before them,

---

[1] A highly useful general work is Louis Henkin, *Foreign Affairs and the Constitution* (Mineola, N.Y.: Foundation Press, 1972).

but that is a different problem and one outside the confines of the present study.

THE NATURE OF FEDERAL POWER

The provisions of the Constitution pertaining to foreign relations all take the form of assignments of particular functions to the various branches of the government. These specifically mentioned powers by no means cover the whole range of foreign affairs, and there is no grant of authority over foreign relations in broad terms comparable, say, with the authorization to regulate commerce among the states. On the other hand there are no provisions expressly denying or limiting the federal government's full authority to conduct external relations as a sovereign nation in a world of sovereign nations.

The framers were in fact well aware that they had no choice in this matter. The central government they were instituting would be fatally disabled if it lacked authority to deal with its peers or to meet the ever-recurring crises arising out of its relations abroad. As Hamilton said in No. 23 of *The Federalist:* "The circumstances that endanger the safety of nations are infinite, and for this reason no constitutional shackles can wisely be imposed on the power to which the care of it is committed." Thus the first principle in this area is that governmental power over foreign relations is plenary. The manner of its exercise is in certain respects specified by the Constitution, and the location of responsibility is defined. But the federal government's basic authority to conduct foreign relations is constitutionally unlimited.

What is the constitutional source of this authority, which goes far beyond the sum of the particular functions mentioned in the document? The answer is that authority over foreign affairs is an inherent power, which attaches automatically to the federal government as a sovereign entity, and derives from the Constitution only as the Constitution is the creator of that sovereign entity. As Justice Sutherland said in *United States v. Curtiss-Wright Export Corporation* (1936): "The investment of the federal government with the powers of external sovereignty did not depend upon the affirmative grants of the Constitution. The powers to declare and wage war, to conclude peace, to make treaties, to maintain diplomatic relations with other sovereignties, if they had never been mentioned in the Constitution, would have vested in the federal government as necessary concomitants of nationality."

For this reason, Sutherland continued, the source of foreign relations authority contrasted sharply with federal power over internal affairs. "In that field, the primary purpose of the Constitution was to carve from the general mass of legislative powers *then possessed by the states* such portions as it was thought desirable to vest in the federal government, leaving those not included in the enumeration still in the states." But the Constitution could not transfer power over external affairs in this way from the states to the nation because "the states severally never possessed international powers." Rather, on the separation of the colonies "acting as a unit" from Great Britain, "the powers of external sovereignty passed from the Crown not to the colonies severally, but to the colonies in their collective and corporate capacity as the United States of America." Even before the Declaration of Independence, the Colonies were acting through a common agency, the Continental Congress, and when "the external sovereignty of Great Britain in respect of the colonies ceased, it immediately passed to the Union." Thus the Union, existing before the Constitution, "was the sole possessor of external sovereignty and in the Union it remained without change save insofar as the Constitution in express terms qualified its exercise."

Presumably the purpose of Sutherland's conceptualistic analysis, which seems strikingly at variance with the actual historical facts of the Revolutionary period,[2] was to establish that the federal government's power over foreign affairs was inherent, plenary, and exclusive, but it seems an unnecessarily involved way of achieving those ends. Surely the inherent nature of the power to conduct foreign affairs can be deduced from the right of a nation to self-preservation in a world of nations, without elaborate hypotheses about the location and transfer of sovereignty in a revolutionary period. That the power is plenary is established by the absence of any expressed constitutional limitations on its exercise. That the power is exclusive as against the states is sufficiently established by Article I, section 10, which flatly forbids states to enter into "any treaty, alliance, or confederation," or to grant "letters of marque and reprisal." The third clause of section 10 carries further prohibitions, though these may be waived with the consent of Congress. The clause reads:

> No state shall, without the consent of Congress, . . . keep troops, or ships of war in time of peace, enter into any agreement or compact . . . with a foreign power, or engage in war, unless actually invaded, or in such imminent danger as will not admit of delay.

In fact, the consent of Congress has never been asked for any of these purposes, and the clause must now be read as an unqualified bar to the acts specified. Thus the complete incapacity of the states for foreign relationships is fully established by the letter of the Constitution and by practice.

Neither is Sutherland's theory necessary to prevent any possible encroachment on federal authority by the states through their "reserved powers" under the Tenth Amendment. In discussing the commerce clause, we saw how the doctrine of dual federalism for a time made reserved state powers an instrument for denying full exercise by the federal government of its directly granted powers to regulate commerce among the states. But dual federalism

---

[2]See the excellent article by Charles A. Lofgren, *"United States v. Curtiss-Wright Export Corporation:* An Historical Reassessment," 83 YALE LAW JOURNAL 1 (1973), in which he concludes that Justice Sutherland's history was "shockingly inaccurate."

never got a foothold in the field of foreign relations, as *Ware v. Hylton* (1796) demonstrates. During the Revolutionary War, Virginia passed a law sequestering British property and providing that debts owed by citizens of the state to British subjects could be discharged by payment to a designated state officer. This statute was clearly a valid exercise of state powers under international law. However, the treaty of peace between the United States and Great Britain controverted this arrangement and preserved the right of British creditors to collect such debts. The Supreme Court held that this exercise by the United States of its treaty power had the effect of nullifying the conflicting Virginia law.

THE ROLE OF THE PRESIDENT

The principal theoretical writers on government whose works were known and read by the framers—Blackstone, Locke, Montesquieu—were unanimous in contending that the power to conduct foreign relations must rest with the executive. In spite of this fact, the Constitution allocated the power to declare war to Congress, where the authority had vested under the Articles of Confederation. It made the Senate's consent necessary to the ratification of treaties, and by a two-thirds vote. It made the Senate's advice and consent a condition to the appointment of ambassadors. When account is taken of the general lawmaking and appropriating powers of Congress, the exercise of which may be essential to the formulation and execution of foreign policy decisions, it is clear that, as Corwin says, "The Constitution, considered only for its affirmative grants of powers capable of affecting the issue, is an invitation to struggle for the privilege of directing American foreign policy."[3]

For this struggle the President is powerfully equipped by the general characteristics of executive power already noted, by his constitutional authority as commander in chief, and by his recognized position as "the Nation's organ for foreign affairs."[4] The Supreme Court has repeatedly recognized the President's primacy and special position in this area, as a further look at the *Curtiss-Wright* decision will demonstrate. The controversy in that case involved a joint resolution adopted by Congress in 1934 authorizing the President by proclamation to prohibit the sale within the United States of arms to certain South American belligerent states. The President promptly issued such a declaration. A conviction for violation of the proclamation and joint resolution was attacked on the ground that the statute constituted an unlawful delegation of legislative power to the President, because action was left to the

[3]Edward S. Corwin, *The President: Office and Powers, 1787-1957*, 4th rev. ed. (New York: New York University Press, 1957), p. 171.

[4]This phrase goes back to a statement made by John Marshall in the House of Representatives in 1799. See ibid., pp. 177–78. See Raoul Berger, "The Presidential Monopoly of Foreign Relations," 71 MICHIGAN LAW REVIEW 1 (1972).

"unfettered discretion" of the executive with no statutory standards to guide his decision.

As noted in Chapter 10, the Court had just used such grounds to invalidate federal statutes in the *Panama Refining, Schechter,* and *Carter Coal Co.* cases. But in *Curtiss-Wright* Justice Sutherland pointed out that the delegations in those three cases had "related solely to internal affairs," whereas the "whole aim" of the resolution challenged here was "to affect a situation entirely external to the United States." In this latter area the President possessed not only the powers given him by statute, but also "the very delicate, plenary and exclusive power of the President as the sole organ of the federal government in the field of international relations." Sutherland went on:

> It is quite apparent that if, in the maintenance of our international relations, embarrassment . . . is to be avoided and success for our aims achieved, congressional legislation which is to be made effective through negotiation and inquiry within the international field must often accord to the President a degree of discretion and freedom from statutory restriction which would not be admissible were domestic affairs alone involved. Moreover, he, not Congress, has the better opportunity of knowing the conditions which prevail in foreign countries. . . . He has his confidential sources of information. He has his agents in the form of diplomatic, consular and other officials.

In the light of these circumstances, the Court concluded that delegations of legislative power to the President in matters involving foreign relations could not be judged by the same standards that would be applied in internal affairs.

More specifically, what powers does the President exercise in his role as "sole organ" of foreign relations for the nation? First of all, he is the channel for communications to and from other nations. He appoints the members of the diplomatic corps through whom official contacts are maintained abroad and receives their reports through the Department of State. Negotiations with foreign countries are conducted under his direction. In collaboration with the secretary of state and his national security adviser, he determines the policies to be followed in dealing with foreign nations.[5]

Second, the power of recognizing foreign governments follows from the presidential role in sending and receiving diplomatic representatives. President Washington established the controlling precedent in this area when he received Citizen Genêt and then some months later demanded his recall by France, without consulting Congress on either occasion. Constitutional authority for decisions on the establishment of diplomatic relations—as in the recognition of Russia in 1933, or the Nixon-Kissinger visit to the People's Republic of

---

[5]During the Nixon administration, Secretary of State William P. Rogers was largely eclipsed by Henry Kissinger, presidential assistant for national security. Kissinger became secretary of state in 1973 but also retained his White House national security post until 1975. Under succeeding presidents, relations between the national security adviser and the secretary of state continued to be strained and were in part responsible for the resignation of Secretary of State Haig in 1982.

China in 1972, or the break with Castro's Cuba—rest on the President alone, as the Supreme Court recognized in *United States v. Belmont* (1937).

Third, the President can use his control of the Armed Forces to implement his foreign policy and to enforce American rights or interests abroad. In 1844 Tyler disposed the naval and military forces so as to protect Texas against Mexican reprisals because of the pending treaty for annexation of Texas to the United States. Theodore Roosevelt in 1903 "took Panama," as he put it, and later sent the fleet around the world to demonstrate American power and interest in world affairs. President Wilson ordered the arming of American merchant vessels as a countermove to German unrestricted submarine warfare in March, 1917. Three Presidents sent troops into the Vietnam quagmire. Ford used air and naval forces in 1975 against Cambodia to rescue the American vessel *Mayaguez*. President Reagan sent military "advisers" into El Salvador in 1981. Troops have been repeatedly employed to protect American lives and property in foreign countries.

These are powers of tremendous impact—so great, in fact, that they largely cancel out the most important grant of external authority to Congress, the power to declare war.

Treaties

On the other hand, the necessity of securing Senate consent by a two-thirds vote for the ratification of treaties has proved in practice to be a real limitation on executive policy making. The framers thought of the Senate as a kind of council with which the President would sit while treaties were under negotiation and from which he would get advice. In fact President Washington tried to use the Senate in this way in August, 1789, going to the Senate chamber in person and presenting seven issues pertaining to a proposed treaty with the Southern Indians on which he wished "advice and consent." The senators preferred not to discuss the matter in the presence of President, and voted to refer it to a committee of five. Washington, quite indignant, exclaimed: "This defeats every purpose of my coming here," and subsequently withdrew with what William Maclay called "a discontented air." Washington did go back two days later for the Senate's answers to his questions, but the whole experience was so unfortunate that the effort has never been repeated.

Treaties are consequently negotiated by the executive, though congressional leaders are normally appointed to the American delegation to important international conferences as well as to the United Nations. When treaties are sent to the Senate in completed form, their fate is unpredictable. John Hay once wrote: "A treaty entering the Senate is like a bull going into the arena; no one can say just how or when the final blow will fall—but one thing is certain, it will never leave the arena alive."[6] This is highly exaggerated, but

---

[6]William R. Thayer, *The Life and Letters of John Hay* (Boston: Houghton Mifflin Company, 1915), II: 393. In 1974 the Senate Foreign Relations Committee voted out the Geneva protocol on chemical warfare, which had been submitted for ratification in 1926.

the shambles that Senate intervention has sometimes made of United States foreign policy has led students to conclude that consent to treaty ratification by a majority vote of the two houses of Congress would be preferable to the present arrangement.

The Senate can defeat a treaty entirely or consent to ratification with amendments. This latter action requires the President, if he still favors the treaty, to secure the acceptance of these amendments by the foreign power involved before the treaty can be ratified. The Senate may also attach reservations, which do not alter the content of the treaty itself but do qualify the obligations assumed under the treaty by the United States.

President Carter secured ratification in 1978 of the controversial Panama Canal Treaty, which yields ownership of the Canal to Panama in the year 2000, but with only one vote to spare, sixty-eight to thirty-two. He had the assistance of the Supreme Court, which rejected several lawsuits by opponents of the treaty, asserting constitutional objections, the principal contention being that the House also had to approve the treaty because the disposition of federal property was involved.[7]

President Carter was unsuccessful in securing Senate ratification of SALT II (Strategic Arms Limitation Treaty) with Russia, which he withdrew from Senate consideration in 1980 following the Soviet invasion of Afghanistan. His major diplomatic triumph in bringing Israel and Egypt into the Camp David Accord of course required no Senate approval.

Constitutional objections were also lodged against Carter's termination of the American mutual defense treaty with Taiwan in 1978. But Senator Goldwater's suit alleging that Senate consent was required for abrogation of the treaty was dismissed by the Supreme Court, seven to two, in *Goldwater v. Carter* (1979), though with some disagreement as to the reasoning. Rehnquist spoke for four justices in regarding this as a classic nonjusticiable political question, and Marshall concurred in the result. But both Brennan and Powell held the dispute justiciable. However, Powell concurred in the dismissal on the ground that the dispute was not ripe for judicial review, while Brennan upheld abrogation as a necessary incident to executive recognition of the Peking government. A sense-of-the-Senate resolution condemning the President's action was adopted in 1979, but it had no legal effect.

Executive Agreements

Partly because of the hazards of Senate treaty approval, the President has made extensive use of "executive agreements" with foreign countries.[8]

---

[7] *Helms v. Vance* (1977); *Idaho v. Vance* (1978); *Edwards v. Carter* (1978).

[8] Congress has periodically but unsuccessfully sought to restrict the use of executive agreements as a means of avoiding submission of treaties to the Senate. The famous Bricker Amendment of the 1950s had this as one of its purposes. In 1972 discovery by the Senate of a number of secret foreign commitments, particularly an agreement permitting use of Spanish bases in return for American grants, led Congress to adopt the so-called Case Amendment, which requires

Since these agreements are not treaties in name, they are not subject to the constitutional requirement of Senate consent. They may be employed for minor matters which it would be inappropriate to embody in a treaty, but in the twentieth century many executive agreements have dealt with matters of major importance. Thus Japanese immigration into the United States was governed for seventeen years by the "Gentlemen's Agreement" of 1907, and the controversial Potsdam and Yalta Pacts were executive agreements.

Executive agreements are often based on acts of Congress authorizing them. If not, they are usually said to find their constitutional authority in the President's power as commander in chief or in his position as the sole organ of international relations.[9] Efforts to distinguish the legal effects of executive agreements from treaties have generally been unsuccessful. One contention has been that the force of an executive agreement terminates with the end of the administration that entered into it, but this is not true. For example, the 1940 destroyer deal with Britain provided for United States leases extending ninety-nine years on the British bases involved.

A further contention is that agreements, unlike treaties, are not "law of the land" unless authorized or approved by Congress, and so not noticeable by the courts. But in *United States v. Belmont* (1937) the Supreme Court specifically denied this view, holding that the recognition of Soviet Russia in 1933 and the accompanying executive agreements constituted an international compact that the President was authorized to enter into without consulting the Senate. Moreover, such agreements had the same effect as treaties in superseding conflicting state laws. To similar effect was the decision in *United States v. Pink* (1942).[10]

CONGRESS AND FOREIGN RELATIONS

In addition to the power of Congress to declare war and the special role of the Senate in ratifying treaties and confirming ambassadorial appointments, Congress can exercise great influence over foreign policy through its general powers of legislation, appropriation, and investigation.[11] Congress early seized power from the President on the matter of neutrality. In 1793 President Wash-

---

the secretary of state to submit to Congress within sixty days the text of any international agreement made by the executive branch.

[9]As noted in Chapter 15, President Carter's executive agreement with Iran for freeing the American hostages was found by the Supreme Court in *Dames & Moore v. Regan* (1981) to be authorized in part by statute and in part by long-continued executive practice in settling claims against American nationals.

[10]The Supreme Court has not determined whether an executive agreement will supersede an earlier act of Congress with which it is in disagreement. See *United States v. Guy W. Capps, Inc.* (1955).

[11]See Arthur Schlesinger, Jr., "Congress and the Making of American Foreign Policy," 51 FOREIGN AFFAIRS 78 (1972).

ington, on the outbreak of war between Britain and France, issued a proclamation asserting the intention of the United States to be "friendly and impartial" toward both belligerents. Hamilton wrote a defense of the constitutional right of the President to issue such a proclamation, but the action was offensive to Jeffersonian views of executive power. In 1794 Congress superseded the executive proclamation by passing the first neutrality act, and this precedent has been subsequently accepted as establishing legislative authority over the neutrality issue.

Congress possesses specific constitutional authority to define and punish offenses against the law of nations as well as to regulate foreign commerce. Congress may use its general lawmaking power to frustrate or limit executive foreign policy. In 1924 Congress adopted the Japanese Exclusion Act over the protests of President Coolidge and Secretary of State Hughes, with damaging effects on American foreign relations. The authority to negotiate reciprocal trade agreements, a basic instrument of foreign policy after 1934, had to be won anew from Congress every two or three years. More recently a favorite legislative device has been to impose statutory bans on trade with, or aid to, countries in congressional disfavor. The 1982 Boland Amendment forbade assistance to forces seeking to overthrow the government of Nicaragua.

Congressional legislative power may also step into the breach caused by failure of the treaty process to function successfully. After the defeat of the Treaty of Versailles, it was a joint resolution of Congress that finally brought American participation in the war against the Central Powers to a legal conclusion in 1921. Moreover, it should be noted that American adherence to the United Nations was accomplished by congressional statute, the United Nations Participation Act of 1945.

The appropriations power gives legislative control over any executive policy that requires funds for its implementation, and the fact that appropriations measures must originate with the House serves somewhat to balance the Senate's special role in the foreign relations field. Since the inauguration of the Marshall Plan in 1947, the appropriation for foreign aid has annually precipitated lengthy and often acrimonious debates over foreign policy, and the executive recommendations are almost invariably substantially reduced.

The House and Senate can also use their general investigatory powers to influence foreign policy. During the 1930s Senator Nye's investigations of the armaments industry did much to encourage an isolationist attitude toward foreign involvements. Senator Fulbright, who was at odds with President Johnson on Vietnam, used his powerful position as chairman of the Senate Foreign Relations Committee to conduct "educational" hearings on China policy and the North Atlantic Treaty Organization as well as Vietnam.

Conscious of the desirability of congressional support for the use of troops outside the country, President Eisenhower in 1955 requested Congress to adopt a joint resolution authorizing his employment of the armed forces to protect Formosa (Taiwan) from Chinese attack. Again in 1957 Congress voted support for the President if he should determine there was necessity for use of force against Communist aggression in the Middle East.

These precedents were utilized by President Johnson in 1964. At a time when there were only 20,000 American troops in Vietnam, and after alleged North Vietnamese torpedo boat attacks on two United States destroyers in the Gulf of Tonkin, the President asked Congress for a joint resolution of support to strengthen his hand in dealing with the Vietnam situation. Almost unanimously Congress adopted the so-called Tonkin Gulf Resolution approving and supporting "the determination of the President, as commander in chief, to take all necessary measures to repel any armed attack against the forces of the United States and to prevent further aggression."

In the aftermath of the Vietnam debacle, Congress undertook to play a more active role in foreign relations, highlighted by an arms embargo against Turkey in 1974 following the Turkish invasion of Cyprus, and a ban on funds and military aid to factions in the Angola civil war in 1975. Both actions were strongly condemned by the executive as congressional meddling in foreign affairs. Disclosure of CIA covert activities and assassination plots abroad led both the House and Senate to create special intelligence committees in 1975 to investigate these reports, and in 1976 the Senate created a select committee charged with oversight of all the nation's secret intelligence services.

The Arms Export Control Act of 1976 requires the President to send Congress an unclassified notice describing major arms sales abroad before he can issue a formal offer to the country buying weapons or services. Congress can block a sale if both houses pass an identical concurrent resolution within thirty days of receiving the notice. But the President can waive the right of congressional veto if he states in his notice that an emergency exists requiring the sale in the interest of national security. In 1981 a sale of sophisticated planes and other air combat equipment totalling $8.5 billion to Saudi Arabia was narrowly approved by the Senate. Congressional concern about repeating the Vietnam disaster generated a variety of limitations and controls over Reagan's involvement in Central America.

CONSTITUTIONAL ASPECTS OF THE TREATY POWER

Article VI provides: "This Constitution, and the laws of the United States which shall be made in pursuance thereof; and all treaties made, or which shall be made, under the authority of the United States, shall be the supreme law of the land." Two problems growing out of this language need consideration here: first, the relationship between treaties and acts of Congress; and second, the relationship of treaties and the treaty-making power to the Constitution itself.

Treaties and Acts of Congress

Article VI sets treaties and acts of Congress on a par—both are "the supreme law of the land." How then are conflicts between treaties and statutes adjusted? First it is necessary to distinguish between "self-executing" and "non-self-executing" treaties. A treaty is self-executing when it requires no congressional legislation to put it into effect. Thus the provisions of a treaty defining the rights of aliens in the United States would automatically become the "supreme law of the land," and the courts would be obliged to enforce them. A non-self-executing treaty is one in which obligations of future action are undertaken by the political departments of the government. A treaty of alliance with a foreign power, or a treaty that required the appropriation of money by Congress would be illustrations. The courts have no power to enforce such treaties should the government fail to honor the obligation it has undertaken.

In general, where a treaty and a statute conflict, the later in point of time supersedes the earlier. There are exceptions, however. All acts of Congress prevail over earlier conflicting treaties, but a non-self-executing treaty does not supersede an earlier conflicting act of Congress.[12]

Constitutional Scope of Treaties

According to Article VI, laws must be made "in pursuance" of the Constitution in order to have status as supreme law of the land, but treaties need be made only "under the authority of the United States." Considerable effort has been made to conjure up from this difference in wording the bogey of a treaty power which is unlimited by the Constitution. Some substance seems to be given to these fears by the fact that the Supreme Court has never held a treaty unconstitutional. But such fears, to the extent that they were genuine, were completely unfounded.

First, the provision that treaties need be made only "under the authority of the United States" was required to validate treaties made *before* the Constitution was adopted, particularly the important peace treaties that concluded the Revolutionary War. Second, the Court has on several occasions clearly announced that the treaty power is subject to the Constitution. Perhaps the most explicit earlier holding to this effect came in *Geofroy v. Riggs* (1890). Justice Field there began by admitting that "the treaty power, as expressed in the Constitution, is in terms unlimited," but he went on to note that it was subject to those implied "restraints which are found in that instrument against the action of the government or of its departments, and those arising from the nature of the government itself and of that of the States." Since this language was a little vague, Field added: "It would not be contended that [the treaty power] extends so far as to authorize what the Constitution forbids, or

[12] See *Head Money Cases* (1884).

a change in the character of the government or in that of one of the States, or a cession of any portion of the territory of the latter, without its consent."

Any doubt that could have remained on the subjection of the treaty power to the Constitution after this decision was completely extinguished by *Reid* v. *Covert* (1957). Justice Black, after quoting Article VI, said:

> There is nothing in this language which intimates that treaties and laws enacted pursuant to them do not have to comply with the provisions of the Constitution. . . . It would be manifestly contrary to the objectives of those who created the Constitution, as well as those who were responsible for the Bill of Rights—let alone alien to our entire constitutional history and tradition—to construe Article VI as permitting the United States to exercise power under an international agreement without observing constitutional prohibitions. In effect, such construction would permit amendment of that document in a manner not sanctioned by Article V.

The Supreme Court's decision in *Missouri* v. *Holland* (1920) dealt with another important aspect of the treaty power. This case arose out of the efforts of the United States to impose limits on the shooting of migratory birds. The first congressional statute passed for this purpose was declared an unconstitutional exercise of federal commerce power in two federal district court decisions, on the ground that the birds were owned by the states in their sovereign capacity for the benefit of their people. The United States then entered into a treaty with Great Britain, reciting the dangers of extermination of birds in their annual migrations between the United States and Canada, providing for closed seasons and other forms of protection, and agreeing that the two powers would take or propose to their legislatures necessary measures for making the treaty provisions effective. In pursuance of this treaty, Congress passed a statute in 1918 prohibiting the killing of migratory birds except in accordance with federal regulations.

The Supreme Court, through Justice Holmes, upheld enforcement of this statute against the charge that the treaty and legislation were an unconstitutional interference with the rights of the states. In part his conclusion rested upon the evanescent nature of the state claim to ownership of the birds. "The whole foundation of the State's rights is the presence within their jurisdiction of birds that yesterday had not arrived, tomorrow may be in another State and in a week a thousand miles away." But more positively his case was based on recognition of the fact that here was "a national interest of very nearly the first magnitude" that could be protected "only by national action in concert with that of another power. . . . But for the treaty and the statute there soon might be no birds for any powers to deal with."

Holmes did not intend to see the only effective means of protecting this national interest frustrated by "some invisible radiation from the general terms of the Tenth Amendment." For "it is not lightly to be assumed that, in matters requiring national action, 'a power which must belong to and somewhere reside in every civilized government' is not to be found.'' In this instance the authority was to be found in the treaty power. Holmes hastened to add that he did not ''mean to imply that there are no qualifications to the treaty-making power'': one such limitation, he suggested, would be any explicit ''prohibitory words . . . found in the Constitution.'' But there were none applicable to this situation. The general deduction which he drew was that ''there may be matters of the sharpest exigency for the national well-being that an act of Congress could not deal with but that a treaty followed by such an act could.''

There is at first glance something startling about a situation whereby ratification of a treaty gives Congress constitutional powers it did not possess in the absence of the treaty. But this result is an inevitable consequence of the plenary nature of federal power over foreign affairs. The division of functions between federal and state governments made by the Constitution relates only to internal affairs. The complete incapacity of the states for foreign relationships requires that the federal government have authority to deal with all matters that are of legitimate concern to American foreign relations.

CONTROL OVER PASSPORTS

The Passport Act of 1856, codified and reenacted in 1926, provides that ''The Secretary of State shall be authorized to grant and issue passports . . . under such rules as the President shall designate and prescribe. . . .'' Subsequent legislation authorized the secretary of state, as incident to the issuance of passports, to control travel by American citizens abroad. Motivated by the cold war after World War II, the State Department in 1947 adopted a policy of refusing passports to members of the Communist party or persons whose travel would ''prejudice the orderly conduct of foreign relations'' or ''otherwise be prejudicial to the interests of the United States.'' During the following decade, a substantial number of persons, most of whom denied being members of the Communist party, were refused passports. In the Internal Security Act of 1950, Congress added statutory support to this policy by forbidding passports to members of Communist organizations ordered to register with the attorney general.

The first test of these restrictions to reach the Supreme Court was *Kent v. Dulles* (1958), in which Justice Douglas held:

> The right to travel is part of the ''liberty'' of which the citizen cannot be deprived without the due process of law of the Fifth Amendment. . . . Freedom of movement across frontiers in either direction . . . was a part of our heritage. Travel abroad . . . may be necessary for a livelihood. It may be as close to the heart of the individual as the choice of what he eats, or wears, or reads.

Having decided this much, the Supreme Court found it unnecessary to take up the more difficult question of how far this liberty might be curtailed without infringing on due process, because five justices concluded that Congress had not authorized the kinds of curtailment that the State Department had been practicing.

The State Department, while announcing that passport applicants would no longer be required to answer questions about Communist party membership, immediately appealed to Congress to adopt legislation confirming the powers it had been exercising. Surprisingly, Congress failed to act. This left, as the only expressly applicable statute, the Internal Security Act, the registration provisions of which the Court held constitutional in 1961.[13] This brought the passport provisions of the act into effect, and the State Department promptly used them to deny passports to two leading American Communists. The Supreme Court held the legislation unconstitutional in *Aptheker v. Secretary of State* (1964).

Justice Goldberg ruled for the Court that the language was unconstitutional on its face because it prohibited the granting of passports to any member of a registered Communist organization, regardless of whether his membership was knowing or unknowing, regardless of his degree of activity in the organization and his commitment to its purpose, or regardless of the purposes for which he wished to travel. After all, he might simply want "to visit a relative in Ireland, or . . . read rare manuscripts in the Bodleian Library of Oxford University." Justice Clark for a three-judge minority thought these were "irrational imaginings" and argued that, at least as applied to admitted Communist leaders, the statute should be upheld.

The Court did not say in *Aptheker* that the right to travel was absolute. It merely held that this particular limitation was too broad and indiscriminate in its scope. In *Zemel v. Rusk* (1965), the Court upheld the State Department's refusal to validate passports for travel to Communist Cuba. The broad language of the Passport Act of 1926, which the Court had held in the *Kent* case did not authorize State Department denial of passports to Communists, was here thought to justify the practice of geographical area limitations on travel. The Court majority found that there had been a frequent practice of area restrictions on passports in the decade prior to 1926; thus it could be inferred that Congress intended by the broad language of the act to maintain such authority in the executive—authority that could be supported by "the weightiest considerations of national security."

Another, and more persuasive, difference from the *Kent* situation was that there the action was taken against an individual because of his views or affiliations, whereas area limitations are imposed "because of foreign policy considerations affecting all citizens." Thus the Court felt there was no possible First Amendment claim that the individual was being restrained from travel because of his views.

Enforcement of these area restrictions proved quite frustrating for the

---

[13]*Communist Party v. Subversive Activities Control Board* (1961).

State Department. A newspaperman who went to Cuba without a passport was indicted on his return under the Immigration and Nationality Act of 1952, which forbids reentry of an American citizen into the United States without a valid passport. The Court of Appeals for the Fifth Circuit held this provision unconstitutional as a denial of the fundamental right of free ingress.[14] Preferring not to take this case to the Supreme Court, the Department of Justice chose to rely instead on a statute forbidding citizens to depart from the country without a valid passport. But there was no specific language in the statute punishing violation of State Department area restrictions, and the Court in *United States v. Laub* (1967) and *Travis v. United States* (1967) held that the criminal indictments must be dismissed. "Crimes are not to be created by inference," said Justice Fortas.

This ruling left open to the State Department the sanction of canceling the passports of persons who visited off-limits countries. But after another court reversal on this issue,[15] the State Department in 1968, while continuing to declare certain countries off limits to American travelers, abandoned its efforts to deny passports to persons wishing to visit those countries or to revoke passports of those who traveled to restricted countries.

In 1981 the Court for the first time upheld revocation of a passport on national security grounds. Philip Agee, an American citizen and former CIA official residing abroad, had over a decade publicly named agents of the CIA working undercover in foreign countries in an avowed effort to disrupt the agency's operations. One murder of an official he had identified was attributed to his actions. In 1979 the State Department revoked his passport, and the Court approved in *Haig v. Agee* (1981). The right to travel, which the Court had strongly defended in earlier rulings, was "subject to reasonable government regulation," wrote Chief Justice Burger. Brennan, dissenting, agreed that Agee was hardly a "model representative of our nation," but contended that the Constitution protects "both popular and unpopular travelers," and that this was a case where "bad facts make bad law."

---

[14] *Worthy v. United States* (1964).
[15] *Lynd v. Rusk* (1967).

17

The President as Commander in Chief

In No. 74 of *The Federalist* Alexander Hamilton wrote: "Of all the cares or concerns of government, the direction of war most peculiarly demands those qualities which distinguish the exercise of power by a single hand." He was defending the "propriety" of the commander-in-chief clause (Art. II, sec. 2), which reads: "The President shall be Commander in Chief of the army and navy of the United States, and of the militia of the several states, when called into the actual service of the United States." This provision, he added, was "so consonant to the precedents of the State constitutions in general, that little need be said to explain or enforce it." It would amount, he said in No. 69, "to nothing more than the supreme command and direction of the military and naval forces, as first general and admiral of the Confederacy," while the more significant powers of declaring war and of raising and regulating fleets and armies were exercised by Congress.

LINCOLN AND THE WAR POWER

Hamilton did not foresee the tremendous reservoir of power that this constitutional language was to provide for the President. It was President Lincoln who, in his resolve to maintain the Union, linked together the Presidential power to take care that the laws be faithfully executed with that of commander in chief to yield a result approaching constitutional dictatorship.[1]

For ten weeks after the fall of Fort Sumter until he called Congress into special session, Lincoln met the emergency by a series of actions that were for the most part completely without statutory authorization, though they were subsequently ratified by Congress. He added 40,000 men to the Army and Navy, closed the Post Office to "treasonable correspondence," paid out $2 million from unappropriated funds in the Treasury, proclaimed a blockade of Southern ports, suspended the writ of habeas corpus in several areas, and caused the arrest and military detention of persons suspected of treasonable practices.

Lincoln's inauguration of military operations without authorization by Congress was upheld by the Supreme Court in the *Prize Cases* (1863). The President had declared a blockade of Confederate ports in April, 1861, and this case concerned four vessels that had been captured and taken as prizes by Union naval vessels. To decide this issue of private rights, the Court had to consider questions of the highest political significance. If it held that the conflict was not a war because it had not been declared so by Congress, then the laws of war would not apply and the prizes would have been illegally taken. If it held that the blockade was legal, but in the process recognized the Confederacy as an independent sovereign, recognition of the Confederate States by foreign governments would be encouraged, with vastly damaging effects for the Union cause.

By a narrow margin the Court avoided both of these positions. Five justices held that the insurrection was a state of war under domestic and international law, so that the President's blockade and the capture of prizes was legitimate. This "greatest of civil wars," Justice Grier said, "sprung forth suddenly from the parent brain, a Minerva in the full panoply of *war*. The President was bound to meet it in the shape it presented itself, without waiting for Congress to baptize it with a name; and no name given to it by him or them could change the fact." Moreover, it was the President who had to determine "what degree of force the crisis demands." The President's blockade proclamation was conclusive evidence for the Court that a state of war existed which demanded recourse to such a measure. At the same time, the Court majority accorded no rights of sovereignty to the South.

The Court thus took the view urged by Richard Henry Dana, one of the counsel in the case, that "War is *a state of things,* and not an act of legislative will." In contrast, the minority contended that the conflict was a "personal war" of the President "until Congress assembled and acted upon this state of things."

---

[1]See James G. Randall, *Constitutional Problems under Lincoln,* rev. ed. (Urbana: University of Illinois Press, 1964).

been presidentially, not judicially, shaped: their exercise is for Congress and the people, not the Court, to oversee''[5]

Efforts to secure judicial review of the constitutionality of the congressionally undeclared war in Indochina were almost uniformly unsuccessful. A variety of tactics were employed to develop litigable cases which the courts might agree to hear. In *Katz v. Tyler* ((1967), a draft objector claimed that the American operation in Vietnam was a war of aggression outlawed by the 1945 Treaty of London.[6] The trial judge dismissed the suit for lack of standing, and the Supreme Court refused to grant certiorari.

In *Mitchell v. United States* (1967) the Court likewise denied certiorari in another case based on the Treaty of London, where the trial judge had barred from evidence any testimony as to the legality of the war or about alleged atrocities by American forces in Vietnam as not germane to the charge of failing to report for induction. Justice Douglas dissented, on the ground that these claims presented ''sensitive and delicate questions'' that should be answered, adding that there is ''a considerable body of opinion that our actions in Vietnam constitute the waging of an aggressive 'war.' ''

The Court also denied certiorari in *Mora v. McNamara* (1967), where three soldiers had refused to go to Vietnam on the ground that it was an illegal war, but this time Justice Stewart joined Douglas in thinking the case should be heard. The appeal, he said, raised questions of great magnitude as to whether the Vietnam action was war in the constitutional sense, and if so, whether the President could send men to fight there when no war had been declared by Congress.

In an effort to force the Supreme Court to confront the Vietnam issue, the Massachusetts legislature in 1970 passed a law providing that Massachusetts servicemen could refuse to take part in armed hostilities in the absence of a declaration of war by Congress. The state attorney general was authorized to bring an action in the name of the state in the original jurisdiction of the Supreme Court, seeking a declaration that the military action in Vietnam was unconstitutional and an injunction forbidding the secretary of defense to send any citizen of Massachusetts to Vietnam until Congress had declared war. The Supreme Court in *Massachusetts v. Laird* (1970) denied the state's motion to file the suit, though Douglas, Harlan, and Stewart dissented.

The case was then filed in federal district court in Boston, but Judge Wyzanski held that the Supreme Court's action meant that Massachusetts lacked standing and that the controversy lacked justiciability. This decision was affirmed by the Court of Appeals for the First Circuit, that body relying principally on the fact that the Vietnam War was ''a product of the jointly

[5]Clinton Rossiter, *The Supreme Court and the Commander in Chief* (Ithaca, N.Y.: Cornell University Press, 1951), p. 126.

[6]The Treaty of London, often called the Nuremberg Charter, was signed by United States representatives but not submitted to the Senate for ratification. It makes soldiers in an aggressive war individually responsible as war criminals, even if they acted under orders.

THE POWER TO DECLARE WAR

The members of the Constitutional Convention had considered the allocation of the war-making power only very briefly. The original draft from the Committee on Detail gave Congress the power ''to make war.'' After a short debate, the word ''make'' was changed to ''declare,'' perhaps to assure the President the power to repel attacks or perhaps to make clear that the President, not Congress, would *conduct* the war. As early as 1793 Hamilton and Madison were disagreeing over the intention of the Convention. Hamilton argued that since war making was by nature an executive function, Congress could exercise only those aspects that the Constitution specifically granted to the legislature. Madison, on the other hand, asserted that war making was a legislative function and that any exceptions in favor of the executive must be strictly interpreted.

This debate has continued over almost two centuries and can never be settled. But Charles Lofgren's careful reexamination of the original understanding convinces him that the intention was to give Congress the power to ''commence'' war, whether declared or not.[2]

In practice, of course, the President's control over the armed forces and responsibility for the conduct of foreign relations has made Congress a distinctly secondary participant in decisions on inauguration of military action. The only wars that Congress declared and that it had a significant role in instigating were the War of 1812 and the Spanish-American War of 1898. In the Mexican War of 1846 and in World Wars I and II Congress simply recognized the existence of a state of war by its declaration.

In the present century, both Roosevelts, Wilson, Truman, Eisenhower, Kennedy, Johnson, Nixon, and Ford have all moved American troops into action or across national frontiers with little or no effort to secure advance congressional assent. Since 1950, there have been presidential moves into Korea, Lebanon, Cuba, the Dominican Republic, Vietnam, Laos, Cambodia, Iran, Nicaragua, and El Salvador—as well as distant naval operations, undercover plots, military advisory programs, and aerial overflights of foreign countries. All these actions risked conflict and gave Congress little or no opportunity for review.

The War in Vietnam

The disastrous American involvement in Indochina was accomplished by the use of commander-in-chief powers by four different Presidents. After the

[2]Charles A. Lofgren, ''War-Making under the Constitution: The Original Understanding,'' 81 YALE LAW JOURNAL 672 (1972). See also Francis D. Wormuth, ''The Nixon Theory of the War Power: A Critique,'' 60 CALIFORNIA LAW REVIEW 623 (1972); and Edward Keynes, *Undeclared War: Twilight Zone of Constitutional Power* (University Park; Pennsylvania State University Press, 1982).

initial commitment of American advisers and a small number of troops in Vietnam by Presidents Eisenhower and Kennedy, President Johnson used the occasion of an alleged, and almost certainly nonexistent, North Vietnamese torpedo-boat attack on two United States destroyers in the Gulf of Tonkin to ask Congress for a joint resolution of support to strengthen his hand. Almost unanimously, Congress adopted the Gulf of Tonkin Resolution approving and supporting ''the determination of the President, as commander in chief, to take all necessary measures to repel any armed attack against the forces of the United States and to prevent further aggression.''

President Johnson subsequently relied on this resolution as authorizing and justifying the tremendous escalation of military operations in Vietnam and the bombing of North Vietnam, whereas many members of Congress came to feel that there had been no such intention and that they had been manipulated into a position where they had to approve the resolution or give an impression of national disunity. Assistant Secretary of State Katzenbach, testifying before the Foreign Relations Committee of the Senate on August 17, 1967, argued that the Gulf of Tonkin Resolution gave the President as much authority as a declaration of war would have. In fact, he alarmed the senators by referring to declarations of war as ''outmoded'' and contended that a declaration of war would not ''correctly reflect the very limited objectives of the United States with respect to Vietnam.''

Efforts by members and committees of Congress to recapture some control of the war-making power were tremendously accelerated in 1970 by President Nixon's precipitate expansion of military activities into Cambodia without any prior consultation with Congress, but they had only limited success. The Cooper-Church Amendment of 1970 banned the use of funds for American ground combat forces in Laos, Thailand, and Cambodia. Later that year Congress repealed the Gulf of Tonkin Resolution, but this had no effect, since by then the official justification for continued military operations was the necessity to protect American troops until they could be withdrawn from Vietnam. Various ''end the war'' and withdrawal resolutions failed, but Congress did eventually order the bombing of Cambodia stopped by August 15, 1973.

The War Powers Act

Ultimately, congressional frustration over its own impotence produced an important new statute, the War Powers Act, passed in 1973 over President Nixon's veto. The law set a sixty-day limit on any presidential commitment of United States troops abroad without specific congressional authorization. The commitment could be extended for another thirty days if necessary for the safe withdrawal of troops. Unauthorized commitments might be terminated prior to the sixty-day deadline through congressional adoption of a concurrent resolution, a measure that does not require presidential signature. Moreover, the

act requires the President to consult with Congress in every possible instance before introducing United States armed forces into hostilities or into situations where imminent involvement in hostilities is clearly indicated. While President Nixon condemned the statute as an unconstitutional and dangerous restriction on the power of the commander in chief to meet emergencies, some members of Congress voted against it on the opposite ground that the statute in fact recognized the President's right to start a war.[3]

As the South Vietnamese regime was collapsing in April, 1975, President Ford felt obliged, because of the limitations imposed by the War Powers Act, to ask Congress for authorization to use United States troops if necessary to evacuate American citizens and their dependents from Saigon. A Vietnam aid bill containing such authority was approved by a conference committee on April 25, but before the House could act on the report, American troops had carried out the evacuation on April 28 and 29. The bill was then defeated on May 1, on the ground that conditions had made it moot.

Within two weeks another situation occurred calling for application of the War Powers Act—the seizure of the American merchant vessel *Mayaguez* by Cambodian naval forces on May 12, 1975. Not until the sea and air rescue operation ordered by President Ford, including bombing of the Cambodian mainland, was under way on May 14 did he ''advice'' congressional leaders of the action. Similarly, when Reagan sent marines into Lebanon in the fall of 1982, he reported the action to Congress as a matter of information, not in compliance with the act, which would have triggered the 60-day limitation.[4] In fact, none of the War Powers Act reports submitted to Congress by Ford, Carter, and Reagan admitted the constitutionality of the act. The 1983 *Chadha* decision against legislative vetoes had the effect of invalidating the concurrent resolution requirement in the act.

The Vietnam War in the Courts

The judiciary has never played an extensive role in determining the constitutional limits of the presidential war power. Summing up his study of the commander in chief, Clinton Rossiter concluded that the Supreme Court has been asked to examine only ''a tiny fraction of [the President's] significant deeds and decisions as commander in chief, for most of these were by nature challengeable in no court but that of impeachment—which was entirely as it should have been. The contours of the presidential war powers have therefore

[3]See Robert Scigliano, ''The War Powers Resolution and the War Powers,'' in Joseph M. Bissette and Jeffrey Tulis, eds., *The Presidency in the Constitutional Order* (Baton Rouge: Louisiana State University Press, 1981), pp. 115–53.

[4]The American operation in Lebanon was the first case under the act in which U.S. forces, equipped for combat, had been introduced into an obviously dangerous environment and maintained for more than sixty days.

supportive actions of the two branches to whom the congeries of the war powers have been committed.'' Only if one of the two branches should be opposed to the continuance of hostilities would the court take a different view of its responsibility. The "steady Congressional support" for the war that the appeals court cited was of course the Gulf of Tonkin Resolution and the appropriations that Congress had consistently voted to finance the war.

Sarnoff v. Shultz (1972) was a suit brought against the secretary of the treasury to enjoin disbursements under the Foreign Assistance Act of 1961 in aid of American military operations in Vietnam. The suit was dismissed on the ground that it presented a "political question" beyond judicial cognizance. The Supreme Court denied certiorari over the dissent of Douglas and Brennan, who thought it presented a spending issue that might be litigable under the doctrine of *Flast v. Cohen* (1968).[7]

In *Holtzman v. Schlesinger* (1973), a federal district judge enjoined the secretary of defense from continuing military action in Cambodia as being unauthorized by Congress. The injunction was promptly stayed by the Court of Appeals for the Second Circuit. Holtzman, a Congresswoman from New York, then appealed on August 1 to Justice Marshall, as circuit justice, to vacate the stay. While granting that the Cambodian war might ultimately be adjudged to have been unlawful, Marshall concluded that granting the application would exceed his legal authority. Holtzman then applied to Justice Douglas who, while recognizing that he owed great deference to Marshall's ruling, nevertheless vacated the stay on August 4, because he regarded this as a capital case in which "someone is about to die" in Cambodia. Later that day Marshall, having communicated with the other members of the Court by phone, reversed Douglas's action and reentered the stay. Douglas dissented, charging that "telephone disposition of this grave and constitutional issue is not permissible." On August 6, when the bomb load of an American B-52 fell short and struck the Cambodian town of Neak Luong, 137 people were killed.

THE STATE OF WAR

The War Power of Congress

There have been several alternative theories about the source of the war power of Congress. In No. 23 of *The Federalist* Hamilton seemed to assume that the war power derived from the specific provisions of Article I, section 8, which in clauses 11 to 14 authorizes Congress:

---

[7]Two additional cases that the Supreme Court declined to review, *Berk v. Laird* (1971) and *Orlando v. Laird* (1971), are discussed in Leon Friedman and Burt Neuborne, *Unquestioning Obedience to the President: The ACLU Case against the Legality of the War in Vietnam* (New York: W. W. Norton & Company, Inc., 1972). See also Michael Tigar, "Judicial Power, the 'Political Question' Doctrine, and Foreign Relations," 17 UCLA LAW REVIEW 1135 (1970).

To declare war, grant letters of marque and reprisal, and make rules concerning captures on land and water;

To raise and support armies, but no appropriation of money to that use shall be for a longer term than two years;

To provide and maintain a navy;

To make rules for the government and regulation of the land and naval forces.

But in *Penhallow v. Doane* (1795), the Supreme Court suggested that the war power was an attribute of sovereignty and so not dependent upon these specific grants. Marshall in *McCulloch v. Maryland* (1819) derived the power to "conduct" a war from the authorization to "declare it."

No matter what the constitutional theory, the judicial result has almost invariably been to support a war power coextensive with war's "felt necessities." Conscription was attacked in the *Selective Draft Law Cases* (1918) on the grounds that the Constitution gave Congress no such power, that conscription amounted to involuntary servitude, and that it encroached on the constitutional power of the states over the militia, but the Court rejected all these contentions.

The war power of course does not require the existence of a state of war for its exercise. Even in the more sheltered times of the nineteenth century, it was necessary to prepare for war in time of peace. The Supreme Court found occasion to defend this obvious principle in *Ashwander v. Tennessee Valley Authority* (1936), where it supported the peacetime maintenance and operation of the Wilson Dam nitrate and power plants, built under the National Defense Act of 1916, on the ground that they were "national defense assets."

After hostilities end, there is necessarily a period before the state of war is legally terminated and the country readjusts to a peacetime economy. Congressional reliance on its war powers to deal with the problems of the postwar period has seldom been questioned. During World War I the so-called Wartime Prohibition Act was passed on November 22, 1918, eleven days after the armistice. In *Hamilton v. Kentucky Distilleries* (1919), the Court unanimously refused to "enquire into the motives of Congress," but noted in support of the legislation "that the treaty of peace has not yet been concluded, that the railways are still under national control by virtue of the war powers, that other war activities have not been brought to a close, and that it cannot even be said that the man power of the nation has been restored to a peace footing." The Court upheld postwar rent control for the District of Columbia in 1921 in *Block v. Hirsh,* though by 1924 it did conclude that the emergency had come to an end, and with it the case for rent control.[8]

Similar questions were raised at the close of World War II. The rent control statute passed in 1947 was upheld in *Woods v. Miller Co.* (1948). Justice Douglas warned, however, that the Court did not intend to permit the war power to "be used in days of peace to treat all the wounds which war

---

[8]*Chastleton Corp. v. Sinclair* (1924).

inflicts on our society,'' to the point where it would ''swallow up all other powers of Congress'' and the Ninth and Tenth Amendments as well.

Another important ruling in this period was *Ludecke v. Watkins* (1948), involving deportation of a German national in 1946 under the Alien Enemy Act of 1798, which was operative only during periods of a ''declared war.'' Five justices held that the Court could not question the President's power to take such action, but Justice Black thought ''the idea that we are still at war with Germany in the sense contemplated by the statute . . . is a pure fiction.''

The Ending of War

In the absence of any constitutional language indicating how wars are to be ended, judicial responsibility has again been to recognize the political decisions. As for the actual cessation of hostilities by armistice or otherwise, that is, of course, a decision for the President to make. Termination of the legal state of war is effected normally by negotiation of a treaty, but there is American experience with other methods. The Civil War was ended by presidential proclamation, World War I by joint resolution of Congress. ''Whatever the mode,'' said the Supreme Court in *Ludecke v. Watkins* (1948), termination of a state of war ''is a political act.''

Occupation of Territory

Territory conquered by the United States comes under the control of the President. In a whole series of controversies arising out of incidents following the Mexican War, the Civil War, and the Spanish-American War, the Supreme Court repeatedly denied any right to review presidential actions in these circumstances. The President's authority to establish a government for conquered territory comes neither from the Constitution nor the laws of the United States, but only from the law of war.

Following a period of military occupation, the President has full authority to establish a system of civil government for conquered territory, which may, however, be superseded by congressional legislation. If the territory is to be retained permanently by the United States, Congress must adopt legislation creating a civil government. But until this is done, the President is the sole source of governmental authority in the area.[9]

THE PRESIDENT AND THE ARMED FORCES

As commander in chief, the President is the ceremonial, legal, and administrative head of the armed forces.[10] He appoints the officers of the services,

[9]The sole exception was the case of *Jecker v. Montgomery* (1851). See *Santiago v. Nogueras* (1909).

[10]The president's position as commander in chief gives him the status of a member of the armed forces. President Lincoln's assassination was treated as a military crime for this reason—

though Congress determines the grades to which appointments may be made and may specify the qualifications of the appointees, who must also be confirmed by the Senate. The President has an unlimited power to dismiss officers from the service in time of war, but in time of peace Congress has provided that dismissal shall be only in pursuance of the sentence of a general court-martial. He may adopt rules and regulations for the government, safety, and welfare of the armed forces, in subordination to Congress's constitutional power "to make rules for the government and regulation of the land and naval forces."

The President may involve himself in such direction of military movements and strategy and the actual conduct of military operations as he sees fit. President Washington accompanied his troops into the field at the time of the Whiskey Rebellion in 1792. One need think only of President Lincoln's telegraphic orders and personal visits to his generals in the field, or President Roosevelt in the chart room of the White House mapping the grand strategy of World War II, or President Johnson personally approving the targets to be bombed in North Vietnam, to appreciate the tremendous potential of the President's role.

As commander of the armed forces the President is in control of the most incomparably powerful machinery of coercion in the country. He may use this power to enforce national laws and treaties within the United States, and he is the agent for enforcing the guarantee that Article IV, section 4, gives to the states against invasion and domestic violence.[11]

THE PRESIDENT AND MARTIAL LAW

Suspension of the Writ of Habeas Corpus

"Martial law" is a general term covering military rule in domestic areas. In varying degrees it involves military assumption of normal civil lawmaking and enforcement functions. A necessary instrument of a system of martial law is suspension of the writ of habeas corpus, which permits civil or military authorities to hold persons in jail indefinitely without placing charges against them or bringing them to trial.

The Constitution provides in Article I, section 9: "The privilege of the writ of habeas corpus shall not be suspended, unless when in cases of rebellion or invasion the public safety may require it." Suspension of the "privilege"

---

the killing of the commander in chief while he was actually in command of the national forces in his headquarters city. A military tribunal of nine officers tried the assassins, and no civil court ever looked into the commission's jurisdiction or proceedings.

[11]Two early Supreme Court decisions, *Martin v. Mott* (1827) and *Luther v. Borden* (1849), dealing with presidential action in calling out the militia, emphasize that the President is not judicially accountable for his emergency use of the armed forces.

of the writ means that, though courts may continue to issue the writ, the jailer to whom the writ is directed is relieved of the responsibility of obeying the order to produce the prisoner in court. The Constitution undoubtedly contemplated that Congress should have power to suspend the writ when required by public safety, since the clause is located in the legislative article of the Constitution. However, President Lincoln, acting on his own authority, suspended it several times during the Civil War. In the Habeas Corpus Act of March 3, 1863, Congress, in carefully chosen language, said that the President was authorized to suspend the writ "during the present rebellion," but without indicating where the authorization came from. Before this act was passed, however, there had been a notable clash between Lincoln and Chief Justice Taney over the issue.

In May, 1861, Taney, sitting in the circuit court in Baltimore, under statutory authority from the Judiciary Act of 1789 granted the writ requested by John Merryman, who had been arrested and confined in Fort McHenry because of his secessionist activities. The military authorities refused to honor the writ, and Taney's effort to arrest the commanding general for contempt was likewise frustrated. Taney wrote an opinion holding unconstitutional Lincoln's suspension of the privilege, and directed the clerk of the court to send a copy to the President. "It will then," he added, "remain for that high officer, in fulfillment of his constitutional obligation to take care that the laws be faithfully executed, to determine what measures he will take to cause the civil processes of the United States to be respected and enforced." Lincoln continued to exercise the power that Taney had held unconstitutional, though Merryman was shortly turned over to civil authorities and indicted for treason.

Military Trials of Civilians

In a proclamation of September 24, 1862, President Lincoln coupled suspension of habeas corpus with an order that all persons "guilty of any disloyal practice affording aid and comfort to rebels" should be liable to trial and punishment by "courts-martial or military commissions." This order was effective throughout the United States and was a direct challenge to the authority of the regular civil courts. Although Congress subsequently ratified the habeas corpus suspension by its act of 1863, it never gave statutory support to trial of civilians by military commissions, which had to rest solely on the President's power as commander in chief.

The Court eventually ruled trial by military commissions unconstitutional, but not until the Civil War had been over for a year, in the case of *Ex parte Milligan* (1866). Milligan was arrested at his home in Indiana late in 1864, tried by a military commission, and sentenced to be hanged. In May, 1865, Milligan got a writ of habeas corpus from the federal court in Indianapolis, and the Supreme Court unanimously ruled that the President had no power to order trial of civilians by military courts in areas where the regular courts were open and operating.

There was a considerable similarity between Lincoln's military commissions and the situation that prevailed in Hawaii during the greater part of World War II. Under authority of the Hawaii Organic Act, the governor of Hawaii declared martial law immediately after the Japanese attack on December 7, 1941; the President approved his action two days later. Civil and criminal courts were forbidden to try cases, military tribunals being set up to replace them. Some criminal cases were still being tried by military courts as late as 1944. In *Duncan v. Kahanamoku* (1946), the Supreme Court held that when Congress had granted the governor of Hawaii the power to declare martial law, it had not meant to supersede constitutional guarantees of a fair trial that apply elsewhere in the United States or to "authorize the supplanting of courts by military tribunals."

THE PRESIDENT AND MILITARY JUSTICE

Military Trials for Military Personnel

The armed forces maintain a system of courts-martial for punishment of offenses by their members, under regulations prescribed by Congress. Articles of War were adopted for the army by Congress in 1789, and for the navy in 1800. The procedures embodied in the articles were those of the Revolutionary War, aimed at enforcing discipline rather than administering justice, and they became increasingly unacceptable to the citizen soldiers of World Wars I and II. These protests were recognized by the adoption in 1950 of the Uniform Code of Military Justice, a sweeping overhaul of military law that gave uniformed personnel more procedural rights than they would have had in civilian courts at that time. In fact, the code anticipated the major Supreme Court decisions of the next decade by providing free legal counsel in general courts-martial, requiring warning of rights before a suspect could be questioned, and providing free transcripts and counsel for appeals.[12]

In general, courts-martial are totally distinct from the civilian courts, constituting completely separate systems of justice. Courts-martial exercise no part of the judicial power of the United States. The decision of a court-martial must be affirmed by the appropriate command officers and in certain cases by a board of review appointed by a judge advocate general, and a final appeal may be taken on matters of law to the Court of Military Appeals. This is a bench of three civilian judges set up by the Uniform Code of Military Justice, appointed for fifteen-year terms by the President with the advice and consent of the Senate.

---

[12]*Middendorf v. Henry* (1976) ruled that counsel need not be furnished to servicemen accused of minor offenses at summary courts-martial. By contrast, *Argersinger v. Hamlin* (1972) held that in the regular courts no person could be imprisoned even for a petty offense unless there had been representation by counsel.

Article 76 of the Code makes the findings and sentences of courts-martial "final and conclusive" and "binding upon all . . . courts . . . of the United States." However, the writ of habeas corpus furnishes a method whereby detention as a result of a court-martial decision can be reviewed by the civil courts. Such review is strictly limited to the issue of jurisdiction of the court-martial, which may be challenged on the ground that the offense charged was not within its cognizance, that the court was not constituted according to law, or that the punishment exceeded the limits imposed by the code. Conformity of court-martial procedures to applicable constitutional standards may also be examined.

The relationship of the guarantees of the Bill of Rights to military trials is somewhat complex. The right to indictment by grand jury is specifically made inapplicable to "cases arising in the land and naval forces," and there is of course no right to trial by jury. Initially it was assumed that only those constitutional rights specifically authorized by Congress applied in courts-martial, and in fact legislation did guarantee the privilege against self-incrimination and the rights to confrontation, counsel, and compulsory process. But in *Wade v. Hunter* (1949) the Supreme Court held that the Fifth Amendment's ban on double jeopardy also applied to courts-martial, and in *United States v. Tempia* (1967) the Court of Military Appeals applied all the standards of the Supreme Court's decision in *Miranda v. Arizona* (1966) for the regular courts to the military legal system. The theory of the *Tempia* decision is that the entire framework of constitutional rights applies in the armed services "except insofar as they are made inapplicable either expressly or by necessary implication."

In addition to absence of grand jury indictment and trial by jury, the principal objection to court-martial procedure has been "command influence." The commanding officer appoints the pretrial investigating officers, authorizes searches and arrests, convenes the court-martial, decides whether the accused shall remain in pretrial confinement, selects the prosecutor and often the defense counsel, chooses the members of the court (the equivalent of jurors), decides whether a sentence to confinement will be deferred pending appeal, and makes the initial review of the case. Proposals have been made in Congress to eliminate command influence by establishing in the armed forces a separate and independent court-martial command, modeled after the civilian courts.[13]

---

[13]Criticism of military justice was heightened by the record in the My Lai atrocity cases. Out of a total of twenty-five enlisted men and officers charged in connection with the 1968 mass murders in Vietnam, only six were brought to trial and only one—Lt. William Calley—was convicted. When widespread public sympathy was manifested for Calley—arising partly from the feeling that he had been made a scapegoat for the misdeeds of his superiors—President Nixon issued a public statement pointing out that as commander in chief he would ultimately review the conviction. This was an extraordinary illustration of "command influence," which the army captain who had prosecuted the Calley case publicly condemned as subjecting military justice to "political influence." Calley's conviction was set aside in 1974 by a federal judge on the ground

On occasions the Supreme Court has been critical of the court-martial system, comparing it unfavorably with the civil courts. In *United States ex rel. Toth v. Quarles* (1955), Justice Black said that "from the very nature of things, courts have more independence in passing on the life and liberty of people than do military tribunals." This attitude motivated the Court in *Toth* to deny the right of the air force to subject a civilian ex-serviceman to court-martial for a crime allegedly committed during his period of military service.

The same inclination to limit the jurisdiction of courts-martial was even more evident in *O'Callahan v. Parker* (1969), where the Court reviewed the conviction of a soldier who, while on an evening pass, had broken into a Honolulu hotel room and assaulted a girl. This time it was Justice Douglas who stressed that courts-martial are not "an independent instrument of justice" but rather a "specialized part of the overall mechanism by which military discipline is preserved." By a vote of six to three, the Court held that where a member of the armed forces was charged with the commission of a crime cognizable in a civilian court, alleged to have been committed off post and while on leave, there was no justification for a court-martial that would deprive the serviceman of his constitutional rights to indictment by grand jury and trial by jury.[14]

The "service-connected" issue was raised again in *Schlesinger v. Councilman* (1975) by a soldier brought before a general court-martial on a marijuana charge, but he also challenged the entire legitimacy of the justice system as denying due process of law. The Court rejected this charge, saying that "implicit in the congressional scheme embodied in the code is the view that the military court system generally is adequate to and responsibly will perform its assigned task. We think this congressional judgment must be respected and that it must be assumed that the military court system will vindicate servicemen's constitutional rights."

For the three dissenters, Brennan denied that this was a service-connected offense. Rather, it was a "common everyday type of drug offense that federal courts encounter all over the country every day." It does not become a service-connected crime "merely because the participants are servicemen." This decision, Brennan held, violated the "basic constitutional tenet that subordinates the military to civil authority—restrict[ing] military cognizance of offenses to the narrowest jurisdiction deemed absolutely necessary, and preclud[ing] expansion of military jurisdiction at the expense of the constitutionally preferred civil jurisdiction."

The unpopular Vietnam War, fought with a largely conscript army, cre-

---

that massive publicity about his case had denied him a fair trial, but this ruling was reversed and the conviction reinstated by the Court of Appeals for the Fifth Circuit in 1975. The Supreme Court refused review; *Calley v. Hoffmann* (1976). See generally Joseph W. Bishop, Jr., *Justice under Fire: A Study of Military Law* (New York: Charterhouse, 1974).

[14]In *Relford v. Commandant* (1971), the Court itemized twelve tests to aid in determining whether an offense was "service-connected."

ated strains within the armed forces, resistance to military discipline, and new claims for First Amendment rights of criticism and free discussion. The best-known case was that of Captain Howard Levy, who talked against the war and refused to teach his medical skills to the Green Berets, an elite combat force, on the ground that they were guilty of calculated atrocities in Vietnam. At his court-martial, Levy's defense charged that two articles of the Uniform Code were unconstitutional as infringing on rights of free speech and also vague and unduly broad in violation of the Fifth Amendment. Article 133, dating back to the Revolutionary War, proscribes "conduct unbecoming an officer and a gentleman," and Article 134 forbids "all disorders and neglects to the prejudice of good order and discipline."

The Supreme Court denied certiorari to review the court-martial verdict of guilt in *Levy v. Corcoran* (1967). Review was then sought by the habeas corpus route, but eventually the Supreme Court ruled against Levy's claims by a vote of five to three in *Parker v. Levy* (1974). For the majority, Justice Rehnquist held that the two questioned articles were neither unduly vague nor overbroad and that Levy's conduct in publicly urging enlisted personnel to refuse to obey orders that might send them into combat was unprotected under the most expansive notions of the First Amendment. Because of the factors differentiating military from civilian society, Congress was permitted to legislate with greater breadth and flexibility, and the standards for judicial review should be those applicable to economic affairs, not First Amendment rights. Justice Stewart, dissenting, said he found it "hard to imagine criminal statutes more patently unconstitutional than these vague and uncertain General Articles. . . ."[15]

Military Trials for Military Dependents

Whether military courts may assert jurisdiction over dependents accompanying American servicemen stationed abroad in occupied territory or at American military bases has given the Supreme Court some trouble. The Uniform Code of Military Justice makes subject to its provisions "all persons serving with, employed by, or accompanying the armed forces without the continental limits of the United States." In *Reid v. Covert* (1957) and *Kinsella v. Krueger* (1957), cases in which wives of military personnel living on American bases in England and Japan had killed their husbands, the Court held that subjecting civilians "accompanying" the armed forces to courts-martial was unconstitutional.

There was some disagreement on the Court as to whether this reasoning was applicable only when capital crimes were involved. However, in *Kinsella v. United States ex rel. Singleton* (1960), the Court majority ruled that military trial of service dependents for noncapital offenses was also unconstitutional. Moreover, American civilian employees of the armed forces abroad cannot be

[15]See also *Secretary of the Navy v. Avrech* (1974); *Greer v. Spock* (1976).

tried by military courts for either capital or noncapital offenses, according to *McElroy v. United States ex rel. Guagliardo* (1960) and *Grisham v. Hagan* (1960).

Military Trials of Enemies

Courts-martial or military commissions have occasionally been set up by the president, under statutory authorization or his inherent powers as commander in chief, to deal with military crimes committed by others than the armed forces of the United States. As already noted, a military commission was created to try the assassins of President Lincoln. In 1942 President Roosevelt established a military commission to try eight German saboteurs who had been landed in this country by submarine with the assignment of blowing up factories and bridges. When the case before the tribunal was nearly completed, counsel for the saboteurs, despite an executive order denying them all access to civil courts, got a writ of habeas corpus contending for their right to trial in a civil court.

The Supreme Court unanimously upheld the military trial in *Ex parte Quirin* (1942). It was unnecessary to determine the extent of presidential authority as commander in chief, since Congress had provided for the trial of offenses against the law of war by such commissions, and the acts charged against the saboteurs were offenses against the law of war. The constitutional requirements of grand jury indictment and jury trial were held inapplicable to the trial of such offenses by military commissions. As for the *Milligan* decision, which was particularly relied on by counsel for the saboteurs, the Court pointed to the obvious factual differences in that case and held it inapplicable. The significance of the *Quirin* decision is its firm establishment of the authority of the civil courts to examine the jurisdiction of presidentially appointed military commissions.

Following World War II certain Japanese generals who had commanded troops in the Pacific theater were placed on trial before an American military commission in the Philippines. The Supreme Court in *In re Yamashita* (1946) again took jurisdiction, and again upheld the authority of the commission. Its procedures had been particularly under attack, for under the regulations prescribed by General MacArthur the commission had admitted hearsay and opinion evidence, and had allowed defense counsel inadequate time to prepare their defense. But the Court majority held that the commission's procedures and its rulings on evidence were reviewable only by the superior military authorities, not by the courts. Justices Murphy and Rutledge, however, filed eloquent dissents objecting to "departures from constitutional norms inherent in the idea of a fair trial."

Hirota v. MacArthur (1948) differed from the *Yamashita* case in that the Japanese defendants involved had been tried for war crimes before a military tribunal set up by General MacArthur as the agent for the Allied Powers, which had defeated Japan. The defendants sought to file habeas corpus petitions directly with the Supreme Court, but their motions were denied on the grounds that courts of the United States could have no jurisdiction over this tribunal because of its international character. It was not "a tribunal of the United States."[16]

THE PRESIDENT AND THE HOME FRONT

Control of the Economy

Insofar as the economic controls increasingly demanded by twentieth-century warfare have been based on congressional enactments, their general judicial ratification has already been noted. There have been some instances, however, where a President has acted without specific statutory support under his general powers as commander in chief.

In both World Wars I and II presidential action was taken to seize industrial plants, an interference with the use of private property which admittedly could be justified only on grounds of wartime necessity. President Wilson's seizures were based on statutory authorization, but from 1941 to 1943 President Roosevelt made numerous seizures without any supporting legislation, simply referring to his general authority as President and commander in chief. The plants seized were ones important to war production in which labor-management disagreements were threatening, or had already resulted in, stoppage of production. Ultimately Congress authorized presidential seizures of manufacturing and production facilities by the Smith-Connally Act of 1943.

Only one court test of these wartime seizures eventuated, and it led to no definitive ruling by the Supreme Court. After a three-year struggle between Montgomery Ward and the War Labor Board, the President in 1944 ordered the secretary of war to take possession of the company's properties. The government itself then went to court, seeking an injunction forbidding the company officers from interfering with the seizure. A federal district judge held that Montgomery Ward was engaged in "distribution," not "production," and consequently the statute did not authorize seizure of its facilities, nor did he think the President could take such action under his general war powers. The court of appeals, however, interpreted production more broadly and thereby found statutory support for the seizure. The Supreme Court accepted the case, but then dismissed it as moot because the army had turned the properties back to the company.[17]

President Truman's seizure of the nation's steel mills in 1952 did not come in a period of declared war, and Justice Black's opinion for the Court

---

[16]See Richard H. Minear, *Victor's Justice: The Tokyo War Crimes Trial* (Princeton, N.J.: Princeton University Press, 1971).

[17]*Montgomery Ward and Co. v. United States* (1945).

in *Youngstown Sheet & Tube Co. v. Sawyer* refused to give any consideration
to claims that the action could be justified by his status as commander in chief.
Justice Jackson undertook a more thoughtful statement of reasons for this
holding.

> We should not use this occasion to circumscribe, much less to contract, the law-
> ful role of the President as Commander-in-Chief. I should indulge the widest
> latitude of interpretation to sustain his exclusive function to command the
> instruments of national force, at least when turned against the outside world for
> the security of our society. But, when it is turned inward, not because of rebellion
> but because of a lawful economic struggle between industry and labor, it should
> have no such indulgence. . . . The purpose of lodging dual titles in one man was
> to insure that the civilian would control the military, not to enable the military
> to subordinate the presidential office. No penance would ever expiate the sin
> against free government of holding that a President can escape control of ex-
> ecutive powers by law through assuming his military role.

The Japanese Evacuation

The enforced evacuation of Japanese and Japanese-Americans from the
West Coast early in World War II by combined executive-legislative action
must be regarded, in spite of its subsequent ratification by the Supreme Court,
as one of the most disastrous episodes in the long history of the war power
under the Constitution. The deeply rooted opposition to Orientals on the West
Coast, combined with the hysteria of the early war period, built up a tremendous pressure to take action against the over 100,000 persons of Japanese
ancestry in the area. On February 19, 1942, President Roosevelt issued an
executive order empowering the secretary of war to designate military areas
from which any or all persons might be excluded in order to prevent espionage
and sabotage. Under this authorization the three West Coast states and part
of Arizona were proclaimed military areas and all persons of Japanese ancestry, 70,000 of whom were American citizens, were cleared from these areas.
Congress on March 21, 1942, passed a law ratifying and confirming the executive order.[18]

The inevitable constitutional tests of this harsh and unprecedented treatment of American citizens and aliens lawfully resident in the United States,
with its untold suffering and loss of property, presented the Supreme Court
with a difficult problem. Was it to hold these procedures contrary to due process, or to justify them on the ground that the responsible civil and military
leaders claimed they were a military necessity? As usual, the law's delays gave
the Court a period of grace before it had to answer. The decision in *Hirabayashi v. United States* did not come until June, 1943. Moreover, the circumstances of the case provided an opportunity for the Court to avoid the

---

[18]See Jacobus Tenbroek, Edward N. Barnhart, and Floyd W. Matson, *Prejudice, War and
the Constitution* (Berkeley: University of California Press, 1954); Morton Grodzins, *Americans
Betrayed: Politics and the Japanese Evacuation* (Chicago: University of Chicago Press, 1949).

more difficult constitutional questions. Shortly before the evacuation program had been undertaken, the army had adopted a curfew regulation requiring all aliens and persons of Japanese ancestry to be in their residences between 8 P.M. and 6 A.M. Hirabayashi, an American-born citizen of alien Japanese parents, was convicted of failure both to obey the curfew and to report for registration for evacuation. Sentence for the two offenses was made to run concurrently.

The Supreme Court took advantage of this fact to limit its review to the curfew, clearly a less drastic interference with liberty than the enforced evacuation, and unanimously upheld it as a temporary emergency war measure. Under the circumstances that existed at the time, the Court concluded that it was not unreasonable for those charged with the national defense to feel that the Japanese constituted a peculiar danger to national security. Racial discriminations are odious and usually unconstitutional, because justified by no proper legislative purpose. But "in time of war residents having ethnic affiliations with an invading enemy may be a greater source of danger than those of a different ancestry."

In *Korematsu v. Unites States,* decided in December, 1944, the constitutionality of the evacuation program, then in effect for over two and a half years, could no longer be avoided, and the Court upheld it by a divided vote. The majority opinion followed the lines of the earlier decision, holding that the military authorities were not unjustified in concluding that the Japanese residents of the Coast area constituted a potentially grave danger to the public safety, a danger so great and pressing that there was no time to set up procedures for determining the loyalty or disloyalty of individual Japanese. Actually the Court made no effort to use that valuable prerogative of judicial review, "the wisdom of hindsight," to challenge the military conclusions, though it certainly was apparent by the end of 1944 that the fears of sabotage and treachery by West Coast residents of Japanese descent were entirely groundless. Only Justice Murphy charged that the case made by the military had not been based on any demonstrated public necessity, but upon "an accumulation of much of the misinformation, half-truths and insinuations that for years have been directed against Japanese Americans by people with racial and economic prejudices." Justices Roberts and Jackson also dissented, the latter suggesting that even if the military decision was justified, the Court should refuse to enforce it, because Court approval would give constitutional sanction to "a military expedient that has no place in law under the Constitution."

The Court partially recouped its reputation as the defender of individual liberties by *Ex parte Endo* (1944), decided the same day as *Korematsu.* Here the Court upheld the right of a Japanese-American woman, whose loyalty to the United States had been established, to a writ of habeas corpus freeing her from a relocation camp. Justice Douglas's opinion avoided any ruling on the constitutionality of the detention program as a whole by pointing out that neither statute nor executive order anywhere specifically authorized detention. Justice Roberts, concurring in the result, thought the Court had ignored its responsibility to meet squarely the constitutional issue created by the government's action in depriving an admittedly loyal citizen of her liberty for a period of years. The weekend before the *Endo* ruling, and apparently in anticipation of it, the army ordered the release of all loyal Japanese-Americans from the relocation camps.

In 1947 President Truman's Commission on Civil Rights described the evacuation as "the most striking mass interference since slavery with the right to physical freedom," and recommended that the evacuees be at least partly compensated for their property losses. Congress responded by passing the Evacuation Claims Act of 1948, under which the totally inadequate sum of $37 million was paid to 26,500 claimants.[19] A congressional Commission on Wartime Relocation and Internment of Civilians concluded in 1983 that the program had been a "grave injustice," motivated by "racial prejudice, war hysteria, and failure of political leadership."[20]

[19]See also *Honda v. Clark* (1967).

[20]*The New York Times*, February 25, 1983. Gordon Hirabayashi and Fred Korematsu, convicted in 1943 and 1944 of curfew and evacuation violations, in 1983 filed suit in Federal Court to have their convictions overturned; *The New York Times*, January 31, 1983.

Appendix: Constitution of the United States

We the people of the United States, in order to form a more perfect union, establish justice, insure domestic tranquility, provide for the common defense, promote the general welfare, and secure the blessings of liberty to ourselves and our posterity, do ordain and establish this Constitution for the United States of America.

ARTICLE I

Section 1. All legislative powers herein granted shall be vested in a Congress of the United States, which shall consist of a Senate and House of Representatives.

Section 2. (1) The House of Representatives shall be composed of members chosen every second year by the people of the several States, and the electors in each State shall have the qualifications requisite for electors of the most numerous branch of the State legislature.

(2) No person shall be a Representative who shall not have attained to the age of twenty-five years, and been seven years a citizen of the United States, and who shall not, when elected, be an inhabitant of that State in which he shall be chosen.

(3) Representatives and direct taxes[1] shall be apportioned among the several States which may be included within this Union, according to their respective numbers, which shall be

---

[1] Modified as to income taxes by the 16th Amendment.

determined by adding to the whole number of free persons, including those bound to service for a term of years, and excluding Indians not taxed, three fifths of all other persons.[2] The actual enumeration shall be made within three years after the first meeting of the Congress of the United States, and within every subsequent term of ten years, in such manner as they shall by law direct. The number of Representatives shall not exceed one for every thirty thousand, but each State shall have at least one Representative; and until such enumeration shall be made, the State of New Hampshire shall be entitled to choose three, Massachusetts eight, Rhode Island and Providence Plantations one, Connecticut five, New York six, New Jersey four, Pennsylvania eight, Delaware one, Maryland six, Virginia ten, North Carolina five, South Carolina five, and Georgia three.

(4) When vacancies happen in the representation from any State, the executive authority thereof shall issue writs of election to fill such vacancies.

(5) The House of Representatives shall choose their Speaker and other officers; and shall have the sole power of impeachment.

SECTION 3. (1) The Senate of the United States shall be composed of two Senators from each State, chosen by the Legislature thereof,[3] for six years; and each Senator shall have one vote.

(2) Immediately after they shall be assembled in consequence of the first election, they shall be divided as equally as may be into three classes. The seats of the Senators of the first class shall be vacated at the expiration of the second year, of the second class at the expiration of the fourth year, and of the third class at the expiration of the sixth year, so that one third may be chosen every second year; and if vacancies happen by resignation, or otherwise, during the recess of the legislature of any State, the executive thereof may make temporary appointments until the next meeting of the legislature, which (see footnote 3) shall then fill such vacancies.

(3) No person shall be a senator who shall not have attained to the age of thirty years, and been nine years a citizen of the United States, and who shall not, when elected, be an inhabitant of that State for which he shall be chosen.

(4) The Vice President of the United States shall be president of the Senate, but shall have no vote, unless they be equally divided.

(5) The Senate shall choose their other officers, and also a president pro tempore, in the absence of the Vice President, or when he shall exercise the office of President of the United States.

(6) The Senate shall have the sole power to try all impeachments. When sitting for that purpose, they shall be on oath or affirmation. When the President of the United States is tried, the Chief Justice shall preside: and no person shall be convicted without the concurrence of two thirds of the members present.

(7) Judgment in cases of impeachment shall not extend further than to removal from office, and disqualification to hold and enjoy any office of honor, trust or profit under the United States: but the party convicted shall nevertheless be liable and subject to indictment, trial, judgment and punishment, according to law.

SECTION 4. (1) The times, places and manner of holding elections for Senators and Representatives, shall be prescribed in each State by the legislature thereof; but the Con-

[2] Replaced by the 14th Amendment.
[3] Modified by the 17th Amendment.

gress may at any time by law make or alter such regulations, except as to the places of choosing Senators.

(2) The Congress shall assemble at least once in every year, and such meeting shall be on the first Monday in December, unless they shall by law appoint a different day.

SECTION 5. (1) Each House shall be the judge of the elections, returns and qualifications of its own members, and a majority of each shall constitute a quorum to do business; but a smaller number may adjourn from day to day, and may be authorized to compel the attendance of absent members, in such manner, and under such penalties as each House may provide.

(2) Each House may determine the rules of its proceedings, punish its members for disorderly behavior, and, with the concurrence of two thirds, expel a member.

(3) Each House shall keep a journal of its proceedings, and from time to time publish the same, excepting such parts as may in their judgment require secrecy; and the yeas and nays of the members of either House on any question shall, at the desire of one fifth of those present, be entered on the journal.

(4) Neither House, during the session of Congress, shall, without the consent of the other, adjourn for more than three days, nor to any other place than that in which the two Houses shall be sitting.

SECTION 6. (1) The Senators and Representatives shall receive a compensation for their services, to be ascertained by law, and paid out of the Treasury of the United States. They shall in all cases, except treason, felony and breach of the peace, be privileged from arrest during their attendance at the session of their respective Houses, and in going to and returning from the same; and for any speech or debate in either House, they shall not be questioned in any other place.

(2) No Senator or Representative shall, during the time for which he was elected, be appointed to any civil office under the authority of the United States, which shall have been created, or the emoluments whereof shall have been increased during such time; and no person holding any office under the United States, shall be a member of either House during his continuance in office.

SECTION 7. (1) All bills for raising revenue shall originate in the House of Representatives; but the Senate may propose or concur with amendments as on other bills.

(2) Every bill which shall have passed the House of Representatives and the Senate, shall, before it become a law, be presented to the President of the United States; if he approve he shall sign it, but if not he shall return it, with his objections to that House in which it shall have originated, who shall enter the objections at large on their journal, and proceed to reconsider it. If after such reconsideration two thirds of that House shall agree to pass the bill, it shall be sent, together with the objections, to the other House, by which it shall likewise be reconsidered, and if approved by two thirds of that House, it shall become a law. But in all such cases the votes of both Houses shall be determined by yeas and nays, and the names of the persons voting for and against the bill shall be entered on the journal of each House respectively. If any bill shall not be returned by the President within ten days (Sundays excepted) after it shall have been presented to him, the same shall be a law, in like manner as if he had signed it, unless the Congress by their adjournment prevent its return, in which case it shall not be a law.

(3) Every order, resolution, or vote to which the concurrence of the Senate and House of

Representatives may be necessary (except on a question of adjournment) shall be presented to the President of the United States; and before the same shall take effect, shall be approved by him, or being disapproved by him, shall be repassed by two thirds of the Senate and House of Representatives, according to the rules and limitations prescribed in the case of a bill.

SECTION 8. (1) The Congress shall have power to lay and collect taxes, duties, imposts and excises, to pay the debts and provide for the common defense and general welfare of the United States; but all duties, imposts and excises shall be uniform throughout the United States;

(2) To borrow money on the credit of the United States.

(3) To regulate commerce with foreign nations, and among the several States, and with the Indian tribes;

(4) To establish an uniform rule of naturalization, and uniform laws on the subject of bankruptcies throughout the United States;

(5) To coin money, regulate the value thereof, and of foreign coin, and fix the standard of weights and measures;

(6) To provide for the punishment of counterfeiting the securities and current coin of the United States;

(7) To establish post offices and post roads;

(8) To promote the progress of science and useful arts, by securing for limited times to authors and inventors the exclusive right to their respective writings and discoveries;

(9) To constitute tribunals inferior to the Supreme Court;

(10) To define and punish piracies and felonies committed on the high seas, and offenses against the law of nations;

(11) To declare war, grant letters of marque and reprisal, and make rules concerning captures on land and water;

(12) To raise and support armies, but no appropriation of money to that use shall be for a longer term than two years;

(13) To provide and maintain a navy;

(14) To make rules for the government and regulation of the land and naval forces;

(15) To provide for calling forth the militia to execute the laws of the Union, suppress insurrections and repel invasions;

(16) To provide for organizing, arming, and disciplining the militia, and for governing such part of them as may be employed in the service of the United States, reserving to the States respectively, the appointment of the officers, and the authority of training the militia according to the discipline prescribed by Congress;

(17) To exercise exclusive legislation in all cases whatsoever, over such district (not exceeding ten miles square) as may, by cession of particular States, and the acceptance of Congress, become the seat of the government of the United States,[4] and to exercise like authority over all places purchased by the consent of the legislature of the State in which the same shall be, for the erection of forts, magazines, arsenals, dockyards, and other needful buildings; and

(18) To make all laws which shall be necessary and proper for carrying into execution the

[4] Modified by the 23rd Amendment.

foregoing powers, and all other powers vested by this Constitution in the government of the United States, or in any department or officer thereof.

SECTION 9. (1) The migration or importation of such persons as any of the States now existing shall think proper to admit, shall not be prohibited by the Congress prior to the year one thousand eight hundred and eight, but a tax or duty may be imposed on such importation, not exceeding ten dollars for each person.

(2) The privilege of the writ of habeas corpus shall not be suspended, unless when in cases of rebellion or invasion the public safety may require it.

(3) No bill of attainder or ex post facto law shall be passed.

(4) No capitation, or other direct, tax shall be laid, unless in proportion to the census or enumeration herein before directed to be taken.[5]

(5) No tax or duty shall be laid on articles exported from any State.

(6) No preference shall be given by any regulation of commerce or revenue to the ports of one State over those of another: nor shall vessels bound to, or from, one State, be obliged to enter, clear, or pay duties in another.

(7) No money shall be drawn from the Treasury, but in consequence of appropriations made by law; and a regular statement and account of the receipts and expenditures of all public money shall be published from time to time.

(8) No title of nobility shall be granted by the United States: and no person holding any office of profit or trust under them, shall, without the consent of the Congress, accept of any present, emolument, office, or title, of any kind whatever, from any king, prince, or foreign State.

SECTION 10. (1) No State shall enter into any treaty, alliance, or confederation; grant letters of marque and reprisal; coin money; emit bills of credit; make anything but gold and silver coin a tender in payment of debts; pass any bill of attainder, ex post facto law, or law impairing the obligation of contracts, or grant any title of nobility.

(2) No State shall, without the consent of the Congress, lay any imposts or duties on imports or exports, except what may be absolutely necessary for executing its inspection laws; and the net produce of all duties and imposts, laid by any State on imports or exports, shall be for the use of the Treasury of the United States; and all such laws shall be subject to the revision and control of the Congress.

(3) No State shall, without the consent of Congress, lay any duty of tonnage, keep troops, or ships of war in time of peace, enter into any agreement or compact with another State, or with a foreign power, or engage in war, unless actually invaded, or in such imminent danger as will not admit of delay.

ARTICLE II

SECTION 1. (1) The executive power shall be vested in a President of the United States of America. He shall hold his office during the term of four years,[6] and, together with the Vice President, chosen for the same term, be elected, as follows:

(2) Each State shall appoint, in such manner as the legislature thereof may direct, a

[5] Modified by the 16th Amendment.
[6] Modified by the 22th Amendment.

number of electors, equal to the whole number of Senators and Representatives to which the State may be entitled in the Congress: but no Senator or Representative, or person holding an office of trust or profit under the United States, shall be appointed an elector.

The electors[7] shall meet in their respective States, and vote by ballot for two persons, of whom one at least shall not be an inhabitant of the same State with themselves. And they shall make a list of all the persons voted for, and of the number of votes for each; which list they shall sign and certify, and transmit sealed to the seat of the government of the United States, directed to the president of the Senate. The president of the Senate shall, in the presence of the Senate and House of Representatives, open all the certificates, and the votes shall then be counted. The person having the greatest number of votes shall be the President, if such number be a majority of the whole number of electors appointed; and if there be more than one who have such majority, and have an equal number of votes, then the House of Representatives shall immediately choose by ballot one of them for President; and if no person have a majority, then from the five highest on the list the said House shall in like manner choose the President. But in choosing the President, the votes shall be taken by States, the representation from each State having one vote; a quorum for this purpose shall consist of a member or members from two thirds of the States, and a majority of all the States shall be necessary to a choice. In every case, after the choice of the President, the person having the greatest number of votes of the electors shall be the Vice President. But if there should remain two or more who have equal votes, the Senate shall choose from them by ballot the Vice President.

(3) The Congress may determine the time of choosing the electors, and the day on which they shall give their votes; which day shall be the same throughout the United States.

(4) No person except a natural born citizen, or a citizen of the United States, at the time of the adoption of this Constitution, shall be eligible to the office of President; neither shall any person be eligible to that office who shall not have attained to the age of thirty five years, and been fourteen years a resident within the United States.

(5) In the case of the removal of the President from office, or of his death, resignation, or inability to discharge the powers and duties of the said office, the same shall devolve on the Vice President, and the Congress may by law provide for the case of removal, death, resignation, or inability, both of the President and Vice President, declaring what officer shall then act as President, and such officer shall act accordingly, until the disability be removed, or a President shall be elected.[8]

(6) The President shall, at stated times, receive for his services, a compensation, which shall neither be increased nor diminished during the period for which he shall have been elected, and he shall not receive within that period any other emolument from the United States, or any of them.

(7) Before he enter on the execution of his office, he shall take the following oath or affirmation:—"I do solemnly swear (or affirm) that I will faithfully execute the office of President of the United States, and will to the best of my ability, preserve, protect and defend the Constitution of the United States."

SECTION 2. (1) The President shall be commander in chief of the army and navy of the United States, and of the militia of the several States, when called into the actual service of the United States; he may require the opinion, in writing, of the principal officer in each of the executive departments, upon any subject relating to the duties of their

---

[7] This paragraph was replaced in 1804 by the 12th Amendment.

[8] Replaced by the 25th Amendment.

respective offices, and he shall have power to grant reprieves and pardons for offenses against the United States, except in cases of impeachment.

(2) He shall have power, by and with the advice and consent of the Senate, to make treaties, provided two thirds of the Senators present concur; and he shall nominate, and by and with the advice and consent of the Senate, shall appoint ambassadors, other public ministers and consuls, judges of the Supreme Court, and all other officers of the United States, whose appointments are not herein otherwise provided for, and which shall be established by law: but the Congress may by law vest the appointment of such inferior officers, as they think proper, in the President alone, in the courts of law, or in the heads of departments.

(3) The President shall have power to fill up all vacancies that may happen during the recess of the Senate, by granting commissions which shall expire at the end of their next session.

Section 3. He shall from time to time give to the Congress information of the state of the Union, and recommend to their consideration such measures as he shall judge necessary and expedient; he may, on extraordinary occasions, convene both Houses, or either of them, and in case of disagreement between them, with respect to the time of adjournment, he may adjourn them to such time as he shall think proper; he shall receive ambassadors and other public ministers; he shall take care that the laws be faithfully executed, and shall commission all the officers of the United States.

Section 4. The President, Vice President and all civil officers of the United States, shall be removed from office on impeachment for, and conviction of, treason, bribery, or other high crimes and misdemeanors.

ARTICLE III

Section 1. The judicial power of the United States, shall be vested in one Supreme Court, and in such inferior courts as the Congress may from time to time ordain and establish. The judges, both of the Supreme and inferior courts, shall hold their offices during good behavior, and shall, at stated times, receive for their services, a compensation, which shall not be diminished during their continuance in office.

Section 2. (1) The judicial power shall extend to all cases, in law and equity, arising under this Constitution, the laws of the United States, and treaties made, or which shall be made, under their authority;—to all cases affecting ambassadors, other public ministers and consuls;—to all cases of admiralty and maritime jurisdiction;—to controversies to which the United States shall be a party;—to controversies between two or more States;—between a State and citizens of another State;[9]—between citizens of different States;—between citizens of the same State claiming lands under grants of different States, and between a State, or the citizens thereof, and foreign States, citizens or subjects.

(2) In all cases affecting ambassadors, other public ministers and consuls, and those in which a State shall be party, the Supreme Court shall have original jurisdiction. In all the other cases before mentioned, the Supreme Court shall have appellate jurisdiction, both as to law and fact, with such exceptions, and under such regulations as the Congress shall make.

---

[9] Restricted by the 11th Amendment.

(3) The trial of all crimes, except in cases of impeachment, shall be by jury; and such trial shall be held in the State where the said crimes shall have been committed; but when not committed within any State, the trial shall be at such place or places as the Congress may by law have directed.

SECTION 3. (1) Treason against the United States, shall consist only in levying war against them, or in adhering to their enemies, giving them aid and comfort. No person shall be convicted of treason unless on the testimony of two witnesses to the same overt act, or on confession in open court.

(2) The Congress shall have power to declare the punishment of treason, but no attainder of treason shall work corruption of blood, or forfeiture except during the life of the person attainted.

ARTICLE IV

SECTION 1. Full faith and credit shall be given in each State to the public acts, records, and judicial proceedings of every other State. And the Congress may by general laws prescribe the manner in which such acts, records and proceedings shall be proved, and the effect thereof.

SECTION 2. (1) The citizens of each State shall be entitled to all privileges and immunities of citizens in the several States.

(2) A person charged in any State with treason, felony, or other crime, who shall flee from justice, and be found in another State, shall on demand of the executive authority of the State from which he fled, be delivered up, to be removed to the State having jurisdiction of the crime.

(3) No person held to service or labor in one State, under the laws thereof, escaping into another, shall, in consequence of any law or regulation therein, be discharged from such service or labor, but shall be delivered up on claim of the party to whom such service or labor may be due.

SECTION 3. (1) New States may be admitted by the Congress into this Union; but no new State shall be formed or erected within the jurisdiction of any other State; nor any State be formed by the junction of two or more States, or parts of States, without the consent of the legislatures of the States concerned as well as of the Congress.

(2) The Congress shall have power to dispose of and make all needful rules and regulations respecting the territory or other property belonging to the United States; and nothing in this Constitution shall be so construed as to prejudice any claims of the United States, or of any particular State.

SECTION 4. The United States shall guarantee to every State in this Union a republican form of government, and shall protect each of them against invasion; and on application of the legislature, or of the executive (when the legislature cannot be convened) against domestic violence.

ARTICLE V

The Congress, whenever two thirds of both Houses shall deem it necessary, shall propose amendments to this Constitution, or, on the application of the legislatures of two thirds of the several States, shall call a convention for proposing amendments, which, in either case, shall be valid to all intents and purposes, as part of this Constitution, when ratified by the legislatures of three fourths of the several States, or by conventions in three fourths thereof, as the one or the other mode of ratification may be proposed by the Congress; Provided that no amendment which may be made prior to the year one thousand eight hundred and eight shall in any manner affect the first and fourth clauses in the ninth section of the first article; and that no State, without its consent, shall be deprived of its equal suffrage in the Senate.

ARTICLE VI

SECTION 1. All debts contracted and engagements entered into, before the adoption of this Constitution, shall be as valid against the United States under this Constitution, as under the Confederation.

SECTION 2. This Constitution, and the laws of the United States which shall be made in pursuance thereof; and all treaties made, or which shall be made, under the authority of the United States, shall be the supreme law of the land; and the judges in every State shall be bound thereby, anything in the constitution or laws of any State to the contrary notwithstanding.

SECTION 3. The Senators and Representatives before mentioned, and the members of the several State legislatures, and all executive and judicial officers, both of the United States and of the several States, shall be bound by oath or affirmation to support this Constitution; but no religious test shall ever be required as a qualification to any office or public trust under the United States.

ARTICLE VII

The ratification of the conventions of nine States, shall be sufficient for the establishment of this Constitution between the States so ratifying the same.

Done in Convention by the unanimous consent of the States present the seventeenth day of September in the year of our Lord one thousand seven hundred and eighty-seven, and of the independence of the United States of America the twelfth. In witness whereof we have hereunto subscribed our names.

Go Washington—
Presidt. and Deputy from Virginia

Articles in addition to and amendment of the Constitution of the United States of America, proposed by Congress, and ratified by the legislatures of the several States, pursuant to the fifth article of the original Constitution.

ARTICLE I[10]

Congress shall make no law respecting an establishment of religion, or prohibiting the free exercise thereof; or abridging the freedom of speech, or of the press; or the right of the people peaceably to assemble, and to petition the government for a redress or grievances.

[10] The first ten Amendments were adopted in 1791.

ARTICLE II

A well regulated militia, being necessary to the security of a free State, the right of the people to keep and bear arms, shall not be infringed.

ARTICLE III

No soldier shall, in time of peace be quartered in any house, without the consent of the owner, nor in time of war, but in a manner to be prescribed by law.

ARTICLE IV

The right of the people to be secure in their persons, houses, papers, and effects, against unreasonable searches and seizures, shall not be violated, and no warrants shall issue, but upon probable cause, supported by oath or affirmation, and particularly describing the place to be searched, and the persons or things to be seized.

ARTICLE V

No person shall be held to answer for a capital, or otherwise infamous crime, unless on a presentment or indictment of a grand jury, except in cases arising in the land or naval forces, or in the militia, when in actual service in time of war or public danger; nor shall any person be subject for the same offense to be twice put in jeopardy of life or limb; nor shall be compelled in any criminal case to be a witness against himself, nor be deprived of life, liberty, or property, without due process of law; nor shall private property be taken for public use, without just compensation.

ARTICLE VI

In all criminal prosecutions the accused shall enjoy the right to a speedy and public trial, by an impartial jury of the State and district wherein the crime shall have been committed, which district shall have been previously ascertained by law, and to be informed of the nature and cause of the accusation; to be confronted with the witnesses against him; to have compulsory process for obtaining witnesses in his favor, and to have the assistance of counsel for his defense.

ARTICLE VII

In suits at common law, where the value in controversy shall exceed twenty dollars, the right of trial by jury shall be preserved, and no fact tried by a jury shall be otherwise reexamined in any court of the United States, than according to the rules of the common law.

ARTICLE VIII

Excessive bail shall not be required, nor excessive fines imposed, nor cruel and unusual punishments inflicted.

ARTICLE IX

The enumeration in the Constitution, of certain rights, shall not be construed to deny or disparage others retained by the people.

ARTICLE X

The powers not delegated to the United States by the Constitution, nor prohibited by it to the States, are reserved to the States respectively, or to the people.

ARTICLE XI[11]

The judicial power of the United States shall not be construed to extend to any suit in law or equity, commenced or prosecuted against one of the United States by citizens of another State, or by citizens or subjects of any foreign State.

ARTICLE XII[12]

The electors shall meet in their respective States and vote by ballot for President and Vice-President, one of whom, at least, shall not be an inhabitant of the same State with themselves; they shall name in their ballots the person voted for as President, and in distinct ballots the person voted for as Vice-President, and they shall make distinct lists of all persons voted for as President, and of all persons voted for as Vice-President, and of the number of votes for each, which lists they shall sign and certify, and transmit sealed to the seat of the government of the United States, directed to the president of the Senate;—The president of the Senate shall, in the presence of the Senate and House of Representatives, open all the certificates and the votes shall then be counted;—The person having the greatest number of votes for President, shall be the President, if such number be a majority of the whole number of electors appointed; and if no person have such majority, then from the persons having the highest numbers not exceeding three on the list of those voted for as President, the House of Representatives shall choose immediately, by ballot, the President. But in choosing the President, the votes shall be taken by States, the representation from each State having one vote; a quorum for this purpose shall consist of a member or members from two thirds of the States, and a majority of all the States shall be necessary to a choice. And if the House of Representatives shall not choose a President whenever the right of choice shall devolve upon them, before

[11] Ratified in 1795; proclaimed in 1798.
[12] Adopted in 1804.

the fourth day of March next following, then the Vice-President shall act as President, as in the case of the death or other constitutional disability of the President.—The person having the greatest number of votes as Vice-President, shall be the Vice-President, if such number be a majority of the whole number of electors appointed, and if no person have a majority, then from the two highest numbers on the list, the Senate shall choose the Vice-President; a quorum for the purpose shall consist of two thirds of the whole number of Senators, and a majority of the whole number shall be necessary to a choice. But no person constitutionally ineligible to the office of President shall be eligible to that of Vice-President of the United States.

ARTICLE XIII[13]

SECTION 1. Neither slavery nor involuntary servitude, except as a punishment for crime whereof the party shall have been duly convicted, shall exist within the United States, or any place subject to their jurisdiction.

SECTION 2. Congress shall have power to enforce this article by appropriate legislation.

ARTICLE XIV[14]

SECTION 1. All persons born or naturalized in the United States, and subject to the jurisdiction thereof, are citizens of the United States and of the State wherein they reside. No State shall make or enforce any law which shall abridge the privileges or immunities of citizens of the United States; nor shall any state deprive any person of life, liberty, or property, without due process of law; nor deny to any person within its jurisdiction the equal protection of the laws.

SECTION 2. Representatives shall be apportioned among the several States according to their respective numbers, counting the whole number of persons in each state, excluding Indians not taxed. But when the right to vote at any election for the choice of electors for President and Vice President of the United States, Representatives in Congress, the executive and judicial offices of a State, or the members of the legislature thereof, is denied to any of the male inhabitants of such State, being twenty-one years of age, and citizens of the United States, or in any way abridged, except for participation in rebellion, or other crime, the basis of representation therein shall be reduced in the proportion which the number of such male citizens shall bear to the whole number of male citizens twenty-one years of age in such State.

SECTION 3. No person shall be a Senator or Representative in Congress, or elector of President and Vice President, or hold any office, civil or military, under the United States, or under any State, who, having previously taken an oath, as a member of Congress, or as an officer of the United States, or as a member of any State legislature, or as an executive or judicial officer of any State, to support the Constitution of the United States, shall have engaged in insurrection or rebellion against the same, or given aid or comfort to the enemies thereof. But Congress may by a vote of two thirds of each House, remove such disability.

[13] Adopted in 1865.
[14] Adopted in 1868.

Section 4. The validity of the public debt of the United States, authorized by law, including debts incurred for payment of pensions and bounties for services in suppressing insurrection or rebellion, shall not be questioned. But neither the United States nor any State shall assume or pay any debt or obligation incurred in aid of insurrection or rebellion against the United States, or any claim for the loss or emancipation of any slave; but all such debts, obligations and claims shall be held illegal and void.

Section 5. The Congress shall have power to enforce, by appropriate legislation, the provisions of this article.

ARTICLE XV [15]

Section 1. The right of citizens of the United States to vote shall not be denied or abridged by the United States or by any State on account of race, color, or previous condition of servitude.

Section 2. The Congress shall have power to enforce this article by appropriate legislation.

ARTICLE XVI [16]

The Congress shall have power to lay and collect taxes on incomes, from whatever source derived, without apportionment among the several States, and without regard to any census or enumeration.

ARTICLE XVII

The Senate of the United States shall be composed of two Senators from each State, elected by the people thereof, for six years; and each Senator shall have one vote. The electors in each State shall have the qualifications requisite for electors of the most numerous branch of the State legislatures.

When vacancies happen in the representation of any State in the Senate, the executive authority of such State shall issue writs of election to fill such vacancies: *Provided,* That the legislature of any State may empower the executive thereof to make temporary appointments until the people fill the vacancies by election as the legislature may direct.

This amendment shall not be so construed as to affect the election or term of any Senator chosen before it becomes valid as part of the Constitution.

ARTICLE XVIII [17]

Section 1. After one year from the ratification of this article the manufacture, sale, or transportation of intoxicating liquors within, the importation thereof into, or the

[15] Adopted in 1870.
[16] Adopted in 1913.
[17] Adopted in 1919. Repealed by Article XXI.

exportation thereof from the United States and all territory subject to the jurisdication thereof for beverage purposes is hereby prohibited.

SECTION 2. The Congress and the several States shall have concurrent power to enforce this article by appropriate legislation.

SECTION 3. This article shall be inoperative unless it shall have been ratified as an amendment to the Constitution by the legislatures of the several states, as provided in the Constitution, within seven years from the date of the submission hereof to the States by the Congress.

ARTICLE XIX [18]

The right of citizens of the United States to vote shall not be denied or abridged by the United States or by any State on account of sex.

The Congress shall have power to enforce this article by appropriate legislation.

ARTICLE XX [19]

SECTION 1. The terms of the President and Vice President shall end at noon on the 20th day of January, and the terms of Senators and Representatives at noon on the 3rd day of January, of the years in which such terms would have ended if this article had not been ratified; and the terms of their successors shall then begin.

SECTION 2. The Congress shall assemble at least once in every year, and such meeting shall begin at noon on the 3rd day of January, unless they shall by law appoint a different day.

SECTION 3. If, at the time fixed for the beginning of the term of the President, the President elect shall have died, the Vice President elect shall become President. If a President shall not have been chosen before the time fixed for the beginning of his term, or if the President elect shall have failed to qualify, then the Vice President elect shall act as President until a President shall have qualified; and the Congress may by law provide for the case wherein neither a President elect nor a Vice President elect shall have qualified, declaring who shall then act as President, or the manner in which one who is to act shall be selected, and such person shall act accordingly until a President or Vice President shall have qualified.

SECTION 4. The Congress may by law provide for the case of the death of any of the persons from whom the House of Representatives may choose a President whenever the right of choice shall have devolved upon them, and for the case of the death of any of the persons from whom the Senate may choose a Vice President whenever the right of choice shall have devolved upon them.

SECTION 5. Sections 1 and 2 shall take effect on the 15th day of October following the ratification of this article.

[18] Adopted in 1920.

[19] Adopted in 1933.

SECTION 6. This article shall be inoperative unless it shall have been ratified as an amendment to the Constitution by the legislatures of three-fourths of the several States within seven years from the date of its submission.

ARTICLE XXI[20]

SECTION 1. The eighteenth article of amendment of the Constitution of the United States is hereby repealed.

SECTION 2. The transportation or importation into any State, Territory or Possession of the United States for delivery or use therein of intoxicating liquors in violation of the laws thereof is hereby prohibited.

SECTION 3. This article shall be inoperative unless it shall have been ratified as an amendment to the Constitution by conventions in the several States, as provided in the Constitution, within seven years from the date of submission hereof to the States by the Congress.

ARTICLE XXII[21]

SECTION 1. No person shall be elected to the office of the President more than twice, and no person who has held the office of President, or acted as President for more than two years of a term to which some other person was elected President shall be elected to the office of the President more than once. But this Article shall not apply to any person holding the office of President when this Article was proposed by the Congress, and shall not prevent any person who may be holding the office of President, or acting as President, during the term within which this Article becomes operative from holding the office of President or acting as President during the remainder of such term.

SECTION 2. This Article shall be inoperative unless it shall have been ratified as an amendment to the Constitution by the legislatures of three-fourths of the several States within seven years from the date of its submission to the States by the Congress.

ARTICLE XXIII[22]

SECTION 1. The District constituting the seat of Government of the United States shall appoint in such manner as the Congress may direct:

A number of electors of President and Vice-President equal to the whole number of Senators and Representatives in Congress to which the district would be entitled if it were a State, but in no event more than the least populous state; they shall be in addition to those appointed by the states, but they shall be considered, for the purposes of the election of President and Vice-President, to be electors appointed by a state; and they shall meet in the District and perform such duties as provided by the twelfth article of amendment.

[20] Adopted in 1933.

[21] Adopted in 1951.

[22] Adopted in 1961.

SECTION 2. The Congress shall have power to enforce this article by appropriate legislation.

ARTICLE XXIV[23]

SECTION 1. The right of citizens of the United States to vote in any primary or other election for President or Vice-President, for electors for President or Vice-President, or for Senator or Representative in Congress, shall not be denied or abridged by the United States or any state by reason of failure to pay any poll tax or other tax.

SECTION 2. The Congress shall have power to enforce this article by appropriate legislation.

ARTICLE XXV[24]

SECTION 1. In case of the removal of the President from office or his death or resignation, the Vice President shall become President.

SECTION 2. Whenever there is a vacancy in the office of the Vice President, the President shall nominate a Vice President who shall take the office upon confirmation by a majority vote of both houses of Congress.

SECTION 3. Whenever the President transmits to the President pro tempore of the Senate and the Speaker of the House of Representatives his written declaration that he is unable to discharge the powers and duties of his office, and until he transmits to them a written declaration to the contrary, such powers and duties shall be discharged by the Vice President as Acting President.

SECTION 4. Whenever the Vice President and majority of either the principal officers of the executive departments, or of such other body as Congress may by law provide, transmit to the President pro tempore of the Senate and the Speaker of the House of Representatives their written declaration that the President is unable to discharge the powers and duties of his office, the Vice President shall immediately assume the powers and duties of the office as Acting President.

Thereafter, when the President transmits to the President pro tempore of the Senate and the Speaker of the House of Representatives his written declaration that no inability exists, he shall resume the powers and duties of his office unless the Vice President and a majority of either the principal officers of the executive department, or of such other body as Congress may by law provide, transmit within four days to the President pro tempore of the Senate and the Speaker of the House of Representatives their written declaration that the President is unable to discharge the powers and duties of his office. Thereupon Congress shall decide the issue, assembling within 48 hours for that purpose if not in session. If the Congress, within 21 days after receipt of the latter written declaration, or, if Congress is not in session, within 21 days after Congress is required to assemble, determines by two-thirds vote of both houses that the President is unable to discharge the powers and duties of his office, the Vice President shall continue to discharge the same as Acting President; otherwise, the President shall resume the powers and duties of his office.

[23] Adopted in 1964.
[24] Adopted in 1967.

ARTICLE XXVI[25]

SECTION 1. The right of citizens of the United States, who are eighteen years of age, or older, to vote shall not be denied or abridged by the United States or by any state on account of age.

SECTION 2. The Congress shall have the power to enforce this article by appropriate legislation.

PROPOSED AMENDMENTS

Representation of the District of Columbia in the Congress

SECTION 1. For purposes of representation in the Congress, election of the President and Vice-President, and Article V of this Constitution, the District constituting the seat of government of the United States shall be treated as though it were a State.

SECTION 2. The exercise of the rights and powers conferred under this article shall be by the people of the District constituting the seat of government, and as shall be provided by the Congress.

SECTION 3. The twenty-third article of amendment to the Constitution of the United States is hereby repealed.

SECTION 4. This article shall be inoperative, unless it shall have been ratified as an amendment to the Constitution by the legislatures of three-fourths of the several States within seven years from the date of its submission. [Proposed by Congress on August 22, 1978.]

Equal Rights Amendment

[Proposed by Congress on March 22, 1972 with a seven-year period for ratification specified in the resolution proposing the amendment. When it appeared that three-fourths of the state legislatures would not ratify by March 22, 1979, Congress extended the period for ratification to June 30, 1982, but efforts to secure sufficient additional ratifications were unsuccessful and the amendment lapsed.]

SECTION 1. Equality of rights under the law shall not be denied or abridged by the United States or by any state on account of sex.

SECTION 2. The Congress shall have the power to enforce, by appropriate legislation, the provisions of this article.

SECTION 3. This amendment shall take effect two years after the date of ratification.

[25] Adopted in 1971.

Index of Cases

Subject Index